CHALLENGING GENETIC DETERMINISM

Challenging Genetic Determinism

New Perspectives on the Gene in Its Multiple Environments

Edited by
LOUIS MAHEU AND
RODERICK A. MACDONALD

McGill-Queen's University Press
Montreal & Kingston • London • Ithaca

ISBN 978-0-7735-3780-4 (cloth)
ISBN 978-0-7735-3813-9 (paper)

Legal deposit third quarter 2011
Bibliothèque nationale du Québec

Printed in Canada on acid-free paper that is 100% ancient forest free (100% post-consumer recycled), processed chlorine free

This book has been published with the help of grants from the Canadian Institutes for Health Research and the Social Sciences and Humanities Research Council of Canada.

McGill-Queen's University Press acknowledges the support of the Canada Council for the Arts for our publishing program. We also acknowledge the financial support of the Government of Canada through the Canada Book Fund for our publishing activities.

Library and Archives Canada Cataloguing in Publication

Royal Society of Canada. Symposium (2007)
Challenging genetic determinism : new perspectives on the gene in its multiple environments / edited by Louis Maheu and Roderick A. MacDonald.

Papers previously presented at the 2007 Fall Symposium of the Royal Society of Canada, under the auspices of the Social Sciences Academy, Academy II.

Includes bibliographical references.

ISBN 978-0-7735-3780-4 (bound). – ISBN 978-0-7735-3813-9 (pbk.)

1. Personality – Genetic aspects – Congresses. 2. Genotype-environment interaction – Congresses. 3. Phenotype – Congresses. 4. Behavior genetics – Congresses. 5. Human genetics – Moral and ethical aspects – Congresses. 6. Human genetics – Research – Congresses. I. Maheu, Louis II. Macdonald, Roderick A. III. Royal Society of Canada. Academy II IV. Title.

QH438.5.R69 2011 576.5'3 C2010-905356-7

This book was typeset by Interscript in 10.5/13 Sabon.

Contents

Preface and Acknowledgments

LOUIS MAHEU AND RODERICK A. MACDONALD

The papers in this collection were initially presented at the 2007 Fall Symposium of the RSC: *The Academies of Arts, Humanities and Sciences of Canada*. The Symposium was organized under the auspices of the Social Sciences Academy (Academy II) of the RSC. Nine papers have been revised for inclusion in this book and the co-editors have written an introduction, a chapter overviewing major advances and paradigm shifts within the research field of genetically and environmentally influenced behaviours, and a conclusion. We are most grateful to these Symposium participants for the additional time they have devoted to preparing their papers for publication.

We also wish to acknowledge the efforts and contributions of many others who have assisted us in bringing this book to print. From the outset, the leadership and staff of the RSC have been unstinting in their support. Dr Patricia Demers, former RSC president, and professor, Department of English, at the University of Alberta devoted enormous energy to supporting the Symposium and liaising with the University of Alberta to ensure its effective material presentation. Dr Debra Osburn, associate vice-president, and Amy Stafford from the Office of External Relations, University of Alberta, were also of great assistance in organizing the Symposium. At the *RSC* head office François Bélisle, Louise Joly, Amy Boughner, and Anne-Marie Marcil were particularly helpful in helping us to move the project forward.

The Symposium and the publication of the collection were generously supported by the Social Sciences and Humanities Research Council of Canada, the Canadian Institutes for Health Research, the University of Alberta, and the RSC. We are most grateful to Dr Chad Gaffield,

SSHRC president, as well as to Dr Alan Bernstein, former CIHR president, both for their efforts in securing a financial contribution to the Symposium from their respective organizations, and for their thoughtful advice as we developed the Symposium theme.

A number of scholars enthusiastically contributed their insights to helping us develop the program. In particular we would like to thank Dr Ronald Barr, centre director, Centre for Community Child Health Research, University of British Columbia; Dr Michael Burgess, professor in biomedical ethics and principal of the College for Interdisciplinary Studies, University of British Columbia; Dr Pierre Chartrand, vice-president of research, CIHR; Dr Monique Ernst, head of Neurodevelopment of Reward Systems, Emotional Development and Affective Neuroscience Branch, Department of Health and Human Services, National Institute of Mental Health, USA; Dr Sherrill E. Grace, Professor, Department of English, British Columbia University, and Past-President RSC–Academy of Arts and Humanities; Dr Rod McInnes, professor, Paediatrics and Molecular Genetics, University of Toronto, scientific director, Institute of Genetics; Dr Daniel S. Pine, chief, Emotion and Development Branch Section on Development and Affective Neuroscience Mood and Anxiety Program, Department of Health and Human Services, National Institute of Mental Health, USA; Dr Daryl Pullman, associate professor of medical ethics, Faculty of Medicine, Memorial University of Newfoundland, co-chair, Genetics and Ethical, Legal and Social Issues, CIHR, Institute of Genetics; Sir Michael Rutter, MD, professor of Developmental Psycho-pathology at the Institute of Psychiatry, Kings College, London; and Dr Christian Sylvain, former director, Policy, Planning and International Affairs, SSHRC.

Colleagues from various fields helped us to identify particular disciplines and sub-fields that were especially relevant for presenting the paradigms and research questions necessary to address the main topics of this book. We also thank them for input that influenced our own writings within this collection: Dr Andrée Demers, professor and chair, Sociology Department, University of Montreal; Dr Eric Lacourse, associate professor, Sociology Department, University of Montreal; Dr Françoise Maheu, research associate, St-Justine Hospital Research Centre and Psychiatry Department, University of Montreal; Dr Fraser Mustard, MD, president Founders' Network, Canada; and Dr Remi Quirion, scientific director, Research Centre, Douglas Institute, professor, Department of Psychiatry,

McGill University, scientific director, Institute of Neurosciences, Mental Health and Addiction (INMHA).

In the latter stages of editing and preparation of this collection we benefitted from the wise counsel of Dr Margaret Lock, Marjorie Bronfman Professor in Social Studies in Medicine, Emerita, McGill University, and the editorial assistance of Claudette Richard, research assistant to Dr Louis Maheu, and Madeleine Macdonald.

Finally, we would like to acknowledge the support and assistance of our publisher, McGill-Queens University Press, and its director, Philip Cercone, for their cheerful assistance in seeing the manuscript through to publication.

L.M.
R.A.M.

Contributors

FRANÇOISE BAYLIS, professor and Canada Research Chair in Bioethics and Philosophy,1234 Le Marchant Street, Dalhousie University, Halifax, Nova Scotia, Canada B3H 3P7
francoise.baylis@dal.ca

YVONNE BOMBARD, postdoctoral fellow, University of Toronto, Faculty of Medicine, Department of Health Policy, Management and Evaluation, Toronto, Ontario, Canada M5T 3M6
yvonne.bombard@utoronto.ca

TIMOTHY CAULFIELD, Canada Research Chair in Health Law and Policy; professor, Faculty of Law and School of Public Health; research director, Health Law Institute, University of Alberta
tcaulfld@law.ualberta.ca

SUZANNE D. CONZEN, MD, associate professor, University of Chicago Medical Center, 5841 S. Maryland Avenue, MC 2115 Chicago, IL 60637
sconzen@medicine.bsd.uchicago.edu

JONATHAN FLINT, head, Psychiatric Genetics Group, Wellcome Trust Centre for Human Genetics, University of Oxford, Roosevelt Drive, Oxford, OX3 7BN, UK
jf@well.ox.ac.uk

SARAH GEHLERT, E. Desmond Lee Professor of Racial and Ethnic Diversity, George Warren Brown School of Social Work, Washington University in St. Louis, Campus Box 1196, One Brookings Drive, St. Louis, MO 63130-4899
sgehlert@wustl.edu

DAVID GOLDMAN, senior investigator, Laboratory of Neurogenetics, National Institute on Alcohol Abuse and Alcoholism, National Institutes of Health, 5625 Fishers Lane, Rockville, MD 20852
davidgoldman@mail.nih.gov

MICHAEL R. HAYDEN, director and senior scientist, Centre for Molecular Medicine and Therapeutics, Department of Medical Genetics, Faculty of Medicine, 950 West 28th Avenue Vancouver, British Columbia V5Z 4H4
mrh@cmmt.ubc.ca

THOMAS KRAUSZ, professor and director, Anatomic Pathology, University of Chicago Hospitals, 5841 S. Maryland Avenue Chicago, IL 60637
thomas.krausz@uchospitals.edu

MARGARET LOCK, Marjorie Bronfman Professor in Social Studies in Medicine, Department of Social Studies of Medicine and Department of Anthropology, McGill University, 805 Sherbrooke Street West, Montréal, Québec H3A 2K6
margaret.lock@mcgill.ca

RODERICK A. MACDONALD, F.R. Scott Professor of Constitutional and Public Law, Faculty of Law, McGill University, 805 Sherbrooke Street West, Montréal, Québec H3A 2K6
roderick.macdonald@mcgill.ca

LOUIS MAHEU, emeritus professor, Department of Sociology, University of Montreal, Box 6128, succursale Centre-ville, Montreal, Québec H3C 3J7,
louis.maheu@umontreal.ca

MARTHA K. MCCLINTOCK, DAVID LEE SHILLINGLAW Distinguished Service Professor in Psychology, Institute for Mind and Biology, Division of the Social Sciences, University of Chicago, 940 E. 57th Street, Chicago, IL 60637
garden@uchicago.edu

OLUFUNMILAYO I. OLOPADE, professor and director, Center for Clinical Cancer Genetics, Department of Human Genetics, 5841 S. Maryland Avenue Chicago, IL 60637
folopade@bsd.uchicago.edu

RICHARD E. TREMBLAY, professor, Department of Psychology, University of Montreal, Box 6128, succursale Centre-ville, Montreal, Québec H3C 3J7,
richard.ernest.tremblay@umontreal.ca

DOUGLAS WAHLSTEN, professor, Department of Psychology, University of North Carolina, Greensboro, NC, USA 27402-6170
dlwahlst@uncg.edu

Introduction

LOUIS MAHEU AND RODERICK A. MACDONALD

The RSC: The Academies of Arts, Humanities and Sciences of Canada is dedicated to the advancement of exceptional learning, research, and accomplishments in the various disciplines of the scientific, cultural, and artistic universes. It strives to promote scholarship and the dissemination of new knowledge in important matters of public interest. The Social Sciences Academy (Academy II) adheres to and pursues these foundational values of the RSC: The Academies. Its members are fully engaged in producing and sharing ideas and understanding, both through their own scholarly activities and through their deep commitment to interdisciplinary dialogue with other scholarly disciplines, which will also inform public intellectual debates and State policy formation.

The Social Sciences Academy assumed, in 2007, responsibility for organizing the annual Fall Symposium of the RSC: The Academies. Academy Fellows charged with planning this event quickly settled on a challenging, multidisciplinary theme for the Symposium. Its title, *Changing Boundaries between Gene Expressions, Behaviours and the Social Fabric*, framed the field of inquiry; its sub-title, *The Social Sciences Confront Modern Genetics Challenges*, the intellectual objective: How, if at all, have contemporary developments in genetics research influenced humanities and social science research into the role of social factors in shaping the behaviour of human subjects? And how, if at all, might humanities and social science research influence the design and execution of genetic research models and the interpretation and extrapolation of research results into estimates of probabilities of individual behaviour and risk situation?

While the formal panels comprised presentations that gave rise to the scholarly essays published here, the Symposium also included a play written by Caryl Churchill entitled *A Number* (Churchill, 2002). This play explores the complex relationship between a father and his "sons." Having survived the death of his wife and children, a father arranges to clone a new child from the one he lost. Thirty years later three of these "sons" encounter their father.

Limitations both material and legal have prevented the inclusion of the play and its text in this collection. But we would be doing a disservice to the multidisciplinary aspirations of the RSC, to its deep commitment to informing public intellectual debate and State policy formation, and to the contributions of our panellists and authors were we not to draw attention to the full artistic as well as scientific dimensions of the 2007 Symposium.

The contributors to this collection are leading scholars drawn from diverse scientific fields and we readily acknowledge that scholars from many other disciplines as well have addressed the themes raised here. Explorations of the relationships among gene expressions, behaviour, and the social fabric also came from artists of various fields. The issues raised in the Symposium are rightly so enlightened by each and all of these scientific and cultural milieus. Our primary hope is that this collection might serve as a provocative stimulus to broader cross-disciplinary inquiry.

The theme of the papers in this volume engages the rich and continuing intellectual debates about the role of human and social factors, as opposed to influences external to them, in shaping the behaviour of human beings. This is a fertile terrain of inquiry, underpinned by conflicting paradigms and competing models, each aimed at explaining a whole range of complex processes and systems – including social behaviours and relationships, personality traits and disorders, epidemiological factors impacting on diseases, and disease-risks.

One longstanding tradition within the social sciences seeks to explain the social by the social. The focus is on how individuals and collectivities are influenced by, for example, family types in which child-rearing and parenting take shape, cultural beliefs and traditions passing from one generation to another, the accessibility of school systems and their educational resources to individuals and groups, and conceptions of what constitutes an appropriate life-style and life-project. Despite this preoccupation with the social, however, the influence of material and natural factors external to the social world could not always be simply dismissed. Natural cataclysms, spatial configuration and constraints, climate changes, and available material resources, to mention only a few such factors, occasionally figured in some analytical models as variables impacting on social processes and systems.

Theoretical debates and paradigm conflicts in the social sciences intensified when the factors opposed to the social were not external material facts, but were related to the innate nature of human beings. These inner dimensions of the human person constitute a vast domain of inquiry that attracts scholars from an array of disciplines. In addition, the domain is infused with complex beliefs, ideologies, and religious dogma about how the inner characteristics of the human condition constrain social processes and systems. Yet, under the impulse of late-nineteenth and early-twentieth century advances in biology, a new era of scientific inquiry exploring the innate nature of human subjects began to take shape. Indeed, within many branches of modern science, conflicting paradigms and competing models tended to reduce the scope of the innate to biological variables.

More significantly still, advances in genetics, buttressed, along with other factors, by the importance given to the brain as a new scientific frontier, have led to the increasing identification of biological variables with genetic factors. Finally, the spectacular advances of molecular genetics, following the full sequencing of the human genome, came to add further weight to genetic explanations of several social processes and systems bearing on human behaviour.

Thus, within modern sciences, biological markers and categories were claimed to have significant causal explanatory power. At the same time, however, leading social scientists strongly denounced the "naturalization" of social categories, processes, and thought. They generally argued for the social construction of distinguishing categories, like race or sex; in this latter case the notion of a socially constructed gender was advanced as a more accurate marker than sex for distinguishing human subjects within societies.

As we shall see in the following chapter, the dawn of the twentieth century saw the emergence of now well-known hyphenated couplets within many branches of modern science. Most prominently, the nature-nurture divide, and its many complex pendulum shifts, played a major role in debates about the respective merits of models putting the emphasis either on natural and biological factors (nature), or on cultural and a whole range of socio-economic dimensions (nurture), in shaping processes or systems under study.

Of course, as is often the case with catchphrases, these two terms conveyed quite different meanings depending on the particular discipline and domain where they were deployed, and on the particular processes and systems that were under investigation.

It is beyond the scope of this book, and especially of its first chapter, to review all the changes, nuances, and variations that this famous couplet went through within different contemporary scientific disciplines. This said, we cannot simply ignore the intellectual debates fuelled by the nature-nurture distinction. Obviously, the changing boundaries between gene expressions, behaviour, and the social fabric are embedded in quarrels regarding competing models meant to explain the respective imprints of biological and/or environmental factors on social processes and systems.

The various contributions to this book document how advances within genetics and molecular genetics gave great impetus to those arguing for the predominance of biological factors (nature) in shaping human behaviour. They also explain how sophisticated genetic determinisms are at work in various scientific and lay discourses. Unfortunately, these advances sometimes nourished the dream of achieving a eugenically driven utopia. Here and there during the twentieth century we can see the effects of a crass linkage of genetic markers to various dimensions of human behaviour, as if genetic engineering could either eradicate disorders and disease-risks or instrumentally control unwanted individual or collective behaviour.

Today, no one doubts that major advances in genetics raise new and crucial social issues. How are we to react, for example, to the possibility of genetic controls for disease-risk, genetically managed death and life, sex selection of children, screening for inheritable defects, food and species transformation prompted by bio or genetic technologies, economic markets and categories, as well as public policies pertaining to genetically influenced behaviours and therapies or genetically modified products and goods?

In the following chapter, we depict a more complex picture of contemporary advances in genetics, and in particular in molecular genetics. We note new ways of thinking and paradigm shifts that have emerged as a result of discoveries by molecular geneticists. We also signal the work of human and social sciences scholars who have been revisiting both the dogmas of modern genetics and the complex matrix of genetically and socially influenced behaviours. We highlight how, in the last decades of the twentieth century, these intellectual debates and competing models about gene and environment interplays led to more nuanced understandings of what previously had been framed as either/or propositions.

The objective of this book is to explore and explain how recent scientific discoveries bear upon current research, debates, and critiques. This book does not, and cannot, cover every dimension of competing models or new discoveries pertaining to the interrelationship of genetic and environmental factors. It aims, rather, to illustrate how genetic-determinist explanatory models have been thoroughly discredited by more sophisticated research. Of course, this does not mean that genetically oriented models can be simply replaced by social factors explanatory models. Rather, various chapters of this book report both environmentally and genetically related processes in areas such as specific personality traits or disorders, gene testing issues for Mendelian-genes or more complex diseases, functional genomics of stress impacts on behavioural variations, anti-social and physical aggression in child development, breast cancer disease disparities.

The emphasis now is on more probabilistic and complex models of gene and environment interrelationships. The boundaries of gene expressions, behaviour, and the social fabric are now changing as a result of more subtle models of the complex pathways, neurobiological and/or behavioural, through which genetic influences are channelled. These boundaries are shaped by the impacts at the organism level of epigenetic regulations, within which environmental factors play a much greater causal role.

There is another significant consequence of reflection on the changing boundaries of gene expressions, behaviour, and the social fabric as explored here. It pushes competing models and intellectual debates beyond the reductionist nature-nurture couplet. What emerges is the need for much more fine-grained scientific strategies and paradigms to combine and couple the respective impacts of genes and environment within both correlation and dynamic interaction models. Through a few revealing studies offered as exemplars, this book shows how human and social scientists and scientists working in modern genetic disciplines are contributing to new ways of addressing gene and environment interplays.

This collection of essays comprises nine thematic chapters divided in three sections. The book's first section presents three papers discussing personality traits or disorder issues, a rather rich, very complex, and hotly debated terrain for exploring complex interplays of genetic and social-environmental factors. This section begins with a piece on the few successes and many shortcomings of studies tying human intelligence inheritance to the exclusive or combined effects of genetic and/or environmental factors. The next paper is a review of a whole range of research strategies and research results, underpinned by reference to the sequencing of the human genome, which try to robustly associate genetic and environmental factors and personality traits. The section ends with a discussion of the potential contribution of a functional genomic approach, which could better highlight the numerous intermediary phenotypes that channel genetic and environmental factors impacting on personalities' stress-related behaviours.

The next section of this book presents three chapters that emphasize social and ethical issues pertaining to the potential genetic and environmental determinants of human behaviour. Its first essay comments on a sophisticated version of genetic determinism that still influences research in modern genetics and feeds the trend to geneticize several modern social processes. A second contribution to this section examines how scientific discussion of whether race is a biological reality or a social construct frequently end up, in popular discourse, as examples of a race geneticization process. The last thematic issue addressed in this section concerns the extent to which genetic predictive tests can result in genetic discrimination that reaches, beyond more usual social areas, into family and primary social relationships as well.

The third and final section of the book also comprises three chapters. It explores new frontiers for more interactive models of the combined effect of genetic and environmental factors on human behaviour. Its first piece looks at advances in experimental prevention analyses that rely upon epigenetic studies renewing explanatory frames applied to adverse rearing effects on child development. The second essay then examines how epigenetic transdisciplinary research challenging accepted gene and environment boundaries can shift the paradigm for understanding genetically sensitive diseases and health disparities. The section concludes with an essay that illustrates, in relation to late-onset Alzheimer's disease genetic testing, how the inconclusive and uncertain character of research outcomes fuels problematic understandings of modern genetic-related issues and of human subjects' identities.

Before presenting these thematic chapters and sections, we begin with a chapter discussing the major advances and strategic paradigm shifts that have occurred within the research field of genetically and environmentally influenced behaviours. Our goal in this first essay is not to provide an in-depth report and review of every discovery or new set of data generated by biological, biomedical, genetic, humanities, and social science research into the unilateral or combined impacts of genes and the environment on human behaviour.

Rather, we seek, without focusing on specific disciplines, to describe a sequence of research questions and advances that have contributed to more sophisticated understandings of the complex interplays between genes and the environment. This modern intellectual and scientific history of research questions, inquiries, and findings obviously concerns biological and genetic sciences; but this intellectual and scientific history also engages somehow the humanities and social sciences as well.

Key paradigm debates and shifts have been stimulated by new theoretical thinking about disease, disease risks, behaviours, and personality traits, which criss-crosses all scholarly disciplines. They have as well been nurtured by advanced research methodologies and technologies applied to observational studies specific to human subjects. Finally, these new paradigms have gained from the recourse to more sophisticated analytical models that dynamically and robustly combine multiple variables and factors in a manner that permits researchers to better decipher complex genetically and environmentally influenced human behaviours.

The conclusion to this collection of essays raises a series of questions about interdisciplinary scholarship of the type undertaken by the contributors. Disciplines will of course still fuel the core of research. However, we argue that interdisciplinarity research has its own major role to play. This requires scholars to adopt appropriate reflexive attitudes towards their respective disciplines and demands that universities and academic organizations like the RSC openly support interdisciplinarity. More generally, we hope that the papers in this collection will not only advance our understanding of the conditions and prospects of interdisciplinary dialogue in the sciences, the humanities and the arts, but will also make an important contribution to advancing our understanding of the relationship among gene expressions, behaviours, and the social fabric.

It would be naïve to think that recent advances in models deciphering the complex interrelationships of genes and environmental factors will end all intellectual debates. For reasons we set out in the following chapter, the future contribution of human and social sciences and modern genetic disciplines to our understanding of such complex issues does not easily lend itself to a dominant and shared integrative paradigm. Within these respective research communities, there still will be proponents of extreme mono-causal models pushing analysis towards a dominant factor, be it genes or socio-economic environments, taken in isolation from the more complex interrelationships between multiple variables discussed here. Likewise, there still will be those who oppose new paradigms that reach beyond our inherited traditional disciplinary categories.

Equally importantly, as the contributors to our book argue, intellectual debates and competing paradigms are still necessary to uncover and develop the foundational ethical and legal principles that are put into play by the manifold processes that reflect a combination of genetic and environmental impacts. Nourishing these ethical debates is a daunting task that confronts several scientific disciplines. For the most part, we have yet to elaborate the required principles to guide moral or norm-regulated behaviour in this rapidly evolving field of inquiry.

In our desire to confront these diverse challenges through the Symposium and the present book following from it, we opted for more rather than less science. It is our deepest conviction that robust and well-founded research strategies, within the humanities and social sciences, as well as modern genetic disciplines, are the best tools we can deploy to generate data, scientific criticisms, intellectual debates, and accurate as well as sophisticated explanatory models to shed brighter light on gene and environment interplays. We also believe that more dialogue across scholarly fields will add value to a scientific enterprise that aims to transcend accepted boundaries among gene expressions, behaviours, and the social fabric.

BIBLIOGRAPHY

Churchill, Caryl. 2002. *A Number*. London. Nick Hern Books Ltd. in association with the Royal Court Theatre.

CHALLENGING GENETIC DETERMINISM

The Changing Boundaries of Genes and Social Environment in Perspective: An Overview

LOUIS MAHEU AND RODERICK A. MACDONALD

The debates and questions thrown up by attempts to explore genetically and environmentally influenced processes and behaviours are, of course, part of the scientific and intellectual history of humanity – a history full of intriguing queries and fantastic discoveries. For many centuries the quest for knowledge and understanding of life's most profound questions was deeply embedded within overarching philosophical discourses, if not entrenched in religious beliefs and dogmas.

Only in the past few centuries has this quest been transformed into an array of systematic scholarly research questions. Indeed, in this universe of intellectual queries and discoveries, as in many other facets of the human experience, what has come to be characterized as the dawn of the modern era represents a crucial dividing line. With modernity a whole range of queries came to be cast in intellectual terms at arm's length from metaphysics or religion.

However, quite often our answers to crucial research questions give rise to big explanations grounded in meta-theories. As complex theoretical discourses, meta-theories do not easily lend themselves up-front to the rigorous experimentation and demonstration that characterizes scientific explanation. They nevertheless are quite helpful as they open the way to theoretically well-grounded hypotheses and to middle-range levels of analysis (Sklair 1987; Keat and Urry 1975). As well, meta-theories may inspire new data collection that can then be rigorously deployed to test more simple explanations and assumptions.

For a very long time, the development of living organisms has stimulated its own intriguing questions. Inquiry into the inheritance sequence of humans, as a discrete species within nature, has obviously been at the forefront of such research. Indeed, the quest to understand inheritance and inter-generational transmission of fundamental traits has been at the very core of meta-theories and research questions and strategies that seek to shed light on how living organisms of the same species develop through time.

THE STUDY OF THE DEVELOPMENT OF LIVING ORGANISMS: A FIELD OF THEORETICAL DEBATES

Throughout history human beings have posed challenging questions about the "real nature" of the development of living organisms. How are living organisms formed? Which relations, if any, link mature final traits to the status or shape of initial organisms? How are fundamental traits transmitted to and inherited by other generations of living organisms of the same species? It is hardly surprising that many different, and ultimately radically opposed, conceptual frames, embedded within philosophical discourses and entrenched in distinct meta-theories, emerged to tackle such queries.

However, as Jacob notes, "at a time when living beings are known by their visible structure alone, what has to be explained about generation (i.e., development) is the maintenance of this primary structure through succeeding generations." For Jacob, the crucial point is to recognize that the final traits of a mature organism, or the "germ" of what is to come has to be contained in the seed; "it has to be 'preformed'" (Jacob 1973; Kendler 2005c).

The term "preformed" is a coded term with a specific theoretical referent: It explicitly refers to developmental theories of "preformationism." And as Kendler suggests, preformationist developmental theories are strongly embedded within a number of philosophical discourses. First articulated by Aristotle, preformationism became particularly influential in the seventeenth century (Magner 1994; Moss 2003; Mayr 1982; Kendler 2005c). According to the preformationist perspective, the individual traits of mature and adult living organisms are the product of a few expanded preformed characteristics or elements, usually called *anlagen*. Before modern times, many different developmental meta-theories flourished, including various sub-currents of the preformationist master-frame, each of which offered a competing explanation of the guiding forces underlying inheritance and the development of living organisms.

Nonetheless, there seems to be a straight-line critical path from preformationist theoretical viewpoints to Mendel's idea of the "elements of inheritance." According to Kendler (2005c) during the nineteenth century, the emerging field of biology entertained a number of theories that still embedded significant preformationist hypotheses and themes (Magner 1994; Dunn 1965). Thus, adds Kendler, "when Mendel's ground-breaking work on genetics (originally published in 1866) was rediscovered in 1900, one common interpretation was that his 'elements of inheritance' were the discrete anlagen predicted by preformationist theories" (2005c; Moss 2003).

For several decades beginning in the late nineteenth century, theoretical conceptualizations increasingly came to rest on ideas that resonated with what had previously been termed *anlagen*. At the turn of the twentieth century, these elements of inheritance were coined "genes" (Kendler 2005c; Dunn 1965). Influential geneticists of that era, encountering Mendelism, set about to reshape preformationist concepts and theories in new theory-building exercises, the cornerstone of which were now "genes." Referring explicitly to deVries and Bateson, for example, Kendler and others (Allen 2003; Dunn 1965; Falk 1995) claim that "the Mendelian anlagen (later genes) could be defined by their relationship to the particular phenotype (or 'unit character') with which it had a privileged causal link. That is, such *genes caused phenotypes* in the same way that the preformationist anlagen prefigured adult traits" (Kendler 2005c).

Under preformationist master-frames the key analytical factor of development and inheritance was conceptualized as the element, the gene, of a visible structure that it causes; and the visible structure so caused – a personality trait, or disorder, or disease – was called a *phenotype*. It is, then, not surprising that in the first part of the twentieth century, theoretical views about genetic effects tended to establish the powerful impact on many outcomes of "nature" – nature standing for these elements (genes) already containing, up-front so to speak, all information needed by mature organisms in their final state. Thereafter, a biologically determined concept of nature, most often uninfluenced by environmental mediation of any kind, crept into scientific conceptual frames and eventually into experiments and demonstrations.

This genetic conception of nature has been a powerful hypothesis for the study of many different dependent variables. Plant and animal development; personality traits; human behaviours and disorders; as well as diseases and disease-risks in immunology were among the more active research fields where such a conception was prevalent. While each field had its own paradigmatic traditions and diversified theoretical sub-currents, each shared the universal emphasis given to nature as being the guiding factor undergirding the development of plants, animals, and human personality and behaviour.

PENDULUM SHIFTS BETWEEN INHERITANCE AND ENVIRONMENT

In the first part of the twentieth century the behavioural sciences both generated and were nourished by analytic trends linking elements of inheritance to personality traits and disorders. Twin and adoptee studies, for example, played important roles in linking genetic inheritance to personality traits or disorders within specific populations at specific times. Genes were overwhelmingly held to be the main causal factor. The notion of genetic effects pervaded a good number of heritability analyses dealing both with intelligence and with personality traits or disorders such as anorexia, schizophrenia, bipolar illness, and attention deficit. Inquiry into the development of organisms adopted and replicated what might be called a "crude genetic determinism" reminiscent of preformationist meta-theories. More-over, in the arena of political policies and practices, with genetic determinism also came eugenic interventions based on the view that genes directly cause various phenotypes (Rutter et al. 2006; Kendler 2005c; Rutter 2006).

In many conceptual frames, the emphasis given to nature is associated with a latent, if not at times explicit, dichotomy. At one pole lie genes. The other pole comprises a series of factors embedded within the general notion of environment. Some speak of the dichotomy of the mind and the body, others of the mental and the functional, or the biological and the organic (Kendler 2005 b). According to Plomin, at the end of the nineteenth century Galton coined the famous hyphenated term: nature-nurture. And he added that "nature prevails over nurture ... when the differences of nurture do not exceed what is commonly to be found among persons of the same rank in the same country" (Galton 1883; Plomin 1994).

Emphasizing nature as an explanatory factor led some scientists to argue that the gene contains all the information needed for the development of a phenotype, for example a personality trait. In so arguing, they implicitly acknowledged only a trivial role for the mind or the environment in developing any given phenotype. Not all scientists who looked through the prism of genetic determinism in the first part of the twentieth century were discreet about the implications of their research. A good number stated loudly and repeatedly that they could not conceive of any important causal role played by factors standing for the environment, or for that matter nurture (Plomin 1994; Rutter et al. 2006; Rutter 2006).

Despite these latter mono-causal claims, the dichotomy between nature and nurture still grounded research activities and debates throughout this period. It played an important role in sustaining sharp paradigmatic conflicts between conceptual frames relating to human development and inheritance. In addition, despite the overall predominance of the nature pole of the dichotomy, it would be misleading to conclude that the nurture pole never assumed the leading position in scholarly inquiry.

By mid-twentieth century, what many saw as outrageous eugenic interventions and misguided views of deterministic genetic effects had led to considerable distrust of genetic thinking and practice, and of behavioural sciences (Rutter et al. 2006). Earlier research results that apparently displayed all the hallmarks of robust and rigorous empirical investigation suddenly appeared to be less convincing and promising. The discovery of a number of theoretical misconceptions, methodological weaknesses, replication failures, and other defects underlying complex research designs seriously compromised the scientific credibility of the crude genetic determinism hypothesis.

Moreover, within the behavioural sciences, many voices pointed to studies showing crucial and significant relationships between various environments and personality traits or disorders. Twin and adoptee studies focusing on experiences, for example, within or outside the family of origin, and on the upbringing of children, mainly in the early years, brought new insights into development, inheritance, and personality traits or disorders. Though they were less influential at the beginning of the twentieth century, theories emphasizing environmental factors achieved significant acceptance by mid-century. According again to Plomin, in 1925, one major proponent of environmentalist views, Watson, took on genetic determinism by explicitly declaring: "There is no such thing as an inheritance of capacity, talent, temperament, mental constitution and characteristics" (Watson 1925; Plomin 1994).

After World War II behaviourism flourished as a coded term meant to account for the powerful imprint of learning and experience on all forms of behaviour (Rutter et al. 2006). Influential scholars contributed to enlarging behaviouristic master-frames within the social sciences (Skinner 1972; Watson 1925, 1928). According to reviewers and commentators who were already aware of the importance of biologically determined factors, the very first decades of the second part of the twentieth century could be labelled a period of "extreme environmentalism" (Rutter et al. 2006; Plomin 1994).

By this point, the pendulum had swung towards acknowledging the key role of multiple guiding forces belonging to the environment. For behavioural scientists, these environmental features clearly bear the mark of social relationships and social context. Whether present either latently or explicitly in various conceptual frames, experiments, and scholarly discussions, the nurture side of the dichotomy reasserted itself, to the point, some would argue, of excluding from certain fields of inquiry research into the impact of nature and its cornerstone – genes.

But in the last quarter of the twentieth century the pendulum swung once again. Major research in behavioural genetics, including psychiatric genetics, made available evidence, again mainly through expanded twin and adoptee studies, about the importance of genetic influences on variations in individual liabilities to personality traits and mental disorders. Not surprisingly, this trend was accompanied by its traditional corollary: A renewed denial of the importance of environmental influences (Rutter et al. 2006). As Kendler also notes (2005c), two books, one by E. O. Wilson (1975) and the other by R. Dawkins (1976), had a significant impact on promoting gene-centred views of the evolution of living organisms.

The resurgence of genetic determinism in the late twentieth century was also fuelled by other factors. Powerful developments in tools, methodologies, and theories of molecular biology assisted scientists in tracking down specific genes and gene mutations that could be responsible for human traits and disorders. These molecular genetic strategies were then applied to psychiatric genetics. Moreover, the extensive publicity afforded to the complete and successful sequencing of the human genome led, both in the scientific literature and the popular media, to the proclamation of a triumphant genetic and neurogenetic determinism (Rutter et al. 2006; Kendler 2005c; Nelkin 1995; Rose 1995).

Genetic determinism, sometimes of a very subtle kind, seems more or less an irreducible component of modern behavioural sciences. As Françoise Baylis argues in her chapter, the disconnect between what we know and we do with respect to genetic and environmental factors bearing on traits and behaviours ultimately nourishes the geneticization of social processes. Such an attitude, prompted by a resilient gene-centric perspective rather than overt genetic determinism, gives priority to specific genotypes for many phenotypes. The disconnect she observes perpetuates itself because social forces, within academic research and more generally within diverse social milieus, including of course business corporations, render it very useful and profitable, especially to pharmaceutical companies.

The trends mentioned by Baylis are also central to Timothy Caulfield's discussion of the reification of race within public representations. In his chapter, Caulfield notes that quarrels and paradigmatic conflicts internal to the research community about whether race is a biological reality or a social construct more often than not end up being publicly expressed as a matter of race geneticization. Market forces and ambiguous research designs contribute, Caulfield argues, to the genetic reification of race in popular discourse. Moreover, provocative (if not sensationalized) media coverage – the BiDil pharmacogenomic drug supposedly helpful in palliating the risk of heart disease among "black" Americans being a paradigmatic example – is a powerful driver of the race geneticization processes.

Looking retrospectively at these intellectual inquiries and research findings, we see a scholarly universe of great diversity at work over an extended period of time. To date, no uniform set of criteria capable of capturing the whole panoply of theoretical and methodological sub-currents and schools of thought has been generally accepted. Yet the search for big explanations – all grounded in conflicting meta-theories – continues to shape the contemporary scientific quest for the role and function of elements of inheritance and/or of mental and environmental factors. Notwithstanding an intellectual context driven by conflicting paradigms, however, numerous scientific milieus have risen to the challenge of designing and executing creative research agenda that in turn have generated robust scholarly outcomes.

A MORE COMPLEX PICTURE OF MODERN GENETICS

The swinging pendulum between meta-theories promoting either nature or nurture is just the visible tip of a stratified iceberg. Obviously, over the past 30 years developments in modern genetics, including behavioural genetics, cannot be reduced to a one-sided or unidimensional description. An increasingly complex scientific field, modern genetics, or more precisely modern molecular genetics, has experienced major paradigmatic changes, some of which continue to have great influence on promising research pertaining to the development of living organisms.

In a programmatic paper published in 2005, Kendler (2005b) called for a number of epistemological improvements in the field of psychiatry. His appeal for a new analytic framework takes direct aim at genetic psychiatry and, more globally, behavioural genetics. Kendler suggested abandoning what he labels the sterile trend to seek out, whatever the cost, big meta-theoretical explanations. He argued for more complex, more grounded and more pluralist explanatory models focused on developing and testing less comprehensive explanations.

Thus, Kendler proposed that dualistic Cartesian thinking and vocabulary, still too entrenched in the way clinical and research problems are addressed, be rejected. In particular, he asserted that the mind-body and nature-nurture dichotomies have to be transcended. Further, he claimed that epiphenomenalism, which lodges causal explanation at the level of the brain function as an organic component, or at the level of living organisms' cells, must be overcome. Living organisms evolve and develop through experiences, thoughts, feelings, impulses, and of course behaviours and relationships with their environment. It follows that causality models looking both at genetic influence on the environment and at the reverse influence of environment on the genes – that is, bidirectional causality models – should provide the necessary underpinning of systematic research programs. According to Kendler, these epistemological improvements will pave the way to more appropriate theory-building, to robust scientific experiments and to more meaningful results within genetic behavioural sciences (Kendler 2005b).

Although Kendler's paper has an obvious programmatic orientation, at the same time it testifies to, and reports, various paradigmatic changes already exemplified by contemporary research strategies. In the following paragraphs, we shall underline some of the most important theoretical developments in modern molecular genetics. These have not, of course, put internal quarrels and conceptual conflicts within and between theoretical and methodological subcurrents to rest. Nevertheless they represent significant advances that offer opportunities for new interdisciplinary dialogue that will highlight the relationship of gene expressions with their environments, including the social environment.

The Promise and Limitations of Quantitative Genetics

During the twentieth century, quantitative genetics was mainly concerned with estimating and predicting the relative strength of genetic effects on the variation of traits or disorders within populations. Its most well-known research outcomes were experiments, usually twin and adoptee studies, that sought, within specific populations at precise time periods, to link genetic factors to psychological traits or mental disorders. The heritability predictions that resulted were not meant to apply to individuals; rather they spoke to variations within specific populations (Rutter 2006).

Until the end of the past century, quantitative genetics data offered, at best, only a description of certain relationships between unspecified genes' effects – "latent omnibus genetic effects" (Moffit et al. 2006) – and some liabilities for certain traits. Moreover, this black box statistical association could not be generalized to larger populations; the results obtained were more or less sample-specific and time-specific (Rutter 2006). In other words, these research outcomes were applicable uniquely to specific populations living in precise period of times, for example monozygotic twins at a precise stage of their development and most often of the same sex within a precise ethnic group. Even then, the statistical genetic differences between individuals within these populations accounted for only a proportion of the variance for personality traits or disorders.

These research results often generated intense debate about their validity and their interpretation. Both the conceptual frames adopted and methodological characteristics of the studies limited the scope of application of these heritability scores. Quantitative genetics asks how much of a trait variation is influenced by genetic factors. It does not explain how these genetic factors operate to condition the distribution of personality traits and disorders. While this branch of genetic research mainly addresses variance proportion for traits or disorders, it also raises questions about the significance that should be attributed to such variations in the overall problematic of gene and environment relationships.

Advances in molecular genetics at the end of the century, however, heralded a move beyond quantitative genetics' known limits. Up till then, the bulk of quantitative genetics research was addressed to discovering latent omnibus genetic effects. The successful sequencing of the human genome helped substitute for these genetically unspecified effects research into measurable effects of identified genes. Thus were highlighted susceptibility genes' impacts on traits, disorders, and behaviours. Consequently, heritability scores for personality traits and disorders were expected to gain significantly in robustness as specific identified genes were co-related to behavioural outcomes.

In following years, research strategies have, predictably, come to focus on tracking identified genes. Association studies determining whether particular traits or disorders are related to a particular gene or genetic allele, e.g., an alternative form of a gene at a particular locus on a chromosome, stimulated renewed quantitative genetic research. As well, linkage studies, usually focusing through whole genome scans on sib pairs to determine potential co-inheritance between a gene locus and a trait, were an important part of these new research strategies. Thus, association and linkage explanatory models pursued this new challenge of linking more or less directly a susceptibility gene to behaviour (Rutter 2006).

After a period of considerable research enthusiasm, however, the revised quantitative genetics approach ultimately did not meet the expectations raised by advances in molecular genetics. Overall, this new brand of quantitative genetics was subject to as much critical commentary as quantitative genetics received during the period when it did not rely upon advances within molecular genetics. Repeated replication failures soon raised major concerns about published association and linkage studies.

In his contribution to this book, Douglas Wahlsten – deploying an approach also followed by Jonathan Flint in his own piece – systematically reviews the theoretical conceptions and methodological characteristics of a good number of association studies with respect to personality traits, and more precisely human intelligence. His conclusion is nuanced and commendable: Any one single gene would at best explain only an insignificant proportion of the phenotypic variation for human intelligence. The point is that personality characteristics are influenced by multiple genes, and each of them exercises very small effects on specific personality traits. As a consequence, on the basis of current knowledge, one must conclude, according to Wahlsten, that genetic influences on personality traits can never serve as robust foundations to any social or policy-oriented intervention.

The genetic influence on personality traits and disorders is thus revealed to be a much more complex matter than would be predicted by most conceptual frames and methodological designs founded on quantitative genetics. Indeed, unreplicated findings have played a crucial role in sowing suspicion of studies purportedly directly connecting identified susceptibility genes to behavioural outcomes (Rutter 2006; Kendler 2005c). While it was at first thought, optimistically, that the era of major advances in molecular genetics, would permit traditional research weaknesses in quantitative genetics to be overcome and to facilitate improvements in research paradigms, in the end this era turned out to be a "dispiriting period" (Rutter et al. 2006).

Quantitative genetics, one may conclude, has objective limits – both as to research design and as to research outcomes. For example, heritability studies depend upon stable conditions for populations sampled, for time periods covered, and for environmental conditions under which they are executed. Still, some researchers continued to insist that rather strong heritability scores were obtained, at least for some mental disorders (Rutter 2006). Others, however, noted what a limited and worrisome proportion of the sample variance could be explained in this way (Plomin et al. 1977; Plomin 1994). In the end, the broader scientific community came to have mixed feelings about the overall results of quantitative genetics research.

At the same time, it would be wrong to declare genetic effects totally innocuous. Their magnitude is nowhere near determinative, but neither is it trivial (Kendler and Prescott 2006). The most obvious conclusion is that there are clear conceptual and analytic limits to calculating heritability scores. At best these estimates testify to some genetic influences that need to be better understood and explained. Progress depends on developing more complex conceptual frames and analytic models that better account for genetic risk factors, environmental risk factors, and their possible interplay in the study of behavioural outcomes.

Serendipity Effect: Environmental Impacts through the Role of Mediating Variables

Despite these disappointments, quantitative genetics nonetheless did produce a crucial serendipity effect that contributed to a paradigm shift and helped generate more nuanced epistemological positions. Behavioural genetic research provided "the best available evidence for the impact of the environment" (Plomin 1994; Rutter 2006): twin and adoptee studies confirmed that usually more than half of the variance for some traits of behavioural development cannot by accounted for by genetic factors (Plomin 1994). As Plomin notes: "However, as the pendulum swings from nurture to nature in many fields such as psychiatry, it is important to emphasize the point just made: the same quantitative genetics data that made the case for the importance of genetic differences also provide strong evidence for the importance of non-genetic factors" (1994).

All environmental measures that have an impact on personality traits, disorders, or behaviours are obviously not genetic in origin. It has been well documented that proximal as well as more or less distal environmental factors influence individuals and communities in their respective developmental trajectories. Still, research advances depended on a further step being taken – namely programmatic suggestions about appropriate conceptual models of the interplay of gene and environment. The serendipity effect arising from quantitative genetics was to focus inquiry on more complex and pluralist explanatory models that required increased attention to be given to the role of the environment in relationship with genetic effects. As we shall see below, Plomin among others (1994) contributed to these advances by proposing correlation models of genes' interplays with environmental factors as a key to explaining how personality traits or disorders are generated.

Another important paradigm shift necessary for the development of more complex models of the interplay of gene and environment involved seriously questioning the propensity of quantitative behavioural genetics to rely on "additive effects" hypotheses for the study of genetic and environmental influences (Rutter 2006; Moffit et al. 2006). Of course, genetic effects can sometimes be added to environmental effects in explaining how some personality traits, disorders, and behavioural outcomes are produced, and therefore the idea of parallel additive influences of gene and environment cannot simply be dismissed (Kendler and Prescott 2006).

Still, even accepting that environmental and genetic factors can exercise parallel additive influences for some behavioural outcomes, it is important to ask if these cases are really the norm. In order to study non-additive synergistic interplays between gene and environment much more sophisticated conceptual frameworks and research strategies are required. These frameworks would generate and propose integrative interplay models and hypotheses (Caspi and Moffit 2006). Such models would emphasize that specific behaviours ultimately are the outcomes of genetic influences only if and when they are also fashioned by facilitative or transformative effects exercised by environmental factors. Of course, the potential for a reverse causality pattern would equally be emphasized in these models: Specific behaviours could stem from environmental factor influences being mediated or moderated by active genetic factors.

The discussion that follows will rapidly detail the differences of and the role played in modern genetics by, on the one hand, correlation models, and on the other hand, synergistic co-action models as better ways to address gene and environment interplays. While these models underpinned conventional research strategies and findings, they also nurtured crucial paradigmatic shifts within modern genetics.

So, for example, Plomin recognizes that the bulk of research in the mid-seventies that was underpinned by correlation models depicted the environment as a mediating stimulus. Family and child-rearing contexts are the classical examples of a passive type of correlation between environment and genes. In this case, at least during early childhood, identified children share heredity and environmental influences with members of their family (Plomin 1994). Passive correlation of genes to environmental factors mostly concern genetic factors characterizing the parents of offspring (Rutter and Silberg 2002). Of course, more complex correlation models of genetic and environmental interplays would also show the relevance of mediating factors related to the contexts within which human subjects act and behave.

Driven by macro-theories (Wachs 1992) and references to Bronfenbrenner's (1989, 1994) ecological model for the study of various environment levels and systems, at least two other correlation pathways among genes and environment were identified. Plomin proposes a distinction between reactive (also called evocative) and active types of genes and environment correlations. According to Plomin (1994), reactive or evocative correlation types would cover environmental mediation for traits, disorders, or behaviours constitutive of a child's experiences that are influenced by reactions of other people to the child's genetic propensities. By contrast, active correlation between genes and environment, which seemed increasingly to drive research towards the end of the past century, presupposes and reveals human subjects as exercising a more autonomous agency. Open to constructionist viewpoints, the active correlation between genes and environment factors puts the emphasis on the notion of experience and on the capacities of actors to select or create environments that are compatible with their own genetic propensities (Plomin 1994; Rutter et al. 2006).

The classic example of the active correlation model of gene and environment factors evokes genetic control of exposure to environmental risk factors. It illustrates how individuals with genetic-specific risk backgrounds for traits or disorders would respond to environmental risk factors, like stressful life events or low social support, through a personality trait, especially neuroticism or extroversion in most studied cases (Kendler and Baker 2007). By definition, not all of these individuals would be sensitive to environmental risk factors such as stressful life events or low social support. To have an impact on behaviour or outcomes, environmental risk factors have to be channelled. Only individuals behaving as neurotic or extroverted personalities, for example, would openly manifest a relevant sensitivity to such environmental risk factors (Caspi and Moffit 2006; Moffit et al. 2006).

On the other hand, environmental risk factors are differently influenced by genetic factors. Thus heritability estimates for some personality traits or behavioural outcomes are conditioned by environmental factors. Overall, these heritability estimates for more or less environmentally mediated personality traits or behavioural outcomes remain significant, although not overwhelming (Kendler and Baker 2007).

Both active and evocative/reactive correlation models of the interplay of genes and environmental factors require the intervention of a mediator variable. More often than not, the intervening mediator variable derives from the behaviour of human subjects. The key causal factor here is how subjects shape and select the different environments in which they will act. They mainly do so through their capacity to act as agents: The behaviour of individual subjects turns environmental dimensions into risk factors (Rutter 2006).

All these studies point to the conclusion that there is no direct relationship of a genotype to an outcome, to a personality trait, to a disorder, or to behaviour. Genes interact with environmental factors through indirect pathways, through behavioural mediating variables. As a result of changing paradigms relating to the interplay of genes and environment, research studies are now quite far removed from the straightforward hypothesis that a gene directly causes a phenotype. Crude genetic determinism or predetermined programming is no longer sustainable in the face of multifactorial environmental indicators sustaining gene and environment correlations. Today research refers rather to probabilistic propensities sustaining complex, sophisticated gene and environment correlations in shaping behavioural outcomes, including personality traits and disorders (Plomin et al. 1977; Plomin 1994; Kendler and Prescott 2006).

From Resistance to the Role of Environmental Factors to Multifactorial Genetic and Environmental Pathways

Correlation models of interplays between gene and environment ultimately emphasize genetic control of exposure to the environment, or environmental factors differently influenced by genetic variables. In such analytic models, environmental factors obviously appear on the radar screen as influential factors for some behavioural outcomes. But this does not mean that the complex and diversified roles of environmental factors have been entirely deciphered. Many questions remain. Can we speak of more direct causal power of environmental factors for some behavioural outcomes mediated by genetic propensities? Can environmentally mediated factors be associated to behavioural outcomes and genotype susceptibility? Can environmental factors modify genotype inheritances?

To address such research questions we need more complex conceptual frames and analytic models. Gene by environment interaction models could of course be relevant for such queries. Before we turn to these models of gene and environment interplays, however, it is useful to consider why there is continued resistance to emphasizing environmental factors in their relationships with genetic factors.

The origin of some of the critical reactions to research proposals that downplay the direct relationship of a genotype to a phenotype, and that acknowledge the active role of environmental factors correlated with genes to shape behavioural outcomes are well known. Single structural gene effects, the effects of those genes often called Mendelian genes, are consistently portrayed as being a direct relationship of a genotype to a phenotype. Such single Mendelian genes are more directly related to rather intensively studied specific diseases: cystic fibrosis, achondroplasia, Huntington disease, etc. Originally seen as significant also for psychiatric disorders, Mendelian structural gene effects however now seem less amenable for the inheritance of multifactorial mental disorders (Rutter 2006, 1994). Most often, however, abnormalities linked to Mendelian inheritance are due to gene mutations that do not appear to require the involvement of any environmental risk experience (Rutter 2006).

Let us, before continuing this discussion of questions concerning the direct relationship of genotypes to phenotypes, note the interesting contribution to an enlarged problematic for assessing Mendelian structural genes that emerges from the essay in this book by Yvonne Bombard and Michael Hayden. Their chapter concerns Huntington Disease (HD), the causation pathways of which tend to show that, at least on the basis of current knowledge in this particular case, genetic factors still exercise much more influence than what could be considered environmental factors. It also is a disease for which predictive gene testing has a longer history. Indeed, it is one of the first diseases to benefit from what are generally deemed accurate predictive tests. These special features of HD present Bombard and Hayden with a rare opportunity to address a more precise and relatively under-studied issue, the link between gene testing and genetic discrimination arising as a consequence of gene testing.

Taking a sample of tested individuals with the genetic HD mutation and of at-HD-risk individuals who have not been tested, their findings show complex experiences of stigmatized identities and life-cycle patterns. As a consequence of diverse manifestations of social stigma often prompted by awareness of previous life events, a peculiar interaction between gene and social environment arises. For individuals suffering genetic discrimination, genetic information and testing are received and managed through a variety of difficult and intricate relationships in diverse social settings. To cope with tension-driven relationships within the workplace and with insurance companies, distinctive types of engagement strategies, involving cognitive and emotional components, are used by affected individuals. Although they are careful to qualify their results and call for further research, Bombard and Hayden argue that these contexts of genetic discrimination tend ultimately to link up with another discriminatory environmental setting that is much less studied – the family and primary social relationships.

Even for Mendelian structural gene effects though, progress in molecular genetics at the end of the twentieth century has contributed to crucial paradigm shifts. For these genes, but much more significantly for genetics effects in general, increasingly fine-grained and accurate research results have tended to establish, at the organism level, more sophisticated and indirect genetic causation pathways. For example, protein coding genes, as a result of mRNA molecule syntheses conditioned by DNA through transcription and translation processes, were shown to explain only a small proportion of genes' effects. Only an astonishingly small amount of the DNA sequence was revealed to give rise to protein-coding genes. As a result, researchers were obliged to pay more attention, beyond protein coding genes, to a large inventory of gene mutations or of gene-related mechanisms, to allelic variations in genes' structure, to differential and more complex gene interactions and to gene expressions.

Gene to gene interactions, the impacts of multiple non-coding genes on transcription and translation processes for coding genes obviously called for additional research. As a consequence, the genetic behavioural sciences were required to pay more rigorous attention to multiple genes with limited single effects, to genes with multiple and different effects (genetic pleiotropy mechanisms), and to gene expression mechanisms. The influential role played by non-protein coding genes within a class of mechanisms called epigenetic mechanisms inspired key research programs. Epigenetic regulation mostly concerns heritable states not depending on the stable DNA sequence of individuals (Rutter 2006). This research revealed that epigenetic regulations were linked to differential effects stemming from environmental factors (Jaenisch and Bird 2003).

Incomplete genetic penetration amongst generations, parental imprinting, and other diversified genetic transcription, regulation, and expression mechanisms reveal the limitations of the single Mendelian genes model, which postulates direct relationships of genotypes to phenotypes (Rutter 2006). Particularly in the crucial field of neurobiology, genes have been found to act through much more complex causal pathways than previously expected.

The term *endophenotype*, or intermediate phenotype, has been coined to identify some complex physiological or cognitive pathways channelling genotype effects on possible behavioural outcomes (Gottesman and Gould 2003). This term was proposed because scholars felt that it might be more productive, within molecular genetics research, to first focus on genes' impacts on biological factors rather than to tie them directly to a personality trait, a disorder, or a disease. Among the key biological factors playing a role in causal mechanisms leading to specific outcomes are the manifold dimensions of brain structure and functioning, though some effective endophenotypes may also be more or less directly influenced by environmental factors (Abbott 2008).

The consequence of this research is that multifactorial explanatory models came to replace more direct genetic-causation approaches. What Kendler and Prescott call the "inside the skin" genetic pathway (2006) can be seen as a set of indirect channels by which genes are related to phenotypes. But the picture still is incomplete. Although visible and active first at the organic molecular level, these more complex and differentiated "inside the skin" genetic pathways are not totally unconnected with the arena of behaviours and their relevant environmental factors. Indeed, they tend to crisscross, to be woven to "outside the skin" webs of pathways for gene and environment interplays (Kendler and Prescott 2006). Inside the skin webs of pathways, as well as a number of outside the skin pathways, highlight the important functions played by intermediate phenotypes, or endophenotypes, within the overall relationship between genotypes and behavioural outcomes.

Petronis (2001) convincingly argues that explanatory models based on multifactorial genetic and environmental factors are unavoidable when it comes to understanding complex diseases. Complex diseases exhibit a heritable component but do not follow Mendel's laws. At both the molecular and behavioural levels, multifactorial explanatory models can enlighten "the dynamic epigenetic inheritance system (that) provides a cohesive explanation for the various features of complex diseases, and epigenetic mechanisms can be a common denominator for the wide variety of epidemiological, clinical, and molecular findings in such diseases" (Petronis 2001; Petronis et al. 2003).

Before presenting some preliminary conclusions about these research advances, let us briefly note their impact on genetically related disease risk issues. This is a question admirably discussed by Margaret Lock in her contribution to this book on the basis of ethnographic findings regarding late-onset Alzheimer's disease genetic testing of individuals who would eventually be at risk. Contrary to what has been previously assumed – and unfortunately continues to be assumed by too many scholars and the public at large – incontrovertible evidence from basic science studies, namely developments in molecular epigenetic research, clearly establish that genome segments are very rarely, if ever, straightforward determinants of disease.

In the case of late-onset Alzheimer's disease, epidemiological research mainly targeting the most popular "susceptibility gene" candidate (APOE) ends up with clearly inconclusive research results. Even though this research unfortunately covers almost exclusively Caucasian populations, these last findings are quite coherent with epigenetic basic science results for a disease that moreover lacks clear diagnosis patterns. At most, this candidate gene is part of a much more complex causation system including gene cluster interactions, human and evolutionary history factors, environmental conditions, individual and collective life-cycle patterns, and other behavioural variations.

Ultimately, this means that in the "risk society" global context we allude to below individuals declared genetically at risk on the basis of knowledge given to them about specifics of their personal genome, confront a more complex problematic of embodied identities. As Lock points out, what genetic testing is bringing to their condition is more uncertainty about their future. According to Lock's ethnographic findings, the genetic information individuals get – information that a good number of them are surprisingly unable to recall or correctly retain – tends to supplement and reinforce rather than negate or displace their existing thoughts and beliefs about embodied identities, and genetically related issues more globally. These beliefs and cultural frames have already been well documented by several interesting human and social sciences studies.

In other words, in this specific context of gene testing, and regardless of the scientific nuances they are presented about the multiple impacts of genetic and environmental factors, people generally still revert to beliefs of an unsophisticated "blended heritance" from both parents when confronting genetic-related issues. As epigenetic research progresses, Lock concludes, we may hope for a broader public dissemination of the understanding that genes are not just an individual matter, but that they respond to a dynamic interpenetration of nature with history, culture, and permeable boundaries of self, as well as other complex relationships.

From this review of studies, we can see that many analysts accepted that new knowledge about complex gene expressions pathways requires, within behavioural sciences, a shift in the research paradigm and a more emphatic rejection of crude genetic and neurogenetic determinism. These latter paradigm shifts, some argued, have opened the way to still more ambitious research undertakings. Beyond gene and environment correlation models, the ambition now is to uncover and explore real, objectively measurable, co-action and interaction models of the interplay between gene expressions and environmental factors.

Moderator Variables Challenging Gene and Environment Interplays

Correlation model interplays between gene and environment have a significant consequence: They nicely illustrate mainly genetic control of exposure to environmental risk factors. In so doing, they clarify how environmental risk factors are influenced by genetic factors. They also highlight the overlap of genetic factors that simultaneously predispose to specific traits, disorders, or behaviours and influence exposure to measured environmental risk factors.

Interestingly, these correlation model interplays have their own serendipity effect: Significant but not overwhelming heritability estimates for genetically influenced differential environmental factors ultimately indicate the influence of other factors on outcomes and behaviours. This conclusion highlights the relevance of gene-environment covariance explanatory models (Kendler and Baker 2007). But when it comes to explaining the respective and combined impact of genetic and environmental factors on behavioural outcomes, correlation model interplays reveal their limits.

To systematically explore the changing boundaries among gene expressions and the social environment, and to give real meaning to interactive relationships between genes and the environment, more complex conceptual frames are needed. These frameworks would generate "gene by environment (GxE)" models moving beyond measuring additive-only effects of genetic and environmental factors, and putting the emphasis on synergetic co-action of genetic and environmental factors in shaping outcomes and behaviours. With research strategies and hypotheses focusing on dynamic bidirectional relationships between environmental and genetic factors, these models tend to explain how specific behaviours are complex interactive outcomes of both genetic and environmental factors. In these back-and-forth interactive outcomes, each factorial category constantly tends to frame and moderate the enduring effects of the other factorial category. Epigenetic regulations of gene expressions, which shall also retain our attention, illustrate at the organism level how the environment can interact with identified genetic factors to pave the way for behaviours.

More sophisticated conceptual frames require correspondingly more robust statistical and mathematical tools. The aim is ambitious: to achieve research advances that will pave the way to modelling not only how environmentally mediated factors alter and moderate genetic effects on outcomes but as well how environmental factors moderate various gene expressions and interactions, and eventually genotype inheritances. Co-action models of interplays between gene and environment require researchers to not only measure the respective roles of complex genetic and environmental factors, but also to measure their combined action.

Thus modern approaches to genetics that seek to go beyond correlation model interplays face major analytic challenges. Gene and environment co-action models are more promising if genetic effects introduced in modelling equations are more than omnibus, latent, inferred genetic effects. While research models using inferred genetic effects may signal the likelihood of gene by environment interaction for some groups of disorders, identified and measured susceptibility genes, sustained by advances specifically in molecular genetics, have to be available if research is to go even further (Rutter et al. 2006). Hence, the crucial role played by identified genes, as well as identified environment risk factors. Clearly, identified single susceptibility genes, working or not in interaction with other genes, are key components for developing improved interplay models of the gene and environment relationship.

As we shall later see, David Goldman's chapter in this book clearly states a conclusion with which many in behavioural genetics would now agree. Indeed, if based on well-selected very large samples, the strategic end-result of current association and linkage studies should be to reliably identify specific candidate genes that could be related, for example, to distinctive personality or disorder traits.

It should thus be acknowledged that studies of gene by environment interplays demand carefully and technically controlled genetic measures and identified and measured environmental risk pathogens. Both are prerequisites to robust and accurate equation modelling of the combined action of environmental and genetic factors (Moffit et al. 2006; Caspi and Moffit 2006; Kendler and Prescott 2006).

Within genetic psychiatry, and in other medical research fields, pioneering research results are now being reported as outputs of gene by environment interactions (Rutter 2006), also called by Kendler and Prescott "genetic control of sensitivity to environmental factors," or "environmental control of gene expression" (Kendler and Prescott 2006). An oft-cited study by Caspi et al. (2003) illustrates how environmentally mediated effects of maltreatment and stressful life events impact on depressive behaviours. The relationship between depressive behaviour and environmental factors is moderated by a specific polymorphism in the promoter region of the serotonin transporter gene. Subjects characterized by one or two copies of the short allele of the serotonin transporter gene are more likely than other subjects to respond to environmental pathogens with depressive behaviours.

Other researchers have sought to establish that children experiencing some forms of maltreatment in their rearing environments and whose genotype conferred low levels of monoamine oxydase A enzyme (MAOA) more often tended to develop conduct disorders and anti-social personalities than subjects characterized by high levels of the same enzyme when confronted with maltreatment. There have also been some preliminary results concerning schizophrenia and the use of cannabis. Adolescent onset cannabis users sensitive to the vanine allele of the cathecol-O-methyltransferase (COMT) gene were likely to subsequently display a range of schizophrenic features. Such schizophrenic features would not characterize adolescent onset cannabis users who were not sensitive to the vanine allele of the COMT (Moffit et al. 2006; Rutter et al. 2006).

It must be emphasized that the pioneering research results cited above are a selection of classical examples of gene by environment interactions. They seek to carefully describe relevant moderator variables channelling the bi-directional influences of genes on the environment and/or of the environment on the genes. As such, they simultaneously identify the roles played by some complex causal intermediate phenotypes or endophenotypes. But these specific pioneering studies have quite uneven replication track records.

Genetic controls of sensitivity to environmental factors or environmental controls of gene expressions are not easy to prefigure in the design of research. Nor are they easy to establish beyond reasonable doubt with robust and unquestionable empirical data. To date, it appears that research referring to moderator variables in the interaction among the serotonin transporter gene, maltreatment, and stressful life events as leading to depressive behaviours are characterized by the strongest replication results (Rutter et al. 2006). Yet the mixed success of current replication studies recalls previous dispiriting periods involving research addressing genetically influenced behavioural outcomes.

In his contribution to this book, Jonathan Flint recollects just how dubious and uncertain genetic associations between identified gene polymorphisms and specific personality traits are. His review of meta-analyses pertaining to numerous whole genome association research strategies and results is truly challenging. Even though these projects have tended to rely upon very large samples, meta-analyses signal multiple methodological weaknesses that compromise hypotheses about the relationship between identified genes and personality behavioural outcomes.

This dubious track record of genetic associations between genes and personalities makes Flint apprehensive about what future gene by environment research strategies will really contribute to our understanding of genetic effects on personality traits. Not only do these research endeavours have to control for and explain complex genetic factor effects, but they also have to highlight equally complex environmental factor effects on personality variations. Moreover, gene by environment interaction studies that until now have usually focused on rather small samples, may well fare no better than earlier large sample genetic association studies. He nonetheless concludes his discussion by considering whether epigenetic regulation of gene expressions can open a brighter future for the understanding of genetic effects on personality traits.

In his chapter, David Goldman proposes a different perspective on gene by environment interactions that may be relevant to the study of personality disorders. Association and linkage studies face obvious statistical constraints and challenges. Genes with multiple pleiotropic functional loci and genes with rare alleles have effects that, by definition, are very difficult to track down statistically. Even with respect to genes with more common functional alleles, in order to make it possible to generate robust statistical replications, it is necessary to locate these on precise chromosomes, or within a small genomic region, with a measurable and measured repetitious local pattern of variation.

Thus, Goldman suggests that we should move beyond the statistical tyranny of association studies and devote more attention in complex molecular genetics to functional validation genomics. In this perspective, the fundamental difference in the validation process lies in the greater emphasis given to directional coherence of alleles' molecular effects on intermediate phenotypes. The molecular effects of alleles on more precisely disease-associated intermediate phenotypes, or endophenotypes, should of course also be assessed.

Goldman then concludes that more incisive studies in the area of stress and behaviour would be good candidates for demonstrating the fruitfulness of functional genomics. Indeed, these could highlight, as a first step, the role played by association studies' discoveries of specific functional genetic loci in improving stress studies. Then appropriate robust research strategies and technologies could functionally validate the strategic molecular action of alleles on disorder resiliency and vulnerability through complex intermediate neurobiological phenotypes. Thus, these cumulated advances would ultimately highlight the complex interplays of stress and environment in behavioural variations.

The gene and environment co-action and interaction models just referred to share important features with the sub-current of modern molecular genetics we have previously alluded to. Indeed, epigenetic regulation studies, much more valued today, mainly address at the organism level gene expressions not depending only on the stable DNA sequence of individuals within species. As shown by etiology studies of complex diseases and behavioural sciences experiments using animal models, epigenetic studies and research strategies explore environmental as well as genetic moderator variables in the complex interplays of gene and the environment. However, they tend, as compared to research studies investigating other interplay models between gene and environment, to give more attention to environmental factors impacting on gene neurobiological expressions and ultimately on behavioural outcomes. But epigenetic research protocols can also do more.

There is one crucial question about how the environment acts in relationship with genes and their multifactorial neurobiological pathways highlighted by epigenetic research protocols. Can epigenetic regulations induce potentially heritable traits that then could be genetically passed to the next generation of individuals within the same species? In most cases, environmentally mediated changes induced by epigenetic regulations would be cancelled since they normally do not enter the inheritance chain of the DNA sequence (Rutter 2006). But in animal epigenetic studies focused on gene and environment interplays, some rather recent research studies conclude otherwise.

A pioneering research study on epigenetic regulation, making use of an animal model, recently established that environmental variations, normal as well as pathological, were associated with behavioural outcomes through genetic pathways. Indeed, lactating mother rats' maternal care – licking and grooming of their offspring – was associated, for example, with individual offspring's low sensitivities with respect to stress behaviour and responses. Such relationships between environmental variation and stressful behaviour did not occur with non-maternal mother rats' offspring, or with the offspring of licking and grooming mothers passed on to these non-maternal rats right after birth.

Even more significantly, these studies tracked down the neurobiological gene expressions involved in these processes. They showed that individual differences in offspring were related to variations in the dopamine neurotransmitter region of the brain, and also established that the role of the rearing environment tended to be more significant than that of the genetic factor. Indeed, the organisms of all offspring that experienced more maternal care, even those offspring of low licking and grooming mothers passed on after birth to high licking and grooming mothers, incorporated specific biological *and* genetic information through gene expression mechanisms. These mechanisms were shown to have an impact on tissue-specific effects located on the specifically identified receptor gene promoter in the brain.

This research strikingly illustrates that low licking mother rats' offspring nurtured by high licking mother rats right after birth incorporated specific biological and genetic information up to the point where, in a very short time period, this first generation offspring passed it on to the next generation. Hence, as illustrated by cumulative and imaginative experimental research designs, new neurobiological information induced by epigenetic regulations did not disappear in the genome cellular division shaping the next generation. Some epigenetically influenced predispositions incorporated by next generation offspring within species are persistent into adult life behaviour (Cameron et al. 2005; Diorio and Meaney 2007).

It must be emphasized that we are at the very beginning of research exploring more ambitious analytic interplay models for co-action and bi-directional relationships between genetic and environmental factors. Epigenetic regulations of gene expressions are at the cutting edge of modern molecular genetics. So far, animal studies under ideal laboratory conditions have generated the most promising results. It is an open question whether environmental factors could, through such epigenetic mechanisms, have forceful impacts on the genetic structure as well as its inheritance in human beings. While the number of uncontested and replicated research results is insufficient to support a clear conclusion, it seems that there are good reasons for optimism (Rutter 2006).

In their contribution to this book, Martha McClintock et al. optimistically call for a paradigm shift in the way scientists and scholars conceptualize genetically sensitive diseases and health disparities. Such a paradigm shift would especially improve studies of genetically dysfunctionally regulated mechanisms, some inherited and some much more frequently related to epigenetic factors (which are at the root of what is called "sporadic cancer"), playing important roles for breast cancer subtype disparities for women of various ethnic backgrounds. A transdisciplinary research strategy already discussed by Françoise Baylis, who convincingly details its promising features, would pave the way, McClintock et al. argue, to the required paradigm shift.

To identify the causes of the prevalence of specific cancer subtypes among African-American women, notably basal-like breast cancer in premenopausal women, Centers for Population Health and Health

Disparities combine approaches and findings generated by diverse research teams. Animal model research results, for example, have proven quite valuable. They highlight the role of social isolation and of some endocrinal, physiological and tissue-level genetic intermediate phenotypes underlying glucocorticoid receptor actions and immune system reactions linked to dysfunctionally regulated stress responses. The richness of outcomes from these animal models suggests the utility of similar data collection and research strategies applied to human subjects. These would include measures of social isolation and of felt loneliness, as well as environmental surveys of the built environment. This research modelling posits a two-way relationship. Thus, disruptions in social networks through relocation that were revealed to be important stressors by interviews with human individuals were then modelled by equivalent research designs in animal studies.

By moving back and forth from animal to human subjects' studies, multiple teams of scholars pull together their disciplinary perspectives to address disparities in the incidence of breast cancer experienced by African-American women. The breadth of knowledge these teams produce captures the interactions among multiple levels of complex relevant epigenetic factors for cancer disparities. Criss-crossing biological and genetic variables with organizational and environmental pathways, ranging from neighbourhood and socio-cultural elements to persons' mental and psychological attributes, enables a much deeper understanding of relevant epigenetic factors. McClintock et al. emphasize how transdisciplinary research coupled to community-based participatory research can shed important light on the etiology, treatment, and prevention of disparities in disease risks induced by interactions between place, ethnicity, stressors, and genetic regulation.

As for Richard Tremblay, he argues in his chapter that current advances in epigenetic studies have the potential to pave the way to prevention of anti-social behaviour. Making cleaver use of a research methodology of modern social sciences to study change through time, i.e., longitudinal studies, Tremblay contests the Rousseauian point of view with respect to child development. He clearly shows that a programmed tendency towards physical aggression from birth can normally be overcome by youths, mostly through learning ways to master it. At the same time, some individuals highly at risk because of an early and then sustained adverse rearing environment are not able to complete this learning process.

Moreover, preliminary studies suggest that adverse rearing environments can induce negative effects on gene expression, in this case regularly aggressive youths having methylated alleles at a precise site on the T cells, and therefore disturb brain development to such an extent that chronic physical aggression cannot normally be prevented. Even though current gene by environment interaction analyses are far from being able to causally explain physical aggression during various phases of childhood, Tremblay draws a provocative conclusion. On the basis of robust data already gathered about numerous impacts of adverse rearing contexts, experimental prevention analyses – optimally from the pre-natal stage and early childhood – should be initiated to both understand basic genetic and environmental mechanisms for chronic physical aggression and use this knowledge to effectively prevent its development.

Yet Jonathan Flint recalls in his chapter that models of gene by environment interactions also face numerous challenges. Is this enthusiasm for explanatory co-action models of measured genes and measured environmental factors, including epigenetic regulation studies at the organism level, really justified? Can available state-of-the-art genetic theoretical and conceptual frames, at both the organic molecular and psychological and societal levels, inspire robust scientific strategies to successfully address such sophisticated integrative interplays between genes and environment? Are the required technological and methodological tools sufficiently developed and sufficiently mastered to enable expert investigators to address these complex research questions? The questions raised by Flint ultimately echo the worries of those scholars who were, at first, more optimistic: Will more ambitious gene by environment interaction explanatory models be a boom or a bust? (Rutter et al. 2006).

The field of gene and environment co-action and interaction is still in its infancy. For this reason, it is hardly surprising that there are only a limited number of published studies that can be characterized as promising. Moreover, these highly complex research projects are embedded within a scientific universe still wracked by critical dialogue, internal quarrels, and paradigmatic conflicts. These theoretical and methodological debates are evidence that there is, as yet, not a unified field of modern molecular genetics. According to Kendler (2005b), genetic psychiatry, and for that matter genetic behavioural sciences globally, are facing the caveats of a Kuhnian "preparadigmatic" (Kuhn 1962) immature state.

In such a state of affairs, effective and productive communication across sub-currents and paradigms and the building of common viewpoints to channel debate, critical dialogue, and conflicts are especially difficult to achieve. Kendler notes, however, that increased "cross-paradigm" discussions and collaborations and the lessening of the ideological rancour that marked earlier debates may pave the way to greater acceptance of "explanatory pluralism" within genetic behavioural sciences. Acceptance of explanatory pluralism would help this research field reach the status of a mature science in which there is broad agreement on basic scientific paradigms (2005b).

EXPANDING THE FRUITFUL DIALOGUE WITH MODERN GENETICS: CHANGING PARADIGMS FOR THE HUMANITIES AND SOCIAL SCIENCES

Modern genetics has been the scene of important debates fuelled in part by dubious findings, but also by more robust research advances. It has as well undergone significant paradigm shifts driven most of the time by molecular biosciences, although scholars from the human and social sciences have also contributed to some of these advances. At the same time, diverse research communities within humanities and social science disciplines were revisiting their own conceptual frames, research strategies, and methodologies to better understand complex social processes, prominent among which have been health and disease issues. This chapter is not the place to review all the insights that humanities and social science disciplines contributed to a better understanding of genetically and/or environmentally determined health, disease, or other human behaviours. This would be an enormous undertaking. But it is helpful to briefly highlight some of the major developments that helped change paradigms and that paved the way for more robust theoretical and methodological explanations of these complex processes.

The contemporary period has rightly been described as the "risk society" (Beck 1992; Giddens 1991). Advanced technologies and sciences and planning exercises embedded within the reflexive monitoring of more and more social processes have contributed to an endless tension within modern societies: the struggle to innovate through risky technologies and decision-making mechanisms as well as path-breaking policy responses, combined on the other hand with the desire to control these risk situations and factors within all spheres of social action. In many segments of contemporary society facing such structural constraints, the logic of managing risk factors locks individual and collective agents as well as institutions into a web of social relationships and reflexive mechanisms. While obviously neither the exclusive site of risk, nor separate from other major risk-embedded social processes, illness, disease, and health nonetheless figure very high on the policy agenda of modern risk societies.

By mid-twentieth century, scholars in the humanities and social sciences began to propose new research questions, strategies, and methodologies to address the multiple risk factors associated with illness and disease. Strong critiques of the medicalization (including what some call the biomedicalization) of social processes and whole societies are a perennial theme within contemporary scholarly and lay literature (Conrad 2000, 2007; Clarke et al. 2003). Invariably, these critical assessments conclude that medicalization and biomedicalization of disease risks and health is reductionist, in that they offer narrow, one-dimensional approaches to the health challenges faced by modern risk societies. Still, the continual flow of scientific discoveries, and especially the highly mediatized advances in molecular genetics, buttresses the powerful narrative presented by medicalization and biomedicalization as meta-theories of health and disease, and more globally of whole areas of human behaviour.

The Medicalization Narrative under Question

In the decades following World War II, a number of "anomalous findings" with respect to disease and health research challenged the traditional biomedical and medical care paradigm. It thus became urgent to rethink and enlarge the conceptual frameworks that were being applied to health and disease issues.

Throughout the second half of the twentieth century, various revisionist sub-currents in modern humanities and social sciences came to acquire a clear and distinctive voice (House 2001; Evans et al. 1994). Studies revealed that a wide range of factors that served to locate the particular position of individuals and groups within overall social relationships had an important impact on disease and health. Scholars in disciplines like anthropology, sociology, psychology, economics, social epidemiology, and population or public health were generating research and publishing data pointing beyond both psychological predispositions of individuals and biological markers and pathways as determinants of health and disease.

These studies established that individual and collective life styles and consumption patterns had much to say about health and disease risk factors. In addition, these studies revealed that social relationships and the character of support that individuals and groups experienced played a role in a person's health and disease outcomes. The same was true of chronic difficulties and stress in (or their absence from) the workplace, family, and primary group relationships. Finally, individual and collective health and disease conditions were shown to be affected by the social status of individuals and groups as an outcome of economic considerations combined with other factors (House 2001; Evans and Stoddart 1994; Kaplan 2004).

This suggests that data stemming from different humanities and social sciences that adopt, among other research strategies, cultural or social epidemiology approaches, could add to our knowledge of a broader universe of determinants of health. A population health perspective as applied, for example, to coronary heart disease has generated robust research findings. For time periods too short to be conditioned by major genetic mutations, social determinants of coronary heart disease could explain a range of cross-cultural variations and mutations in the etiology of the disease (Marmot and Mustard 1994). At a significant critical distance from former bio-medical and medical care conceptual frames, such findings now open the way to new narratives about health and disease. They do so by establishing, against excessively narrow biological and medicalization paradigms, how relevant factors, embedded mainly within social and environmental determinants, contextually condition disease and health issues.

These advances did not totally overcome conflicts between research paradigms and put to rest internal quarrels within the humanities and social sciences or, as was more often the case, quarrels between these disciplines and bio-medical sciences. But at the same time, integrative conceptual frames do point to socio-economic status, education, employment, revenues, and social capital as factors that condition access to health conditions and markers by individuals, collectives, ethnic groups, and races (House 2001; Evans et al.1994). Nonetheless, these integrative conceptual frames also have to take into consideration the cultural frames and narratives that individuals, collectives, and ethnic groups use to identify and label disease, disease risks, and health (Corin 1994).

It is noteworthy that the population health paradigm acknowledges the continuing pertinence of biological markers and pathways. Hence, the key research question is how integrative socio-economic status factors influence health conditions through diverse biological pathways. The common framework sought by some scholars would look at how specific social determinants interact with other factors to affect health. Likewise, this framework would explore how the impact of these social determinants is channelled by various biological pathways, for example, immune or endocrine, nervous and brain systems (Evans and Stoddart 1994; Evans et al. 1994).

It must, however, be recognized that scholarly efforts, to which diverse humanities and social science disciplines contributed so much, that sought to socially and culturally contextualize health and disease issues once more suffered hard times during the apogee of the molecular genetic revolution. As briefly mentioned earlier, this scientific revolution bears a number of characteristics.

Many contributors to this book have acknowledged the huge effects produced by the sequencing of the genome and the molecular genetic advances it precipitated. These effects were visible not only within contemporary biosciences and more globally the scientific scene, but also in general public opinion. As a result, the door was opened to scientific proclamations of a radically renewed genetic determinism. Contributors to this collection of essays have also emphasized how this gene-centric perspective quickly invaded explanatory models of human behaviour, most notably in connection with the popular field of personality traits and disorders. In producing this last effect, renewed genetic determinism moved onto a terrain that is sustained by a powerful cultural matrix and that modern individuals see as especially crucial.

Modern societies, or what some call late modern societies, constitutive of our contemporary scene, tend to value agents who position themselves through a strong affirmative and radical self. As Charles Taylor argues (1989) this radical self typically characterizes modern identity. As a consequence, identity and intimacy issues, and individualization patterns tend to over-determine the processes by which specific late modern societies construct their own characteristic social structures and cultural beliefs (Giddens 1991, 1992). An emphasis on the exposure of the self and on the radically individualistic nature of several behavioural patterns tends increasingly to negate what the construction of the self, of the personality, owes to more global and comprehensive social contexts where this construction takes place.

This type of cultural trend is fertile ground for the sustained popular upsurge of belief in radical genetic determinism of the personality and the self. Obviously, gene-centric explanations add scientific weight to social and cultural trends already working within modern societies to erect barriers between, on the one hand, social and cultural contexts and, on the other, the construction of identity and personality.

In such narratives, identity and personality are portrayed as totally isolated from their nurturing social and cultural contexts; they are literally decontextualized. To better understand these developments, contributors to this book refer to the problematic of decontextualized embodied identities; a problematic admirably explored by scholars in the humanities and social sciences. Other contributors speak rather of the geneticization of social processes to emphasize fairly similar processes. These contributions offer some key examples of current conceptual schemes and research developments found within, among other disciplines, biological and cultural anthropology, bio-ethics, law, and the sociology of health and medicine.

Diverse humanities and social sciences disciplines, already committed to contextualized disease and health issues, brought intense attention and rigorous scientific analysis to push back against genetically deterministic views of the self, of personality traits and disorders, and more generally of human behaviours. Without totally dismissing the influence of biological or genetic variables, they nonetheless proposed a broader view of personality building. Indeed, in the last decades or so, as documented also by contributors to this book, several scholars within humanities and social science disciplines have been actively engaged, with uneven success, datasets, and quality of research, in explaining that personality building and the whole area of social relationships involved therein are also highly embedded within social and environmental variables (Ehrlich and Feldman 2003; Lock 2005; Alper et al. 2004).

Time and Space Categories in Health Issue Narratives

The strategic conceptual advances that have enabled a fruitful dialogue among scholars working in the humanities, social sciences, and modern genetics also speak to theory-building about how time and space categories affect social processes and behaviours. After all, time and space constitute foundational features of the human and social environment (Giddens 1984). Theoretical considerations like these are evident in more robust epidemiological and longitudinal studies that better capture the impact of time and space categories on human behaviour. These research trends are especially visible within disciplines like developmental psychology, medical sociology and anthropology, population and public health, and social and cultural epidemiology, to name only a few.

Since the mid-twentieth century, humanities and social science disciplines have displayed increasing openness to investigating complex research questions, and to deploying methodologies that account for time measurements. Individual and collective life cycles and trajectories extend into distinct time periods. Thus, attempts to address life cycles and trajectories require the theoretical and methodological tools to follow the same individual or collective actors over extended periods of time. They also require mastering measures applied to broader and complex historical conjunctures and contexts. For active subjects within societies, significant historical periods are characterized by distinctive means for action, by constraints as well as opportunity structures and assets around which social relationships are constructed and experienced.

This is why longitudinal studies have been extraordinarily useful for addressing the time component of social processes and behaviours. They criss-cross time dimensions with life cycles and trajectories as these cycles bear on the relationships of individuals and groups among themselves and with their socio-economic environment. These studies cover, for long periods of time, diverse population cohorts composed, as much as possible, of the same individual subjects selected at the onset of a study. With the crucial input of longitudinal studies facilitated by better data collection technologies and equipment, scholars in the humanities and social sciences are able to address change within social processes and behaviours in an entirely new light.

Social behaviours and relationships owe, on the other hand, some of their fundamental characteristics to the geopolitical, economic, and cultural regional as well as local spaces where they are nurtured. However, improved space measures require mastering data sets from multiple and different space-embedded communities and networks, as well as collective ecological studies relating to distinct and stratified societies. Moreover, given the comparative dimension that has always figured in research in the humanities and social sciences, these space measures also require upgrading research programs so as to make better use of cross-cultural studies that address salient characteristics of distinctive regional and national spaces. Today, the globalization of social processes, exchanges, and relationships cannot be denied. But at the same time, we know that local and regional spaces still matter. Embedded within and shaped by their own basic cultural characteristics and social structures, local and regional spaces in our global era nonetheless influence human behaviour. Humanities and social science disciplines now cope with this challenge first, by developing sophisticated analytic models and statistical technologies to master huge epidemiological data sets and second, by undertaking studies more sensitive to space and cross-cultural dimensions.

More sophisticated data collection permits renewed epidemiological and longitudinal studies, and opens the way to a better dialogue between social sciences and modern genetics. Such dialogue is also conditioned by advances with respect to data analysis protocols and to relevant matches between theory building exercises and analytic models supported by adequate mathematical and statistical tools. Today it is beyond question that those modern humanities and social sciences disciplines in closest interaction and dialogue with modern genetics are increasingly conscious of the theoretical and methodological conditions needed to nurture such paradigmatic relationships. Not only are these disciplines more prone to reconsider the design of their research studies, their methodologies, and their protocols, they can now profit from more relevant expert knowledge in the area of model building, research methods, and technological tools.

Advances in Sampling Technologies and in Modelling Roles of Complex Mediator and Moderator Variables

The sampling technology of many contemporary gene and environment interplay research studies is frequently criticized for methodological defects. Quite often these critiques focus on the size of the samples being used. Far too many published studies are being rightly challenged for their lack of robust samples and defects in sampling techniques. Some scholars propose meta-analyses as a response to these critiques, but this would be, at best, only a partial solution.

Major meta-analyses normally depend on the existence of a number of specific and distinct already completed, if not already published, studies on highly comparable research questions and topics. That is, the relevant research dimensions of the aggregated studies must be objectively comparable and equivalent if not similar: independent and dependent variable definitions; measured and control group samples; analytic models and statistical tools used for data analyses. Hence, the feasibility of successful meta-analyses is conditional upon the availability and quality of complete detailed information pertaining to the research design of already completed studies normally regrouped within major meta-analyses.

Among the various defects relating to samples and sampling techniques that might affect studies is the difficulty of comparing the characteristics of the sample group with the characteristics of control groups. This difficulty constitutes the major challenge for observational studies of human subjects. By contrast with rigorously and more easily controlled population units of "ideal" experimental research, as in animal studies, observational studies of human subjects look at measured populations or groups within which the selection of individuals for sampling matters is severely constrained. Personality disorders, diverse kinds of abuses, or consequential risk of diseases faced by the sample groups, as well as ethical problems raised by the inclusion of such populations in field research, compromise almost every process for selecting individuals to participate in sample populations or groups. It follows that observational studies unavoidably confront those sample selection and comprehensive data collection problems that are inherent in complex population units operating in more or less normal daily life situations.

These difficulties also have a significant impact on how control groups are, quantitatively and qualitatively, designed and selected. It is a truism to say that sample and control groups must overlap with respect to multivariate background characteristics. Without such overlap, studies cannot generate a reasonably rigorous estimate of the effects of mediating and dependent variables on outcomes. Fortunately, sampling designs and techniques have recently become an increasingly innovative and refined area of expert knowledge.

A specific relevant dimension for which improvements in sampling techniques are now available is the field of matched sampling as it applies to observational studies. "Matched sampling attempts to choose the controls for further study so that they are similar to the treated subjects with respect to background variables measured on all subjects" (Rosenbaum and Rubin 2006). Quite often these matching sample exercises will encompass multivariate characteristics for both the sampled and control groups. Theoretical expertise and technical know-how about matching samples are becoming more advanced and available. Moreover, for controlling bias that could result from confounding unmeasured variables effects, the combination within specific research studies of, on the one hand, regression adjustments to multiple variables, and on the other hand, matched samples for many covariates applied to both sample and control groups is a superior strategy to either of these techniques used alone (Rubin 2006).

Scholars studying the correlation and interaction interplays between components like genes and environment are now in a position to take advantage not only of advanced sampling techniques, but also of many other advances in research design. In so doing, specific humanities and social science disciplines that have the potential to make significant contributions to epidemiological and longitudinal studies will be able to nurture a richer dialogue still with modern genetics.

Advances in theory building and methodological strategies permit, for example, a better understanding of both correlation models and integrative co-action models. Correlation models emphasize the analytic role of mediator variables between genes and environmental factors. On the other hand, interaction models refer normally to moderator variables to address the synergetic co-action relationships of genetic and environmental factors.

For studies focusing on interplay models between multiple genetic and environmental variables and various behavioural outcomes, the prerequisites relating to the measurement of mediator or moderator variable roles, as well as to their possible combination are now more clearly formulated. Expert knowledge and techniques are currently available to strengthen studies high-lighting mediation or moderation mechanisms uniting complex independent variables and equally complex behavioural outcomes (Baron and Kenny 1986; McClelland, Judd 1993). Such knowledge should enrich understanding of correlation and interaction interplays among gene expressions and the social environment.

Advances in molecular genetics that substitute specific measured genes for omnibus latent and inferred genetic factors have helped to improve studies of correlation, as well as interaction-model interplays between genes and the environment. Unfortunately, these advances have often led to an unfortunate analytic imbalance since more attention was given to conceptual and methodological requirements, as well as weaknesses, relative to genetic factors. Equivalent difficulties and potential refinements pertaining to the conception and measurement of environmental factors were less noticed.

As already noted, theory building and methodological constructs with respect to environmental factors *per se* are, however, prerequisites to discerning more robust correlation and interaction interplays among genes and environmental factors (Wachs 1992; Friedman and Wachs 1999). One promising approach involves the use of instrumental ecological models. For example, Bronfenbrenner's (1989, 1994) ecological model applied to the environments of behaviours already engaged different levels of environmental context to be distinguished. This model recognizes how many environmental layers, from proximate to quite distant from an individual subject, can each have a distinct but important role in shaping individual and group behaviours.

However, for humanities and social science studies, the most important feature is what are called the "niche effects" that can be observed with respect, for example, to how specific multiple dimensions belonging to one single environmental level can be linked with each other. Niche effects can also stem from interrelations between numerous levels of environmental factors over a specific observational time period. Thus complex environmental factors of social behaviours are increasingly understood as multivariate niche elements whose structuring relationships must be explained. They can obey more or less additive rules, the impact of one level of environmental factors being added to other levels' factors. More often than not they exercise some influence through level combination rules pertaining to correlation or interaction interplays that encompass multiple levels of environmental factors. Of course, the interplay between environmental factor levels can also be plotted on a hierarchical scale: A particular environmental factor level can have more influence on an outcome than another.

It is also noteworthy that such niche dimensions are not only restricted to environmental factors and dimensions. Theoretical and methodological constructs of the various characteristics of a single personality as a complex and dynamic variable can also be sensitive to comparable niche effects. Indeed, contemporary social research is more and more open to research strategies and designs that address individual personalities through theory and methodology constructs that distinguish, and then combine, various but still clearly identified components of a personality. It follows that these theory-building exercises depend on the adoption of methodological devices and statistical tools that are specific to them. Expert knowledge advances are available to better master relevant dimensions within both person-oriented research designs and the classical variable-oriented approaches. Moreover, where appropriate, both person-oriented and variable-oriented approaches can be combined (Bergman and Trost 2006; Magnuson 1999; Bergman 2001).

Within social research of the last twenty years or so, there is one area that has undergone a tremendous advance in sophisticated expert knowledge. Mathematical and statistical models and tools to address hierarchical data sets and structures clearly constitute, over the last decades, one of the most visible and significant areas of new and sophisticated knowledge. Hierarchical data sets are data structures addressing directly various and distinct niches or levels of multidimensional complex social processes or behaviours. Hierarchical modelling frameworks are now available to rigorously study processes and behaviours mainly characterized by their hierarchically ordered structuring dimensions (Raudenbush and Bryk 2002).

Called multi-level linear models, or mixed-effects or random-effects models, or random-coefficient regression models, an integrated set of methods that apply to multiple-variable relationships belonging to a niche hierarchical structure have been recently developed. Not only can they help scholars to master the inter-relationship of variables within one level of environmental factors, but more importantly they highlight relationships among factors impacting on a behavioural outcome across different environmental levels. These methods support analytical models to study complex interactions within and between levels of environmental factors while at the same time permitting researchers to assess the amount of variation proper to each of these levels. In this, these methods overcome the limitations of conventional regression models, which cannot properly highlight hierarchical relationships among dimensions of outcomes (Raudenbush and Bryk 2002).

The methodological and statistical opportunities provided by non-linear dynamical systems methodology within structural differential equation modelling can also be quite useful for specific research designs (Boker and Nesselroade 2002). This is certainly the case, for example, for person-oriented approaches where the focus is on the development and interaction of distinct components constitutive of the individual as a system (Bergman and Trost 2006). But these are not the only situations of research relating to gene and environment interplays where such specialized modelling, whether or not in combination with other approaches, could open up new explanatory horizons. Gene by environment interaction models that dynamically couple multifactorial genetic and environmental factors, where each category of variables is quite sensitive to time variations, could be strengthened through the use of nonlinear dynamical systems methodology and differential equations within structural equation modelling.

One may conclude as follows. It is crystal clear that these specific improvements within the theoretical and statistical literature in the humanities and social sciences have already had, and will continue in the future to have, a major impact in helping to conceive more powerful research strategies for investigating the interplay of gene expressions and social environment. They obviously make their unique contribution to other research advances that bear on the changing boundary between gene expressions and the social environment. Every one of these scholarly developments facilitates and enhances the current dialogue between scholars in the humanities and social sciences and those working in the field of modern genetics.

BIBLIOGRAPHY

Abbot, A. 2008. News Feature: The brains of the family. *Nature,* 454(10) July:154-7.

Allen, G.E. 2003. Mendel and modern genetics: The legacy for today. Endeavour, 27:63-8.

Alper, J.S., Ard, C., Asch., A., Beckwith., J., Conrad., P., Geller, L.N., eds. 2004. *The Double-Edged Helix; Social Implications of Genetics in a Diverse Society*. Baltimore: John Hopkins University Press.

Baron, R.B., Kenny, D.A. 1986. The moderator-mediator variable distinction in social psychological research: Conceptual, strategic, and statistical considerations. *Journal of Personality and Social Psychology,* 51(6):1173-82.

Beck, U. 1992. *Risk Society: Towards a New Modernity*. London: Sage.

Bergman, L.R. 2001. A person approach in research on adolescence: Some methodological challenges. *Journal of Adolescents Research,* 16(1):28-53.

Bergman, L.R., Trost, K. 2006. The person-oriented versus the variable-oriented approach: Are they complementary, opposites, or exploring different world? *Merrill-Palmer Quarterly,* 52(3):601-32.

Boker, S.M, Nesselroade, J.R. (2002) A method for modeling the intrinsic dynamics of intraindividual variability: Recovering the parameters of simulated oscillators in multi-wave data, *Multivariate Behavioral Research,* 37:127–60.

Bronfenbrenner, U. 1989. Ecological systems theory. *Annals of Child Development, 6:187-249.*

– 1994. Ecological models of human development, in T. Husten, T.N. Postlethewaite, eds. *International Encyclopaedia of Education*, 2nd ed, 3. New York: Elsevier Science.

Cameron, N.M., Parent, C., Champagne, F.A., Fish, E.K., Ozaki-Kuroda, K., Meaney, M.J. 2005. The programming of individual differences in defensive responses and reproductive strategies in the rat through variations in maternal care. *Neuroscience and Biobehavioral Review,* 29:843-65.

Caspi, A., Sugden, K., Moffitt, T.E., Taylor, A., Craig, I.W., Harrington, H.L., McClay, J., Mill, J., Martin, J., Braithwaite, A., Poulton, R. 2003. Influence of life stress on depression: Moderation by a polymorphism in the 5-HTT gene. *Science,* 301:386-9.

Caspi, A., Moffit, T.E. 2006. Gene-environment interactions in psychiatry: Joining forces with neuroscience. *Nature Reviews/Neuroscience, 7:583-90.*

Clarke, A.E., Shim, J.K., Mamo, L., Fosket, J.R., Fishman, J.R. 2003. Biomedicalization: Technoscientific transformations of health, illness, and US Biomedicine. *American Sociological Review, 68(2):161-94.*

Conrad, P. 2000. Medicalization, genetics and human problems, in C. E. Bird, P. Conrad, A. Fremont, eds. *Handbook of Medical Sociology,* Thousand Oaks, CA: Sage.

– 2007. *The Medicalization of Society; On the Transformation of Human Conditions into Treatable Disorders*. Baltimore: John Hopkins University Press.

Corin, E. 1994. The social and cultural matrix of health and disease, in R.G. Evans, M.L. Barer, T.R. Marmor, eds. *Why Are Some People Healthy and Others Not?* New York: Aldine de Gruyter.

Dawkins, R. 1976. *The Selfish Gene*. New York: Oxford University Press.

Diorio, J., Meaney, M.J. 2007. Maternal programming of defensive responses through sustained effects on gene expression. *Journal of Psychiatry Neuroscience*, 32(4):275-84.

Dunn, L. 1965. *A Short History of Genetics*. New York: McGraw-Hill.

Ehrlich, P., Feldman, M. 2003. Genes and cultures: What creates our behavioural phenome? *Current Anthropology*, 44(1):87-107.

Evans, R.G., Barer, M.L., Marmor, T.R., eds. 1994. *Why Are Some People Healthy and Others Not?* New York: Aldine de Gruyter.

Evans, R.G., Stoddart, G.L., 1994. Producing health, consuming health care, in R.G. Evans, M.L. Barer, T.R. Marmor, eds. *Why Are Some People Healthy and Others Not?* New York: Aldine de Gruyter.

Falk, R. 1995. The struggle for genetics independence. *Journal of Historical Biology*, 28:219-46.

Friedman, S.L., Wachs, T.D. 1999. eds, *Measuring Environment Across the Life Span; Emerging Methods and Concepts*. Washington: American Psychological Association.

Galton, F. 1883. *Inquiries into Human Faculty and its Development*. London: Macmillan.

Giddens, A. 1984. *The Constitution of Society. Outline of the Theory of Structuration*. Berkeley: University of California Press.

– 1990. *The Consequences of Modernity*. Stanford: Stanford University Press.

– 1991. *Modernity and Self-Identity. Self and Society in the Late Modern Age*. Stanford: Stanford University Press.

– 1992. *The Transformation of Intimacy. Sexuality, Love and Eroticism in Modern Societies*. Stanford: Stanford University Press.

Gottesman, H., Gould, T. D., 2003. The endophenotype concept in psychiatry: Etymology and strategic intentions. *American Journal of Psychiatry*, 160(4):636-45.

House, J.S. 2001. Understanding social forces and inequalities in health: 20th century progress and 21st century prospects. *Journal of Health and Social Behavior*, 43:125-42.

Jacob, F. 1973, *The Logic of Life: A History of Heredity*. New York: Pantheon Books.

Jaenisch, R., Bird, A. 2003. Epigenetic regulation of gene expression: How the genome integrates intrinsic and environmental signals. *Nature Genetics Supplement*, 33:245-54.

Kaplan, G.A. 2004. What's wrong with social epidemiology, and how can we make it better? *Epidemiologic Reviews*, 26:124-35.

Keat, R., Urry, J. 1975. *Social Theory as Science*. London: Routledge and Kegan Paul.

Kendler, K.S. 2005a. Psychiatric genetics: A methodologic critique. *American Journal of Psychiatry*, 162(1):3-11.

– 2005b. Toward a philosophical structure for psychiatry. *American Journal of Psychiatry*, 162(3):433-40.

– 2005c. 'A gene for...': The nature of gene action in psychiatric disorders. *American Journal of Psychiatry*, 162(7):1243-52.

Kendler, K.S., Baker, J.H. 2007. Genetic influences on measures of the environment: A systematic review. *Psychological Medicine*, 37:615-26.

Kendler, K.S., Prescott, C.A. 2006. *Genes, Environment, and Psychopathology: Understanding the Causes of Psychiatric and Substance Use Disorders*. New York: The Guilford Press.

Kuhn, T.S. 1962. *The Structure of Scientific Revolutions*. Chicago: University of Chicago Press.

Lacourse, E., Gendreau, P.L. 2007. Boys' biopsychosocial difficulties during the teenage years; Canadian state of affairs for the 21st century. Discussion Paper. Ottawa, Government of Canada, Policy Research Initiative.

Lakatos, I., Musgrave, A. 1970. Eds, *Criticism and the Growth of Knowle*dge. Cambridge, Cambridge University Press.

Lock, M. 2005. Eclipse of the Gene and the Return of Divination. *Current Anthropology, 46(Supplement)*:S47-S70.

Magner, L. 1994. *A History of the Life Sciences*. New York: Marcel Dekker.

Magnuson, D. 1999. On the individual: A person-oriented approach to developmental research. *European Psychologist*, 4:205-18.

Marmot, M.G., Mustard, F. 1994. Coronary hearth disease from a population perspective, in R.G. Evans, M.L. Barer, T.R. Marmor, eds. *Why Are Some People Healthy and Others Not?* New York: Aldine de Gruyter.

Mayr, E. 1982. *The Growth of Biological Thought*. Cambridge, Mass: Belknap Press.

McClelland, G.H., Judd, C.M. 1993. Statistical difficulties of detecting interactions and moderator effects. *Psychological Bulletin*, 114:376-90.

Moffit, T.E., Caspi, A., Rutter, M. 2006. Measured gene-environment interactions in psychopathology; Concepts, research strategies, and implications for research, intervention, and public understanding of genetics. *Perspectives on Psychological Science*, 1(1):5-27.

Moss, L. 2003. *What Genes Can't Do*. Cambridge, Mass: MIT Press.

Nelkin, D., Lindee, M.S. 1995. *The DNA Mystique: The Gene as a Cultural Icon*. New York: W.H. Freeman.

Petronis, A. 2001. Human morbid genetics revisited: Relevance of epigenetics. *Trends in Genetics,* 17(3):142-46.

Petronis, A., Gottesman, I.I., Kan, P., Kennedy, J.C., Basile, V.S., Paterson, A.D., Popendikyte, V. 2003. Monozygotic twins exhibit numerous epigenetic differences: Clues to twin discordance? *Schizophrenia Bulletin,* 29:169-78.

Plomin, R. 1994. *Genetics and Experience: The Interplay between Nature and Nurture.* Thousands Oaks: CA: Sage.

Plomin, R., Defries, J.C., Loehlin, J.C. 1977. Genotype – environmental interaction and correlation in the analysis of human behavior. *Psychological Bulletin,* 84:309-22.

Raudenbush, S.W., Bryk' A.S., 2002 *Hierarchical Linear Models; Applications and Data Analysis Methods,* 2nd edition, London, Sage Publications.

Reichborn-Kjennerud, T., Czajkowski, N., Neale, M.C., Orstavik, R.E., Torgersen, S., Tambs, K., Roysamb, E., Harris, J.R., Kendler, K.S. 2007. Genetic and environmental influences on dimensional representations of DSM-IV cluster C personality disorders: A population-based multivariate twin study, *Psychological Medicine,* 37:645-53.

Rose, S. 1995. The rise of neurogenetic determinism. *Nature,* 373.

Rosenbaum, P.R., Rubin, D.B. 2006 Constructing a Control Group Using Multivariate Matched Sampling Methods That Incorporate the Propensity Score, in Rubin, D.B., Editor, *Matched Sampling for Causal Effects,* New York: Cambridge University Press.

Rubin, D.B., 2006. ed., *Matched Sampling for Causal Effects,* New York: Cambridge University Press.

– 2006. William G. Cochran's Contributions to the Design, Analysis, and Evaluation of Observational Studies, in Rubin, D.B., ed., *Matched Sampling for Causal Effects,* New York: Cambridge University Press.

Rutter, M. 1994. Psychiatric genetics: Research challenges and pathways forward. *American Journal of Medical Genetics (Neuropsychiatric Genetics),* 54:185-98.

– 2006. *Genes and Behavior: Nature-Nurture Interplay Explained.* Oxford, UK: Blackwell.

– 2007a. Gene-environment interdependence, *Developmental Science,* 10(1):12-18.

– 2007b. Resilience, competence and coping, *Child Abuse and Neglect,* 31:205-9.

Rutter, M., Moffit, T.E., Caspi, A. 2006. Gene-environment interplay and psychopathology: Multiple varieties but real effects. *Journal of Child Psychology and Psychiatry,* 47(3/4):226-61.

Rutter, M., Silberg, J. 2002. Gene-Environment interplay in relation to emotional and behavioral disturbance, *Annual Review of Psychology*, 53:463-90.

Skinner, B.F. 1972. *Beyond Freedom and Dignity*. London: Cape.

Sklair, L. 1987. Métathéorie, théorie et recherche empirique: l'analyse de la dépendance et du «gender» en sociologie du développement, *Sociologie et Sociétés*, 19(2):51-64.

Taylor, C. 1989. *Sources of the Self: The Making of the Modern Identity*. Cambridge, MA: Harvard University Press.

Wachs, T.D. 1992. *The Nature of Nurture*. London: Sage.

Watson, J.B. 1925. *Behaviorism*. New York: Norton.

– 1928. *Psychological Care of Infant and Child*. New York: Norton.

Wilson, E.O. 1975. *Sociology: The New Synthesis*. Cambridge, Mass: Belknap Press of Harvard University Press.

SECTION ONE
Genes and Personality Traits

This first section presents papers discussing personality traits or disorder issues, a complex terrain embedded in a long tradition of advances and debates regarding interplays of genetic and social-environmental factors.

This section begins with Douglas Wahlsten's thorough survey of studies linking human intelligence inheritance to the exclusive or combined effects of genetic and/or environmental factors. Given the numerous shortcomings and limited advances that characterize these studies, Wahlsten, not surprisingly, calls for more sophisticated explanatory models to adequately address this question and its potential social impacts for individuals and collectivities.

Jonathan Flint reviews a whole range of research designs, methodologies, and findings that associate genetic and environmental factors with personality traits. No doubt, this literature gained in momentum with the sequencing of the human genome without however reaching more robust advances. Flint ultimately concludes that research prompted by epigenetic regulation advances may eventually fare better than the numerous prior efforts to find a robust undisputed link between combined genetic and environmental factors and personality traits.

Finally, David Goldman discusses how a functional genomic approach could improve the already promising field of stress and environment behavioural interrelationships. In such a research strategy, he argues, more emphasis would be given to the role of numerous intermediary phenotypes in the complex interplays of genetic and environmental factors impacting on stress-related behavioural variations.

Special Challenges of Complex Behavioural Traits: Gene Discovery and Applications

DOUGLAS WAHLSTEN

Major advances in molecular genetics make headlines almost every day when one human characteristic or disease after another is reported to depend on some gene. Media coverage spawns hope that genetic science may before too long lead to cures or treatments for major medical disorders. At the same time, fears of a renewed genetic determinism and even eugenics are stoked by journalists and enthusiastic scientists hyping the latest discoveries. As scientists, we welcome this increased level of interest in our work, along with the increased funding for our research that accompanies it, while as citizens we worry that public discourse may be galloping far ahead of what is warranted by a more sober and rigorous assessment of progress in the genetic analysis of human behaviours and abilities, especially intelligence, the focus of this chapter.

POTENTIAL BENEFITS OF KNOWING ROLES OF SPECIFIC GENES

Two broad categories of claims can be discerned in recent debates. One extols the benefits for society of a better understanding of the actions of specific, identified genes. Knowing that a specific gene contributes to disease creates possibilities for devising therapies aimed directly at the molecular cause of the problem (Wahlsten 1999). Thus, gene-based treatments should benefit the afflicted individual as well as the broader society. The major drawbacks in this realm are the difficulties in finding an effective treatment, even with the aid of better genetic knowledge, and the likelihood of extremely costly therapies.

A positive example is the screening of newborn infants for a defect in the phenylalanine hydroxylase (PAH) gene, which when present in two abnormal copies and untreated leads to a clinically significant metabolic abnormality (phenylketonuria or PKU), impaired brain development, and mental deficiency (www.pku.com). As shown in figure 1, the metabolic pathways are well known. Protein in the diet is broken down into its constituent amino acids in the digestive tract, and these amino acids are then absorbed into the blood and circulated to all organs of the body. One of these amino acids, phenylalanine, can be obtained only from the diet. Normally it is kept within tolerable limits in the blood, even when at high levels in the diet, because any excess can be converted to the amino acid tyrosine in the liver and used in many kinds of cells or excreted. When both inherited copies of the PAH gene are defective, however, the infant cannot convert phenylalanine to tyrosine and the levels of phenylalanine increase to toxic levels that impair brain development. The excess phenylalanine also leads to high levels of metabolites that give the infant a peculiar musty odour.

The PAH defect provides a classical example of gene-environment interaction. Genetically normal infants are able to regulate phenylalanine levels despite wide variations in the dietary input of phenylalanine, whereas for infants with two defective PAH genes the blood level of phenylalanine is closely related to dietary levels. This fact can be utilized to treat the disorder simply by giving the infant a special formula (Lofenalac) that is low in phenylalanine (Lyman and Lyman 1960), rather than nurturing it with mother's milk. In this way, the negative symptoms of PKU can be prevented. The newborn screening program has been a great success, and clinical PKU is now virtually absent in Canada (Fisch et al. 1997; Scriver 2001).

Knowing both the gene and how it works in a metabolic pathway are the keys to the treatment. The defect arises from just one specific gene, but the larger picture is far from simple because of the way PAH functions as part of a system (Scriver and Waters 1999). When the child has passed a sensitive period for brain development, he or she can begin to consume a normal diet without suffering major harm. Nevertheless, trouble arises if a woman with two defective PAH genes becomes pregnant (Hanley, Clarke, and Schoonheyt 1987). Although

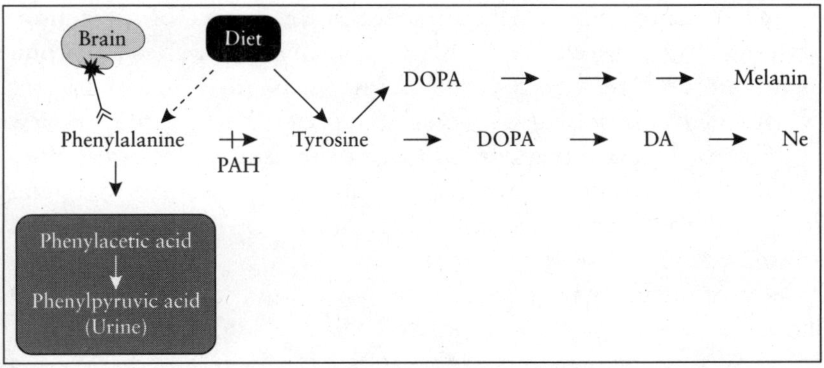

Figure 1. The amino acid phenylalanine is obtained from protein in the diet and is abundant in mother's milk. Normally, excessive levels of phenylalanine are converted to the amino acid tyrosine by the enzyme phenylalanine hydroxylase (PAH). Tyrosine then can be converted by several other enzymes to the pigment melanin and the neurotransmitter molecules dopamine (DA) and norepinephrine (NE). The PAH gene codes for the structure of that enzyme. If a child has two mutant copies of the PAH gene, he or she cannot convert phenylalanine to tyrosine, and the level of phenylalanine in the bloodstream becomes so high that brain development is impaired. This clinical syndrome, known as phenylketonuria, can be easily prevented by screening for the defect at birth and feeding the infant a special formula (Lofenalac) low in phenylalanine.

her high blood level of phenylalanine does not impair her own mental function, it can harm the brain development of her fetus, even though the fetus has a normal PAH gene from the father. This negative consequence can be avoided if the mother returns to the diet low in phenylalanine after becoming pregnant (Gambol 2007).

PERILS OF SWEEPING CLAIMS ABOUT NON-SPECIFIC GENETIC EFFECTS

A second kind of claim makes vague, general assertions about intelligence, for example, on the basis of poorly substantiated, nonspecific genetic involvement in brain function. This kind of crude genetic determinism misleads public debate about government policies and is actually harmful to individuals who suffer subnormal mental ability. Because the claims are not founded on reliable knowledge of any specific gene, no help can be offered by genetics to disadvantaged persons.

Numerous examples of bad science in the service of a reactionary political agenda can be cited. In 1969, an article published prominently in the *Harvard Educational Review* asserted that Americans of African ancestry are less successful in society because they possess inferior intelligence as a consequence of inferior genes and it suggested that "current welfare policies, unaided by eugenic foresight, could lead to the genetic enslavement" of African-Americans (Jensen 1969). *The Bell Curve* in 1994 put forward a similar genetically based argument against social assistance for the poor, especially those with dark skin (Herrnstein and Murray 1994). More recently, James Watson, winner of the Nobel prize for his role in discovering the structure of DNA in 1953, announced to a journalist that he was "inherently gloomy about the prospect of Africa" because intelligence testing says their intelligence is not the same as that of whites, and that he doubts the wisdom of policies that are based on the idea that "their intelligence is the same as ours" because "people who have to deal with black employees find this is not true" (Nugent 2007).

Watson repeated the mistake of some recipients of high honours who believe they are masters of fields beyond the scope of their real expertise. In an interview on the occasion of the fiftieth anniversary of the discovery of the structure of DNA, he said that, were he to start a career in science today, he would "be working on something about connections between genes and behaviour. You can find genes for behaviors ... " (Rennie 2003). Concerning bird migration, he alleged that "the mother bird isn't telling the young one where to go! So it's got to be inherited." His prejudice and lack of knowledge of behaviour genetics is painfully obvious here. Decades of research on the genetic aspects of animal behaviour have taught us well that *no* behaviour is inherited in any simple manner and environmental influences are involved to some extent in virtually all behaviours of any degree of complexity. As for bird migration, where to fly is indeed learned by many songbirds while in the nest by observing the rotation of stars around the north pole star Polaris (Emlen 1967).

These three examples from Jensen, *The Bell Curve,* and Watson share several flaws. They fail to cite one specific gene that is known to influence the degree of human intelligence; hence, there is no reliable genetic basis for their claims. They make a big fuss about so-called racial differences at a time when anthropologists and geneticists have largely abandoned the race concept because they recognize that lines of demarcation among populations are arbitrary and that the vast majority of genetic variation resides within geographic populations rather than between (Cavalli-Sforza 2000; Cavalli-Sforza, Menozzi, and Piazza 1994). They also ignore a vast amount of evidence showing that intelligence depends strongly on environmental factors and that the structure of the brain itself is sculpted by experience (Wahlsten 2002).

An egregious instance of the misapplication of genetics is apparent in the Alberta government's program of eugenic sterilization in which, from 1929 to 1971, 2,832 children confined to the Provincial Training School for Mental Defectives (PTS) were surgically sterilized (Wahlsten 1997). Many were also subjected to crude experiments with powerful psychiatric drugs (Le Vann 1959, 1961, 1968, 1971). The rationale for the eugenics program was a simple-minded belief that bad genes determine low intelligence and will be passed to the next generation unless the state intervenes. Decisions about reproduction of innocent children were made by a Eugenics Board that lacked even the most rudimentary expertise in genetics. Many children in the PTS in fact were in the normal range of intelligence but were sterilized anyway, and many came from severely impoverished families, a fact blithely ignored by the Eugenics Board. This shameful history came to light when one of the victims, Leilani Muir, sued the Alberta government and won. In the press conference following the decision by Madame Justice Joanne Veit that Muir was of normal intelligence and had been wrongly sterilized, Muir expressed her contempt for those who deprived her of motherhood: "They called me a moron, so what does that make them?" (The National Film Board of Canada 1996). She subsequently ran for a seat in the provincial legislature as a candidate for the New Democratic Party, addressed conferences of geneticists in France and the United States, and wrote her autobiography.

These negative examples of the abuse of genetic science need to be kept in mind when considering future applications of genetics. Leading scientists have a social responsibility to expose and oppose wrongful applications of unsubstantiated claims about the role of genes in human behaviours and abilities, and to ensure that public discourse is based firmly on well established facts and principles. In this regard, it is apparent that certain kinds of genetic investigations hold considerable promise for important advances, whereas others are leading to a scientific and practical dead end.

THREE KINDS OF REAL GENETIC INFLUENCES

When considering bona fide genetic involvement in mental development, it is important to distinguish three general kinds of genetic influences: (i) Mendelian genetic disorders involve a major defect in one specific gene; (ii) Complex psychiatric disorders involve the combined actions of a small number of abnormal genes, each of which has a relatively modest effect; (iii) Continuous characteristics have a wide range of normal values and the outcome is influenced by a large number of genes, each with a small effect. It should be emphasized that all three kinds of phenomena are subject to environmental influences. It is generally not true that a disorder caused by a mutation in a single gene is therefore rendered impervious to environmental modification. On the contrary, as shown vividly by the example of PKU, a genetic mutation can make an individual *more* sensitive to environmental perturbations.

Single gene defects can now be diagnosed with certainty from the DNA sequence. They often result in severe, even fatal abnormalities, and consequently they are kept at low frequencies by natural selection. Well-known examples include Huntington Disease, the topic of the chapter by Bombard and Hayden in this volume, and cystic fibrosis. Colour blindness occurs in several forms that are determined by defects in different genes, and its relatively mild consequences allow relatively high frequencies of these gene defects to persist in many populations (Sacks 1998). Mental deficiency is one consequence of many different genetic mutations (Inlow and Restifo 2004; Raymond and Tarpey 2006); hence, it is clear that the activity of numerous genes is essential for normal mental development. Knowing the nature of a genetic defect can, in principle, provide important clues that may lead to a treatment or cure for the malady, but it must be acknowledged that cures have eluded science in most cases. Sickle-cell anemia was first identified as a genetic disorder of hemoglobin function in 1949 (Pauling et al. 1949), whereas 60 years later the symptoms can be ameliorated to some extent but there is still no cure (http://www.nhlbi.nih.gov/health/dci/Diseases/Sca/SCA_Treatments.html). The molecular causes of Huntington Disease are well understood, yet there is currently no way to impede the progression of the disease, which is why so many potential carriers decline to be tested to see if they have the bad gene (Bombard and Hayden, this volume). For these kinds of single-gene disorders, there is considerable promise in creating animal models in order to explore the molecular consequences of the defect and find ways to treat it.

Complex psychiatric disorders such as alcoholism, drug abuse, schizophrenia, depression, and impulsive violence clearly have some genetic basis, as shown by studies with twins and parent-offspring resemblance. There are reasons to believe that defects in a small number of genes may make a person susceptible to environmental factors that provoke or exacerbate a clinically significant disorder (Cicchetti 2007). Because the consequences of any one genetic anomaly tend to be mild, these kinds of genetic defects can persist in the population at relatively high frequencies. The small effect of any one gene, combined with major effects of environmental factors, make it difficult but not impossible to detect the culprit genes, as discussed by Goldman (this volume). Recent research has indicated that individuals with certain genotypes may be more sensitive to harmful effects of negative life experiences (Caspi et al. 2003; Cicchetti and Rogosch 2007; Cicchetti, Rogosch, and Sturge-Apple 2007; Eley et al. 2004; Enoch 2006; Jabbi et al. 2007), which suggests that attempts to identify specific genes may be more successful if the studies take into account the experiences of both vulnerable and resistant individuals. Complex disorders diagnosed on the basis of symptoms often are heterogeneous, so individuals may end up with the same clinical diagnosis for different genetic reasons, as can happen with Alzheimer's disease (Lambert and Amouyel 2007) and autism (Eichler and Zimmerman 2008).

It has been suggested that genetic analysis of psychiatric disorders may be more successful with physiological or anatomical measures (phenotypes) that mediate the effects of genes on behaviour (Gottesman and Gould 2003; Gould and Gottesman 2006). Data on these endophenotypes are discussed by Goldman (this volume). A recent meta-analysis, however, found no noteworthy difference in the degree of genetic influence on measures of overt psychiatric functioning versus the putative endophenotypes believed to be especially relevant for mental disorders (Flint and Munafo 2007). It appears that there will be no shortcut around the difficult genetic analysis of traits caused by multiple genes interacting with their environments.

Continuous characteristics such as intelligence and personality traits (see Flint, this volume) differ among people only in degree, and they have a wide range of values in the population. Test scores often show a normal or bell-shaped distribution (figure 2); only the most extreme manifestations below an arbitrarily defined level of 2.0 standard deviations from the population average are considered really abnormal. There is generally little relation between scores on a psychological test of these characteristics and reproductive success, which helps to explain why such great individual variation persists generation after generation. Although studies of twins, adoption, and parent-offspring resemblance suggest that genetic variation is an important source of differences among people in these characteristics, just how important it may be in comparison with effects of environmental differences is controversial and has proven difficult to judge (Devlin, Daniels, and Roeder 1997; Wahlsten 1994). It is widely accepted that any genetic influence is very complex, involving large numbers of genes that interact with each other and with a variety of environmental factors. These features make the detection of genes contributing to individual differences in the normal range a daunting task. They make it even more difficult, even impossible, to utilize this genetic knowledge for the benefit of those who have low test scores or for the improvement of human society.

How to detect the presence of a form of a specific gene that may increase or decrease human intelligence by a small amount is a highly technical subject whose mastery requires knowledge of advanced mathematics. The two major approaches, genetic association and linkage with markers, are broadly summarized here.

Genetic association studies examine the relation between test scores and known variations in genes (Ramoz and Gorwood 2007). Suppose there is a genetic locus, a specific place along a DNA molecule in a chromosome where a gene resides, that we will name gene A. Suppose further that two forms (alleles, expressed in italics here) of the gene are present in the population, the dominant allele *A* and the recessive allele *a*. Because each person receives one copy of the gene from each parent, three genotypes are possible: *AA*, *Aa*, and *aa*. Let us confine our attention to the two genotypes *AA* and *aa*. The researcher can determine the person's genotype with a biochemical test and then measure the phenotype with a psychological test. If the mean scores of those with genotype *AA* is X_{AA} and with *aa* is X_{aa}, then an association study asks whether the difference ($X_{AA} - X_{aa}$) is large enough to justify a conclusion that the gene probably caused the test scores to differ. Such a conclusion would be drawn only if it could be shown that no other factor was correlated with the *AA* versus *aa* genotypic difference. Usually this can be done only if the

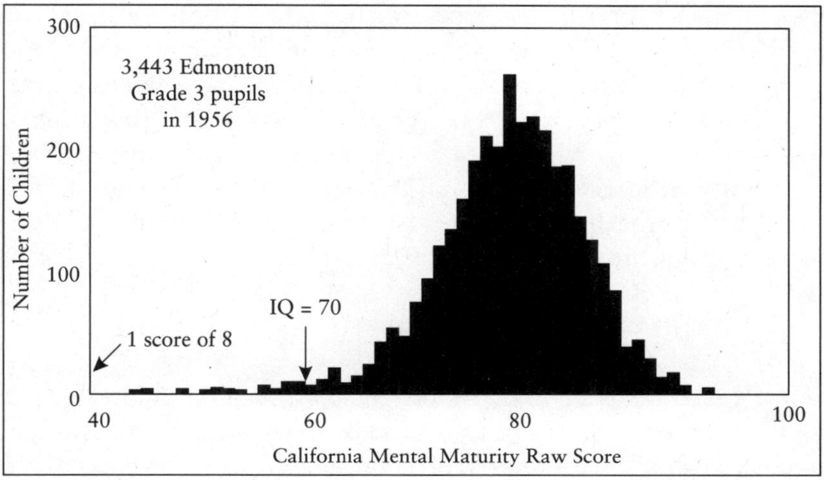

Figure 2. The bell-shaped distribution of scores on the California Mental Maturity test of mental ability that was taken by all children in the Edmonton, Alberta, schools in 1956 (original data in Coull 1956). Almost all scored in the normal range, from about 60 to 95 points on that test, and very few were below the score equivalent to an IQ (intelligence quotient) of 70.

people in the study are from the same ethnic group and live in very similar environments. The genetic association study is limited to research with genes that are already known to have genetic polymorphisms in the population. The numbers of such genes is increasing in the wake of the completion of the human genome sequence, but the full extent of human genetic variation in genes with clear functions is not yet known.

Genetic linkage studies examine the relation between test scores and variations in pieces of DNA that have no known function at all or variants in the gene that do not affect its function and can therefore serve as more or less neutral markers of location along a chromosome (Almasy and Blangero 1999). These kinds of neutral markers are much more likely to show polymorphisms in a population than are real genes with important functions. Suppose there is a marker M that occurs in two forms, m_1 and m_2. If marker M and the gene A are close together on the same chromosome, they will usually be inherited together and will not recombine during the generation of egg and sperm through meiosis. If the marker M is close to the gene at locus A that has a real effect on a psychological characteristic, then there should be a difference in average test scores between people with different genotypes (m_1m_1, m_1m_2, or m_2m_2) at the marker locus. Because so many markers are usually assessed in a single study, researchers must be very careful to avoid false positive associations that occur merely by chance. The only way to do this is to demand strong evidence of test score differences among those with different marker genotypes (Lander and Kruglyak 1995). This statistical approach cannot conclusively eliminate false positive associations but can only reduce their frequency.

DANGERS OF FALSE POSITIVE ASSOCIATIONS

When a research team finds an intriguing association of intelligence with a marker or with alleles of a known gene, the result is often publicized and over-interpreted in the mass media by journalists with little understanding of statistical association and the laws of chance. A prime example was a statistically significant association between intelligence test score and a chromosomal region containing the "insulin-like growth factor receptor-2" (IGF2R) gene (Chorney et al. 1998). Journalists privy to a pre-publication version of the paper lauded this as being "the first specific gene for human intelligence" and speculated that the finding "could settle the debate about whether genetics or education and lifestyle determine human intelligence" (*The Globe and Mail*, Nov. 17, 1997). One study author, Robert Plomin, told the *Daily Telegraph* (Nov. 20, 1997) that those who emphasize the role of environment will have trouble now because "it is harder to argue with a piece of DNA." The enthusiasm of some readers was later dampened when the full article in *Psychological Science* appeared in 1998 and it was learned that the IGF2R polymorphism could, at most, account for only 4 per cent of the variation in human intelligence in the population. It was also apparent from databases of gene expression (www.genecards.org) that the IGF2R gene is widely expressed in many tissues in the body, including heart, lung, kidney, and gall bladder, while its level of expression is lower in the brain than in most other organs. It could not be a gene *for* intelligence. Furthermore, subsequent efforts by the same group of researchers to replicate this tantalizing report with a larger sample ended in failure (Hill et al. 2002). Although the supposed connection of IGF2R with intelligence was still being cited in 2003 (Payton et al. 2003), the claim that the IGF2R gene is important for human intelligence was quietly withdrawn by those in the know.

A current search of the Online Mendelian Inheritance in Man database (OMIM; www.ncbi.nlm.nih.gov/sites) for genes related to human intelligence does not return IGF2R, and the entry for IGF2R indicates the gene's protein product is a receptor involved in intracellular trafficking of lysosomal enzymes. There is no mention of the history of claims concerning the gene and intelligence. The GeneCards database (www.genecards.org) does return IGF2R when searching for "intelligence," but this is an artefact arising from inclusion of IGF2R in a study that found positive association of intelligence with variants of the CTSD gene.

THE QUEST FOR GENES HAVING SMALL EFFECTS ON INTELLIGENCE

One real benefit of the Human Genome Project is the discovery of vast numbers of small genetic variants, presently numbering more than 4,671,723 locations along the DNA molecules (www.ncbi.nlm.nih.gov/projects/SNP/snp_summary.cgi), that are spread widely over all of the human chromosomes. It is now possible to conduct a comprehensive, whole genome scan by assessing several thousand markers spaced fairly evenly along every chromosome. If there is a gene with two or more alleles that influence human intelligence, for example, then intelligence test scores should differ substantially for people with certain DNA variants on a chromosome, while they will show minimal differences in intelligence with respect to hundreds of other DNA variants elsewhere in the genome.

Five whole genome studies of human intelligence were published in 2005 and 2006 (Buyske et al. 2006; Dick et al. 2006; Luciano et al. 2006; Posthuma et al. 2005; Wainwright et al. 2006), results of which are summarized in figure 3. Several important conclusions are warranted from these studies. First, a surprising number (eleven) of previously reported significant associations of intelligence with some specific gene were not replicated by these more powerful studies. Genes once so promising but now tossed into the garbage bin of false positives include IGF2R, BDNF (brain-derived neurotrophic factor), COMT (catechol-o-methyl transferase), DRD2 (dopamine receptor type D2 (Moises et al. 2001), and APOE (apolipoprotein E). Second, very few clearly significant associations of intelligence with markers in a particular region were seen anywhere in the genome by any study. Only regions on chromosomes 2, 6, and 14 met reasonable criteria for significant linkage in at least one study. Third, most regions of the chromosomes that were identified as possibly harbouring a gene important for differences in intelligence were reported by only one or two of the five studies, which pointed to a remarkable lack of agreement. Fourth, only one region, the distal portion of the p arm of chromosome 6, was identified as probably being important in a majority of the studies. Because of the sample sizes and numbers of markers employed in these studies, the region of interest is quite broad and contains dozens of genes (Dick et al. 2006). If there is a polymorphic gene lurking therein that causes differences in intelligence, it will be exceedingly difficult to pinpoint it.

Scientists reviewing these and other whole genome scans have been quite forthright about their frustrations over lack of agreement among studies. Regarding earlier claims about specific genes supposedly related to intelligence, Gray and Thompson (2004) noted that "none of these associations has yet been replicated." This concern was repeated with exclamation marks after the 2006 genome scans became known. Plomin (Plomin, Kennedy, and Craig 2006) noted that the studies "have not yielded ... associations that consistently replicate." Payton (2006) lamented the "inconsistency within the literature," while Posthuma and de Geus (2006) acknowledged that "poor replication ... is a common concern," and Dreary, Spinath and Bates (2006) observed that most associations "have yet to be replicated."

There are two possible explanations for the disappointing results of these large and expensive research projects. Perhaps there are flaws with the methodology that obscure real genetic effects. This does not seem likely, given the large increase in number of genetic markers examined with sophisticated statistical methods in recent studies. Alternatively, perhaps the genes that are related to variations in human intelligence are very large in number but very small in their individual effects. Collectively, they might exert an important influence on mental development, while nevertheless remaining unseen or only briefly glimpsed in the swirl of interactions with fluctuating environments. This latter possibility seems most likely. Reviewing several studies of genes and intelligence, Dreary et al. (Dreary, Spinath, and Bates 2006) concluded that any one gene is likely to alter intelligence by no more than one-tenth of a standard deviation and account for less than 1 per cent of the phenotypic variance in intelligence in the population. A DNA variant associated with a small quantitative effect on IQ is termed a Quantitative Trait Locus or QTL. An effect size of 0.1 standard deviation is very, very small

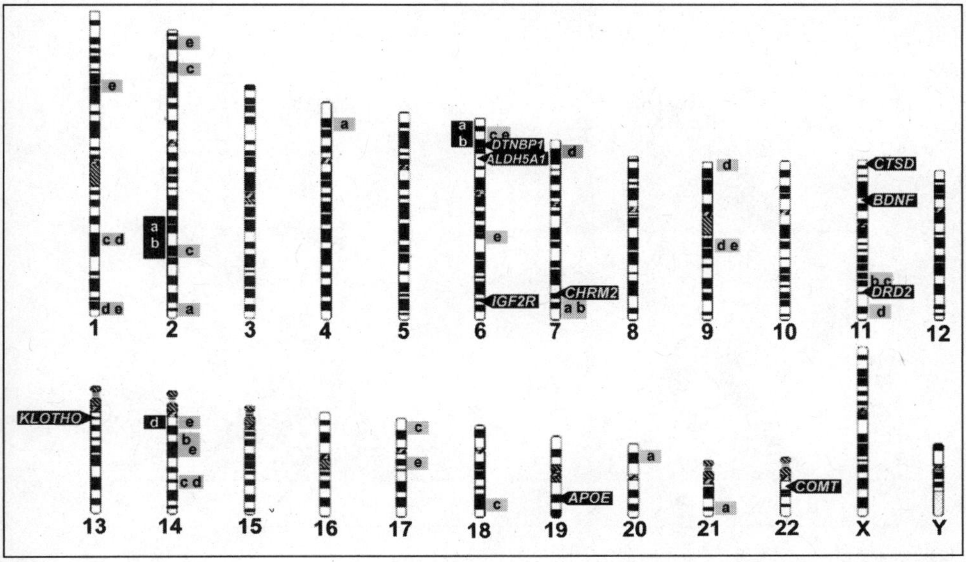

Figure 3. Summary of findings from five whole-genome scans of genetic markers located on all 22 human chromosomes as well as the X and Y chromosomes in relation to intelligence, modified with permission from Posthuma and de Geus (2006). Regions of a chromosome possibly containing a gene or genes relevant to IQ score are indicated by the letters a through e, denoting the studies by Posthuma et al. (2005), Luciano et al. (2006), Wainwright et al. (2006), Buyske et al. (2006), Dick et al. (2006), respectively. Regions showing statistically significant linkage with IQ are shown by a black bar on the left side of a chromosome, whereas those with grey bars indicate suggestive evidence of linkage. Gene symbols in capital letters on a dark background denote genes previously reported in the literature to be possibly important for variations in IQ.

indeed (figure 4), and extraordinarily large samples of subjects must be examined in order to identify such an effect (Wahlsten 1991, 2000, 2005). Plomin et al. (Plomin, Kennedy, and Craig 2006) concurred that human intelligence is influenced by "many more QTLs of much smaller effect size than previously imagined." They estimated that it would be necessary to assess 100,000 genetic markers in at least 2,000 people at a cost of $1,800 per person in order to detect a significant relation with a gene having such a small effect.

NO REAL VALUE IN KNOWING GENES WITH TRIVIALLY SMALL EFFECTS

If the statistical obstacles can be surmounted and one or a few genes pertinent to intelligence can finally be specified with confidence and universal acclaim, the question then arises as to how this knowledge

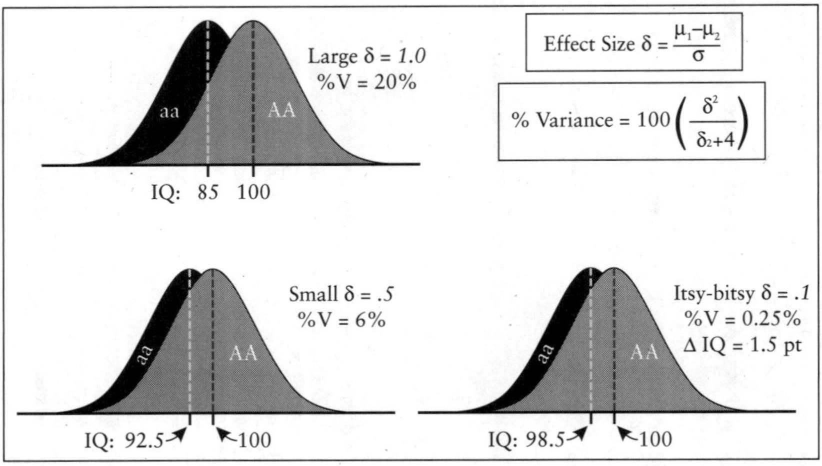

Figure 4. Effect sizes, expressed as the fraction of a standard deviation by which group means differ. Effect size is related to the degree of overlap between two distributions of scores and the percentage of variation in the two groups combined that can be attributed to the difference between group means. Based on standards proposed by Wahlsten (2007).

can be applied for the practical benefit of individuals and society. Here we confront a challenge that most likely can never be overcome. Genes work in highly specific ways at the chemical and neural levels. There are many reasons that something can go wrong with a gene and have an impact on intelligence. Consider table 1 where the functions of four genes mentioned in the review by Posthuma and de Geus (2006) and shown in figure 3 are described. No two of them work in the same physiological pathway. Each does its own unique thing. Thus, if several genes relevant for human intelligence could eventually be identified, any realistic intervention would need to be adapted to a baffling variety of gene combinations in real people.

Consider some simple models of how the effects of multiple genes combine to influence intelligence. Suppose we know that five genes (A, B, C, D and E) are relevant and each has two alleles (*A* and *a*, *B* and *b*, etc.). Suppose further that having two dominant genes at one locus (*AA*, *BB*, etc.) increases test scores by an average of 2 units, having one (*Aa*, *Bb*, etc.) increases the score by 1 unit and having all recessive alleles (*aa*, *bb*, etc.) does not augment intelligence. This is one of many possible models of gene effects, and it is not overly realistic, but lacking more definitive guidance from the data, it is

Table 1
Genes believed to have possible relevance for human intelligence, and their physiological functions

Gene symbol	*Chromosome: site*	*Gene name*	*Functions*
MYCN	2: p24.1	Myelocytomatosis viral oncogene	Immune system, neuroblastoma, leukemia
ALDH5A1	6: p22.2	Aldehyde dehydrogenase 5 type A1	Mitchondrial metabolism of GABA
DTNBP1	6: p22.3	Dystobrevin binding protein 1	Melanosomes, lysosomes, maybe schizophrenia
CHRM2	7: q31	Cholingeric receptor, muscarinic type 2	Heart muscle contraction, smooth muscles, bladder

Source: www.ncbi.nlm.gov/sites/entrez.

good enough to make the explanatory point. Once we have a model of genetic effects at individual loci, it is essential to specify how they combine across the five genes. Are their effects additive or multiplicative or do they operate according to some more intricate pattern? The proper answer to this question depends on the nature of the biochemical and physiological pathways uniting their effects (figure 5). If they act in parallel and are effectively independent, an additive model may be appropriate, whereas action in series warrants a multiplicative model. Under a simple additive model, the genotype *AA Bb CC Dd Ee* would have the value 2 + 1 + 2 + 1 + 1 = 7, whereas with the multiplicative model it would score 2(1)(2)(1)(1) = 4. A slight genetic change at locus B that makes the genotype *AA bb CC Dd Ee* would decrease the score by one unit to 6 under the additive model, but it would be reduced by three units to 0 under the multiplicative model.

This scheme can be extended to many combinations of alleles at the five loci. The graphs in figure 6 show the frequency of different genotypic values under two models when each locus has two equally common alleles in the population. There are 5^3 = 125 possible genotypes in the population but only 11 possible genotypic scores under the additive model and 15 possible scores under the mixed model. Note that under the additive model, there are 15 different genotypes

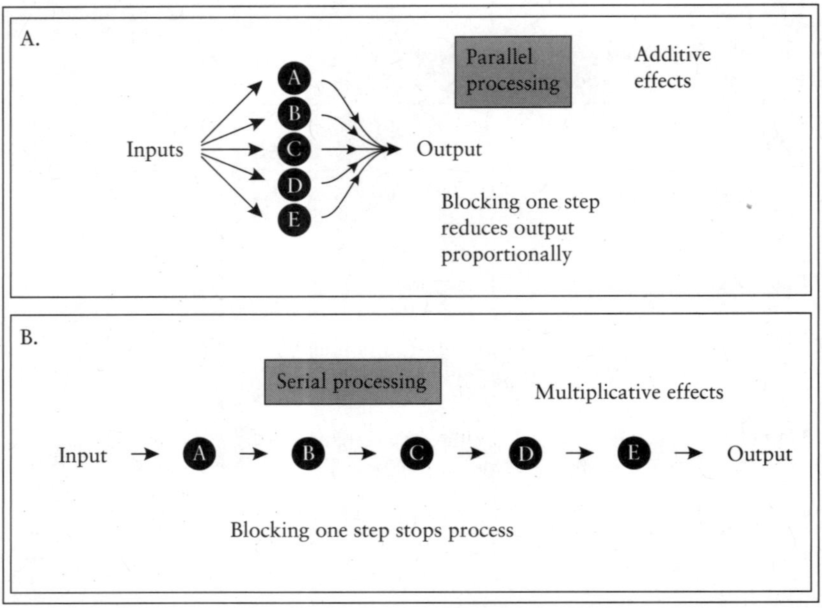

Figure 5. Two models of how the effects of the proteins specified by five genes combine at the physiological level. When the five processes function in parallel, the combined effects may be summarized by an additive algebraic model, whereas proteins working in series are more realistically described by a multiplicative model.

with the same genetic value of 8 units, whereas with the mixed model there are 24 genotypes with a score of 8 units. Thus, regardless of how gene effects combine across multiple loci, many different genetic combinations yield the same phenotypic effect, and different individuals can have the same intelligence test score for a multitude of qualitatively different biochemical, physiological, and psychological reasons.

Because of the very complex and interacting genetic and environmental influences on intelligence, there is no simple way to determine whether a child who seems to be lagging a little behind his or her peers in school does so for genetic or environmental causes. Even if the child is found to possess alleles at two or three loci that are likely to reduce intelligence by a small amount, this cannot serve as proof that environment is not the culprit in the specific instance. Lacking a firm scientific basis for accusing the genes of malfeasance, the medical profession would likely not be authorized to prescribe molecular devices to correct the allelic imbalances.

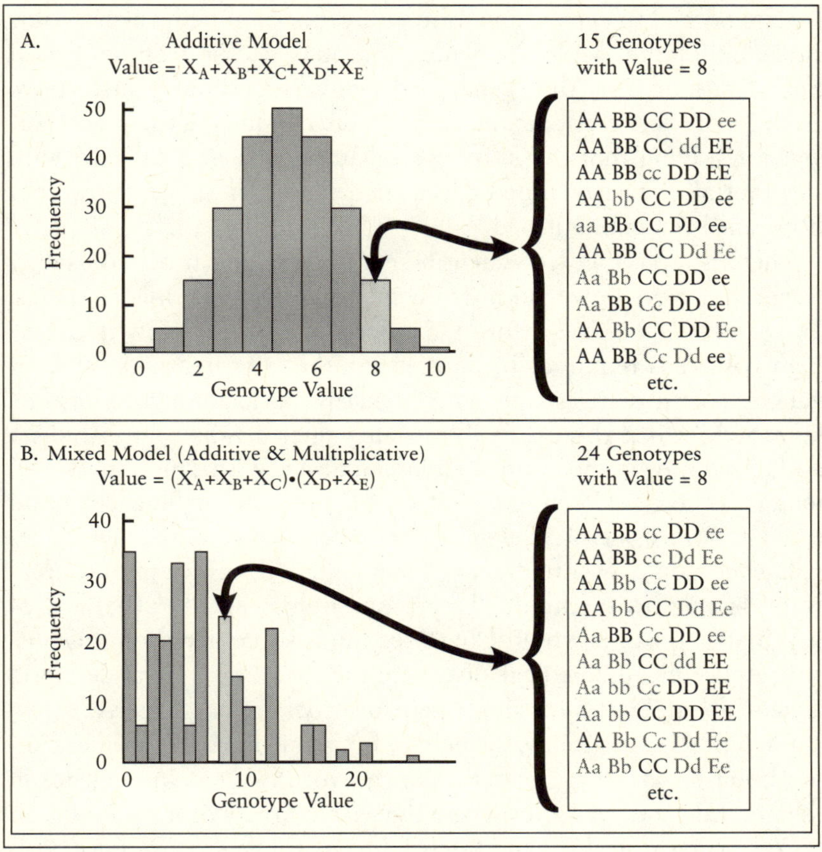

Figure 6. Combined quantitative genetic effects of a system of five genes (A, B, C, D, and E) under two models of how those effects combine. It is assumed here that each gene is present in the population in two equally frequent alleles, and each copy of the dominant allele possessed by an individual augments the score from that gene by 1 point. A. For the additive model, genotypic values range from 0 to 10, and there are 15 different genotypes that all yield the same genotypic value of 8. B. For the mixed additive and multiplicative model, genotypic values range from 0 to 24, and there are 24 different genotypes that yield the same genotypic value of 8. For clarity of the argument, environmental effects are omitted from these models, but the same argument could be made for influences of a range of environmental factors, namely, that several different combinations can yield the same quantitative effect on a test score.

The study of genes pertinent to human intelligence is thus beset by a conundrum. Each of those genes most certainly has an almost trivially small effect by itself. Hence, the sample sizes and expense of studies needed to detect each gene's influence on intelligence become shockingly large, while the benefit that may accrue from increased knowledge of how that gene works hovers perilously just above zero. Before the recent genome scans were conducted, there was reason for hoping that the scans would uncover a gene or two with substantial effects on intelligence in the normal range. Now that hope has been extinguished.

There is a basic law of scientific methodology that demands ever larger and more powerful instruments to detect ever smaller things. To see details within a neuron, an electron microscope with a very high voltage is required. To photograph the faint light from distant galaxies, a huge telescope with a nearly perfect mirror must be launched into earth's orbit. To visualize finer details of metabolism and blood flow in the brain, an imaging device with a more powerful magnet is needed. Phenotypic effects of genes on intelligence are no exception. In principle, the very small effects of several genes on intelligence could eventually be documented if sufficient resources were devoted to the hunt. The big question is whether the field of psychiatric genetics would like to see funds squandered on this pursuit while serious medical disorders still are not well understood genetically and cures for single-gene disorders remain elusive.

As matters stand today, the field of human behaviour genetics cannot point to one single gene that unequivocally alters intelligence in the normal range of scores where the vast majority of the population resides. Time after time, an initial claim has proven to be a false positive result that cannot be replicated. Given this unhappy history, we ought to receive new reports with a greater degree of skepticism, if not outright trepidation, than in the past. An apparently significant association of intelligence with some gene may warrant publication in a scientific journal so that colleagues can attempt to replicate and verify the finding, but surely the news should be read with a cautious and critical eye.

NEW HOPES FROM STUDIES OF GENE-ENVIRONMENT INTERACTION

Consider a report published in the prestigious *Proceedings of the National Academy of Science USA* (Caspi et al. 2007) that found a clear but modest 5 to 7 IQ point benefit of breast-feeding on human intelligence in infants with the "C" allele (genotypes CC or CG) of the FADS2 gene (fatty acid desaturase type 2) but no such benefit in infants lacking that allele and having two copies of the "G" allele. The genotype-dependent effect was seen in two independent samples of children and their mothers. This is a clear instance of gene-environment interaction, and without taking the dependence on nursing environment into account, there would have been no evidence that the FADS2 gene polymorphism had any relevance to intelligence. In fact, when data were combined for infants with and without breast feeding, there was no difference in average IQ score for those with CC, CG and GG genotypes. The FADS2 gene did not affect intelligence per se; instead, it affected fatty acid metabolism which in turn appeared to influence brain development.

The electronic version of the *PNAS* article was made available on the Internet on November 5, 2007. The media pounced on the news and, amidst a frenzied rush to be the first to cover the story, crafted some clever headlines. One Internet news site proclaimed the discovery of the "breast-feeding IQ gene" (www.inthenews.co.uk for November 6). Another mused metaphorically that "mother's milk may pump up baby's IQ" (www.sciam.com for November 7). Xinhua News termed the allele associated with the positive breast-feeding effect a "helpful" genetic variant (news.xinhuanet.com for November 7) when the data actually showed that breast feeding is helpful in almost all infants, save the 10 per cent with the GG genotype. Below the headlines was some real wisdom. *Inthenews* interviewed Terrie Moffit, a study author, who pointed out that "The argument about adult intelligence has been about nature versus nurture for at least a century. We're finding that nature and nurture work together."

Indeed they do, but how they do is not at all obvious. Interpretation of the study was rendered difficult because the mothers of infants who were breast-fed also had considerably more education and higher IQ scores than those who did not breast-feed, regardless of the infant's genotype. It seems unlikely that the experience of breast-feeding itself increases maternal intelligence; rather, mothers with greater education and family income are more likely to breast feed their infants for a longer period. Consequently, it is a major challenge to determine what aspect of the child's intelligence test score reflects the breast feeding advantage or some other factors, even genes, associated with higher maternal education and intelligence. Several previous studies of breast feeding used multiple regression analysis, first estimating child IQ from indicators of maternal environment, education and/or intelligence and then computing a second equation with an additional term to account for any breast feeding effect. If the added term did not improve the amount of variance explained by the regression equation, then investigators concluded that there was no breast feeding effect independent of other maternal factors. The statistical method can also be used to adjust group means for maternal education and IQ. Taking maternal factors into account reduced the statistical estimate of the breast feeding effect in all previous studies (table 2), and the effect vanished altogether in two studies that had measures of maternal IQ in addition to indicators of maternal education and social standing, indicators that are only moderately correlated with IQ.

The Caspi et al. study also measured maternal IQ, and that IQ was considerably higher for mothers who breast-fed their infants, regardless of infant genotype at the FADS2 gene. But child IQ was not higher as a consequence of breast feeding in those with the GG pair of alleles, despite the propitious combination of higher maternal IQ *and* copious breast feeding in a portion of those infants. For GG infants, average maternal IQ scores were 102.6 and 91.8 for infants that were or were not breast-fed, respectively, in one of the samples. It was not simply a matter of the extra nutrients in mother's milk not aiding brain development in GG infants; none of the other factors associated with breast feeding, including maternal intelligence, enhanced IQ in those infants either. The absence of an IQ different in these GG infants defies a large literature on parent-offspring intelligence correlations and begs some explanation.

This fascinating and sophisticated report of gene-environment interaction cannot be the final word on this matter. Just as for a linkage study of genetic markers and intelligence, readers will insist that the gene-related effect of breast feeding and that of maternal intelligence itself, however interesting and theoretically satisfying they may seem, should be replicated by other groups of investigators before they are taken very seriously. Modest effects of any environmental treatment on intelligence, be they gene related or not, need to be verified before they are granted a special place in behavioural and social science. Just because the finding qualifies as gene-environment interaction does not render it immune to being a false positive result. I say this as one with a long history of promoting an interactionist view of development (Wahlsten 1979, 1990).

Table 2
Difference between mean IQ test scores of children who were breastfed and those who were not, either unadjusted means or mean difference statistically adjusted for several maternal and family variables.[a]

Study	*Total sample*	*Child age (yrs)*	*IQ test*	*Maternal IQ measured*	*IQ difference, unadjusted*	*IQ difference, adjusted for maternal factors*
Anderson et al. 1999	7,235	Several	Several	Some	5.3	3.2
Jacobson et al. 1999	322	4	PPVT-R	Yes	6.4	NS
Jacobson et al. 1999	279	11	WISC-R	Yes	4.8	NS
Mortensen et al. 2002	973	27	WAIS	No	8.9	5.5
Mortensen et al. 2002	228	19	BPP	No	8.0	5.2
Auestad et al. 2003	87	3.2	St-Binet	No	5	2
Gibson-Davis & Brooks-Gunn 2006	1645	3	PPVT-III	Yes	6.6	1.7[NS]
Der et al. 2006	5,475	5-14	PIAT	Yes	4.7	0.5[NS]
Caspi et al. 2007	775	7-13	WISC-R	Yes	6.5	?
Caspi et al. 2007	1,724	5	WPPSI-R	Yes	7.0	?

[a] NS indicates the mean difference was not statistically significant. IQ test abbreviations: PPVT-R, Peabody Picture Vocabulary Test – Revised; WISC-R, Wechsler Intelligence Scale for Children – Revised; WAIS, Wechsler Adult Intelligence Scale; BPP, Borge Preins Prove; PPVT-III, the PPVT third edition; PIAT, Peabody Individual Achievement Test; WPPSI-R, Wechsler Preschool and Primary Scale of Intelligence – Revised..

Presuming that the gene-related interaction is substantial in magnitude and easily observed by other investigators, the interactionist approach offers a way out of the chartless tangle of nature-nurture debates that have occupied psychology for many decades. In the case of the FADS2 genetic polymorphism, taking the genetic variable into account offers a more powerful and refined way to study the environment. Presumably many of the previous studies of breast feeding and IQ contained a substantial fraction of subjects with the GG genotype, which would necessarily have attenuated the apparent effect of the environment on many of the children. An interaction with a known gene also provides a major clue about what kinds of improvements to infant formula might be most beneficial to a wide range of children. Thus, studies of gene-environment interaction have the potential to improve child development through environmental changes, and the genetic tool can aid the task of the nutritionist and the developmental psychologist.

CONCLUSIONS

Numerous rare genetic mutations that substantially impair mental development and neural function have been documented, but little therapeutic benefit has yet been realized from this genetic knowledge. Meanwhile, large studies of variation in mental functioning in the normal range of psychological test scores have heretofore not conclusively identified even one relevant gene, principally because the individual genes have vanishingly small effects. Because the effects of genetic variants in the normal range of psychological functioning are so small, little or no practical benefit to individuals or society is likely to accrue from this line of investigation. Instead, it appears that resources could be more fruitfully deployed in seeking better treatments or outright cures for well-documented genetic disorders. Recent evidence suggests that the impact of certain environmental influences on psychological development may depend substantially on child genotype. Research that takes both genetic and relevant environmental variations into account also appears to be more promising than studies that focus narrowly on genes.

Based on a paper presented 16 November 2007, in Edmonton, Alberta, at the Royal Society of Canada Annual Symposium on *Changing Boundaries between Gene Expressions and the Social Fabric: The Social Sciences Confront Modern Genetic Challenges*.

BIBLIOGRAPHY

Almasy, L., Blangero, J. 1999. Linkage strategies for mapping genes for complex traits in man. In *Handbook of molecular-genetic techniques for brain and behavior research*, Eds W.E. Crusio and R. Gerlai: 100-12. Amsterdam: Elsevier.

Anderson, J.W., Johnstone, B.M., Remley, D.T. 1999. Breast-feeding and cognitive development: a meta-analysis. *American Journal of Clinical Nutrition* 70:525-35.

Auestad, N., Scott, D.T., Janowsky, J.S., Jacobsen, C., Carroll, R.E., Montalto, M.B., Halter, R., Qiu, W., Jacobs, J.R., Connor, W.E., Connor, S.L., Taylor, J.A, Neuringer, M., Fitzgerald, K.M., Hall, R.T. 2003. Visual, cognitive, and language assessments at 39 months: a follow-up study of children fed formulas containing long-chain polyunsaturated fatty acids to 1 year of age. *Pediatrics* 112 (3 Pt 1):e177-e183.

Buyske, S., Bates, M.E., Gharani, N., Matise, T.C., Tischfield, J.A., Manowitz, P. 2006. Cognitive traits link to human chromosomal regions. *Behavior Genetics* 36 (1):65-76.

Caspi, A., Sugden, K., Moffitt, T.E., Taylor, A., Craig, I.W., Harrington, H., McClay, J., Mill, J., Martin, J., Braithwaite, A., Poulton, R. 2003. Influence of life stress on depression: Moderation by a polymorphism in the 5-HTT gene. *Science* 301 (5631):386-9.

Caspi, A., Williams, B., Kim-Cohen, J., Craig, I.W., Milne, B.J., Poulton, R., Schalkwyk, L.C., Taylor, A,, Werts, H., Moffitt, T.E. 2007. Moderation of breastfeeding effects on the IQ by genetic variation in fatty acid metabolism. *Proc. Natl. Acad. Sci. U. S. A* 104 (47):18860-5.

Cavalli-Sforza, L.L. 2000. *Genes, Peoples, and Languages*. Berkeley: University of California Press.

Cavalli-Sforza, L.L., Menozzi, P., Piazza, A. 1994. *The History and Geography of Human Genes*. Princeton, NJ: Princeton University Press.

Chorney, M.J., Chorney, K., Seese, N., Owen, M.J., McGuffin, P., Daniels, J., Thompson, L.A., Detterman, D.K., Benbow, C.P., Lubinski, D., Eley, T.C., Plomin, R. 1998. A quantitative trait locus associated with cognitive ability in children. *Psychological Science* 9:159-66.

Cicchetti, D. 2007. Gene-environment interaction. *Dev. Psychopathol.* 19 (4):957-9.

Cicchetti, D., Rogosch, F.A. 2007. Personality, adrenal steroid hormones, and resilience in maltreated children: a multilevel perspective. *Dev. Psychopathol.* 19 (3):787-809.

Cicchetti, D., Rogosch, F.A., Sturge-Apple, M.L. 2007. Interactions of child maltreatment and serotonin transporter and monoamine oxidase A polymorphisms: Depressive symptomatology among adolescents from low socio-economic status backgrounds. *Dev. Psychopathol.* 19 (4):1161-80.

Coull, W.H. 1956. A normative survey of reading achievement of Alberta children in relation to intelligence, sex, bilingualism, and grade placement. A normative survey of reading achievement of Alberta children in relation to intelligence, sex, bilingualism, and grade placement, University of Alberta.

Der, G., Batty, G.D., Dreary, I.J. 2006. Effect of breast feeding on intelligence in children: Prospective study, sibling pairs analysis, and meta-analysis. *British Medical Journal* 10.1136 (bmj.38978.699583.55):1-6.

Devlin, B., Daniels, M., Roeder, K. 1997. The heritability of IQ. *Nature* 388 (6641):468-71.

Dick, D.M., Aliev, F., Bierut, L., Goate, A., Rice, J., Hinrichs, A., Bertelsen, S., Wang, J.C., Dunn, G., Kuperman, S., Schuckit, M., Nurnberger, J. Jr., Porjesz, B., Beglieter, H., Kramer, J., Hesselbrock, V. 2006. Linkage analyses of IQ in the collaborative study on the genetics of alcoholism (COGA) sample. *Behavior Genetics* 36 (1):77-86.

Dreary, I.J., Spinath, F.M., Bates, T.C. 2006. Genetics of intelligence. *European Journal of Human Genetics* 14:690-700.

Eichler, E.E., Zimmerman, A.W. 2008. A hot spot of genetic instability in autism. *New England Journal of Medicine* 10.156 epub.

Eley, T.C., Sugden, K., Corsico, A., Gregory, A.M., Sham, P., McGuffin, P., Plomin, R., Craig, I.W. 2004. Gene-environment interaction analysis of serotonin system markers with adolescent depression. *Mol. Psychiatry* 9 (10):908-15.

Emlen, S.T. 1967. Migratory Orientation in the indigo bunting, Passerina cyanea: Part I: Evidence for Use of Celestial Cues. *The Auk* 84:309-42.

Enoch, M.A. 2006. Genetic and environmental influences on the development of alcoholism: Resilience vs. risk. *Annals of the New York Academy of Sciences* 1094:193-201.

Fisch, R.O., Matalon, R., Weisberg, S., Michals, K. 1997. Phenylketonuria: Current dietary treatment practices in the United States and Canada. *J. Am. Coll. Nutr.* 16 (2):147-51.

Flint, J., Munafo, M.R. 2007. The endophenotype concept in psychiatric genetics. *Psychol. Med.* 37 (2):163-80.

Gambol, P.J. 2007. Maternal phenylketonuria syndrome and case management implications. *Journal of Pediatric Nursing* 22:129-38.

Gibson-Davis, C.M., Brooks-Gunn, J. 2006. Breastfeeding and verbal ability of 3-year-olds in a multicity sample. *Pediatrics* 118 (5):e1444-e1451.

Gottesman, I.I., Gould, T,D. 2003. The endophenotype concept in psychiatry: Etymology and strategic intentions. *Am. J. Psychiatry* 160 (4):636-45.

Gould, T.D., Gottesman, I.I. 2006. Psychiatric endophenotypes and the development of valid animal models. *Genes, Brain and Behavior* 5 (2):113-19.

Gray, J.R., Thompson, P.M. 2004. Neurobiology of intelligence: science and ethics. *Nat. Rev. Neurosci.* 5 (6):471-82.

Hanley, W.B., Clarke, J.T., Schoonheyt, W. 1987. Maternal phenylketonuria (PKU)-a review. *Clin. Biochem.* 20 (3):149-56.

Herrnstein, R.J., Murray, C. 1994. *The Bell Curve: Intelligence and Class Structure in American Life*. New York: Free Press.

Hill, L., Chorney, M.J., Lubinski, D., Thompson, L.A., Plomin, R. 2002. A quantitative trait locus not associated with cognitive ability in children: A failure to replicate. *Psychological Science* 13 (6):561-2.

Inlow, J.K., Restifo, L.L. 2004. Molecular and comparative genetics of mental retardation. *Genetics* 166 (2):835-81.

Jabbi, M., Korf, J., Kema, I.P., Hartman, C., van der P.G., Minderaa, R.B., Ormel, J., den Boer, J.A. 2007. Convergent genetic modulation of the endocrine stress response involves polymorphic variations of 5-HTT, COMT and MAOA. *Mol. Psychiatry* 12 (5):483-90.

Jacobson, S.W., Chiodo, L.M., Jacobson, J.L. 1999. Breastfeeding effects on intelligence quotient in 4- and 11-year-old children. *Pediatrics* 103 (5):e71.

Jensen, A. 1969. How much can be boost IQ and scholastic achievement? *Harvard Educational Review* Reprint series no. 2:1-123.

Lambert, J.C., Amouyel, P. 2007. Genetic heterogeneity of Alzheimer's disease: complexity and advances. *Psychoneuroendocrinology* 32 Suppl 1:S62-S70.

Lander, E., Kruglyak L. 1995. Genetic dissection of complex traits: Guidelines for interpreting and reporting linkage results. *Nature Genetics* 11:241-7.

Le Vann, L.J. 1959. Trifluoperazine dihydrochloride: An effective tranquilizing agent for behavioural abnormalities in defective children. *Canadian Medical Association Journal* 80:123-4.

– 1961. Thioridazine (Mellaril) a psychosedative virtually free of side effects. *Alberta Medical Bulletin* 26:144-7.

– 1968. A new butyrophenone: trifluperidol. A psychiatric evaluation in a pediatric setting. *Canadian Psychiatric Association Journal* 13:271-3.

– 1971. Clinical comparison of haloperidol and chlorpromazine in mentally retarded children. *American Journal of Mental Deficiency* 75:719-23.

Luciano, M., Wright, M.J., Duffy, D.L., Wainwright, M.A., Zhu, G., Evans, D.M., Geffen, G.M., Montgomery, G.W., Martin, N.G. 2006.

Genome-wide scan of IQ finds significant linkage to a quantitative trait locus on 2q. *Behavior Genetics* 36 (1):45-55.

Lyman, F.L., Lyman, J.K. 1960. Dietary management of phenylketonuria with lofenalac. *Arch. Pediatr.* 77:212-20.

Moises, H.W., Frieboes, R.M., Spelzhaus, P., Yang, L., Kohnke, M., Herden-Kirchoff, O., Vetter, P., Neppert, J., Gottesman, I.I. 2001. No association between dopamine D2 receptor gene (DRD2) and human intelligence. *Journal of Neural Transmission* 108:115-221.

Mortensen, E.L., Michaelsen, K.F., Sanders, S.A., Reinisch, J.M. 2002. The association between duration of breastfeeding and adult intelligence. *JAMA* 287 (18):2365-71.

National Film Board of Canada, The. 1996. The sterilization of Leilani Muir. Montreal: The National Film Board of Canada.

Nugent, H. 2007. Black people "less intelligent" scientist claims. *Timesonline*, 2007.

Pauling, L., Itano, H.A., Singer, S.J., Wells, I.C. 1949. Sickle cell anemia, a molecular disease. *Science* 110:543-8.

Payton, A. 2006. Investigating cognitive genetics and its implications for the treatment of cognitive deficit. *Genes, Brain and Behavior* 5 Suppl 1:44-53.

Payton, A., Holland, F., Diggle, P., Rabbitt, P., Horan, M., Davidson, Y., Gibbons, L., Worthington, J., Ollier, W.E., Pendleton, N. 2003. Cathepsin D exon 2 polymorphism associated with general intelligence in a healthy older population. *Mol. Psychiatry* 8 (1):14-18.

Plomin, R., Kennedy, J.K.J., Craig, I.W. 2006. The quest for quantitative trait loci associated with intelligence. *Intelligence* 34 (6):513-26.

Posthuma, D., de Geus, E.J.C. 2006. Progress in the molecular-genetic study of intelligence. *Current Directions in Psychological Science* 15 (4):151-5.

Posthuma, D., Luciano, M., de Geus, E.J., Wright, M.J., Slagboom, P.E., Montgomery, G.W., Boomsma, D.I., Martin, N.G. 2005. A genomewide scan for intelligence identifies quantitative trait loci on 2q and 6p. *American Journal of Human Genetics* 77 (2):318-26.

Ramoz, N., Gorwood P. 2007. The role of association studies in psychiatric disorders. In *Neurobehavoral genetics. Methods and applications*, eds B.C. Jones and P. Mormede, 169-82. Boca Raton: CRC Taylor and Francis.

Raymond, F.L., Tarpey, P. 2006. The genetics of mental retardation. *Human Molecular Genetics* 15:R110-R116.

Rennie, J. 2003. A conversation with James D. Watson. *Scientific American*, 2003, 67-9.

Sacks, O. 1998. *Island of the Colorblind*. New York: Knopf Publishing Group.

Scriver, C.R. 2001. Human genetics: lessons from Quebec populations. *Annu. Rev. Genomics Hum. Genet.* 2:69-101.

Scriver, C.R., Waters, P.J. 1999. Monogenic traits are not simple – lessons from phenylketonuria. *Trends in Genetics* 15:267-72.

Wahlsten, D. 1979. A critique of the concepts of heritability and heredity in behavioral genetics. In *Theoretical Advances in Behavioral Genetics*, eds J.R. Royce and L. Mos, 425-81. Alphen aan den Rijn, the Netherlands: Sijthoff and Noordhoff.

– 1990. Insensitivity of the analysis of variance to heredity-environment interaction. *Behavioral and Brain Sciences* 13:109-61.

– 1991. Sample size to detect a planned contrast and a one degree-of-freedom interaction effect. *Psychological Bulletin* 110:587-95.

– 1994. The intelligence of heritability. *Canadian Psychology* 35:244-58.

– 1997. Leilani Muir versus the Philosopher King: Eugenics on trial in Alberta. *Genetica* 99:185-98.

– 1999. Single-gene influences on brain and behavior. *Annual Review of Psychology* 50 (1):599-624.

– 2000. Planning genetic experiments: power and sample size. In *Neurobehavioral Genetics. Methods and Applications*, eds B Jones and P Mormède, 31-42. New York: CRC Press.

– 2002. The theory of biological intelligence: history and a critical appraisal. In *The general factor of intelligence: how general is it?*, eds R Sternberg and E Gigorenko, 245-77. Mahwah, NJ: Erlbaum.

– 2005. Sample size requirements for experiments on laboratory animals. In *Neurobehavioral Genetics: Methods and Applications, 2nd edition*, eds P Mormède and BC Jones. Boca Raton, FL: CRC Press.

– 2007. Sample size requirements for experiments on laboratory animals. In *Neurobehavioral Genetics: Methods and Applications*, eds BC Jones and P Mormede, 149-68. Boca Raton, FL: CRC Taylor and Francis.

Wainwright, M.A., Wright, M.J., Luciano, M., Montgomery, G.W., Geffen, G.M., Martin, N.G. 2006. A linkage study of academic skills defined by the Queensland core skills test. *Behavior Genetics* 36 (1):56-64.

Personality Genetics

JONATHAN FLINT

I'm going to use personality as an exemplar of the possibilities that molecular genetic approaches open up for investigating the biology of behaviour. As I suppose is true in all scientific fields, research is driven by the tools we have available, and when transformational technologies come along transformations do occur. The genetics tools we have in biological research seem never to stop transforming the way we do science: from the era *BC* (before cloning) to the near future when we will routinely sequence the genomes of individuals (a current project at the Sanger Institute outside Cambridge aims to sequence 1,000 people). And because my training and research area is in genetics, I don't want to forget the capacity we now have to peer into the workings of people's minds (a technology that might appear close to nineteenth-century phrenology); nor to ignore our increasing capacity to visualize and analyze tissues, cells, and their components; nor to overlook the critically important role that the access to cheap, fast, and extensive computing resources has had in biology. Exploiting these tools fully demands mastery of a wide set of skills, or good collaborators, in other words, interdisciplinary action.

I've chosen personality because it touches many of the themes discussed in this book. Because everyone has a personality, concerns over the implications of what genetic analysis means, ethically and legally, will of course touch us all. There will also be cultural differences (genetic factors are not the major determinants of personality), and there will be environmental effects, so that potentially there are many opportunities to investigate interactions between environment and genes. For these reasons, exploring the causes of individual differences in personality is an ideal place to illuminate the issues raised in this book.

Personality appears to be so central to humanity that it is something we cannot imagine being without. There is a considerable literature by psychologists on ways to assess personality, which I will not review here, but it is as well to have some idea of the problems and the disputes that have arisen. Almost all of the assessments have used self-administered questionnaires. One of the most contentious issues has been the state dependence of the personality assessment: For instance, people may answer the same question in very different ways depending on the circumstances in which they find themselves. In fact this does not turn out to be as insuperable an objection as it might appear: Questionnaire assessments turn out to be remarkably consistent. For example, we found correlations in excess of 0.9 when the same questionnaire was administered after an interval of more than 2 years (Willis-Owen et al. 2005).

A more taxing problem is how to interpret the answers. Most people assume when they come across a personality questionnaire for the first time that the meaning of the question is important and that the value of the response depends on the extent to which how truthfully it has been answered. It is easy to see the problem with this interpretation. Here's an example that Hans Eysenck, gives: "One might see some unfortunate individual sitting down with the questionnaire, his hands trembling and sweating with excitement, his face getting pale and flushed alternately, and his tongue licking his lips, his whole body in a tremor of nervousness; on going over to reassure him, one would find after the question, 'Are you generally a nervous sort of person?' he had boldly put the answer 'No'" (Eysenck 1957).

There are two important features about personality questionnaires. The first is that in order to get any sense out of personality questionnaires we have to abandon the idea that the answer a person gives should be interpreted as a truthful self-revelation. Instead we must treat the answers in the same way we do any other scientific observation, as a pattern of responses. The second important feature is that psychologists do not use the individual items of the questionnaire, but use what are called *factors*. Consider these two questions: "Are your feelings hurt?" and "Do ideas run through your head so that you cannot sleep?" There's no reason why you should not answer yes to the first and no to the second. But in fact people who answer yes to the first tend to answer yes to the second, and vice versa. And, since this is true for other questions, it is possible to pull out a set of correlated answers. The correlations allow us to recover a relatively small number (usually five) of correlated responses, or factors.

There is a general consensus that the structure of normal personality contains five factors (Costa and McCrae 1992; Deary and Matthews 1993; Digman 1990, 1997). The five-factor model (FFM) divides personality into the five dimensions of Neuroticism, Extraversion, Openness to Experience, Agreeableness, and Conscientiousness (Costa and McCrae 1992), easily remembered by the acronym OCEAN. The FFM is hierarchical, that is to say, each broad trait dimension may contain more specific features of personality. For example, Neuroticism contains personality features such as anxiety, angry hostility, depression, self-consciousness, impulsiveness, and vulnerability.

But what use are the factors if they cannot be interpreted? Here's an example that Eysenck provides to answer that question (Eysenck 1957): During the First World War, the army became worried about the number of soldiers who developed neurotic disorders and wanted a selection procedure to screen out neurotic soldiers, who were costing them a lot in time and money. The person to whom this task was entrusted was an American psychologist, Woodworth, who drew up a questionnaire of the same yes and no format as the personality questionnaire that asked about all the symptoms of neurosis that Woodworth could find in psychiatry text books. In fact the war came to an end before the screening questionnaire was used, but you can see why the army would like it. By not recruiting soldiers likely to develop neurotic symptoms, the army could become much more efficient.

Personality factors have important correlates with other psychological and physiological phenomena. For instance, we know that levels of neuroticism predict the onset and subsequent episodes of major depression (Angst and Clayton 1986; Kendler et al. 1993) and are associated with symptoms of depression and anxiety in the general population (Cox et al. 2004; Jylha and Isometsa 2006). However, does this mean that personality factors have no value in their own right? This has struck a number of investigators as unlikely, since, assuming that the concordance between personality dimensions is meaningful, "the probability is that they are based on the way in which our biology has evolved to cope with the extraordinary range of social structures and physical environments on this planet" (Zuckerman 1992).

Personality is not restricted to our own species. Behavioural observation of a number of species has shown that personality-like variation of behavioural profiles exists. The idea that animals have personality is not new: "If the impression has been given that the personality of the chimpanzee is relatively uniform and constant, violence has been done to the facts, for there are individual patterns and types. One may as readily identify a familiar ape among many by its personality as mirrored in behaviour as by its physical appearance. The student comes soon to recognize his subjects as in varying degrees patient, tractable, docile, suggestible, gentle, friendly, trustworthy or the opposite" (Yerkes 1939). Yerkes' anecdotal account was succeeded by more rigorous assessments, using methods similar to those used for our own species, including factor analyses that pull out features which, on the face of it, are similar to those found in human studies. For example, factor analysis of octopuses suggests they vary on three dimensions, which were designated Activity, Reactivity, and Avoidance (Mather and Anderson 1993).

Gosling's review of animal personality literature up to 2001 concluded that a number of dimensions appeared repeatedly across multiple species, including a dimension reflecting an individual's reaction to novel stimuli or situations (termed Reactivity, Emotionality, or Fearfulness and possibly homologous to neuroticism) (Gosling 2001). According to Gosling, "The FFM dimensions of Extraversion, Neuroticism, and Agreeableness showed considerable generality across the 12 species included in their review ... The way these personality dimensions are manifested, however, depends on the species. For example, whereas a human scoring low on Extraversion stays at home on Saturday night or tries to blend into a corner at a large party, the octopus scoring low on Boldness stays in its protective den during feedings and attempts to hide itself by changing color or releasing ink into the water" (Gosling 2001).

A powerful impetus for interpreting personality constructs has been the finding that the factors are heritable. Twin studies have been instrumental in demonstrating that about 40 per cent of variation in personality is due to genetic variation (this figure varies between factors, though not substantially) (Eaves et al. 1989; Floderus-Myrhed et al. 1980; Lake et al. 2000; Loehlin 1992). Alone, heritability does not prove anything. In fact, as Tooby and

Cosmides argue, it is consistent with personality being a sort of evolutionary noise: "Selection, interacting with sexual recombination, tends to impose relative uniformity at the functional level in complex adaptive designs, suggesting that most heritable psychological differences are not themselves likely to be complex psychological adaptations. Instead, they are mostly evolutionary by-products, such as concomitants of parasite-driven selection for biochemical individuality" (Tooby and Cosmides 1990). There are problems with using heritability to validate personality constructs; many valid psychological processes don't have a heritability (for instance variation in which language you speak) while many trivial processes do (such as the sort of car you own).

Heritability studies raise one immediate question, often ignored when the hunt for the molecular determinants began. This is the difficulty of explaining why there should be a genetic contribution at all. From an evolutionary perspective, variation is always in need of explanation since evolutionary theory tells us that heritable traits, linked to survival or fitness, will be purged of variation: Individuals with the characteristics that maximize their chances of reproduction will dominate a population. Personality traits are heritable and they are linked to survival: Sensation seekers will be eaten by predators.

Ecologists provide one possible solution. Consider what happens when there is a trade-off between early versus late reproductive strategies. Individuals who postpone reproduction are likely to have more resources, to be larger, richer, and so on, but they will have lived longer to achieve these advantages. Consequently they should be generally risk-averse; the opposite is true for those who reproduce early. In this situation stable individual differences in risk-taking behaviours can evolve and be maintained (Wolf et al. 2007). A similar argument can be made for a trade-off between growth and mortality as a mechanism that favours the evolution of personality. Suppose there is a choice between growing fast, which carries the risk of dying young, or growing slowly, with less risk of dying young. Behavioural variation can result if the two strategies have equal fitness, owing to a trade-off with mortality (Stamps 2007).

The combination of heritability, a concordance between personality dimensions measured by different questionnaires, and evidence that other species have similar, if not identical, personality dimensions has been instrumental in promoting a biological interpretation of personality (Depue and Collins 1999). Gray, arguing for a congruence between animal models of trait anxiety and human neuroticism (Gray 1982, 1987; Gray and McNaughton 2000), put forward the view that there are two interrelated but separable brain systems that subserve both human and rodent traits. The first system, which he terms the fight/flight system, subserves flight, defensive aggression, freezing, and associated autonomic activity. The second system, termed the behavioural inhibition system, subserves the cognitive and information processing aspects of anxiety. Within Gray's theory, neuroticism or emotional stability was seen as a measure of sensitivity to reinforcing events.

Cloninger has argued strongly that personality factors reflect the action of neurobiological systems (Cloninger et al. 1993). He identifies three independent and heritable dimensions of personality: (i) novelty seeking: Frequent exploratory activity and excitement in response to novel stimuli; (ii) harm avoidance: The tendency to respond intensely to aversive stimuli and to learn to avoid punishment and novelty; (iii) reward dependence: The tendency to respond intensely to reward. Cloninger associates each with a different neurobiological system: Novelty seeking with low basal dopaminergic activity, harm avoidance with high serotonergic activity, and reward dependence with low basal noradrenergic activity (Cloninger et al. 1993).

Molecular genetic analysis was not available when these theories were first formulated. It provides one way of testing their adequacy. Could variants in genes in the relevant pathways contribute to personality variation? I believe the answer to this question is no, but there has been considerable debate and it has to be admitted that we do not know the answer for certain. Two examples illustrate the problem.

The central serotonin system plays an important role in emotional behaviour and genes that affect serotonergic function therefore represent good candidate genes for anxiety-related personality traits, such as neuroticism. The serotonin transporter is the target for effective anti-depressants, the serotonin reuptake inhibitors, a class of drug that includes Prozac. The serotonin transporter gene has attracted considerable interest since a report in 1996 that it is associated with neuroticism (Lesch et al. 1996). A 44 base pair insertion/deletion polymorphism in the promoter of the gene (a DNA sequence involved in initiating the processes that produce a functional protein) alters the rate of gene expression, so its association with neuroticism immediately suggests a mechanism by which the gene might act. It is worth pointing out that the direction of action is opposite to that expected from the pharmacology: Prozac inhibits the transporter and reduces anxiety; the allele that inhibits transcription (and therefore leads to the production of less serotonin transporter) is associated with higher neuroticism scores (or higher trait anxiety). Since first reported by Lesch and colleagues, evidence has accumulated for a genetic association between this polymorphism (often called 5-HTTLPR) and neuroticism or harm avoidance. However, results varied between studies, some showing a significant association, others not (Greenberg et al. 2000; Jorm et al. 1998; Mazzanti et al. 1998; Murakami et al. 1999).

We attempted to resolve these discrepancies in two ways. First we applied meta-analytic techniques to the data. Meta-analysis is a method of combining results from independent studies to acquire a much larger data set from which more robust conclusions can be drawn than are obtainable from each of the smaller component studies. When we did this, taking into account sources of heterogeneity, we could find no evidence of association (Munafo et al. 2003). Of course the statistical evidence does not exclude an effect altogether; rather it says that if the 5-HTTLPR *does* underlie variation in neuroticism its impact is likely to be extremely small.

We next undertook a large well-powered study of neuroticism. We chose ethnically homogeneous populations from England (Day et al. 1999; Martin et al. 2000) where we had access to tens of thousands of samples. We worked out the power that our large sample had to detect an effect, and our estimates indicated that if the 5-HTTLPR does impact on neuroticism, assessed by Eysenck's questionnaire (Eysenck and Eysenck 1975), the genotypic effect must account for less than 0.5 percent of variance. Indeed, by combining all samples we estimated that we could have detected an effect accounting for just 0.05 per cent of variance (Willis-Owen et al. 2005).

Unfortunately these results did not bring the debate to a close. When we carried out the meta-analysis we did not include the type of questionnaire as a source of heterogeneity, since we accepted the general agreement in the field that different questionnaires measure the same personality construct. Two other groups independently carried out meta-analyses of the 5-HTTLPR data and investigated the impact of questionnaire type: Both Schinka and colleagues (Schinka et al. 2004) and Sen and colleagues (Sen et al. 2000) reported that 5-HTTLPR was significantly associated with neuroticism as measured using personality questionnaires derived from Costa and McCrae's five-factor model of personality (Costa and McCrae 1992), but was not associated with harm avoidance as measured using the class of questionnaires derived from Cloninger's tridimensional theory of personality (Cloninger 1986). Is there a genetic effect specific to the questionnaire? It's not impossible, but if so, it undermines the assumptions about what different questionnaires measure and takes us back to the beginning of the discussion in this chapter.

We found similar problems when we looked at approach-related traits which, broadly defined, encompass novelty seeking, sensation seeking, extraversion, and impulsivity traits. Extraversion, as measured using questionnaires derived from Costa and McCrae's (Costa and McCrae 1992), and Eysenck's (Eysenck and Eysenck 1975) models of personality, reflects gregariousness, sensation seeking, and high levels of activity. Novelty seeking, as measured using questionnaires derived from Cloninger's (Cloninger 1986) theory of personality, reflects sensitivity to novelty and signals of reward. While extraversion and novelty seeking are not identical constructs, they are correlated (Nigg and Goldsmith 1998).

Dopaminergic genes are candidates for novelty seeking or extraversion. The dopaminergic system is involved in appetitive and motivational behaviours (Comings and Blum, 2000), and pharmacological challenge studies indicate a relationship between dopaminergic hyperactivity and reward seeking, as well as motivational factors associated with both extraversion and novelty seeking (Netter 2006). A number of dopaminergic genes have been investigated by genetic association, among which a receptor (the dopamine D4 receptor (*DRD4*)) has attracted considerable attention. The gene is highly polymorphic, although research has focused largely on a polymorphism in exon III, and in particular the presence or absence of a 7-repeat ("long") allele. The gene also includes a single nucleotide polymorphism in the promoter region which is associated with variation in expression of the D4 receptor (Okuyama et al. 1999; Ronai et al. 2001).

Our meta-analysis did not support an association of the *DRD4* VNTR polymorphism with approach-related traits, but did indicate evidence of association with the C-521T polymorphism (Munafo et al. 2007b). As before, we were not able to confirm these findings using our large sample. However, in a revised meta-analysis of the C-521T polymorphism including our new data, there was evidence of association for measures of novelty seeking and impulsivity, but not extraversion, again raising the unwanted spectre of association with a particular questionnaire, rather than with a personality construct (Munafo et al. 2007b).

The debates about just two genes do not exclude the possibility that there is a much more robust association somewhere else in the genome, for example between another serotoninergic gene and neuroticism. Candidate gene studies give no idea about the genetic architecture of personality, about how many genes are involved and how big an effect each one has. Recently this question has become tractable with the advent of micro-array methods of genotyping, in which hundreds of thousands of genetic variants can be assayed at one time. These methods, while still expensive, have already been used to show that the genetic architecture of complex diseases (like hypertension, diabetes, and obesity) consists of the conjoint action of hundreds of variants, presumably acting in a complex manner to produce disease (Wellcome-Trust-Case-Control-Consortium 2007).

We applied a whole genome association method to investigate the genetic basis of neuroticism, again using our large sample (Shifman et al. 2007). In this case we used DNA from 1,200 individuals with high and 1,200 individuals with low Neuroticism scores. The results of our work confirm that the genetic effects contributing to heritability of neuroticism are small. We looked at more than 600,000 genetic variants which was performed and identified just one, rs702543, which we were able to replicate in a separate sample. This is hardly robust evidence of genetic association. But the negative evidence is important. Since we had failed to find any genetic variants accounting for more than 1 per cent of the variance, it is likely that the 40 per cent heritability of neuroticism arises from many loci explaining much less than 1 per cent.

Two other issues need to be addressed. One is whether the questionnaire data are the right point from which to embark on molecular studies. So far all we have seen are the problems that questionnaires impose on us. Perhaps, as some have argued, they should be used simply as a pointer to more biologically grounded measures that will be more genetically tractable. The argument appears to ignore the original problem (which was the lack of any good biological correlates other than genetics) by assuming that other new technologies, foremost among them imaging, would yield a valid correlate. A good example is the activation of particular brain regions in response to novel or frightening stimuli. For instance, functional magnetic resonance imaging of the brain can be used to visualize specific activation of the amygdala when subjects are shown emotional stimuli: Viewing of negative, compared to neutral, pictures or words, (Canli et al. 2005; Heinz et al. 2004) and matching of fearful and angry faces (compared to geometric shapes) in healthy (Hariri et al. 2002; Pezawas et al. 2005) and in phobia-prone individuals (Bertolino et al. 2005).

These measures, and others like them, called endophenotypes (Gottesman and Gould 2003), are believed to improve the chances of detecting the genetic variants that contribute to personality because they lie in the gap between gene and phenotype (Freimer and Sabatti 2003). Endophenotypes provide a genetically tractable target because they "represent more defined and quantifiable measures that are envisioned to involve fewer genes, fewer interacting levels and ultimately activation of a single set of neuronal circuits. The fewer the pathways that give rise to an endophenotype, the better the chances of efficiently discovering its genetic and neurobiological underpinnings" (Gottesman and Gould 2003).

One example of how endophenotypes might be used to find genetic effects is yet another attempt to implicate the serotonin transporter gene in neuroticism. Hariri and colleagues reported that the 5-HTTLPR was associated with the response of the amygdala to fearful stimuli (Hariri et al. 2002). The means of the two groups of fourteen individuals who differed at this locus were 0.28 (standard deviation 0.22) and 0.03 (standard deviation 0.19). This represents an enormous effect size (equivalent to approximately 40 per cent of phenotypic variance). A subsequent study of ninety-two individuals (including nineteen from the first study) carried out by the same group again showed a significant effect, but with a reduction in the effect size (an effect size of just over 10 per cent of the phenotypic variance)(Hariri et al. 2005).

It remains unclear, however, whether endophenotypes will deliver the goods. Large effects are frequently found in initial publications, effect sizes that are found to be over-estimates as subsequent replications are published. Our own meta-analyses of a number of different published endophenotypes suggested that the genetic dissection of endophenotypes will prove to be just as complicated as genetic dissection of the parent phenotypes (in this case personality).

The second issue is the importance of gene by environment interaction in personality studies. We all know that different people, faced with the same stressful situation, react differently and it is scarcely controversial to assert that this variation has, in part, a genetic origin. But, while few doubt that gene by environment interaction exists, its importance has been difficult to assess. The older literature was not optimistic: Jinks and Fulker (Jinks and Fulker 1970) using the correlation between identical twin intrapair differences and pair sums found little evidence for genotype environment interaction for cognitive and personality traits.

More recently, the tide has turned. In an influential article from 1994, Bronfenbrenner and Ceci argue strongly that interaction needs to be taken into account in behavioural genetic studies: "The mechanisms by which genotypes actualize into phenotypes vary as a function of environmental context. When proximal processes are weak, that is when the environment is not conducive to expression of that genotype, heritability is low, as genetic potential is not realized" (Bronfenbrenner and Ceci 1994). A study of cognitive ability in seven-year old children from the National Perinatal Collaborative Project found that for disadvantaged children, environmental influences accounted for nearly 60 per cent of the variance in IQ, while genetic factors accounted for negligible variance. However in advantaged children, the pattern was almost reversed, good evidence therefore of an interaction (Turkheimer et al. 2003), a finding that has been replicated in an independent study (Harden et al. 2007).

In a cross-fostering analysis (Cloninger et al. 1982), crime rates in male Swedish adoptees were found to be greatest when both heritable and environmental influences were present, with the interaction accounting for twice as much crime as is produced by genetic and environmental influences alone. Cadoret and colleagues (Cadoret et al. 1995) studied adoptees whose either parents had antisocial personality and found that an adverse adoptive home environment interacted with adult antisocial personality in predicting increased aggression in the offspring.

Given that the interactions are there and are important, could it be the case that molecular variants will not be found unless gene by environment interaction is taken into account? Perhaps modelling the joint effects of genes and environment is necessary to obtain sufficient statistical power to detect the effect. Empirical evidence in favour of this view comes, yet again, from a study of the 5-HTTLPR. Caspi and colleagues reported that carriers of the 5-HTTLPR short variant are twice as likely to become depressed after stressful events such as bereavement, romantic disasters, illnesses or job loss; and childhood maltreatment significantly increases this probability (Caspi et al. 2003).

Studies of a variant of 5-HTTLPR in nonhuman primates support this finding. In rhesus monkeys, maternal separation during the first months of life adversely affects later social interaction behaviour. As in humans, there is a repeat length variation in the promoter of the serotonin transporter gene (the variant is called *rh5-HTTLPR)*. The rh5-HTTLPR genotype interacts with deleterious early rearing experience to influence attentional and emotional behaviour, stress reactivity, and alcohol preference and dependence (Bennett et al. 2002).

The trouble with this argument is that the environmental causes of personality variation are frequently as mysterious as the genetic. Where the environmental effect *is* known, then increased power might be obtainable, but what happens if we are not so sure? This problem is well known to epidemiologists, who have been struggling for some years to detect subtle environmental effects (Taubes 1995).

David Clayton and Paul McKeigue, in a discussion of the value of gene by environment studies, argue as follows: "If we could specify in advance that the effect of the environmental factor on disease risk would be restricted to a subgroup of individuals with a particular genotype, there would, of course, be a gain in power from testing only this subgroup for the effect of the environmental factor. In practice, such an extreme situation is unlikely to be frequently encountered in the study of complex diseases, and entails a level of knowledge of underlying biology which would probably render epidemiological studies redundant. In less extreme situations, and where previous knowledge is more limited, a combined test would need to be done for the main effect of environmental exposure and its interaction with genotype. Since such tests have multiple degrees of freedom, the gain in power is much reduced; indeed, power might even be lost" (Clayton and McKeigue 2001).

As an example consider the problem of defining environmental effects on depression, a phenotype that is genetically closely related to neuroticism. Here we know that stressful life events (SLE) have an important role in the onset of depression (Kendler et al. 1999), but the temporal relationship between the two is less well characterized. The largest effect is seen in the month succeeding the SLE, but this depends on the type of event (Kendler et al. 1998), raising the possibility that a gene by environment effect will depend on the type of SLE. Some people might be genetically predisposed to wether a marriage breakup better than others, but not to deal so well with the death of a spouse. As important subgroups of each SLE are found we may be faced with an exponentially increasing list of environmental effects to investigate, with consequent disastrous consequences for our power to detect anything at all.

The literature in support of the detection of gene by environment effects at individual loci looks qualitatively very similar to the initial reports of genetic association studies (Munafo et al. 2003; Munafo et al. 2007a): There have been a small number of high profile findings, followed by a mixture of replications and non-replications (reviewed in Uher and McGuffin 2007). The pattern appears to be pervasive and indicates that the current studies of gene by environment effects are underpowered. It is worth noting that the largest studies of putative gene by environment effects to date have largely produced null results (e.g., Surtees et al. 2006), suggesting that findings in smaller studies may represent false positives. In short, we do not yet know whether gene by environment studies will fare any better than other, simpler-designed genetic association studies.

A critical question is the likely size of a gene by environment interaction effect. If we knew this, we could assess whether published findings are false positives (or negatives) and design replication studies appropriately. Unfortunately we face a problem that can be explained in terms of the "winner's curse" (Capen et al. 1971). In cases where power is low, successful studies are more likely to report a large effect. This ascertainment bias, resulting in overestimates of genetic effects, has been known for some time (Goring et al. 2001). For example, in a meta-analysis of 301 association studies, replication studies reported lower odds ratios than the initial report at 24 out of 25 loci (Lohmueller et al. 2003). There is no reason to think that gene by environment studies are any different, and it is therefore possible that the effects reported in these early studies are overestimates.

Successful, replicated genetic association studies have used sample sizes in the thousands (Zeggini et al. 2007) and tens of thousands (Cox et al. 2007). Compared to these sample sizes, gene by environment studies are relatively small. With the exception of one study of over 4,000 individuals (Surtees et al. 2006), the average size of the 18 studies of the serotonin transporter is 600 (Uher and McGuffin 2007). Even larger samples than the tens of thousands now being used for association studies of simple genetic effects will be necessary if we are to establish beyond doubt that an effect of a molecular variant is manifested through the modification of an environmental effect.

Using simulations from the epidemiological literature as a guide, we can obtain estimates of the sample sizes required (Brookes et al. 2001). Assume we carry out a study searching for the main effect of a genetic variant on a personality trait, and we then ask whether there is also an interaction effect. If the interaction is the same magnitude as the main effect, the sample size must be increased fourfold (assuming we want to maintain power at the same level) (Brookes et al. 2001). But this "increased dramatically to 100 or greater for more subtle interactions that were smaller than 20 per cent of the overall effect" (Brookes et al. 2001).

What other possibilities are there for how genetic effects operate on personality? Here one example from animal work may be relevant. Meaney and colleagues have reported that heritable differences in stress reactivity in rats depend on variation in parenting, not variation in DNA (Francis et al. 1999). Adult offspring of mothers that show higher levels of licking, grooming, and arched-back nursing (high-LG-ABN) are less fearful and show more modest hypothalamic-pituitary axis responses to stress than offspring of "low-LG-ABN" mothers (Meaney 2001). How are these maternal effects, or other forms of environmental programming, sustained over the lifespan of the animal?

Variations in maternal care were found to alter the methylation status of a promoter of the glucocorticoid receptor gene. Central infusion of a histone de-acetylase inhibitor enhanced histone acetylation of the glucocorticoid receptor promoter in the offspring of the low-LG-ABN mothers. Analysis of the promoter showed that CpG dinucleotides were hypomethylated. In consequence, the maternal effect on hippocampal glucocorticoid receptor expression and the hypothalamic-pituitary axis response to stress were both eliminated (Weaver et al. 2004). This finding suggests that there is a causal relation between epigenetic modifications, glucocorticoid receptor expression, and the maternal effect on stress responses (Meaney and Szyf 2005). Whether this same process occurs in humans is unknown, but it is certainly worth investigating.

My coverage of the large area of personality genetics has been partial. I admit I have not quantitatively assessed all papers in this field. My aim has rather been to identify some key features of the intrusion of genetics into personality. I wanted to question certain assumptions about how genetics acts on personality, and therefore on how personality itself is biologically grounded. A similar review undertaken twenty years ago would scarcely have mentioned genetics, perhaps largely to dismiss its importance. Now a new consensus has emerged with genetics in a central position, not only as a main effect on construing personality, but also as a mediator of environmental effects. In part these views have arisen because of the powerful new genetic technologies placed in the hands of psychologists. In part they represent our desire to find the simplest solution to a problem. As I have tried to point out, while the existence of genetic effects on personality is indubitable, their number and the complexity of their action is still much greater than we would like to believe. I think it is quite possible that the current reports of gene by environment interaction will turn out to be false positives. While this would of course be disappointing, we must be alive to this possibility in order to prevent the excessive enthusiasm and false hope which occurred around the time of the first reports of genetic associations with behavioural and psychiatric phenotypes, and which subsequently proved to be unfounded and misplaced.

BIBLIOGRAPHY

Angst, J., Clayton, P. 1986. Premorbid personality of depressive, bipolar and schizophrenic patients with special reference to suicidal issues. *Comprehensive Psychiatry* 27:511-32.

Bennett, A.J., Lesch, K.P., Heils, A., Long, J.C., Lorenz, J.G., Shoaf, S.E., Champoux, M., Suomi, S.J., Linnoila, M.V., Higley, J.D. 2002. Early experience and serotonin transporter gene variation interact to influence primate CNS function. *Mol Psychiatry* 7:118-22.

Bertolino, A., Arciero, G., Rubino, V., Latorre, V., De Candia, M., Mazzola, V., Blasi, G., Caforio, G., Hariri, A., Kolachana, B., et al. 2005. Variation of human amygdala response during threatening stimuli as a function of 5-HTTLPR genotype and personality style. *Biol Psychiatry* 57:517-25.

Bronfenbrenner, U., Ceci, S.J. 1994. Nature-nurture reconceptualized in developmental perspective: A bioecological model. *Psychol Rev* *101*:568-86.

Brookes, S.T., Whitley, E., Peters, T.J., Mulheran, P.A., Egger, M., Davey Smith, G. 2001. Subgroup analyses in randomised controlled trials:

Quantifying the risks of false-positives and false-negatives. *Health Technol Assess* 5:1-56.

Cadoret, R.J., Yates, W.R., Troughton, E., Woodworth, G., Stewart, M.A. 1995. Genetic-environmental interaction in the genesis of aggressivity and conduct disorders. *Arch Gen Psychiatry* 52:916-24.

Canli, T., Omura, K., Haas, B.W., Fallgatter, A., Constable, R.T., Lesch, K.P. 2005. Beyond affect: A role for genetic variation of the serotonin transporter in neural activation during a cognitive attention task. *Proc Natl Acad Sci USA* 102:12224-9.

Capen, E.C., Clapp, R.V., Campbell, W.M. 1971. Competitive bidding in high-risk situations. *J Petrol Technol* 23:641-53.

Caspi, A., Sugden, K., Moffitt, T.E., Taylor, A., Craig, I.W., Harrington, H., McClay, J., Mill, J., Martin, J., Braithwaite, A., et al. 2003. Influence of life stress on depression: Moderation by a polymorphism in the 5-HTT gene. *Science* 301, 386-9.

Clayton, D., McKeigue, P.M. (2001). Epidemiological methods for studying genes and environmental factors in complex diseases. *Lancet* 358:1356-60.

Cloninger, C.R. 1986. A unified biosocial theory of personality and its role in the development of anxiety states. Psychiatr Dev 4:167-226.

Cloninger, C.R., Sigvardsson, S., Bohman, M., von Knorring, A.L. (1982). Predisposition to petty criminality in Swedish adoptees. II. Cross-fostering analysis of gene-environment interaction. *Arch Gen Psychiatry* 39:1242-7.

Cloninger, C.R., Svrakic, D.M., Przybeck, T.R. (1993). A psychobiological model of temperament and character. *Archives of General Psychiatry* 50:975-89.

Comings, D.E., Blum, K. (2000). Reward deficiency syndrome: Genetic aspects of behavioral disorders. *Prog Brain Res* 126:325-41.

Costa, P.T., McCrae, R.R. (1992). *Revised NEO Personality Inventory (NEO-PI-R) and NEO Five-Factor Inventory (NEO-FFI) professional manual* (Odessa, FL, Psychological Assessment Resources, Inc.).

Cox, A., Dunning, A., Garcia-Closas, M., Balasubramanian, S., Reed, M.W.R., Pooley, K.A., Scollen, S.S., Baynes, C., Ponder, B.A.J., Chanock, S., et al. 2007. A common coding variant in CASP8 is associated with breast cancer risk. *Nature Genet* 39:352-7.

Cox, B.J., McWilliams, L.A., Enns, M.W., Clara, I.P. 2004. Broad and specific personality dimensions associated with major depression in a nationally representative sample. *Compr Psychiatry* 45:246-53.

Day, N., Oakes, S., Luben, R., Khaw, K.T., Bingham, S., Welch, A., Wareham, N. 1999. EPIC-Norfolk: Study design and characteristics of the cohort. European Prospective Investigation of Cancer. *Br J Cancer 80 Suppl 1*:95-103.

Deary, I.J., Matthews, G. 1993. Personality traits are alive and well. *The Psychologist*, 299-311.

Depue, R.A., Collins, P.F. 1999. Neurobiology of the structure of personality: Dopamine, facilitation of incentive motivation, and extraversion. *Behav Brain Sci* 22:491-517; discussion 518-69.

Digman, J.M. 1990. Personality structure: Emergence of the 5-factor model. *Annual Review of Psychology* 41:417-40.

– 1997. Higher-order factors of the Big Five. *J Pers Soc Psychol* 73:1246-56.

Eaves, L.J., Eysenck, H.J., Martin, N.G. 1989. *Genes, Culture and Personality: An Empirical Approach*. London: Academic Press, Harcourt Brace Jovanovich.

Eysenck, H.J. 1957. *Sense and Nonsense in Psychology*. Harmondsworth: Penguin Books.

Eysenck, H.J., Eysenck, S.B.G. 1975. *Manual of the Eysenck Personality Questionnaire*. San Diego: CA, Educational and Industrial Testing Service.

Floderus-Myrhed, B., Pedersen, N., Rasmuson, I. 1980. Assessment of heritability for personality, based on a short form of the Eysenck Personality Inventory. *Behav Gen* 10:153-62.

Francis, D., Diorio, J., Liu, D., Meaney, M.J. 1999. Nongenomic transmission across generations of maternal behavior and stress responses in the rat. *Science* 286:1155-8.

Freimer, N., Sabatti, C. 2003. The human phenome project. *Nat Genet* 34:15-21.

Goring, H.H., Terwilliger, J.D., Blangero, J. 2001. Large upward bias in estimation of locus-specific effects from genomewide scans. *Am J Hum Genet* 69:1357-69.

Gosling, S.D. 2001. From mice to men: What can we learn about personality from animal research? *Psychol Bull* 127:45-86.

Gottesman, I.I., Gould, T.D. 2003. The endophenotype concept in psychiatry: Etymology and strategic intentions. *Am J Psychiatry* 160:636-45.

Gray, J.A. 1982. *The Neuropsychology of Anxiety: An Enquiry into the Function of the Septo-hippocampal System*. Oxford, Oxford University Press.

– 1987. *The Psychology of Fear and Stress*, 2nd edn. Cambridge, Cambridge University Press.

Gray, J.A., McNaughton, N. 2000. *The Neuropsychology of Anxiety.* Oxford: OUP.

Greenberg, B.D., Li, Q., Lucas, F.R., Hu, S., Sirota, L.A., Benjamin, J., Lesch, K.P., Hamer, D., Murphy, D.L. 2000. Association between the serotonin transporter promoter polymorphism and personality traits in a primarily female population sample. *Am J Med Genet 96*:202-16.

Harden, K.P., Turkheimer, E., Loehlin, J.C. 2007. Genotype by environment interaction in adolescents' cognitive aptitude. *Behav Genet 37*:273-83.

Hariri, A.R., Drabant, E.M., Munoz, K.E., Kolachana, B.S., Mattay, V.S., Egan, M.F., Weinberger, D.R. 2005. A susceptibility gene for affective disorders and the response of the human amygdala. *Arch Gen Psychiatry 62*:146-52.

Hariri, A.R., Mattay, V.S., Tessitore, A., Kolachana, B., Fera, F., Goldman, D., Egan, M.F., Weinberger, D.R. 2002. Serotonin transporter genetic variation and the response of the human amygdala. *Science 297*:400-3.

Heinz, A., Braus, D.F., Smolka, M.N., Wrase, J., Puls, I., Herman, D., Klein, S., Grusser, S.M., Flor, H., Schumann, G., et al. 2004. Amygdala-prefrontal coupling depnds on a genetic variation of the serotin transporter. *Nat Neurosci*, 1-2.

Jinks, J.L., Fulker, D.W. 1970. Comparison of the biometrical genetical, MAVA, and classical approaches to the analysis of human behavior. *Psychol Bull 73*:311-49.

Jorm, A.F., Henderson, A.S., Jacomb, P.A., Christensen, H., Korten, A.E., Rodgers, B., Tan, X., Easteal, S. 1998. An association study of a functional polymorphism of the serotonin transporter gene with personality and psychiatric symptoms. *Molecular Psychiatry 3*:449-51.

Jylha, P., Isometsa, E. 2006. The relationship of neuroticism and extraversion to symptoms of anxiety and depression in the general population. *Depress Anxiety 23*:281-9.

Kendler, K.S., Karkowski, L.M., Prescott, C.A. 1998. Stressful life events and major depression: Risk period, long-term contextual threat, and diagnostic specificity. *J Nerv Ment Dis 186*:661-9.

– 1999. Causal relationship between stressful life events and the onset of major depression. *Am J Psychiatry 156*:837-41.

Kendler, K.S., Neale, M.C., Kessler, R.C., Heath, A.C., Eaves, L.J. 1993. A longitudinal twin study of personality and major depression in women. *Archives of General Psychiatry 50*:853-62.

Lake, R.I., Eaves, L.J., Maes, H.H., Heath, A.C., Martin, N.G. 2000. Further evidence against the environmental transmission of individual differences in neuroticism from a collaborative study of 45,850 twins and relatives on two continents. *Behav Genet* 30:223-33.

Lesch, K.P., Bengel, D., Heils, A., Sabol, S.Z., Greenberg, B.D., Petri, S., Benjamin, J., Muller, C.R., Hamer, D.H., Murphy, D.L. 1996. Association of anxiety-related traits with a polymorphism in the serotonin transporter gene regulatory region. *Science* 274:1527-31.

Loehlin, J.C. 1992. *Genes and Environment in Personality Development.* Newbury Park, CA: Sage Publications.

Lohmueller, K.E., Pearce, C.L., Pike, M., Lander, E.S., Hirschhorn, J.N. 2003. Meta-analysis of genetic association studies supports a contribution of common variants to susceptibility to common disease. *Nat Genet* 33:177-82.

Martin, N., Goodwin, G., Fairburn, C., Wilson, R., Allison, D., Cardon, L.R., Flint, J. 2000. A population based study of personality in 34,000 sib-pairs. *Twin Research* 3:310-15.

Mather, J.A., Anderson, R.C. 1993. Personalities of Octopuses (Octopus rubescens). *Journal of Comparative Psychology* 107:336-40.

Mazzanti, C.M., Lappalainen, J., Long, J.C., Bengel, D., Naukkarinen, H., Eggert, M., Virkkunen, M., Linnoila, M., Goldman, D. 1998. Role of the serotonin transporter promoter polymorphism in anxiety- related traits. *Arch Gen Psychiatry* 55, 936-40.

Meaney, M.J. 2001. Maternal care, gene expression, and the transmission of individual differences in stress reactivity across generations. *Annu Rev Neurosci* 24:1161-92.

Meaney, M.J., Szyf, M. 2005. Maternal care as a model for experience-dependent chromatin plasticity? *Trends Neurosci* 28:456-63.

Munafo, M.R., Clark, T.G., Moore, L.R., Payne, E., Walton, R., Flint, J. 2003. Genetic polymorphisms and personality in healthy adults: A systematic review and meta-analysis. *Mol Psychiatry* 8:471-84.

Munafo, M.R., Matheson, I.J., Flint, J. 2007a. Association of the DRD2 gene Taq1A polymorphism and alcoholism: A meta-analysis of case-control studies and evidence of publication bias. *Mol Psychiatry* 12:454-61.

Munafo, M.R., Yalcin, B., Willis-Owen, S.A., Flint, J. 2007b. Association of the dopamine D4 receptor (DRD4) gene and approach-related personality traits: Meta-analysis and new data. *Biol Psychiatry*.

Murakami, F., Shimomura, T., Kotani, K., Ikawa, S., Nanba, E., Adachi, K. 1999. Anxiety traits associated with a polymorphism in the serotonin transporter gene regulatory region in the Japanese. *J Hum Genet* 44:15-17.

Netter, P. (2006). Dopamine challenge tests as an indicator of psychological traits. *Hum Psychopharmacol* 21:91-9.

Nigg, J.T., Goldsmith, H.H. 1998. Developmental psychopathology, personality, and temperament: Reflections on recent behavioral genetics research. *Human Biology* 70:387-412.

Okuyama, Y., Ishiguro, H., Toru, M., and Arinami, T. 1999. A genetic polymorphism in the promoter region of DRD4 associated with expression and schizophrenia. *Biochem Biophys Res Commun* 258:292-5.

Pezawas, L., Meyer-Lindenberg, A., Drabant, E.M., Verchinski, B.A., Munoz, K.E., Kolachana, B.S., Egan, M.F., Mattay, V.S., Hariri, A.R., Weinberger, D.R. 2005. 5-HTTLPR polymorphism impacts human cingulate-amygdala interactions: A genetic susceptibility mechanism for depression. *Nat Neurosci* 8:828-34.

Ronai, Z., Szekely, A., Nemoda, Z., Lakatos, K., Gervai, J., Staub, M., Sasvari-Szekely, M. 2001. Association between novelty seeking and the -521 C/T polymorphism in the promoter region of the DRD4 gene. *Mol Psychiatry* 6:35-8.

Schinka, J.A., Busch, R.M., Robichaux-Keene, N. 2004. A meta-analysis of the association between the serotonin transporter gene polymorphism (5-HTTLPR) and trait anxiety. *Mol Psychiatry* 9:197-202.

Sen, S., Burmeister, M., Ghosh, D. 2000. Meta-analysis of the association between a serotonin transporter promoter polymorphism (5-HTTLPR) and anxiety-related personality traits. *American Journal of Medical Genetics* Part B: Neuropsychiatric Genetics.

Shifman, S., Bhomra, A., Smiley, S., Wray, N.R., James, M.R., Martin, N.G., Hettema, J.M., An, S.S., Neale, M.C., van den Oord, E.J., et al. 2007. A whole genome association study of neuroticism using DNA pooling. *Mol Psychiatry*.

Stamps, J.A. 2007. Growth-mortality tradeoffs and "personality traits" in animals. *Ecol Lett* 10:355-63.

Surtees, P.G., Wainwright, N.W., Willis-Owen, S.A., Luben, R., Day, N.E., Flint, J. 2006. Social adversity, the serotonin transporter (5-HTTLPR) polymorphism and major depressive disorder. *Biol Psychiatry* 59:224-9.

Taubes, G. 1995. Epidemiology faces its limits. *Science* 269:164-9.

Tooby, J., Cosmides, L. 1990. On the universality of human nature and the uniqueness of the individual: The role of genetics and adaptation. *J Pers* 58:17-67.

Turkheimer, E., Haley, A., Waldron, M., D'Onofrio, B., Gottesman, II 2003. Socio-economic status modifies heritability of IQ in young children. *Psychol Sci* 14:623-8.

Uher, R., McGuffin, P. 2007. The moderation by the serotonin transporter gene of environmental adversity in the aetiology of mental illness: Review and methodological analysis. *Mol Psychiatry*.

Weaver, I.C., Cervoni, N., Champagne, F.A., D'Alessio, A.C., Sharma, S., Seckl, J.R., Dymov, S., Szyf, M., Meaney, M.J. 2004. Epigenetic programming by maternal behavior. *Nat Neurosci* 7:847-54.

Wellcome-Trust-Case-Control-Consortium 2007. Genome-wide association study of 14,000 cases of seven common diseases and 3,000 shared controls. *Nature* 447:661-78.

Willis-Owen, S.A., Turri, M.G., Munafo, M.R., Surtees, P.G., Wainwright, N.W., Brixey, R.D., Flint, J. 2005. The serotonin transporter length polymorphism, neuroticism, and depression: A comprehensive assessment of association. *Biol Psychiatry* 58:451-6.

Wolf, M., van Doorn, G.S., Leimar, O., Weissing, F.J. 2007. Life-history trade-offs favour the evolution of animal personalities. *Nature* 447:581-4.

Yerkes, R.M. 1939. The life history and personality of the chimpanzee. *The American Naturalist* 73:97-112.

Zeggini, E., Weedon, M.N., Lindgren, C.M., Frayling, T.M., Elliott, K.S., Lango, H., Timpson, N.J., Perry, J.R., Rayner, N.W., Freathy, R.M., et al. 2007. Replication of genome-wide association signals in UK samples reveals risk loci for type 2 diabetes. *Science* 316:1336-41.

Zuckerman, M. (1992). What is a basic factor and which factors are basic? Turtles all the way down. *Personality and Individual Differences* 13:675-81.

Gene x Stress Interactions: An Integrative Perspective

DAVID GOLDMAN

This chapter describes discoveries of functional loci that influence behaviour through the stress domain, with validation through the coherent, multi-level effects of these alleles not only on complex behaviour but also on intermediate phenotypes reflective of the intervening steps between gene and behaviour. This discussion addresses the process and results of discovery for several functional loci which were validated during the first decade of this century, and including functional variants at the monoamine oxidase A gene (MAOA), neuropeptide Y (NPY), catechol-O-methyl-transferase (COMT), and the serotonin transporter (SLC6A4). Other examples are also listed. This functional genomics/intermediate phenotype approach is contrasted and to some extent meshed with linkage and association studies, and their meta-analyses, which are primarily focused on statistical replication, rather than validation.

The utility of statistical analyses of gene/phenotype relationships is not in question, and it is not the purpose of this chapter to dismiss the contributions of statistical genetic analysis in unravelling the causation of variation in behaviour. A gene x environment (GxE) interaction is inherently a marginal interaction effect detected by statistical analysis, and ultimately it is vital to quantitate the amount of variance in complex phenotypes that is attributable to gene variants and GxE effects. As will be discussed, those gene effects on complex phenotypes are likely to be smaller and less reliably tied to the functional gene variants, and still less so to genetic markers that serve as indicators of functional genetic variants.

However, the two types of analysis, statistical linkage and functional, go hand in hand. As applied genome-wide with very large panels of genetic markers, association analyses of complex psychiatric diseases and behavioural traits are generating statistical signals identifying many new targets amenable to functional genetic analysis. The power of genome–wide association studies to identify new targets for psychiatric disease would be enhanced by inclusion of information on gene x stress interactions. Finally new tools are being developed for genome-wide functional genomic analysis, thus paving the way for more rapid identification and validation of functional loci and beginning to free the field of psychiatric genetics from the "tyranny of the p-value."

GENETIC STUDIES IN THE ETIOLOGIC REDEFINITION OF PSYCHIATRIC DISEASE

Psychiatric diseases and broadly defined variations in cognition and personality are moderately to highly heritable. This one fact strongly supports the inference that a key step in understanding, and potentially intervening in these phenotypes, is the identification of the functional genetic variants that influence the inter-individual variation. However, this conclusion is not universally accepted.

There has been considerable discussion concerning the relative priority of genetic research for psychiatric diseases and it has even been suggested that diseases that theoretically are already preventable by an environmental intervention (e.g., abstinence) do not require intensive genetic study despite the high mortality and disability attributable to addictions (Merikangas and Risch 2003) including alcoholism and nicotine addiction. However, the majority of common complex diseases have volitional components, for example the risk of heart disease and many cancers are profoundly influenced by lifestyle choices, and it is likely that public education and preventative efforts will always remain only partially effective in inducing people to make the best lifestyle choices in terms of diet and exercise. Many aspects of the human environment are controllable in theory, but this is not always the case in practice. With specific regard to addictions, which are moderately to highly heritable (Goldman et al. 2005), access to alcohol was (remarkably) already the subject of two amendments to the United States Constitution, the Eighteenth Amendment and the Twenty-First Amendment, which repealed it. It is unlikely that the consumption of alcohol or nicotine will be banned in the United States and most Western societies. Furthermore, there is no hopeful trend for an overall decrease in exposures to other addictive agents, including gambling.

As will be discussed, the risk of most psychiatric diseases is dramatically elevated by exposure to early life stress, including childhood sexual abuse and other trauma. However, the force of law has not succeeded in eliminating such trauma – a third or more of women have suffered sexual abuse, and family violence is common. In a twenty-first century world, increased access to an ever-widening range of exposures including new drugs, new ways of traumatizing whole populations, and new addictions has accompanied better public education and prevention efforts. All available tools are therefore needed to elucidate pathways of vulnerability and resilience and to improve treatment when prevention fails, as it often will.

Finally, and as will be the major focus of this chapter, the genetic analysis of behaviour will not in the end be compartmentalized by disease or by other relatively crude external phenotypes, although many of the initial linkage studies have proceeded on that basis. Instead, genetic variations will be more directly tied to brain mechanisms that underlie behaviour. One important result of this will be the refinement and parsing of psychiatric diagnosis using genetic and neurobehavioural indicators, much as more refined indicators have been used to identify discrete diagnoses within other common medical disorders that are now recognized as groups of diseases: the cancers, the anemias, the immunodeficiencies, the pneumonias, the ear infections, etc. Ultimately, the increased precision leads to an improvement in the targeting of intervention, and to the development of interventions.

WHOLE GENOME ASSOCIATION (WGA) TO IDENTIFY NEW TARGETS

The availability of large panels of single nucleotide polymorphisms (SNPs) genotyped simultaneously via arrays has enabled the scanning of the genome for loci that influence complex traits, in hypothesis-free fashion. The WGA method depends on the fact that moderately common functional alleles (variants) are found on chromosomes in which the local pattern of variation (haplotype) is conserved, enabling even small effects of these functional alleles to be captured by studying large populations. This methodology has now been applied to more than thirty common, complex traits and diseases, yielding many new targets for functional analysis. A particular strength of the method, as compared to linkage in families, is that the implicated genomic region is much smaller. Also, smaller allele effects are detectable. However, WGA is not a panacea.

For Crohn's Disease, one of the complex diseases which has been most carefully and successfully studied using WGA, less than 10 per cent of the genetically attributable variance was accounted for via the identification of some thirty putative loci (Barrett et al. 2008). The majority of statistical signals detected by WGA have yet to be validated and translated to the level of utility, via the identification of functional loci, and this may be in part because many of the functional loci causing complex diseases apparently are not in the coding regions of genes. If there are multiple functional loci within a gene the alleles may be found on different haplotypes, leading to a failure to detect association when linkage would be found in families. At this point the method has primarily been applied to detect the effects of relatively common alleles (i.e., > 5%), and detection of effects of rarer alleles could require much larger populations, and even then they may fail. With regard to the problem of uncommon alleles, large scale re-sequencing of DNA offers an important complementary strategy.

STATISTICAL REPLICATION VERSUS FUNCTIONAL VALIDATION AND PREDICTIVE VALIDITY IN COMPLEX GENETICS

In genetic analysis a tension exists between statistical identification and replication vs functional validation and predictive validity. Many of the methodologies of genetics require robust statistics. The need is especially acute for methods such as WGA where a million or more markers may be tested, with a requirement for stringent statistical thresholds (e.g., p values $<10^{-7}$ for genome wide significance) and robust analytical methods (e.g., correction for ethnic stratification between cases and controls, which otherwise can produce thousands of false positives). There is also a need for sound statistical methods in the diverse analyses that comprise functional genomics: whether one is analyzing the effect of an allele on mRNA level, peptide expression, brain morphometry, or some intermediate response of the brain (for example via neuroimaging or electrophysiology).

However, a fundamental difference is that in functional genomics there is a greater emphasis on directional coherence of allele effects using a functionally informed understanding of the relationship between things.

Also, there are situations where validation is non-statistical in nature. There may be predictive validity, for example in the phenotype of a genetic model created, or found, in a different species. A gene difference that may have been observed in only one individual may be compellingly linked to function. Obviously, this sort of approach cannot be carried too far. How compelling, or important, is a finding if it cannot be translated to larger populations of individuals or demonstrated in other ways, for example in an animal model? On the other hand, the tendency to discount findings not reaching some level of statistical significance, and to overly rely on scientific methodologies that are inherently capable of generating those statistics or well-suited to meta-analytical combination, may be called the "tyranny of the p value." Ultimately, the role of statistical methodologies is to generate targets for functional validation and to ultimately enable a quantitative understanding of the roles of various factors in the complex phenotype.

FROM COMPLEX PHENOTYPE TO FUNCTIONAL LOCUS, AND BACK

Functional alleles have been associated with complex behavioural phenotypes with at least partial retracing of the molecular action of the allele back to behaviour.

As shown in the figure, some of the alleles are rare and uncommon (e.g., MAOA, HTT, HPRT, ERBA for which the frequencies of the alleles, sometimes multiple, are less than 1/1,000) and some of the alleles are common. The seven genes at the bottom of the figure have functional loci with frequencies of greater than 20 per cent, with the ALDH2 and ADH1B alleles having such abundance in particular populations. Several of the genes – MAOA, NPY and HTT – have multiple functional loci, of different types. Resequencing of each gene in thousands of individuals will identify large numbers of additional rare functional variants, but the number of common functional variants will of course be more restricted. For some of these genes, all the common functional variants may be known, however this is

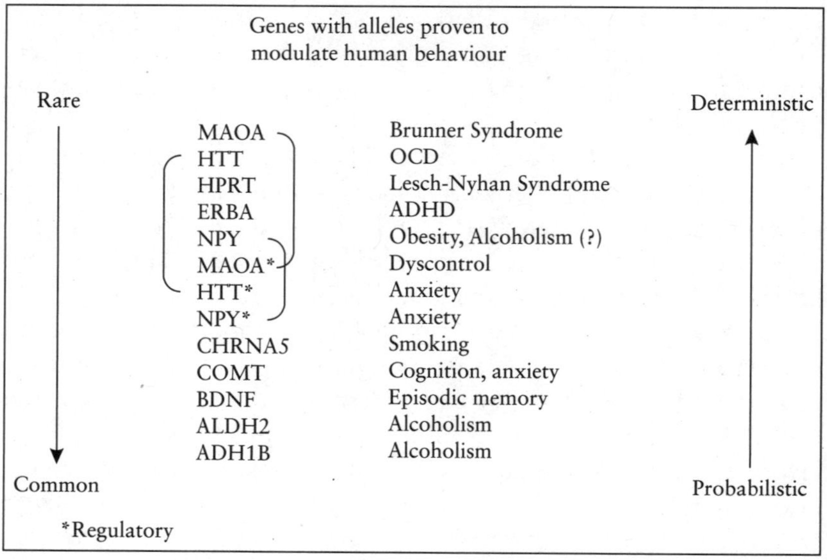

Figure 1. Alleles predisposing to differences in complex behaviour may be rare or common, found in coding or non-coding sequences, and deterministic or probabilistic in action. MAOA: Monoamine Oxidase A. Rare stop codon variant (Brunner et al.) and common functional VNTR (Sabol et al. 1998); HTT: Serotonin transporter. Rare missense variant and common HTTLPR functional promoter alleles (Lesch et al. 1996; Hu et al.2006); HPRT: Hypoxanthine guanine phosphoribosyltransferase. Multiple rare missense variants (Wilson et al. 1983); ERBA: Thyroid hormone receptor. Multiple rare missense variants (Hauser et al. 1993); NPY: Neuropeptide Y: Moderately common missense variant (Karvonen et al. 1998) and common promoter variant (Zhou et al. 2008); CHRNA5: Nicotinic acetylcholine receptor 5. Common missense variant (Bierut et al, 2008); COMT: Catechol-O-methyltransferase. Common missense variant (Lachman et al. 1996) and common alleles epistatically altering mRNA translatability (Nackley et al. 2006); BDNF: Brain-derived neurotrophic factor. Common missense variant (Egan et al. 2003); ALDH2: Aldehyde dehydrogenase 2. Common missense variant, in some populations (Yoshida et al. 1984); ADH1B: Alcohol dehydrogenase 1B. Common missense variant (Thomasson et al. 1995). Note: This is only an illustrative listing of functional loci altering behaviour, and references provided are representative or intended to represent primary discovery of function/phenotype relationship.

uncertain due to our imperfect understanding of the effects of non-coding variants and synonymous substitutions which can alter mRNA processing, stability, or translatability (Nackley et al. 2006). An implication of the varied frequencies and nature of effect of alleles in behaviour is that different strategies are required for discovery and validation.

ALLELES THAT MODULATE RESILIENCY AND VULNERABILITY TO PSYCHIATRIC DISEASE

To understand the role of genetic vulnerability factors in behaviour it is important to identify alleles that modulate response to stress, including the ways that stressful and painful events are emotionally evaluated. Logistic regression analyses have revealed that the odds of various psychiatric diseases are increased two to five times by severe early trauma or neglect. Such trauma is frequent, helping to accounts for high prevalences of post-traumatic stress disorder, anxiety disorders, depression, antisocial personality disorder, alcoholism, and other addictions in the general population and still higher prevalences in particular populations with high exposure to trauma (see for example, Robin et al. 1997; Koss et al. 2003). Specific exposures that can cause profound activation of the brain stress axis include childhood sexual abuse (Robin et al. 1997; Koss et al. 2003), chronic pain, and addictions. The effect of addictions to disrupt the normal homeostatic set point of mood such that the individual is forced to maintain a new allostatic set point of mood is shown in figure 2, from Koob and Le Moal (2001).

A series of common functional alleles whose effects are stress-modulated, altering emotional response and behaviour, have been identified. Table 1 lists these. Excluded from the table are genes for which there is a linkage signal or even a functional haplotype, such as GTP cyclohydrolase (Tegeder et al. 2006), but for which the functional locus is unknown.

Several of the genes listed in the table alter multiple complex behaviours. Such pleiotropy is expected because of action of the same gene in different regions and because of the multiple functions of many brain regions. In this regard, psychiatric diseases are more complex manifestations of neural functions, which themselves are amazingly variable and un-amenable to easy categorization. The difficulty of categorization does not diminish the value of categorization. Disease categories provide a basis for clinical decision-making. Within disease categories, other variables, including dimensional variables (e.g., blood pressure, platelet count, heart rhythm, level of consciousness), guide decisions, particularly day-to-day decisions. By its nature, inherited variation may point to etiologic categorization. However, as revealed by gene x stress and gene x endocrine interactions, genotype is

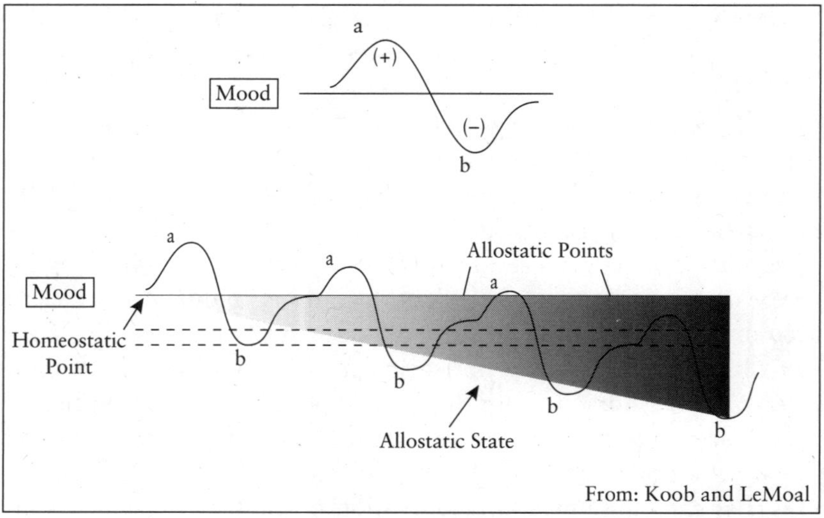

Figure 2. After repeated cycles of drug exposure and withdrawal, the individual is no longer able to maintain the normal allostatic set point of mood (Koob and LeMoal, 2001). Functional alleles modulate both the pre-drug set point of mood and the progression to allostasis determining inter-individual variation in mood.

important for understanding, and predicting, clinical response in a fashion that is somewhat distinct from diagnosis.

Several pharmacogenetic predictors in neuropsychiatry are themselves fairly independent from the role of these genotypes in a disease process, or, if the effect is the same, that may be a coincidence. This is the case for both the COMT and SLC6A4 polymorphisms listed in the table. The low expression COMT Met158 allele, coherent with its effect to increase dopamine concentrations in the frontal cortex, predicts better cognitive performance at baseline. However, cognitive performance in individuals with Val158 genotypes is more likely to show augmentation of cognitive performance after amphetamine, consistent with the inverted U relationship of frontal dopamine to tuning of frontal cortical circuits (Goldberg et al. 2003). SLC6A4 reduction of function genotypes (genotypes containing the S allele and also the L_G allele) are very mildly predictive of depression but also tend to predict worse response to SSRI (serotonin-specific reuptake inhibitor) drugs that act at the serotonin transporter level (Serretti et al. 2005) but possibly via increased side effects and treatment tolerability in individuals carrying reduction-of-function genotypes (Hu et al. 2006).

Table 1
Six genes with common functional alleles altering stress response, emotion, and other phenotypes.

Gene	*Locus or loci*	*Rarer allele*	*Phenotypes*	*GxE Signal*	*Reference*
SLC6A4 (HTT)	HTTLPR	0.5	Brain connectivity Brain volume Emotional fMRI Anxiety Drug response	Yes	Lesch et al. 1996 Hariri et al. 2002 Caspi et al. 2003
MAOA	VNTR	0.3	Dyscontrol Emotional fMRI	Yes	Caspi et al. 2002 Buckholtz et al. 2008
COMT	Val158Met Haplotype	0.4	Cognition Anxiety Pain Emotional fMRI Pain PET Drug response		Egan et al. 2001 Enoch et al. 2003 Zubieta et al. 2003 Meyer-Lind-enberg, et al.2005
NPY	-399T/C Leu6Pro	0.3	Metabolism Anxiety Emotional fMRI Pain PET		Karvonen et al. 1998 Zhou et al. 2008
FKBP5			PTSD Dexamethasone response		Binder et al. 2008
BDNF	Met66Val	0.2	Episodic memory Hippocampal volume Anxiety		Egan et al. 2003 Chen et al. 2006

The DRD3 dopamine receptor has a common missense variant, Ser9Gly, that is moderately predictive of risk of tardive dyskinesia in individuals treated with antipsychotic medications (Lehrer et al. 2002), but is not predictive of psychosis. A *mu* opioid receptor variant Asn40Asp that alters endomorphin binding predicts therapeutic response in alcoholics treated with naltrexone (Oslin et al. 2003; Anton et al. 2008), although the relationship of this polymorphism to the liability to addiction vulnerability is itself controversial. The discovery of such markers is reminiscent of useful findings for other medical diseases: the discovery of fast and slow acetylators, or detection of breast cancers that are estrogen-sensitive and non-sensitive. Genetic findings enable more refined diagnoses guiding treatment, for example by targeting a specific etiology. Other genetic markers enable the better use of treatments that depend on particular molecular targets or that are altered in their efficacy by pharmacokinetic genetic differences or by side effects unrelated to the etiology of the disease.

INTERMEDIATE PHENOTYPES

An intermediate phenotype (table 2) is a phenotype that accesses molecular expression or one or more of the steps between allele and complex phenotype. Such phenotypes are useful because of the advantages of specificity and larger allele effect sizes. The advantage of specificity is sometimes overlooked. An intermediate phenotype that enables a group of individuals with a common trait to be dissected into more homogeneous subgroups is highly useful. For example, the genetic analysis of short stature associated with somatostatin receptor deficiency represents an enormous simplification, and immediately guides the analysis to a gene and a predicted effect. In addition, the effect of a functional allele is usually diluted, or at least altered, as one progresses from molecular phenotypes to phenotypes in the cellular, systems biology, and disease domains. For example, a receptor allele reducing mRNA expression by 50 per cent may show a modified effect at the level of receptor expression due to compensating effects on receptor trafficking to the membrane, receptor down-regulation, or changes in signal transduction. At the cellular and systems levels there may be compensatory changes in synapse formation, neuronal networks, or even behaviour of the animal. At the disease level there may be no phenotypic effect except in particular circumstances, and in this regard most common functional alleles probably exert their effects in probabilistic fashion and by altering the reaction range and risk density distribution of individuals who carry that genotype.

In certain instances a functional allele may account for more of the variance in a complex phenotype than any intermediate phenotype. A codominant molecular or cellular effect may lead to a dominant or recessive effect at the level of the more complex phenotype, due to thresholding. From one molecular level to the next the mode of effect of the allele can even change. For example, at the MRNA and protein subunit level the ALDH2 Glu487Lys polymorphism acts codominantly: a heterozygote will express equal amounts of the

Glu487 and Lys487 mRNA and protein subunits. However, the active enzyme is tetrameric and the presence of one inactive Lys487 subunit drastically reduces activity. Random assembly of the tetramers leads to only one in sixteen being fully active, and a dominant mode of allele action, at the enzyme level, that also translates into a dominant mode of action of Lys487 in predicting alcohol-induced flushing, and protection against alcoholism.

The effects of some functional alleles also seem paradoxical. For example, the reduction-of-function serotonin transporter (SLC6A4) alleles predict higher levels of anxiety and emotionality, contrary to what might have been expected from the therapeutic efficacy of SSRI drugs in anxiety and depression. The paradoxical effect is perhaps due to the developmental expression of the serotonin transporter consistent with mice whose SLC6A4 ortholog has been knocked out and consistent with developmental effects of SSRI exposure in developing rats (Ansorge et al. 2004), and consistent with effect of the reduction of function SLC6A4 genotypes to lead to lower brain connectivity correlating with emotional dysregulation (Pezawas et al. 2005; Heinz et al. 2005).

An endophenotype (table 2) is a heritable intermediate phenotype that is disease-associated (Gottesman and Gould 2003). Intermediate phenotypes that meet these additional criteria are likely to be highly useful in genetic analyses. Many intermediate phenotypes that do not meet these criteria are also highly useful. For example, any intermediate phenotype that reduces heterogeneity may be useful, regardless of disease association. An example is the flushing response just mentioned. Flushing is less common among alcoholics. It is a protective intermediate phenotype, but useful. Also, in many populations flushing is rare, but if identified it would serve as a useful clue to genetic etiology.

The heritability requirement is also deserving of a little more careful scrutiny. First, the heritability of many useful intermediate phenotypes has never been demonstrated via twin or family studies; but it is presumable. Second, non-heritable intermediate phenotypes can be invaluable, especially if they identify non-genetic subgroups (phenocopies) but also if they clarify interactions of environmental exposures with alleles.

Whole genome association, and other types of genetic analysis, can be married with endophenotypes. For example, we recently conducted a WGA study of resting EEEG power in a relatively small

Table 2
Intermediate phenotypes and endophenotypes*

Type of phenotype	*Heritable*	*Disease-associated*	*Mechanism-informative*
Intermediate	Not necessarily	Not necessarily	Perhaps
Endophenotype	Yes	Yes	Perhaps

Source: Gottesman and Gould, 2003.

dataset, numbering 324 individuals (Hodgkinson et al, 2010). Several genome-wide significant loci affecting the EEEG were detected, including two that converged on the locations of top hits from the few family linkage studies that have so far been performed on resting EEG.

Numerous molecular intermediate phenotypes are available that enable environmental exposures to be tracked and thereby facilitate genetic studies. An example of the importance of considering endocrine context is the finding that the low-expression monoamine oxidase A variant, which can lead to impulsivity, is much stronger in males with higher testosterone levels, a gene x endocrine interaction; or, to put it another way, the higher testosterone levels that correlated with impulsivity showed that correlation only in the context of the genotype leading to low MAOA expression (Sjöberg et al, 2008). These findings may be explained by a functional androgen responsive element located in the promoter region of MAOA and may relate to the much higher frequency of dyscontrol behaviours (e.g., murder, assault) in males.

A variety of endocrine measures enable effects of stress to be tracked. A variety of toxin exposures ranging from heavy metals to drugs can be captured by direct measurement. Infection and inflammation lead to the release of mediators such as interleukins and higher titres of specific antibodies, as well as changes in type and number of leukocytes. Nutritional deficiencies can be captured by a variety of specific measures including levels of essential minerals, cofactors synthesized from vitamins, and levels of essential fatty acids.

Looking to the near future, gene technologies will provide a new array of highly specific molecular measures indicating history of different environmental exposures via genome-wide and transcriptome-wide approaches. For example, the quantitative and qualitative changes in the transcriptome (the total complement of expressed messenger RNAs) are assessable both via hybridization arrays that interrogate known transcripts and transcript variants and also via new methods including the detection of sequence tags via sequencing (for example by the SAGE method) and via high throughput sequencing of the whole transcriptome using so called "next-generation" sequencers capable of simultaneously sequencing gigabases (billions of nucleotides – the human genome is approximately three gigabases in size) of DNA, or cDNA made from mRNA, on a single array.

The enhanced capability in DNA sequencing also revolutionizes capability to detect epigenetic changes that follow environmental exposures. An epigenetic variation in the DNA is a change in structure that does not depend on DNA sequence. Two types of epigenetic variations are differences in CpG methylation and variations in the histone packaging of DNA. Regarding CpG methylation, methylcytosines (due to their relatively high mutation rate and tendency to be eliminated) are concentrated in island regions of the genome, in proximity to genes. When methylated, these cytosines often silence transcription, providing a mechanism for long-lasting gene regulation. At the glucocorticoid receptor, a CpG methylation is altered by maternal behaviour, leading to long-lasting behavioural change as observed in rats.

DNA is packaged with protein as chromatin, the DNA being wound around nucleosome cores comprised of histones. Variations in histones include differences in methylation of key lysines and differences in acetylation that are under the control of an array of enzymes including histone deacetylatases. Recently, the activity of a particular histone deacetylase was linked to adaptive changes occurring during addiction (Renthal et al. 2007). A methodology known as ChIP-Seq, which is based on chromatin immunoprecipitation with specific antibodies followed by identification of the immunoprecipitated DNA by next generation sequencing, is enabling the genome-wide mapping of the histone composition of the genome, with the ability to identify changes in chromatin structure that reflect gene activation and suppression of transcription. Such technology will transform the ability to define the imprint of environmental exposure on the DNA, as well as opening a new category of molecular intermediate phenotypes altered by allele effects.

NEUROPEPTIDE Y: DILUTION OF EFFECTS FROM GENE TO COMPLEX PHENOTYPE

Neuropeptide Y is a thirty-six-amino acid neuropeptide synthesized as a larger propeptide and widely expressed in a variety of brain regions, especially the emotion and stress responsive amygdala and the adrenals and pancreatic islet cells (Novartis mRNA array expression data, as posted on the Santa Cruz genomics resource website). Expression in pancreatic islet cells is coherent with the function of this neuropeptide in the lipostat system where it regulates metabolism and appetite. The moderately abundant (0.05) Leu7Pro missense variant found in the cleaved propeptide region of NPY predicted high serum cholesterol and LDL cholesterol levels (Karvonen et al. 1998). The Pro7 allele apparently alters processing and secretion of the NPY (Kallio et al. 2001), explaining its effects on physiology. Expression in the brain and adrenal gland reflects the role of NPY as an anxiolytic neuropeptide released following stress and countering effects of the corticotrophin-releasing hormone.

In that regard, the ability to release NPY predicts relative resilience against deleterious effects of stress, for example post-traumatic stress disease (PTSD) occurring amongst veterans (Rasmussen et al. 2000; Yehuda et al. 2006). A convergence of NPY's effects on behaviour and metabolism is seen in stress-exposed individuals who as a consequence of enhanced NPY release may suffer from metabolic syndrome and obesity (Kuo et al. 2007) and cardiovascular disease (Callanan et al. 2007).

A relatively common (frequency 0.44) NPY haplotype was identified that tags at least one variant in the NPY promoter which alters expression of this gene (Zhou et al. 2008). As shown in figure 3, lower genotype-predicted NPY expression predicts stronger responses in a variety of experimental paradigms that access anxiety and emotion (Zhou et al. 2008). Using functional magnetic resonance imaging (fMRI) of brain metabolic activity, it was observed that responses to emotional stimuli are enhanced in key regions of the brain that are involved in the registration of emotion, including the assignment of magnitude and valence in emotional responses to stimuli, which in this case were pictures selected for their ability to elicit different emotions.

Via a different brain imaging method it was also shown that the low expression NPY genotype predicted diminished resilience to pain

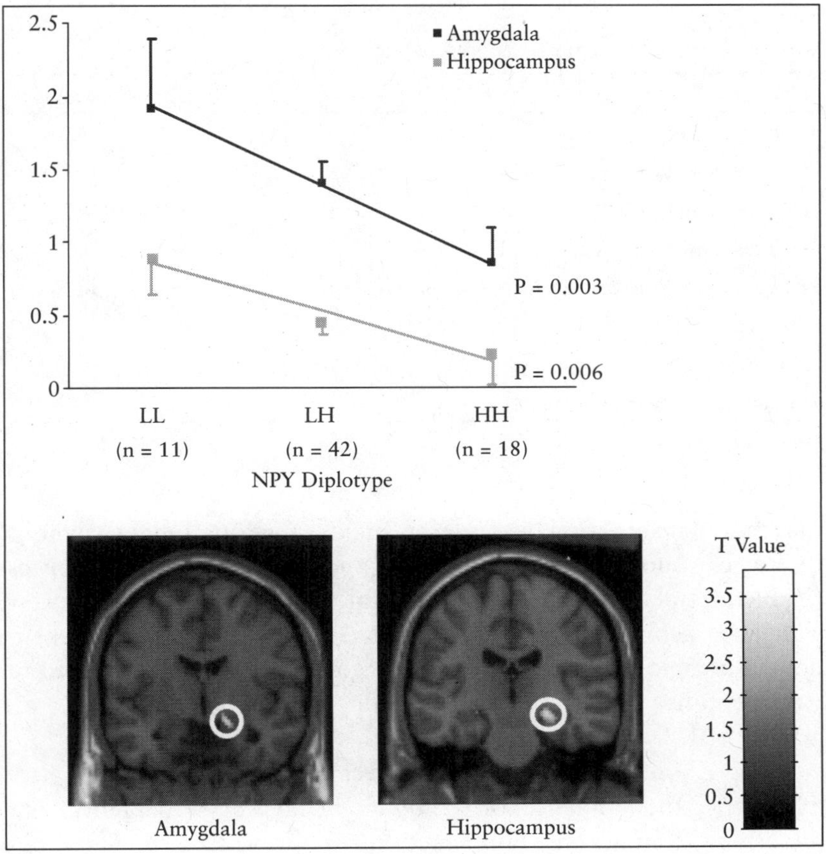

Figure 3. Low expression neuropeptide Y genotypes predict increased emotion-induced fMRI activations in both the amygdala and hippocampus (Zhou et al. 2008).

(table 3). Using a positron emission tomography (PET) approach and a specific labelled ligand for mu opioid receptors (^{11}C-Carfentanil), it was possible to visualize the brain's response to a painful stimulus, namely an infusion of hypertonic saline into the masseter muscle of the jaw. There is considerable inter-individual variation in pain threshold and affective response to pain. That variation is moderately predicted by the ability to release endogenous opioids following a painful stimulus. In this PET brain imaging method, the opioid release is revealed by displacement of the exogenous ^{11}C-Carfentanil from mu opioid receptors. People who release less endogenous opioids after a painful stimulus tend to have both a lower pain threshold and stronger affective responses to pain; and genetic variants

Table 3
Variance attributable to functional NPY haplotypes

Phenotype	*Variance*
mRNA expression in lymphoblastoid cell lines	0.28
Plasma NPY in healthy controls	0.17
Plasma NPY in alcohol dependent patients	0.06
fMRI response to emotional probe	0.09
Pain-induced opioid displacement (PET)	0.37
Affective response to pain	0.05
Pain threshold	0.03
Trait anxiety (Harm avoidance)	0.03

Source: Zhou et al. 2008.

that modulate emotional responses, such as the functional variant of COMT, can modulate these objective and subjective pain responses (Zubieta et al. 2003). After the painful stimulus, the lower expression NPY genotype predicted impaired ability to activate the endogenous opioid system in multiple regions of the brain involved in pain response and the affective component of pain (Zhou et al. 2008).

In the Zhou et al. study on the effect of the low expression NPY haplotype, the influence on complex behaviours emergent from underlying changes in brain function was also assessed. These behaviours included trait anxiety in normal controls as measured by Harm Avoidance measures from the Tridimensional Personality Questionnaire, and anxiety disorders as determined by psychiatric interview. Lower expression NPY genotypes predicted higher trait anxiety levels and increased propensity to anxiety disorders (table 3). However, only a small percentage of inter-individual variation in trait anxiety is influenced by neuropeptide Y genotype.

This is not surprising given the larger number of genes that can influence the complex trait and the importance of environmental exposures such as stress in determining behaviour. Scrutiny of the relationship of NPY to different phenotypes reveals that the effect of this functional polymorphism is progressively diluted as one moves from the molecular level (e.g., mRNA expression and neuropeptide levels) to the level of brain responses (e.g., fMRI and PET brain imaging responses) to the level of emergent behaviour (e.g., trait anxiety, pain threshold, anxiety disorders). These are the types of observations that encourage an analysis of intermediate phenotypes for the purposes of discovery and validation of gene effects, and that also encourage the use of intermediate phenotypes to understand the mechanisms of gene effects, including the moderating influences of the environment on complex behaviours that may emerge as a result of the molecular action of an allele.

THE SEROTONIN TRANSPORTER AND MONOAMINE OXIDASE A: GENE X STRESS INTERACTIONS

The literature on the effects of functional polymorphisms at the serotonin transporter (*SLC6A4*) and monoamine oxidase A (*MAOA*) genes is now large and extraordinarily complex. These represent the first two genes for which gene x stress interactions were demonstrated and this was accomplished in two seminal papers (Caspi et al. 2002; Caspi et al. 2003), both of which made use of the Dunedin, New Zealand, prospective longitudinal cohort. At both of these genes there are much rarer alleles that exert stronger functional effects – a stop-codon variant in MAOA found in one family (Brunner et al. 1993) and a rare missense variant at SLC6A4 (Ozaki et al. 2003). These rare variants are strong, or perhaps one could say deterministic, in action. In contrast, the common SLC6A4 and MAOA alleles are probabilistic in their effect of complex behaviour. For example, the functional HTTLPR polymorphism in the promoter region of SLC6A4 modifies brain function such that individuals tend to be more anxious, however the effect is modest. Each copy of the S allele is associated with a 0.1 standard deviation increase in trait anxiety measured as Harm Avoidance, as discussed earlier, or measured as Neuroticism with a different personality scale (Sen et al. 2004).

In fact the effect of these alleles is tenuous at the level of the complex trait. In a recent meta-analysis (Munafo et al. 2008) it was concluded that the effects of HTTLPR on risk of depression, including the effects mediated by GxE interaction, were negligible, and compatible with chance. There is every indication that the problem lies in the small effect sizes and between-study sources of heterogeneity in the association studies with the complex trait. The best evidence is that HTTLR alters serotonin transporter binding in postmortem brains (Little et al. 1998) and in living brains (Heinz et al. 2000). As a consequence there are HTTLPR-predicted differences in emotional fMRI responses (Hariri et al. 2002) and with many subsequent replications including studies demonstrating a perhaps more fundamental effect on connectivity of brain regions (Heinz et al. 2005; Pezawas et al. 2005) and gene x gene interactions (Smolka et al. 2007) between HTTLPR and other genes, including catechol-O-methyltransferase (COMT) that also alter brain emotional and pain responses, again with neuroimaging phenotypes (Zubieta et al. 2003).

CONCLUSIONS

Gene x environment studies in the area of stress and behaviour are becoming more incisive. First there is an increasing ability to obtain relevant measures that predict the ability of the functional allele to exert an effect on complex behaviour. These would include brain imaging and electrophysiological measures of brain function, as exemplified by a recent EEG WGA study, but also measures of specific small molecules including hormones and small molecules (e.g., NPY, cortisol). As an example of the use of small molecule measures, the availability of CSF testosterone levels enabled the discovery that low expression MAOA genotype is permissive for the effect of testosterone to increase dyscontrol behaviours, a phenotype influenced by the low-activity MAOA allele (Sjoberg et al. 2008).

A second advance in GxE studies is the capture of effects of exposures via studies, some longitudinal, on large, well-defined cohorts and also samples enriched for particular experiences. These datasets are essential both for discovery, to accurately measure effects of functional loci on complex phenotypes, and for moving towards the redefinition of some of those complex phenotypes into phenotypes that are more etiologically homogeneous and clinically more predictive.

Third, animal models are powerfully used both at the front-end of the discovery process in terms of defining genes that are involved in GxE and also in the stages of validation and explication of findings. In particular, the existence of orthologous functional polymorphic loci in non-human primates has proven to be a valuable tool, enabling the GxE effects of the MAOA and HTTLPR loci to be substantially validated via a model in which infant monkeys are peer-reared, constituting an early life stress model (for example, Barr et al. 2004, and reviewed Barr et al. 2006). Via this model, the role of a mu opioid receptor polymorphism in attachment behaviour (which is measured by observing vocalizations and stress behaviours) was uncovered

(Barr et al. 2006). The demonstration that the vasopressin receptor influences attachment behaviour in the vole has similarly now led to the discovery that genetic variation in the human vasopressin receptor influences attachment behaviour in human couples (Walum et al. 2008). Actions of various polymorphisms including the HTTLPR and COMT polymorphisms have been to some extent duplicated and better explained via studies on mice engineered for altered expression of those genes (e.g., Huotari et al. 2002; Zhao et al. 2006).

Finally, the ability to assess chromatin structure and mRNA transcript abundances on a genome-wide level enabled by next generation (>1 gigabase) sequencing technologies is producing a revolution in our understanding of the functionality of the human genome sequence and its sequence variants via the ENCODE project (Encode Project Consortium, 2004) and as applied to the functional significance of sequence variation (Giardine et al. 2007). Early-life environmental exposures, for example altered maternal behaviour, reprogram gene expression via specific epigenetic changes including DNA CpG methylation (Weaver et al. 2004) and changes in histone structure. The next few years will see a revolution in our understanding of the genome-wide changes that are induced by environmental exposures, including stress, with an ability to resolve both the *cis* (local and same-chromosome) and *trans* (pleiotropic and genome-wide) effects of functional polymorphisms that intersect with those exposures to alter behaviour.

Despite the obstacles in the analysis of complex behaviour, considerable progress has been made in understanding the interaction of stress and environment in behavioural variation. Using statistical linkage and association, multiple functional genetic loci have been discovered that interact with stress and other environmental exposures to produce disease vulnerability. In addition, other gene regions have been discovered that are likely to harbour functional loci influencing stress response. However, effects on complex behavioural phenotypes are quantitatively modest as compared to actions of the functional alleles on intermediate molecular and neurobiological phenotypes. Increasingly the process of validation has shifted to the intermediate phenotype level, where explication of effects is also possible.

A new generation of gene x environment studies is enabled by the collection of very large and longitudinal datasets, intermediate phenotypes ranging from neuroimaging to small molecules, animal models targeting particular genes and controlling environmental exposures, and genome-wide capture of epigenetic variation in DNA methylation and chromatin. This new generation of studies will transform our understanding of gene x stress interactions, moving the discussion beyond the statistical sphere into that of function.

BIBLIOGRAPHY

Ansorge, M.S., Zhou, M., Lira, A., Hen, R., Gingrich, J.A. 2004. Early-life blockade of the 5-HT transporter alters emotional behavior in adult mice. *Science* 306(5697):879-81.

Anton, R.F., Oroszi, G., O'Malley, S., Couper, D., Swift, R., Pettinati, H., Goldman, D. 2008. An evaluation of mu-opioid receptor (OPRM1) as a predictor of naltrexone response in the treatment of alcohol dependence: Results from the Combined Pharmacotherapies and Behavioral Interventions for Alcohol Dependence (COMBINE) study. *Arch Gen Psychiatry* 65(2):135-44.

Barr, C.S., Goldman, D. 2006. Non-human primate models of inheritance vulnerability to alcohol use disorders. *Addict Biol* 11(3-4):374-85.

Barr, C.S., Newman, T.K., Shannon, C., Parker, C., Dvoskin, R.L., Becker, M.L., Schwandt, M., Champoux, M., Lesch, K.P., Goldman, D., Suomi, S.J., Higley, J.D. 2004. Rearing condition and rh5-HTTLPR interact to influence limbic-hypothalamic-pituitary-adrenal axis response to stress in infant macaques. *Biol Psychiatry* 55(7):733-8.

Barrett, J.C., Hansoul, S., Nicolae, D.L., Cho, J.H., Duerr, R.H., Rioux, J.D., Brant, S.R., Silverberg, M.S., Taylor, K.D., Barmada, M.M., Bitton, A., Dassopoulos, T., Datta, L.W., Green, T., Griffiths, A.M., Kistner, E.O., Murtha, M.T., Regueiro, M.D., Rotter, J.I., Schumm, L.P., Steinhart, A.H., Targan, S.R., Xavier, R.J.; NIDDK IBD Genetics Consortium, Libioulle, C., Sandor, C., Lathrop, M., Belaiche, J., Dewit, O., Gut, I., Heath, S., Laukens, D., Mni, M., Rutgeerts, P., Van Gossum, A., Zelenika, D., Franchimont, D., Hugot, J.P., de Vos, M., Vermeire S., Louis, E.; Belgian-French IBD Consortium; Wellcome Trust Case Control Consortium, Cardon, L.R., Anderson, C.A., Drummond, H., Nimmo, E., Ahmad, T., Prescott, N.J., Onnie, C.M., Fisher, S.A., Marchini, J., Ghori, J., Bumpstead, S., Gwilliam, R., Tremelling, M., Deloukas, P., Mansfield, J., Jewell, D., Satsangi, J., Mathew, C.G., Parkes, M., Georges, M., Daly, M.J. 2008. Genome-wide association defines more than 30 distinct susceptibility loci for Crohn's disease. *Nat Genet* 40(8):955-62. Epub 2008 Jun 29.

Bierut, L.J., Stitzel, J.A., Wang, J.C., Hinrichs, A.L., Grucza, R.A., Xuei, X., Saccone, N.L., Saccone, S.F., Bertelsen, S., Fox, L., Horton, W.J., Breslau, N., Budde, J., Cloninger, C.R., Dick, D.M., Foroud, T., Hatsukami, D., Hesselbrock, V., Johnson, E.O., Kramer, J., Kuperman, S., Madden, P.A., Mayo, K., Nurnberger, J. Jr, Pomerleau, O., Porjesz, B., Reyes, O., Schuckit, M., Swan, G., Tischfield, J.A., Edenberg, H.J., Rice, J.P., Goate, A.M. 2008. Variants in nicotinic receptors and risk for nicotine dependence. *Am J Psychiatry.* 165(9):1163-71.

Binder, E.B., Bradley, R.G., Liu, W., Epstein, M.P., Deveau, T.C., Mercer, K.B., Tang, Y., Gillespie, C.F., Heim, C.M., Nemeroff, C.B., Schwartz, A.C., Cubells, J.F., Ressler, K.J. 2008. Association of FKBP5 polymorphisms and childhood abuse with risk of posttraumatic stress disorder symptoms in adults. *JAMA* 299(11):1291-305.

Brunner, H.G., Nelen, M., Breakefield, X.O., Ropers, H.H., van Oost, B.A. 1993. Abnormal behavior associated with a point mutation in the structural gene for monoamine oxidase *A. Science* 262(5133):578-80.

Buckholtz, J.W., Callicott, J.H., Kolachana, B., Hariri, A.R., Goldberg, T.E., Genderson, M., Egan, M.F., Mattay, V.S., Weinberger, D.R., Meyer-Lindenberg, A. 2008. Genetic variation in MAOA modulates ventromedial prefrontal circuitry mediating individual differences in human personality. *Mol Psychiatry* 13(3):313-24. Epub 2007 May 22.

Callanan, E.Y., Lee, E.W., Tilan, J.U., Winaver, J., Haramati, A., Mulroney, S.E., Zukowska, Z. 2007. Renal and cardiac neuropeptide Y and NPY receptors in a rat model of congestive heart failure. *Am J Physiol Renal Physiol* 293(6):F1811-17. Epub 2007 Sep 5.

Caspi, A., McClay, J., Moffitt, T.E., Mill, J., Martin, J., Craig, I.W., Taylor, A., Poulton, R. 2002. Role of genotype in the cycle of violence in maltreated children. *Science* 297(5582):851-4.

Caspi, A., Sugden, K., Moffitt, T.E., Taylor, A., Craig, I.W., Harrington, H., McClay, J., Mill, J., Martin, J., Braithwaite, A., Poulton, R. 2003. Influence of life stress on depression: Moderation by a polymorphism in the 5-HTT gene. *Science* 301(5631):386-9.

Chen, Z.Y., Jing, D., Bath, K.G., Ieraci, A., Khan, T., Siao, C.J., Herrera, D.G., Toth, M., Yang, C, McEwen, B.S., Hempstead, B.L., Lee, F.S. 2006. Genetic variant BDNF (Val66Met) polymorphism alters anxiety-related behavior. *Science* 314(5796):140-3.

Ducci, F., Enoch, M.A., Hodgkinson, C., Xu, K., Catena, M., Robin, R.W., Goldman, D. 2008. Interaction between a functional MAOA locus and childhood sexual abuse predicts alcoholism and antisocial personality disorder in adult women. *Mol Psychiatry* 13(3):334-47. Epub 2007 Jun 26.

Ducci, F., Enoch, M.A., Funt, S., Virkkunen, M., Albaugh, B., Goldman, D. 2007. Increased anxiety and other similarities in temperament of alcoholics with and without antisocial personality disorder across three diverse populations. *Alcohol* 41(1):3-12.

Egan, M.F., Goldberg, T.E., Kolachana, B.S., Callicott, J.H., Mazzanti, C.M., Straub, R.E., Goldman, D., Weinberger, D.R. 2001. Effect of COMT Val108/158 Met genotype on frontal lobe function and risk for schizophrenia. *Proc Natl Acad Sci U S A* 98(12):6917-22. Epub 2001 May 29.

Egan, M.F., Kojima, M., Callicott, J.H., Goldberg, T.E., Kolachana, B.S., Bertolino, A., Zaitsev, E., Gold, B., Goldman, D., Dean M., Lu, B., Weinberger, D.R. 2003. The BDNF val66met polymorphism affects activity-dependent secretion of BDNF and human memory and hippocampal function. *Cell* 112(2):257-69.

ENCODE Project Consortium. 2004. The ENCODE (ENCyclopedia of DNA Elements) Project. *Science* 306(5696):636-40.

Enoch, M.A., Xu, K., Ferro, E., Harris, C.R., Goldman, D. 2003. Genetic origins of anxiety in women: A role for a functional catechol-O-methyltransferase polymorphism. *Psychiatr Genet* Mar;13(1):33-41.

Giardine, B., Riemer, C., Hefferon, T., Thomas, D., Hsu, F., Zielenski, J., Sang, Y., Elnitski, L., Cutting, G., Trumbower, H., Kern, A., Kuhn, R., Patrinos, G.P., Hughes, J., Higgs, D., Chui, D., Scriver, C., Phommarinh, M., Patnaik, S.K., Blumenfeld, O., Gottlieb, B., Vihinen, M., Väliaho, J., Kent, J., Miller, W., Hardison, R.C. 2007. PhenCode: connecting ENCODE data with mutations and phenotype. *Hum Mutat* 28(6):554-62.

Goldberg, T.E., Egan, M.F., Gscheidle, T., Coppola, R., Weickert, T., Kolachana, B.S., Goldman, D., Weinberger, D.R. 2003. Executive subprocesses in working memory: Relationship to catechol-O-methyltransferase Val158Met genotype and schizophrenia. *Arch Gen Psychiatry* 60(9):889-96.

Goldman, D., Oroszi, G., Ducci, F. 2005. The genetics of addictions: Uncovering the genes. *Nat Rev Genet* 6(7):521-32. Review.

Gottesman, I.I., Gould, T.D. 2003. The endophenotype concept in psychiatry: Etymology and strategic intentions. *Am J Psychiatry* 160(4):636-45.

Hariri, A.R., Mattay, V.S., Tessitore, A., Kolachana, B., Fera, F., Goldman, D., Egan, M.F., Weinberger, D.R. 2002. Serotonin transporter genetic variation and the response of the human amygdala. *Science* 297(5580):400-3.

Hauser, P., Zametkin, A.J., Martinez, P., Vitiello, B., Matochik, J.A., Mixson, A.J., Weintraub, B.D. 1993. Attention deficit-hyperactivity disorder in people with generalized resistance to thyroid hormone. *N Engl J Med* 328(14):997-1001.

Heinz, A., Braus, D.F., Smolka, M.N., Wrase, J., Puls, I., Hermann, D., Klein, S., Grüsser, S.M., Flor, H., Schumann, G., Mann, K., Büchel, C. 2005. Amygdala-prefrontal coupling depends on a genetic variation of the serotonin transporter. *Nat Neurosci* 8(1):20-1. Epub 2004 Dec 12.

Heinz, A., Jones, D.W., Mazzanti, C., Goldman, D., Ragan, P., Hommer, D., Linnoila, M., Weinberger, D.R. 2000. A relationship between serotonin transporter genotype and in vivo protein expression and alcohol neurotoxicity. *Biol Psychiatry* 47(7):643-9.

Hodgkinson, C.A., Enoch, M.A., Srivastava, V., Cummins-Oman, J.S., Ferrier, C., Iarikova, P., Sankararaman, S., Yamini, G., Yuan, Q., Zhou, Z., Albaugh, B., White, K.V., Shen, P.H., Goldman D. 2010. Genome-wide association identifies candidate genes that influence the human electroencephalogram. *Proc Natl Acad Sci USA.* 107(19):8 695-700.

Hu, X.Z., Lipsky, R.H., Zhu, G., Akhtar, L.A., Taubman, J., Greenberg, B.D., Xu, K., Arnold, P.D., Richter, M.A., Kennedy, J.L., Murphy, D.L., Goldman, D. 2006. Serotonin transporter promoter gain-of-function genotypes are linked to obsessive-compulsive disorder. *Am J Hum Genet* 78(5):815-26. Epub 2006 Mar 28.

Huotari, M., Gogos, J.A., Karayiorgou, M., Koponen, O., Forsberg, M., Raasmaja, A., Hyttinen, J., Männistö, P.T. 2002. Brain catecholamine metabolism in catechol-O-methyltransferase (COMT)-deficient mice. *Eur J Neurosci* 15(2):246-56.

Kallio, J., Pesonen, U., Kaipio, K., Karvonen, M.K., Jaakkola, U., Heinonen, O.J., Uusitupa, M.I., Koulu, M. 2001. Altered intracellular processing and release of neuropeptide Y due to leucine 7 to proline 7 polymorphism in the signal peptide of preproneuropeptide Y in humans. *FASEB J* 15(7):1242-4.

Karvonen, M.K., Pesonen, U., Koulu, M., Niskanen, L., Laakso, M., Rissanen, A., Dekker, J.M., Hart, L.M., Valve, R., Uusitupa, M.I. 1998. Association of a leucine(7)-to-proline(7) polymorphism in the signal peptide of neuropeptide Y with high serum cholesterol and LDL cholesterol levels. *Nat Med* 4(12):1434-7.

Koob, G.F., Le Moal, M. 2001. Drug addiction, dysregulation of reward, and allostasis. *Neuropsychopharmacology* 24(2):97-129.

Koss, M.P., Yuan, N.P., Dightman, D., Prince, R.J., Polacca, M., Sanderson, B., Goldman, D. 2003. Adverse childhood exposures and alcohol dependence among seven Native American tribes. *Am J Prev Med* 25(3):238-44.

Kuo, L.E., Kitlinska, J.B., Tilan, J.U., Li, L., Baker, S.B., Johnson, M.D., Lee, E.W., Burnett, M.S., Fricke, S.T., Kvetnansky, R., Herzog, H., Zukowska, Z. 2007. Neuropeptide Y acts directly in the periphery on fat tissue and mediates stress-induced obesity and metabolic syndrome. *Nat Med* Jul;13(7):803-11. Epub 2007 Jul 1. Erratum in: Nat Med. 2007 13(9):1120.

Lachman, H.M., Papolos, D.F., Saito, T., Yu, Y.M., Szumlanski, C.L., Weinshilboum, R.M. 1996. Human catechol-O-methyltransferase pharmacogenetics: Description of a functional polymorphism and its potential application to neuropsychiatric disorders. *Pharmacogenetics* 6(3):243-50

Lerer, B., Segman, R.H., Fangerau, H., Daly, A.K., Basile, V.S., Cavallaro, R., Aschauer, H.N., McCreadie, R.G., Ohlraun, S., Ferrier, N., Masellis, M., Verga, M., Scharfetter, J., Rietschel, M., Lovlie, R., Levy, U.H., Meltzer, H.Y., Kennedy, J.L., Steen, V.M., Macciardi, F. 2002. Pharmacogenetics of tardive dyskinesia: Combined analysis of 780 patients supports association with dopamine D3 receptor gene Ser9Gly polymorphism. *Neuropsychopharmacology* 27(1):105-19.

Lesch, K.P., Bengel, D., Heils, A., Sabol, S.Z., Greenberg, B.D., Petri, S., Benjamin, J., Müller, C.R., Hamer, D.H., Murphy, D.L. 1996. Association of anxiety-related traits with a polymorphism in the serotonin transporter gene regulatory region. *Science* 274(5292):1527-31.

Little, K.Y., McLaughlin, D.P., Zhang, L., Livermore, C.S., Dalack, G.W., McFinton, P.R., DelProposto, Z.S., Hill, E., Cassin, B.J., Watson, S.J., Cook, E.H. 1998. Cocaine, ethanol, and genotype effects on human midbrain serotonin transporter binding sites and mRNA levels. *Am J Psychiatry* 155(2):207-13.

Merikangas, K.R., Risch, N. 2003. Genomic priorities and public health. *Science* 302(5645):599-601.

Meyer-Lindenberg, A., Kohn, P.D., Kolachana, B., Kippenhan, S., McInerney-Leo, A., Nussbaum, R., Weinberger, D.R., Berman, K.F. 2005. Midbrain dopamine and prefrontal function in humans: Interaction and modulation by COMT genotype. *Nat Neurosci* 8(5):594-6. Epub 2005 Apr 10.

Munafò, M.R., Durrant, C., Lewis, G., Flint, J. 2008. Gene x Environment Interactions at the Serotonin Transporter Locus. *Biol Psychiatry* Aug 6. [Epub ahead of print]

Nackley, A.G., Shabalina, S.A., Tchivileva, I.E., Satterfield, K., Korchynskyi, O., Makarov, S.S., Maixner, W., Diatchenko, L. 2006. Human catechol-O-methyltransferase haplotypes modulate protein expression by altering mRNA secondary structure. *Science* 314(5807):1930-3.

Oslin, D.W., Berrettini, W., Kranzler, H.R., Pettinati, H., Gelernter, J., Volpicelli, J.R., O'Brien, C.P. 2003. A functional polymorphism of the mu-opioid receptor gene is associated with naltrexone response in alcohol-dependent patients. *Neuropsychopharmacology* 28(8):1546-52. Epub 2003 Jun 18.

Ozaki, N., Goldman, D., Kaye, W.H., Plotnicov, K., Greenberg, B.D., Lappalainen, J., Rudnick, G., Murphy, D.L. 2003. Serotonin transporter missense mutation associated with a complex neuropsychiatric phenotype. *Mol Psychiatry* 8(11):933-6.

Pezawas, L., Meyer-Lindenberg, A., Drabant, E.M., Verchinski, B.A., Munoz, K.E., Kolachana, B.S., Egan, M.F., Mattay, V.S., Hariri, A.R., Weinberger, D.R. 2005. 5-HTTLPR polymorphism impacts human cingulate-amygdala interactions: A genetic susceptibility mechanism for depression. *Nat Neurosci* 8(6):828-34. Epub 2005 May 8.

Rasmusson, A.M., Hauger, R.L., Morgan, C.A., Bremner, J.D., Charney, D.S, Southwick, S.M. 2000. Low baseline and yohimbine-stimulated plasma neuropeptide Y (NPY) levels in combat-related PTSD. *Biol Psychiatry* 47(6):526-39.

Renthal, W., Maze, I., Krishnan, V., Covington, H.E. 3rd, Xiao, G., Kumar, A., Russo, S.J., Graham, A., Tsankova, N., Kippin, T.E., Kerstetter, K.A., Neve, R.L., Haggarty, S.J., McKinsey, T.A., Bassel-Duby, R., Olson, E.N., Nestler, E.J. 2007. Histone deacetylase 5 epigenetically controls behavioral adaptations to chronic emotional stimuli. *Neuron* 56(3):517-29.

Robin, R.W., Chester, B., Rasmussen, J.K., Jaranson, J.M., Goldman, D. 1997. Prevalence, characteristics, and impact of childhood sexual abuse in a Southwestern American Indian tribe. *Child Abuse Negl* 21(8):769-87.

Sabol, S.Z., Hu, S., Hamer, D. 1998. A functional polymorphism in the monoamine oxidase A gene promoter. *Hum Genet* 103(3):273-9

Sen, S., Burmeister, M., Ghosh, D. 2004. Meta-analysis of the association between a serotonin transporter promoter polymorphism (5-HTTLPR) and anxiety-related personality traits. *Am J Med Genet B Neuropsychiatr Genet* 127B(1):85-9.

Serretti, A., Benedetti, F., Zanardi, R., Smeraldi, E. 2005. The influence of Serotonin Transporter Promoter Polymorphism (SERTPR) and other polymorphisms of the serotonin pathway on the efficacy of antidepressant treatments. *Prog Neuropsychopharmacol Biol Psychiatry* 29(6):1074-84. Review.

Sjöberg, R.L., Ducci, F., Barr, C.S., Newman, T.K., Dell'osso, L., Virkkunen, M., Goldman, D. 2008. A non-additive interaction of a functional MAO-A VNTR and testosterone predicts antisocial behavior. *Neuropsychopharmacology* 33(2):425-30. Epub 2007 Apr 11

Smolka, M.N., Bühler, M., Schumann, G., Klein, S., Hu, X.Z., Moayer, M., Zimmer, A., Wrase, J., Flor, H., Mann, K., Braus, D.F., Goldman, D., Heinz, A. 2007. Gene-gene effects on central processing of aversive stimuli. *Mol Psychiatry* 12(3):307-17. Epub 2007 Jan 9.

Tegeder, I., Costigan, M., Griffin, R.S., Abele, A., Belfer, I., Schmidt, H., Ehnert, C., Nejim, J., Marian, C., Scholz, J., Wu, T., Allchorne, A., Diatchenko, L., Binshtok, A.M., Goldman, D., Adolph, J., Sama, S., Atlas, S.J., Carlezon, W.A., Parsegian, A., Lötsch, J., Fillingim, R.B., Maixner, W., Geisslinger, G., Max, M.B., Woolf, C.J. 2006. GTP cyclohydrolase and tetrahydrobiopterin regulate pain sensitivity and persistence. *Nat Med* 12(11):1269-77. Epub 2006 Oct 22.

Thomasson, H.R., Beard, J.D., Li, T.K. 1995. ADH2 gene polymorphisms are determinants of alcohol pharmacokinetics. *Alcohol Clin Exp Res* 19(6):1494-9.

Walum, H., Westberg, L., Henningsson, S., Neiderhiser, J.M., Reiss, D., Igl, W., Ganiban, J.M., Spotts, E.L., Pedersen, N.L., Eriksson, E., Lichtenstein, P. 2008. Genetic variation in the vasopressin receptor 1a gene (AVPR1A) associates with pair-bonding behavior in humans. *Proc Natl Acad Sci U S A* 105(37):14153-6. Epub 2008 Sep 2.

Weaver, I.C., Cervoni, N., Champagne, F.A., D'Alessio, A.C., Sharma, S., Seckl, J.R., Dymov, S., Szyf, M., Meaney, M.J. 2004. Epigenetic programming by maternal behavior. *Nat Neurosci* 7(8):847-54. Epub 2004 Jun 27.

Wilson, J.M., Young, A.B., Kelley, W.N. 1983. Hypoxanthine-guanine phosphoribosyltransferase deficiency. The molecular basis of the clinical syndromes *N Engl J Med* 309(15):900-10.

Yehuda, R., Brand, S., Yang, R.K. 2006. Plasma neuropeptide Y concentrations in combat exposed veterans: Relationship to trauma exposure, recovery from PTSD, and coping. *Biol Psychiatry* 59(7):660-3. Epub 2005 Dec 1.

Yoshida, A., Huang, I.Y., Ikawa, M. 1984. Molecular abnormality of an inactive aldehyde dehydrogenase variant commonly found in Orientals. *Proc Natl Acad Sci USA* 81(1):258-61.

Zhao, S., Edwards, J., Carroll, J., Wiedholz, L., Millstein, R.A., Jaing, C., Murphy, D.L., Lanthorn, T.H., Holmes, A. 2006. Insertion mutation at the C-terminus of the serotonin transporter disrupts brain serotonin function and emotion-related behaviors in mice. *Neuroscience* 140(1):321-34. Epub 2006 Mar 20.

Zhou, Z., Zhu, G., Hariri, A. R., Enoch, M-A., Scott, D., Sinha, R., Vikkunen, M., Mash, D.C., Lipsky, R.H., Hu, X-Z., Hodgkinson, C.A., Xu, K., Buzas, B., Yuan, Q., Shen, P-H., Ferrell, R.E., Manuck, S.B., Brown, S.M., Hauger, R.L., Stohler, C.S., Zubieta, J-K., Goldman, D. 2008. Genetic variation in human NPY expression affects stress response and emotion, *Nature* 1038 (06858) Epub 2008 Apr 2.

Zubieta, J.K., Heitzeg, M.M., Smith, Y.R., Bueller, J.A., Xu, K., Xu, Y., Koeppe, R.A., Stohler, C.S., Goldman, D. 2003. COMT val158met genotype affects mu-opioid neurotransmitter responses to a pain stressor. *Science* 299(5610):1240-3.

SECTION TWO

Social and Ethical Issues Challenging Genes and Environment Interplays

This section comprises three chapters starting with Françoise Baylis' contribution. She argues that a resilient form of gene-centric perspective, acting as a sophisticated version of genetic determinism, still tends to influence much current research in the field of modern genetics. Thus, according to Baylis, the gap between what we know and what we do with respect to genetic and environmental factors' respective impacts on human behaviour nurtures the sustained geneticization narrative of the contemporary human condition.

This remark is taken on board by Timothy Caulfield. His chapter discusses the reification processes applied to race within current powerful public representations. Endless discussions about whether race is a biological reality or a social construct more often than not open the way, in popular discourse if not public policies, to a race geneticization process.

In the third essay of this section Yvonne Bombard and Michael Hayden make use of the longer history of genetic predictive tests for Huntington Disease to address the relatively understudied issue of genetic discrimination. Diverse social environment settings play here the role of complex relationship matrices through which genetic testing, information, and eventually discrimination are experienced by concerned individuals for whom, surprisingly, family and primary social relationships may also be an important discriminative setting.

Gene-Environment Interaction: The Gulf Between What We Know and What We Do

FRANÇOISE BAYLIS

This chapter critically examines the gulf between what we – scientists and ethicists – know about the limits of genetics and genetic research and the myriad ways in which what we do belies this knowledge. For example, we know that genes acting alone or in concert are not sufficient for development, yet we enthusiastically report on, read about, and sometimes even celebrate discoveries of this or that gene for this or that trait. Taken together, our words and actions contribute to geneticization and genetic essentialism. The challenge before us then is to take development seriously and to expose the ways in which genes must be deeply contextualized. Next, this chapter explores the gulf between what we know about the merits of the dialectical process for knowledge production, and the cavalier manner in which we dismiss (or worse, denigrate) views that are not consonant with our own. Of particular concern is the trend towards crosstalk, caricature, and *ad hominem* at the expense of engaged and respectful discourse about scientific prowess and progress, economic advantage, social justice, and ethical obligations to future generations. The chapter ends with a brief comment on the gulf between the anticipated benefits of transdisciplinary research, and the challenges we face in moving beyond multidisciplinary and interdisciplinary research in our efforts to dissolve disciplinary boundaries and reap the full benefits of genuinely collaborative interactive research among disciplinary and interdisciplinary researchers.

The year is 2000. The date is June 26th. The occasion is the US/UK press conference announcing the working draft of the human genome sequence (Office of the Press Secretary 2000). President Clinton has informed the audience that "[w]e are here to celebrate the completion of the first survey of the entire human genome. Without a doubt, this is the most important, most wondrous map ever produced by humankind." Prime Minister Tony Blair praised the research community for piecing together "a working blueprint of the human race." In a similar vein, Francis Collins, Director of the International Human Genome Project (and Director of the National Human Genome Research Institute of the National Institutes of Health), enjoined us to celebrate "the revelation of the first draft of the human book of life."

The final speaker is Craig Venter, President and chief scientific officer of Celera Genomics, who is widely described as a "maverick molecular biologist," (Olson 2002) and a "biogenetic buccaneer" (Nerlich, Dingwall, and Clarke 2002) for his role in leading the private sector challenge to the publicly funded Human Genome Project. Venter's reductionist metaphor of choice is "the human genetic blueprint." In his remarks, however, Venter acknowledges: "We're clearly much, much more than the sum total of our genes … Our physiology is based on complex and seemingly infinite interactions amongst all our genes and the environment" (Office of the Press Secretary 2000). But a few sentences later, he undermines what might otherwise be interpreted as a pre-emptive strike against genetic reductionism, (Nerlich, Dingwall, and Clarke 2002) by adding, "*[w]hen life is reduced to its very essence*, we find that we have many *genes* in common with every species on Earth, and that we're not so different from one another" (Office of the Press Secretary 2000; emphasis added).

Meanwhile across the Atlantic on the occasion of this same celebration John Sulston, Director of the Wellcome Trust Sanger Institute, announces that, "[o]ver the decades and centuries to come this sequence will inform all of medicine, all of biology, and will lead us to a total understanding of not only human beings but all of life" (Press Office 2000). Michael Dexter, Director of the Wellcome Trust, affirms that "the immediate impact of the project [i.e., the Human Genome Project] is a deeper recognition of what it means to be human … this code is the essence of mankind … Our genes make us what we are as human beings. It's these genes working together that maintain a healthy functioning body. Our genes make us susceptible or resistant to disease; tolerant or intolerant of medicines." (Dexter 2000). With these statements Sulston and Dexter echo the more dramatic, but equally reductionist, claim by James Watson (who along with Francis Crick described the double helix of DNA): "We used to think our fate was in our stars. Now we know, in large measure, our fate is in our genes" (Jaroff 1989).

Now the temptation, for many, will be to set aside Watson's remark as but one of many "unguarded Watsonisms" (McElheny 2003) and to dismiss the various deterministic metaphors and statements by prominent political figures and scientists as excessive (and forgivable) political posturing on a momentous occasion. To do so, however, is to elide the truth that while many readily admit genes are not sufficient for development, and that development is not unaffected by environmental changes, genes are still granted privileged causal status. This privileging, which occurs despite important research on the wildly complex interactions among genes, regions of DNA void of genes, and environmental factors, amounts to a kind of genetic determinism – regardless of the contributions that our physical, social, and cultural environments make to the complexity and mystery that is us, at some level the belief remains that "our genes make us what we are." A similar privileging of genes as causes can be found in the bioethics literature. For example, in his book *Redesigning Humans*, Gregory Stock, biophysicist and Director of the Program on Medicine, Technology and Society at the School of Medicine at UCLA, writes: "The power of our genes to mold us does not stop with our physical attributes and disease susceptibilities. Our genes are the most important single factor in determining great swaths of "normal" personality too ... our genetic makeup strongly influences the defining aspects of personality and temperament ... Remember, however, that heritability is not absolute; it refers only to relative genetic influences within a particular range of environments" (Stock 2002).

And, on the topic of human cloning, Leon Kass, biochemist turned ethicist and past Chair of the US President's Council on Bioethics writes: "Since the birth of Dolly, there has been a fair amount of double-speak on this matter of genetic identity. Experts have rushed in to reassure the public that the clone would in no way be the same person, or have any confusions about his or her identity ... [T]hey are pleased to point out that the clone of Mel Gibson would not be Mel Gibson. Fair enough. But one is shortchanging the truth by emphasizing the additional importance of the intrauterine environment, rearing and social setting: genotype obviously matters plenty. That, after all, is the only reason to clone, whether human beings or sheep. The odds that clones of Wilt Chamberlain will play in the NBA are, I submit, infinitely greater than they are for clones of Robert Reich" (Kass 1997).

To be sure, scientists and ethicists who are knowledgeable about genetics and genetic research disavow genetic determinism, and explicitly recognize the importance of environmental factors. As we have seen, however, they also speak or write about the centrality or primacy of genes in understanding, predicting, and controlling human physical or behavioural traits and variations. Jonathan Kaplan explains this phenomenon in *The Limits and Lies of Human Genetic Research,* wherein he identifies three different strands of genetic determinism (Kaplan 2000). There is the "complete information" strand of genetic determinism according to which genes alone determine organismal development. According to this view, "everything about us (including, on some interpretations, our behaviour) is predictable, or at least in some way determined or dictated by our genes" (Kaplan 2000).

As Kaplan notes, this view is trivially false and, not surprisingly, universally denied. A less outrageous and more common understanding of genetic determinism is that of "intervention as useless." In this view, we are stuck with our biological nature and no amount of (environmental) intervention will ever make a difference to what is dictated by our genes. Kaplan suggests that when scientists and ethicists deny genetic determinism, it is this strand of genetic determinism that they object to, as they do not believe that genetics precludes intervention.

Kaplan then further suggests that among those who deny the second strand of genetic determinism, there are those who remain committed to the view that "traits with partial genetic etiologies are best understood as being *primarily* genetic" (Kaplan 2000). David Lykken, for example, is a psychologist and behavioural geneticist who maintains a gene-centric perspective on behavioural development. He writes, "Were it not for ideological prejudice, any rational person looking at the evidence would agree that human aptitudes, personality traits, many interests and personal idiosyncrasies, even some social attitudes, owe from 30 to 70 per cent of their variation across people to the genetic differences between people." He maintains that "[a] better formula than Nature versus Nurture would be Nature via Nurture ... the genetic influences are strong and most of us develop along a path determined mainly by our personal genetic steersmen." (Lykken 1998)

And, in somewhat more colloquial terms, Thomas Goetz writes, "[s]crape below the skin and we're flesh and bone; scrape below that and we're code" (Goetz 2007). This sort of gene-centrism, rightly identified by Kaplan as another strand of genetic determinism, helps to explain the emerging success of retail genomics – the marketing of personal DNA information. In the fall of 2007, no less than three companies – deCODEgenetics, 23andMe, and Navigenics – announced that for about $1,000 (US) individuals could purchase an analysis of their DNA[1] that could be used to research their ancestry, physical or behavioural traits, and medical conditions.

GENES FOR THIS OR THAT[2] -> GENETICIZATION -> GENETIC ESSENTIALISM

Nearly twenty years ago, as the project to map the human genome began in earnest, George Cahill, then vice president at the Howard Hughes Medical Institute, predicted, "It's going to tell us everything. Evolution, disease, everything will be based on what's in that magnificent tape called DNA"(Cahill quoted in Jaroff 1989). A quick online survey of media reports of genes for this or that physical or behavioural trait confirms the prophetic nature of these remarks:

> Bad-tempered women "can blame it on genes." – Ever wonder why some women seem to be more ill-tempered than others? The answer may partly lie in their genes, according to a study that suggests a blood test could one day be developed to detect feminine belligerence. [University of Pittsburgh researchers] report that anger, hostility and pugnacity may be genetic, rooted in variations in a serotonin receptor gene. (Highfield 2007)

> "Fat" gene found by scientists. – A gene that contributes to obesity has been identified for the first time, promising to explain why some people easily put on weight while others with similar lifestyles stay slim ... The findings provide the first robust link between a common gene and obesity, and could eventually lead

1 Two years later (November 2009), the same product was for sale at half the price ($499 US) through 23andMe.

2 This locution is borrowed from Lisa Gannett, "Human Genome Project," *The Stanford Encyclopedia of Philosophy*.

> to new ways of tackling one of the most significant causes of ill health in the developed world. (Henderson 2007)
>
> Gene for depression discovered. – In a significant break-through, researchers identify P2RX7 as the gene responsible for major depressive disorders and, surprisingly, find it has no link with serotonin. ("Gene for depression" 2006)

Now some will instinctively criticize these media excerpts as misleading headlines and quotations that inappropriately distort scientific findings. This criticism would be somewhat misplaced, however. For example, much of the text from the first news item about women and aggression (which appeared in several media reports) is taken verbatim from the press release issued by the University of Pittsburgh (University of Pittsburgh 2007). As such, the quotation is not a case of some "dumb-ass" reporter or media outlet getting it wrong, except insofar as the report merely adapts material from a press release. The second quotation mentions the assumed background environment of similar lifestyles, and this is entirely consistent with scientific practice. Only the third quote provides a little too much hoopla, and yet it too is consistent with less circumspect comments by scientists and ethicists.[3] Setting aside debate about the quality of science reporting, these media excerpts effectively showcase how contemporary gene discoveries contribute to the phenomena of geneticization and genetic essentialism.

Geneticization is the term coined by Abby Lippman to refer to the "ongoing process by which differences between individuals are reduced to their DNA codes ... [and] interventions employing genetic technologies are adopted to manage problems of health" (Lippman 1991). In explaining the phenomenon of geneticization, Lisa Gannett argues that "[g]enes are singled out as causes not only because they are amenable to technological control but because they are perceived to be more tractable than their non-genetic counterparts and therefore the best means to various ends" (Gannett 1999). According to Gannett, our "increased capacity to manipulate DNA in the laboratory and in the clinic, and not ... an advancement in our theoretical

3 Thanks are owed to Lisa Gannett for drawing this to my attention and for a number of helpful comments on an earlier draft of this chapter.

understanding of 'the way things really are'" explains the phenomenon of geneticization (Gannett 1999).

Consider the public reporting on the discovery of "a gene that contributes to obesity" (Frayling et al. 2007; Henderson 2007). In the news item cited above, reporter Mark Henderson carefully notes that the gene called FTO "will not be the only gene that influences obesity, and inheriting a particular variant will not necessarily make anyone fat" [4] (Henderson 2007). He also quotes the principal investigator, Mark McCarthy, insisting that "[t]his is not a gene for obesity." And yet, geneticization, whereby health problems are reduced to genetic problems for which genetic (technological) solutions must be found, is in evidence. According to McCarthy, "[t]he research involved too many people to control for exercise and diet, so it is not yet known whether FTO affects how much people eat or how active they are." With these remarks, McCarthy privileges the causal role of genes, and thereby provides manifest evidence of the relative importance of genetics and the relative unimportance of environment in explaining obesity. In his view, a gene (or genes) may yet be found that control(s) for eating and exercise. Further to Lippman's point about geneticization, it is worth noting that members of the research team hope that as they increase their understanding of the biological function of the FTO gene, they will be able to develop drug-based therapies to help people control their weight.

A sure benefit of research on the heritability of obesity, weight, and body fat is the calling into question of negative moralizing attitudes towards persons who are overweight as "lazy, undisciplined and self-indulgent" (Kassirer and Angell 1998). On the darker side, however, such research contributes to the geneticization of obesity and weight, and a shift in responsibility from societal conditions to the individual, in the belief that solutions to the "problem of obesity" are easier to find at the genetic level. Indeed, the tendency is to emphasize gene-level interventions (such as genetically tailored

4 About a year later, British researchers reported the discovery of six genes that increase the risk of obesity. Five of these six genes are active in the brain, suggesting that some people may be hardwired to overeat "through genes that control appetite, energy expenditure and other behavioural aspects." (30) Wilker, Cristen, Speliotes, Loos et al. (2009). Six new loci associated with body mass index highlight a neuronal influence on body weight regulation. *Nature Genetics* 41(1), 25-34.

pharmaceuticals, gene transfer, and pre-implantation diagnosis for reproductive decision-making), instead of alternative measures that might involve personal lifestyle changes, as well as changes to environmental factors and socio-economic structures.

In affluent societies such as North America these factors may have to do with changes to the availability of cheap, poor quality food, the pace and nature of work, and the dominant image of ideal body types (especially for women). On this last point about body image, Kaplan astutely notes, "[o]nce obesity is identified as a treatable medical condition it becomes much more difficult to claim that current standards of weight in, say, American culture are unrealistic, and that a substantial portion of what is currently regarded as 'overweight' should be accepted as part of the normal variation in human weights" (Kaplan 2000). Kaplan does not deny the health risks associated with certain forms of obesity, which he lists as hypertension, angina, congestive heart failure, diabetes, osteoarthritis, esophageal reflux, somnolence, and cerebrovascular disease. He merely asserts that there are body types that we currently label as obese because they are outside medicalized standards of ideal weights, and not because they involve increased medical or health risks.

As a counterweight to geneticization (with its focus on the heritability of obesity and the need to identify gene-level treatments), we need to promote increased tolerance for different body types, and to improve education about the potential benefits of modifying eating habits and increasing physical activity. As well, we need to change environmental factors and socio-economic structures that make it difficult to adopt and maintain a healthy lifestyle. In an environment "characterized by an essentially unlimited supply of convenient, relatively inexpensive, highly palatable, energy-dense foods, coupled with a lifestyle requiring only low levels of physical activity for subsistence" education about behaviours that may protect against obesity can only have a limited impact (Hill and Peters 1998).

Next, consider how the discovery of "P2RX7 as the gene responsible for major depressive disorders" contributes to the geneticization of depression (Barden et al. 2006; "Gene for depression" 2006). Though it is widely acknowledged that mood-affective disorders are complex traits involving both genetic and environmental factors, depressed persons are now commonly perceived as individuals who are genetically predisposed to a biochemical brain disorder. In a social context where there is limited public will to deal with problems of mental illness, the individual's temperament is now conveniently identified as the loci of treatment. This process is facilitated by the tractability of genes and the belief that it is easier to change genes (as when genetic expression is modulated through medication or genetic material is incorporated into the genome using gene transfer technology), or to eliminate genes (using preimplantation genetic diagnosis or prenatal selection), than it is to change physical, social, and cultural environments (presuming we even knew what environmental changes were needed).

Geneticized understandings of depression, however, do not adequately account for the socio-economic context of depression. There is, for example, ample evidence that socio-economic status (measured in terms of education, income and social status), poverty (within families or neighbourhoods), the psychosocial work environment, and social networks/social support influence mental health. Indeed, on this last point, we know that instrumental, emotional, and informational supports not only help to mitigate the adverse effects of stressful life events, they also help to prevent the onset of depression (Kawachi and Berkman 2001).

A further problem with the geneticization of mental illness (as with obesity) is that focusing on the individual and not the environment diminishes the patient's ability to name the environment as problematic:

> With this conviction that biochemistry is both the culprit and the place at which to generate cures comes a decreasing sophistication in dealing with other potential sources of the alleviation of the psychological pain associated with mood-affective disorders, as drugs become the first-line treatment and, at least partially because they are the first thing tried, the treatment with the highest success rate. The story that is told surrounding depression, then, becomes one of genes, brain chemistry, and the clever pharmacologists whose drugs can alleviate those biochemical problems the unfortunate person's genotype has left him with ... Once the story of mood-affective disorders as a class of biochemically based diseases resulting from genetic conditions becomes entrenched, and once the pharmaceutical treatments of these so-called diseases become sophisticated and popular enough, no other stories can be told. (Kaplan 2000)

As the examples of obesity and depression clearly show, the identification of genes as the *primary* cause of illness results in a shift away from shared communal responsibility for health and well-being. Individual accountability replaces collective responsibility and attention is deflected away from the social, political, and cultural environments in which individuals act. This shift effectively negates our common vulnerability to illness and disease, and sharpens the focus on our individual genetic heritage (our genetic luck) and the potential benefits of gene-level interventions. Our individual DNA, not our larger socio-economic environment, is "the place at which to generate cures." The problem here is in our failure to take development seriously and to properly contextualize the genetic contribution to behaviour (Robert 2004).

Further, when we celebrate the discovery of a new gene for this or that physical or behavioural trait – even when scientists and reporters take care to (re)describe so-called genetic causes, as genetic tendencies and predispositions in a "typical" environment – we not only contribute to geneticization, we further entrench inchoate beliefs about *genetic essentialism*. *Genetic essentialism* is the term used by Dorothy Nelkin and M. Susan Lindee to describe the role of genes and genetic explanations in popular culture:

> In supermarket tabloids and soap operas, in television sitcoms and talk shows, in women's magazines and parenting advice books, genes appear to explain, obesity, criminality, shyness, directional ability, intelligence, political leanings, and preferred styles of dressing. There are selfish genes, pleasure-seeking genes, violence genes, celebrity genes, gay genes, couch-potato genes, depression genes, genes for genius, genes for saving, and even genes for sinning. These popular images convey a striking picture of the gene as powerful, deterministic, and central to an understanding of both everyday behavior and the "secret of life." (Nelkin and Lindee 1995)

Genetic essentialism, a version of biological determinism, "reduces the self to a molecular entity, equating human beings, in all their complexity, with their genes." (Nelkin and Lindee 1995)

A striking example of this essentialism is the November 17, 2007, front-page story of the *New York Times*, "My Genome, Myself: Seeking Clues in DNA," which celebrates mail-order genome scans, while seeming to ignore the complex interactions between genes and environment that account for most human behaviours and traits (Harmon 2007). Harmon writes about her genes:

> I had refused to drink milk growing up. Now, it turns out my DNA is devoid of the mutation that eases the digestion of milk after infancy, which became common in Europeans after the domestication of cows ... I don't like Brussels sprouts. Who knew it was genetic? But I have the snippet of DNA that gives me the ability to taste a compound that makes many vegetables taste bitter. I differ from people who are blind to bitter taste — who actually like Brussels sprouts — by a single spelling change in our four-letter genetic alphabet: somewhere on human chromosome 7, I have a G where they have a C ... I tragically lack the predisposition to eat fatty foods and not gain weight. But people who, like me, are GG at the SNP known to geneticists as rs3751812 are 6.3 pounds lighter, on average, than the AA's. Thanks, rs3751812! And if an early finding is to be believed, my GG at rs6602024 mean that I am an additional 10 pounds lighter than those whose genetic Boggle served up a different spelling. Good news, except that now I have only my slothful ways to blame for my inability to fit into my old jeans ... And although there is great controversy about the role that genes play in shaping intelligence, it was hard to resist looking up the SNPS that have been linked — however tenuously — to I.Q. Three went in my favor, three against. But I found hope in a study that appeared last week describing a SNP strongly linked with an increase in the I.Q. of breast-fed babies. (Harmon 2007)

As Peter Conrad succinctly notes in summarizing the phenomenon of genetic essentialism, "[g]enetics wears the mantle of scientific objectivity and has the virtue of simplicity in explanation, so it often is taken as *the* cause, submerging the interactive or even primary effects of social environment" (Conrad 1996; emphasis in original). In part, this explains popular public perceptions of how genes work: "*So now they know the cause of that!*" or, "*How terrible that people with the gene are doomed to be like that!*" (Kitcher 1996). Contributing to these misperceptions are media reports announcing new direct-to-consumer genetic tests that will answer questions such as: "What are the chances that you will get heart disease, or

Alzheimer's? Or that you'll get fat?" (Winslow 2007). Clearly the underlying belief is that "we are our genes, our genes are us." Or, to quote Harmon: "My genome, myself."

A MULTI-TRILLION-DOLLAR INDUSTRY

To this point in the chapter, we have seen how the disconnect between what we know and what we do with respect to gene-environment interaction contributes to geneticization and genetic essentialism, and makes individuals rather than societies in general the target of interventions. To summarize, we know that all human traits involve both genetic and environmental contributions. On this basis, we confidently deny genetic determinism narrowly defined as the belief that genes alone explain our development. For pragmatic reasons, however, we practise an alternate form of genetic determinism in which we privilege genes as *primary* causes of human traits. We do so not because we know this causal story to be true, but because it is useful and simple – genes "are amenable to technological control [and] … are perceived to be more tractable than their non-genetic counterparts" (Gannett 1999); moreover, genetics wears "the mantle of scientific objectivity and has the virtue of simplicity in explanation" (Conrad 1996). But there is more to this causal story, considerably more – this story is not just useful and simple, it is also potentially very profitable. Indeed, the socio-economic context (and in particular the patentability of genes and the marketability of gene products) contributes to the singling out of genes as causes: "The practical context for the "molecularization" and geneticization of disease extends far beyond making individual patients better and furthering disciplinarian professional interests. It incorporates the wider social and economic interests of molecular geneticists, other investors in the biotechnology industry, university and private patent-holders, and government" (Gannett 1999).

Governments, persuaded that the life sciences are the engine of the new knowledge economy (and, as such, will contribute to growth, productivity, job creation and international competitiveness), actively support the biotechnology industry through various mechanisms, including research funding (Kalil 2006; Masood 1998) Biotechnology and pharmaceutical companies in search of profit invest heavily in genetic, genomic, and proteomic projects ranging from toolmaking to drug discovery (Malakoff and Service 2001; Office of Science 2005). Research-intensive universities and teaching hospitals, in partnership with industry, contribute to the commercialization of bioscience research under the banner of knowledge transfer (Bok 2003; Krimsky 2003). And, finally, academic researchers in their new role as entrepreneurs (and often in collaboration with industry) focus more narrowly on applied areas of research, patent their findings, market their discoveries, and launch start-up companies (Frankel and Garfinkel 2003; Williams-Jones 2005).

This thorough commercialization of research raises a number of ethical concerns about the many ways in which economic interests potentially threaten the scientific and social goals of publicly funded research (Downie and Herder 2007; Lewis et al. 2001). There is, for example, significant concern about the free flow of ideas: "When researchers are encouraged to place economic value on their discoveries and patent them to facilitate innovation, other researchers become less able to access this knowledge or build upon it (despite patent rules that require "disclosure"). The most blatant examples include patents on DNA, genes, and other biological materials, which block downstream research by radically increasing the transaction costs and making some areas of research not worth investigating" (Williams-Jones 2005).

Additional potential threats to knowledge production include non-disclosure agreements with industry partners, as well as agreements to delay publication until patents have been filed. The underlying issue here is one of conflict of interest where the pursuit of profit threatens the intellectual integrity and scientific independence of academic researchers and publicly funded research institutions.

A related concern is control of the research agenda. In the past twenty to thirty years university-industry partnerships have increased exponentially, resulting in significant changes with respect to who controls decision-making about where to invest intellectual and financial resources. As academic researchers and their institutions, in pursuit of commercial advantage, cede control of the research agenda to industry, various social priorities are put at risk. Among these social priorities are values at the heart of the academic mission, including the search for knowledge and pursuit of the public interest. Indeed, as Derek Bok poignantly noted some years ago with reference to academic institutions traditionally dedicated to the pursuit of knowledge for its own sake, "commercialization threatens to change the character of the university in ways that limit its freedom, sap its effectiveness, and lower its standing in society" (Bok 2003).

Concern about agenda setting applies at several levels. There is concern about the increased emphasis on genetic rather than non-genetic causes of human physical and behavioural traits. Within genetic research, there is concern about the shift away from fundamental research to applied research that is more easily commercialized (but perhaps scientifically less important). Within applied genetic research there is concern about the shift away from rare debilitating single gene disorders for which there is no lucrative market, to research on more common conditions with a higher probability of significant return on investment. At all levels the key issue is: Who decides which questions are worthy of research (and research funding) and on what basis?

In recent years, peer review criteria for publicly funded research have expanded beyond scientific excellence to include management skills and experience, networking, interdisciplinarity, training for graduate students, marketability, and co-funding (from governments, private foundations, and industry). This last criterion is particularly controversial, especially with respect to co-funding requirements stipulated by Genome Canada, as noted in a letter to *Science* by some of Canada's preeminent scientists in the life sciences: "By eschewing scientific excellence as the primary consideration, co-funded programs imperil scientific credibility and fail to engage the breadth and depth of national scientific expertise. We encourage governments, scientific administrators, and scientists in Canada and other countries not to succumb to the superficial allure of co-funding but rather to evaluate and fully fund research on its own merits" (Tyers et al. 2005).

In support of this view, Jason Scott Robert and I argued that science should not take a backseat to economics; but ours was not a clarion call from the days of old when scientific merit was the sole funding criterion. Rather, we insisted that government funding agencies should not "privilege economic impact over and above other social values of relevance to Canadians" (Robert and Baylis 2005). In brief, we insisted that "when it comes to funding research, value should count." In turn, John Polanyi also argued against co-funding by industry, but he insisted that "we undermine science if we over manage research … [e]xcellence [in science] is a rare and precious resource, wasted if redefined as relevance … What is excellent, by contrast, is a revelation" (Polanyi 2005).

In disagreeing with us, Polanyi discounts the view that while validity and value are both elements of scientific worth, the concept of value has purchase beyond the realm of science. In effect, he rejects the idea that addressing "a priority problem might in itself enhance [a study's] value, *ceteris paribus*" (Freedman 1987). Further, in insisting on the difference between "excellence as revelation" and "excellence as relevance," Polanyi implicitly appeals to the distinction between basic and applied research thereby focusing on science as the engine that propels technology, when the heart of the matter is science as the engine that propels the economy.

The difference in perspective between Polanyi, Nobel laureate in chemistry and champion of basic science, and philosophers trained in ethics who worry deeply about who controls the research agenda (whether industry partners or the scientific elite), provides a nice transition to the second part of the chapter, which looks at the gulf between what we know about the merits of the dialectical process for knowledge production, and the cavalier manner in which we dismiss (or worse, denigrate) views that are not consonant with our own. The perspective here is that of a philosopher; no doubt a scientist would tell a different tale.

CROSSTALK, CARICATURE, AND AD HOMINEM

Research in the sciences, the social sciences, and the humanities typically relies on different theories and uses different methods. In some instances, this is where misunderstanding or disagreement between disciplinary researchers begins. Consider, for example, the following private comment from a senior researcher with the UK Genomics Network, "social scientists still have difficulty speaking a language that scientists can relate to. 'There's still a huge credibility gap ... Their methodologies don't align well'" (Macilwain 2009).

In other instances, problems between professionals have more to do with the goals of research and the research findings. Nik Brown, a UK sociologist, worries that scientists have false expectations of social scientists: "'There's a misperception that our main role is to ease the interaction between scientists and the public ... What we want to do is understand the science, and how it is constructed – which is not a public-understanding-of-science question'" (Macilwain 2009). Indeed, it is widely perceived that the role of ELSI (ethical, legal, and social issues) researchers is primarily to ease the ethics/regulatory/policy pathways:[5] "Scientists don't especially want to know whether their work produces an ethical dilemma... Questions about societies' concerns don't always weigh heavily on their minds" (Macilwain 2009). Meanwhile, there are scientists who lament the lack of critical engagement between philosophers and scientists. For example, evolutionary biologist Ford Doolittle recognizes that "biologist don't think very much about philosophy. We impose patterns on nature for philosophical reasons and then deny that philosophy is important. Philosophers care about the structure of arguments and it is a very good exercise for scientists to start looking at this too." (Macilwain 2009)

That scholars and thinkers should disagree on important matters, or on what matters are important, is not in itself problematic. The use of crosstalk (undesired ancillary conversation), caricature (distorted representation), and *ad hominem* argument (personal attack) in effort to privilege certain disciplinary perspectives is. The dialectical process of knowledge production depends on respectful discourse.

In 1985 Susan Oyama, philosopher of biology, published *The Ontogeny of Information* – a critique of gene-centrism and an introduction to developmental systems theory – a collection of theoretical concepts and perspectives that insists on the reciprocal nature of gene environment exchanges in development and evolution. With developmental systems theory, the unit of inheritance is more than DNA. In addition to genes, organisms inherit other information from the cell, protoplasm, organelles, and the environment. Some fifteen

5 The Canadian Stem Cell Network (SCN) (a cluster of nationally funded stem cell researchers) has a Strategic Program on Public Policy and Ethical, Legal, and Social Issues that focuses "on projects that are of interest to policymakers and to an ELSI core facility." Priority is given to projects "where the Network can have the most impact in easing the ethics/regulatory/policy pathways." The quoted text was on the SCN website until recently. The text was removed following a critique of this statement in: Baylis, F. and M. Herder (2009) 'Policy Design for Human Embryo Research in Canada: An Analysis (Part 2 of 2) Bioethical Inquiry 6:351–65. The text cited can be retrieved through www.archive.org by: (i) inserting http://www.stemcellnetwork.ca/ (ii) selecting the date 26 May 2008 and (iii) following the 'Research' link.

years later, in *Evolution's Eye*, Oyama elaborates on her earlier work; she also reports that a common (somewhat ironic) response to developmental systems theory is "That's completely crazy, and besides, I already knew it" (Oyama 2000).

From one perspective, this type of response should come as no surprise given general skepticism on the part of some (many) about the value of philosophy (of science). According to Nobel physicist Steven Weinberg, for example, philosophy of science is "at best ... a pleasing gloss on the history and discoveries of science. But we should not expect it to provide today's scientists with any useful guidance about how to go about their work or about what they are likely to find" (Weinberg quoted in Pigliucci 2004). This perspective, however, significantly misunderstands philosophy of science, which neither aspires to offer career advice for scientists (telling them how to do their work), nor to engage in fortune-telling by predicting what scientists are likely (or not) to discover. Philosophers of science are interested in how science works (or doesn't), how research questions are framed (and addressed), which perspectives are privileged (and why), and so on.

In important respects, applied ethics (which is interested in similar questions albeit from a different perspective) is no more immune from misunderstanding and criticism than philosophy of science. In particular, scathing critiques of bioethics and bioethicists abound.

In the category of crosstalk, Jason Scott Robert explains how respectful discussions about the ethics of controversial science can effectively be displaced by divisive "us versus them" debates. In some instances, these debates focus on bioethicists who, all too enthusiastically and uncritically, embrace the sciences to the point of "proselytizing rather than critically probing, in pursuit of victory at the expense of truth" (Robert 2009). In other instances, these debates focus on bioethicists who stand in the way of scientific progress. And, ironically, sometimes these discrete debates overlap. As Robert astutely notes, "[D]espite the evangelism of some bioethicists, scientists are typically quick to judge bioethicists as impediments to scientific progress. Scientists often see bioethicists as ... moral police, on patrol to curb the bad behavior of scientists, or as moral firefighters, called in to quell the flames of moral dispute" (Robert 2009). From a still more negative perspective, there are those who see bioethicists as no more than gadflies intent on annoying clinicians and scientists.

In the category of caricature, Leigh Turner explains how it is commonplace in social science critiques of bioethics "to characterize bioethicists as servants of established social and economic authorities. Handmaidens, servants, balm, show dogs, institutional graphite – these evocative terms capture the notion of the bioethicist as servant, parasite, shill, and sellout" (Turner 2009). In commenting further on the critiques of bioethicists as self-serving "false prophets, corporate tools, and accomplices to biomedicine," Turner notes how castigating bioethicists typically serves the dual purpose of uplifting social scientists, in particular medical anthropologists and medical sociologists: "Though bioethicists are cast as witting or unwitting dupes of established social authorities, social scientists are invested with a special purchase on moral authority and social insight. While bioethicists nestle comfortably inside the belly of the whale of medicine, social scientists perch uneasily "on the margins" maintaining their critical lenses sparkling, apparently uninfluenced by power, money, and the prospect of influence" (Turner 2009). Lastly, in the category of *ad hominem* argument, Daniel Callahan explains that whereas, "in the late 1960s and early 1970s, it was considered perfectly acceptable for liberals to be skeptical of science and willing to oppose research directions that might be hazardous ... [at present] everyone now seems expected to get on board the medical progress express. Critics are berated as Luddites at least and at the worst as threats to the glorious future of research (not to mention as a danger to the beleaguered, oh-so-defenseless multibillion dollar research industry)" (Callahan 2005).

From a similar perspective, Edmund Pellegrino insists that arguments should be judged on their own merits and not mired in polemics: "We must deal with the argument, whatever its source, not reject it because of its source. One thinks here of disposing of an argument by labelling it as "conservative" or "liberal," "religious" or "secular," "red" or "blue," "progressivist" or "retrogressive" (Pellegrino 2006).

Sadly, with the increasingly vociferous debates on the ethics of genetics, genomics, and stem cell research, there has been a marked increased in the use of crosstalk, caricature, and *ad hominem* attacks to discredit the motives and arguments of bioethicists, at the expense of engaged and respectful discourse about scientific prowess and progress, economic advantage, social justice, and ethical obligations to future generations. A personal anecdote serves to illustrate the point.

From 2001 to 2005 I was a principal investigator with the Canadian Stem Cell Network. I resigned quietly in 2005 because of certain Network activities, including "the apparent unwillingness to engage in thoughtful, open-ended debate about the ethics and politics of stem cell research" (Robert 2008). About a year later, in December 2006, I was appointed to the inaugural Board of Directors of Assisted Human Reproduction Canada (whose mandate includes the oversight of genetic testing and screening, as well as embryo research). My appointment to the Board was publicly criticized by Michael Rudnicki, the scientific director of the Stem Cell Network, in articles published in the *Globe and Mail* (Abraham 2006) and the *Canadian Medical Association Journal (CMAJ)* (Eggerston 2007). In the *Globe and Mail* article the following quote is attributed to Rudnicki: "She [Françoise Baylis] has some extreme views that I would say are outside of the mainstream. She is very suspicious of the motivations of scientists" (Rudnicki quoted in Abraham 2006). And, in the *CMAJ* article, Rudnicki attempts to marginalize my work by questioning my expertise (and that of three other Board members, all of us having been identified as "social conservatives"). According to Rudnicki, "It was supposed to be an expert [board] and these are not experts. These are people who have agendas and opinions" (Rudnicki quoted in Eggerston 2007).

To say the least, I was surprised by these criticisms for at least two reasons. First, the last time I had spoken with Rudnicki, in the Fall of 2005, he had assured me that I was making important contributions to the Stem Cell Network, and he asked me to reconsider my planned resignation. Why now the palpable contradiction? Second, I could not fathom what in my work would justify the allegations of "social conservatism" and "extreme views outside the mainstream"? Human pluripotent stem cell research is both scientifically complex and ethically contentious. On the one hand, there is the promise of cures and increased understanding of human development. On the other hand, there is the destruction of human embryos, the potential coercion and exploitation of women, the commodification of reproductive tissues, and the creation of part-human chimeras and hybrids. For my part, I have always acknowledged the promise of human pluripotent stem cell research (Baylis 2002a, 2002b). This endorsement, however, has not led me to support unfettered research. For example, I don't agree with cloning-based human embryonic stem cell research in pursuit of personalized medicine. I consider this an unrealistic objective that potentially threatens the Canadian government-funded health care system and that comes with significant opportunity costs in relation to foregone research (Baylis 2005; Baylis and Downie 2005; Giacomini, Baylis, and Robert 2007).

I also worry about the potential coercion and exploitation of women who are solicited to provide eggs for cloning-based stem cell research, just as I worry about the commodification of reproductive labour and tissues as stem cell researchers seek to redress the chronic shortage of eggs for research by offering to pay women (handsomely) for their eggs (Baylis and McInnes 2007; McLeod and Baylis 2007; and Baylis and McLeod 2007). It doesn't follow from any of this that I am a "social conservative," that my views are "outside the mainstream," or that I am "very suspicious of the motivations of scientists."

This brings us to the last part of the chapter on the gulf between the anticipated benefits of transdisciplinary research and the academic silos in which we continue to work while periodically engaging in multidisciplinary and interdisciplinary research.

INTERDISCIPLINARITY IN RESEARCH

Interdisciplinarity can be (and often is) used interchangeably with *multidisciplinarity* and *transdisciplinarity*. Others insist, however, that there are important conceptual differences: Multidisciplinarity occurs when scholars from two or more disciplines work together without integration; interdisciplinarity is when scholars from multiple disciplines work across those disciplines on a common problem to create and apply new knowledge; and transdisciplinarity is when scholars transcend disciplinary boundaries and develop a new process of collaboration opening up new possibilities for knowledge production (Rosenfield 1992).

The potential value of transdisciplinary research involving the health and social sciences was first identified in the early 1990s as the limits of multidisciplinary and interdisciplinary research were becoming apparent. These research methods were found to be "very useful for short-term problem solving, less so for longer-term programmatic changes, especially beyond the health sector, and even more limited in impact on theory building for coping with the changing human condition" (Rosenfield 1992). Failure to transcend disciplinary boundaries was identified as a key problem, and from this emerged a call for transdisciplinary research that would remove disciplinary impasses, transcend cognitive boundaries, develop new methods, and provide new theoretical frameworks.

Unfortunately, more than fifteen years later, very little progress has been made towards this laudable goal despite considerable enthusiasm and apparent good will. Consider the following statement from the Canadian Institutes of Health Research:

> The current revolution in health research is being driven by the convergence of a wide array of disciplines and approaches. For example, new fields and new technologies, such as gene chips, population health, bioinformatics and health informatics, genetic epidemiology, bioethics, health economics, medical anthropology, nanotechnology, and medical imaging are the results of the convergence of two or more disciplines. *To increase our lead in this revolution*, Canada must act on two fronts. First, we need to make it easy to assemble teams of diverse and highly skilled researchers that can learn from each other and overcome cultural differences between disciplines and geographic distances to address complex scientific and technological challenges. Second, we need to develop ways to train a new generation of researchers who will be comfortable moving across disciplines. (Canadian Institutes of Health Research 2001, emphasis added)

Arguably, this excerpt indicates a keen interest in multi- and interdisciplinary research. It also makes transparent, however, one of the most likely reasons for the apparent failure of these research methodologies to makes serious inroads in health research – namely, that enthusiasm for these methodologies is often motivated by their perceived instrumental, rather than intrinsic, value (viz., CIHR's valuing of multi- and interdisciplinary research as a means to the end of increasing Canada's lead in the current revolution in health research). This is not only counterproductive relative to the eventual goal of fostering meaningful transdisciplinary research, it is also unlikely to promote the goal of sound ethics research.

More recently, and with specific reference to the need for transdisciplinary research in the study of gene-environment interactions, the Institute of Medicine of the National Academies (IOM) recommends a shift from interdisciplinary research (which it describes as research on questions of mutual concern to different disciplinary researchers), and multidisciplinary research (which it describes as research on questions of both mutual and separate concern to disciplinary researchers), to transdisciplinary research where the research questions transcend the individual disciplines. Quoting from an earlier IOM Report, *Who will keep the public healthy?* (2003), in the IOM Report on *Genes, behavior, and the social environment*, transdisciplinary research is described with reference to the "conception of research questions that transcend the individual departments or specialized knowledge bases because they are intended to solve research questions that are, by definition, beyond the purview of the individual disciplines" (Institute of Medicine 2006). In support of this recommendation, the IOM further recommends expanding and enhancing training for transdisciplinary researchers as well as creating incentives to foster transdisciplinary research (Institute of Medicine 2006). In this way it hopes to address the current lack of adequate research infrastructure including time, space, personnel, start-up costs, and qualified peer review (both for grants and career progression) (Giacomini 2004).

These proposed initiatives are undeniably positive steps in the right direction. In my view, however, they are not up to the task of transforming the research culture. If we are to move from an additive to an interactive research model where we step outside our intellectual comfort zones, reach beyond our disciplinary boundaries, and begin to frame complex problems in novel and creative ways, then we need a sustainable research culture of respectful collaboration, one steeped in mutual esteem and trust. Without this there truly is no hope of developing research alliances where disciplinary commitments can be set aside, and the overarching unity of knowledge can be fully embraced.

To further explain this point, knowledge production perforce involves testing out (sometimes radically) new ideas, concepts, methods, theories, etc. This process raises the possibility of error as well as the possibility of undue deference. In turn, these two possibilities bring into sharp relief the critical importance of mutual esteem and trust among research colleagues committed to the transformative ideal of transdisciplinary research as a means to knowledge production. When testing out new ideas, for example, errors, missteps, and misunderstandings by an esteemed and trusted colleague (a peer, and possibly even a friend) can become sources of insight. The same contribution from someone who is *perceived* to be a competitor, a dilettante or, worse, an idiot, can only result in frustration (and perhaps even ridicule) as a result of which opportunities for insight are lost.

At the other extreme, without mutual esteem and trust we are unlikely to avoid the problem of undue deference. If those in the "soft" sciences allow themselves to be "co-opted" or "captured" by others in the "hard" sciences (on whom they depend for professional respect) they cannot meaningfully contribute to the process of knowledge production. A critical stance towards science and medicine is needed in order that false beliefs may be identified as such and not shielded from critical scrutiny. In the area of ethics, the problem of capture by scientists, medical professionals, and biotechnology entrepreneurs is manifest in the move away from the normative question, "Is *x* ethically acceptable?" or "Is *x* right or wrong, good or bad?" to the procedural, public policy-type question, "How can we do *x* in an ethically acceptable way?" With this more practical question, the pursuit of *x* as right and good is given – not open to critical question. There is no room for sustained discourse, discussion, or reflection about what ought to be done, only about how best to do it. As Pellegrino rightly remarks, however, "No system of ethics can survive without some 'stop' signs" (Pellegrino 2000, 669).

The promise of transdisciplinary research is considerable. I am not persuaded, however, that this promise can be realized without further attention to the challenges of respectful collaboration across disparate disciplines. To be sure, we have had important successes with multidisciplinary and interdisciplinary research to date. Indeed, there are excellent examples of such research on gene-environment interactions in this volume. However, we are still a long way away from genuinely collaborative transdisciplinary research as an established and valued research methodology. Indeed, we are still learning the contours of each other's areas of disciplinary expertise, and we still face considerable challenges in understanding each other's disciplinary cultures – language, mannerisms, methods, goals, knowledge, and values (Giacomini 2004). Until we better understand and value the differences in research cultures, we cannot hope to develop mutual esteem and trust. Without this, we cannot build the genuinely collaborative research alliances that we need to succeed at transdisciplinary research.

CONCLUSION

In closing, I want to briefly summarize the chapter in reverse order. I believe that we cannot realize the promise of genuinely collaborative transdisciplinary research unless we value this research for its own sake, and do a better job of identifying and addressing the intellectual, interpersonal, and institutional demands of transdisciplinary research. The biggest challenge here will be in creating a sustainable, respectful research culture steeped in mutual esteem and trust (including self-trust) where scholars from all disciplines can effectively contribute to knowledge production. Creating and maintaining such a culture will not be possible if disciplinary and interdisciplinary scholars cannot engage in respectful, well-informed discourse.

Unfortunately, when there is disagreement we often talk past each other, ridicule views that are not consonant with our own, and resort to personal attacks instead of addressing the substance of the argument. This is ultimately unhelpful. Instead, time and care should be taken to listen attentively and with humility and, as appropriate, to dialogue and even debate. Were we able to do so in an open and inviting manner, we might actually succeed in bridging the gulf between what we know and what we do in relation to gene-environment interaction. A first step in this direction would involve taking development seriously (Robert 2004), and challenging the geneticization and genetic essentialism that threatens important (deeply cherished) social values.

Taking development seriously does not mean assigning causal primacy to the environment instead of genes. Rather, it means embracing the notion that "genes must be deeply contextualized" (Robert, Hall and Olson 2001; Robert 2003). Following Oyama, "If development is to re-enter evolutionary theory, it should be development that integrates genes into organisms, and organisms into the many levels of the environment that enter into their ontogenetic construction" (Oyama 2000, 113). Only in taking development seriously might we, once and for all, set aside the nature-nurture debate about the relative contributions of each and begin to fully appreciate how genes and environments are interdependent, co-determining causal factors. This, without a doubt, would be a great project for transdisciplinary research.

BIBLIOGRAPHY

Abraham, C. 2006. Critics troubled by new fertility panel: Social conservatives on oversight board for stem-cell research, reproduction laws. *Globe and Mail*, 23 December, A1.

Assisted Human Reproduction Canada. 2006. Mission and mandate. http://www.hc-sc.gc.ca/hl-vs/reprod/agenc/mission/index_e.html

Barden, N., Harvey, M., Gagné, B., Shink, E., Tremblay, M., Raymond, C., Labbé, M., Villeneuve, A., Rochette, R., Bordeleau, L., Stadler, H., Holsboer, F., Müller-Myhsok, B. 2006. Analysis of single nucleotide polymorphisms in genes in the chromosome 12Q24.31 region points to P2RX7 as a susceptibility gene to bipolar affective disorder. *American Journal of Medical Genetics. Part B, Neuropsychiatric Genetics* 141B:374-82.

Baylis, F. 2005. The impossible dream. *University Affairs*, August-September, 14-16. http://www.universityaffairs.ca/issues/2005/augsept/impossible_dream_01.html.

– 2002a. Our ethics are embryonic. *Globe and Mail*, 2 March, A17.

– 2002b. Parliament's call for moratorium on stem cell research perplexing. *The Hill Times*, 6 May, 30.

Baylis, F., McInnes, C. 2007. Women at risk: Embryonic and fetal stem cell research in Canada. *McGill Health Law Publication* 1:53-67.

Baylis, F., McLeod, C. 2007. The stem cell debate continues: The buying and selling of eggs for research, *Journal of Medical Ethics* 33:726-31.

Baylis, F., Downie, J. 2005. An embryonic debate. *Literary Review of Canada* 13 (2):11-13.

Bok, D. 2003. *Universities in the Marketplace*. Princeton: Princeton University Press.

Callahan, D. 2005. Bioethics and the culture wars. *Cambridge Quarterly of Healthcare Ethics* 14:424-31.

Canadian Institutes of Health Research. 2001. Revolution: CIHR: Towards a national health research agenda. Ottawa: Canadian Institutes of Health Research. http://www.irsc.gc.ca/e/26539.html.

Conrad, P. 1996. Review of *The DNA mystique: The gene as a cultural icon,* by Dorothy Nelkin and M. Susan Lindee. *Contemporary Sociology* 25 (1):124-5.

Dexter, M. 2000. Comment by Dr Michael Dexter, director, The Wellcome Trust. 26 June. http://www.wellcome.ac.uk/doc_wtd002950.html.

Downie, J., Herder, M. 2007. Reflections on the commercialization of research conducted in public institutions in Canada. *McGill Health Law Publication* 1:23-44.

Eggerston, L. 2007 New reproductive technology board belies expert selection process. *Canadian Medical Association Journal* 176(5): 611-12.

Frankel, M.S., Garfinkel, M.S. 2003. "To market, to market": Effects of commerce on cross-generational genetic change. In *Designing our descendants: The promises and perils of genetic modifications*, ed. by Audrey R. Chapman and Mark S. Frankel, 311-25. Baltimore: John Hopkins University Press.

Frayling, T.N., Timpson, N.J., Weedon, M.N., Zeggini, E., et al. 2007. A common variant in the FTO gene is associated with body mass index and predisposes to childhood and adult obesity. *Science* 316 (5826):889-94.

Freedman, B. 1987. Scientific value and validity as ethical requirements for research: A proposed explication. *IRB* 9 (6):7-10.

Gannett, L. Forthcoming 2007. Human genome project. *The Stanford Encyclopedia of Philosophy*. http://plato.stanford.edu/.

– 1999. "What's in a cause? The pragmatic dimensions of genetic explanations," *Biology and Philosophy* 14:349-74.

Gene for depression. 2006. *Scientist Live*, May. http://www.scientistlive.com/15895/gene-for-depression-discovered.thtml.

Giacomini, M. 2004. Interdisciplinarity in health services research: Dreams and nightmares, maladies and remedies. *Journal of Health Services Research and Policy* 9 (3):177-83.

Giacomini, M., Baylis, F., Robert, J.S. 2007. Banking on it: Public policy and the ethics of stem cell research and development. *Social Science and Medicine* 65:1490-1500.

Goetz, T. 2007. 23AndMe Will Decode Your DNA for $1,000. Welcome to the Age of Genomics. *Wired Magazine* 15 (12) http://www.wired.com/medtech/genetics/magazine/15-12/ff_genomics

Harmon, A. 2007. My genome, myself: Seeking clues in DNA. *The New York Times*, 17 November, 1.

Henderson, M. 2007. "Fat" gene found by scientists. *Times Online*, 13 April. http://www.timesonline.co.uk/tol/news/uk/health/article1647517.ece.

Highfield, R. 2007. Bad-tempered women "can blame it on genes." *Telegraph*, 10 March. http://www.telegraph.co.uk/news/main.jhtml?xml=/news/2007/03/09/nwomen09.xml.

Hill, J.O., Peters, J.C. 1998. Environmental contributions to the obesity epidemic. *Science* 280 (5368):1371-4.

Institute of Medicine, Committee on assessing interactions among social, behavioral, and genetic factors in health. 2006. *Genes, behavior, and the social environment: Moving beyond the nature/nurture debate*. Ed. Lyla M. Hernandez and Dan G. Blazer. Washington, DC: National Academies Press. http://www.nap.edu/catalog/11693.html.

International Society for Stem Cell Research. 2006. *Guidelines for the conduct of human embryonic stem cell research*. Version I: 21 December 2006. http://www.isscr.org/guidelines/index.htm.

Jaroff, L. 1989. The gene hunt. *Time,* 20 March. http://www.time.com/time/magazine/article/0,9171,957263-1,00.html.

Kalil, T. 2006. Planning for US science policy in 2009. *Nature* 443:751-2.

Kaplan, J.M. 2000. *The limits and lies of human genetic research: Dangers for social policy.* New York: Routledge.

Kass, L.R. 1997. The wisdom of repugnance: Why we should ban the cloning of human beings. *The New Republic* 216 (22):17-26.

Kassirer, J.P., Angell, M. 1998. Losing weight – an ill-fated New Year's resolution. *The New England Journal of Medicine* 338 (1):52-6.

Kawachi, I., Berkman, L.F. 2001. Social ties and mental health. *Journal of Urban Health* 78 (3):458-67.

Kitcher, P. 1996. *The Lives to Come: The Genetic Revolution and Human Possibilities*. New York: Touchstone.

Krimsky, S. 2003. *Science in the Private Interest*. Lanham: Rowman and Littlefield.

Lewis, S., Baird, P., Evans, R., Ghali, W., Wright, C., Gibson, E., Baylis, F. 2001. Dancing with the porcupine: Rules for governing the university-industry relationship. *Canadian Medical Association Journal* 165:783-5.

Lippman, A. 1991. Prenatal genetic testing and screening: Constructing needs and reinforcing inequities. *American Journal of Law and Medicine* 17 (1-2):15-50.

Lykken, D.T. 1998. How can educated people continue to be radical environmentalists? *The Third Culture*, 20 June. http://www.edge.org/3rd_culture/lykken/index.html.

Macilwain, C. 2009. Watching science at work. Nature 462: 840-2.

Malakoff, D., Service, R.F. 2001. Genomania meets the bottom line. *Science* 291 (5507):1193-1203.

Masood, E. 1998. Britain embraces knowledge economy. *Nature* 396:714-15.

McElheny, V.K. 2003. *Watson and DNA: Making a Scientific Revolution.* Cambridge: Perseus Publication.

McLeod, C., Baylis, F. 2007. Donating fresh versus frozen embryos to stem cell research: In whose interests? *Bioethics* 21:465-77.

Nelkin, D., Lindee, M.S. 1995. *The DNA Mystique: The Gene as a Cultural Icon.* New York: W. H. Freeman.

Nerlich, B., Dingwall, R., Clarke, D. 2002. The book of life: How the completion of the Human Genome Project was revealed to the public. *Health: An Interdisciplinary Journal for the Social Study of Health, Illness and Medicine* 6 (4):445-69.

Office of Science, US Department of Energy Office of Science. 2005. The Human Genome Project and the private sector: A working partnership.

http://www.ornl.gov/sci/techresources/Human_Genome/project/private-sector.shtml.

Office of the Press Secretary, The White House. 2000. Remarks made by the President [Bill Clinton], Prime Minister Tony Blair of England (via satellite), Dr. Francis Collins, Director of the National Human Genome Research Institute, and Dr. Craig Venter, President and Chief Scientific Officer, Celera Genomics Corporation, on the Completion of the First Survey of the Entire Human Genome Project. National Human Genome Research Institute, 26 June. http://www.genome.gov/10001356 .

Olson, M.V. 2002. The Human Genome Project: A player's perspective. *Journal of Molecular Biology* 319:931-42.

Oyama, S. 2000. *Evolution's Eye: A Systems View of the Biology-Culture Divide*. Durham: Duke University Press.

– 1985. *The Ontogeny of Information: Developmental Systems and Evolution.* Cambridge: Cambridge University Press.

Pellegrino, E. 2006. Bioethics and politics: "Doing ethics" in the public square. *Journal of Medicine and Philosophy* 31 (6):569-84.

– 2000. Bioethics at century's turn: Can normative ethics be retrieved? *Journal of Medicine and Philosophy* 25 (6):655-75.

Pigliucci, M. 2004. [Book Review] Embryology, epigenesis, and evolution: Taking development seriously. By Jason Scott Robert. Cambridge and New York: Cambridge University Press. *The Quarterly Review of Biology.* 79 (4):423-5.

Polanyi, J. 2005. We undermine science if we overmanage research. *Globe and Mail,* 7 July, A15.

Press Office, The Wellcome Trust. 2000. The first draft of the *Book of Humankind* has been read. 26 June. http://www.sanger.ac.uk/HGP/draft2000/mainrelease.shtml.

Robert, J.S. 2003. Developmental systems and animal behaviour. *Biology and Philosophy* 18:477-89.

– 2004. *Embryology, epigenesis, and evolution: Taking development seriously.* Cambridge and New York: Cambridge University Press.

– 2008. Nanoscience, nanoscientists, and controversy. In F. Allhoff and P. Lin (Eds), *Nanotechnology and society: Current and emerging ethical issues* (225-39). New York: Springer.

– 2009. Toward a better bioethics: Commentary on "Forbidding science: some beginning reflections" *Science and Engineering Ethics* 15: 283-291.

Robert, J.S., Baylis, F. 2005. When it comes to funding research, value should count. *Globe and Mail*, 4 July, A13.

Robert, J.S., Hall, B.K., Olson, W.M. 2001. Bridging the gap between developmental systems theory and evolutionary developmental biology. *Bioessays*. 23 (10):954-962.

Rosenfield, P.L. 1992. The potential of transdisciplinary research for sustaining and extending linkages between the health and social sciences. *Social Science and Medicine* 35(11):1343-57.

Stock, G. 2002. *Redesigning Humans: Our Inevitable Genetic Future*. Boston: Houghton Mifflin Co.

Turner, L. 2009. Anthropological and sociological critiques of bioethics. *Bioethical Inquiry* 6(1): 83-98.

Tyers, M., Brown, E., Andrews, D.W., et al. 2005. Problems with co-funding in Canada. *Science* 308 (5730):1867.

University of Pittsburgh Schools of the Health Sciences. 2007. Anger and aggression in women: Blame it on genetics. *Science Daily*, 10 March. http://www.sciencedaily.com/releases/2007/03/070309103136.htm.

Williams-Jones, Bryn. 2005. Knowledge commons or economic engine – What's a university for? *Journal of Medical Ethics* 31 (5):249-50.

Winslow, R. 2007. Is there a heart attack in your future? *Wall Street Journal*, 6 November, D1.

Public Representations of Genetics: Reifying Race?

TIMOTHY CAULFIELD

INTRODUCTION

As I was moving across Canada to take up my first research position in 1993, I read Ruth Hubbard and Elijah Wald's book, *Exploding the Gene Myth* (1993). The book still sits on a shelf in my office. At the time, I had not yet done much of my own work on the ethical, legal, and social issues associated with genetic research, and this accessible book seemed like a good place to get some background regarding emerging concerns. Immediately after I finished that book, I read Troy Duster's *Eugenics through the Backdoor* (1990). These books provided a provocative and particular introduction to the social issues associated with genetic research. Indeed, these books and a few others with similar themes, such as *The DNA Mystique: The Gene as a Cultural Icon* by Dorothy Nelkin and Susan Lindee (1996), have become emblematic of the early concerns about the social impact of a new "genetic revolution." The books heavily criticize the framing of genetics research and provide speculation about the impact it might have on social perceptions. In particular, they helped to place at the fore concerns about the potential of public representations to feed an inappropriately deterministic vision. And, in addition, they raised questions about the ways in which the new genetics might stigmatize particular populations.

If you pick the start of the Human Genome Project as roughly 1989, the current "genetic revolution" has been with us for more than two decades (Cook-Deegan 1994) and it has been almost ten years since the announcement of the completion of the first map of the entire human genome (Venter 2001). With the passage of time we can now reflect on these early concerns and consider them in the context of what is now happening in the area of genetics. We can see the emergence of trends and an accumulation of empirical data that inform the ethics debates.

In this chapter, I draw on these data and history and consider a specific social concern associated with genetics research: that popular representations of genetics will reify the notion of race and, as a result, increase racist attitudes. This is a concern that was touched on in much of the early literature, including the books noted above, and which has remained a topic of policy debate, garnering recent international press coverage (Crompton 2007; Harmon 2007).

The proposition in this chapter is simple. Despite claims that genomic research will lead to an enlightened view of genetic difference, thus erasing the biological foundations of race, there are numerous social forces that seem likely to reinforce biological views. This is a pessimistic story, but one that I believe is supported by the available evidence, and thoughtful speculation. The chapter starts with a brief review of the recent history of the race debate in the context of genetic research. This is followed by a discussion of three social forces – the use of race in research, market pressures, and media representations – that will influence the nature of popular representations. The interesting story of the development and marketing of the drug BiDil, the first "race-based" pharmaceutical, is used as a current example of possible future trends (Kahn 2007). I conclude with a consideration of the possible impact of popular representations on public attitudes.

DEFINING RACE

It remains accepted by most, of course, that whether biologically determined or not, the construct of "race" has deep cultural and health care significance. There are profound health disparities between socially defined "races" and a significant amount of important health research is aimed at exploring these disparities. But despite its ubiquitous use in both public discourse and health research, race is a concept that is notoriously difficult to define, biologically or socially. What is a "race"? Even in its crudest form, racial categories are far from clear. Demarcations are foggy and shift with perspective (e.g., self identification versus socially ascribed). Anthropologist Duana Fullwiley has noted that "race is a thing of our world like no other" (2007). There is a complex interaction – or, as Hacking (1995) describes it, a "looping effect" – between the use of the social label "race" and the impact the label has on how we see the world. We create a category and then fit people into it (Fullwiley 2007). And, as we will see, scientists are no different.

In this chapter, I will make no effort to explore the various definitions of race – a complex task that has been handled by others (Lee, Mountain, and Koenig 2001; Pigliucci and Kaplan 2003). Here, the references to "race" will mean the broad, historical categories most commonly associated with the notion, such as Black, White, and Asian. Not only are these the categories with the most cultural traction and used the most in common parlance, they are the categories that have the most history – at least in the Western world. In 1758, for instance, Carolus Linnaeus, the Swedish botanist that named us *Homo sapiens*, divided the species in the subcategories of "red Americans, yellow Asians, black Africans, and white Europeans" (Olson 2001). I also believe that these broad categorizations are the ones with the least biological and most social significance.

But it is important to remember that when exploring the biological legitimacy of the notion of race, the scope of the definition is a key variable – a point noted by Massimo Pigliucci and Jonathan Kaplan (2003). While biology "cannot underwrite the sort of racial concepts that have usually been applied to humans" (ibid., 1166), there still may be biologically significant differences between specific subpopulations in relation to very discrete traits. Here, I am focusing on the application of the notion of race not to these narrow descriptive categories (which, I believe, would reflect a relatively selective use of the term), but to the larger social classifications with which we are most familiar.

THE GENETICS OF DIFFERENCE

Not long after the start of the Human Genome Project, Nelkin suggested that simplistic media presentations of the biology of difference, fuelled by excitement associated with genetic research, could result in an affirmation of existing racial categories (2001). In Nelkin's view, the media tends to oversimplify the relationship between genetic difference and the social construct of "race," thus inappropriately implying that the existing social views of race have a biological foundation.

Indeed, over the past two decades there has been much speculation about the ways in which science may be reifying a biological view of population difference. In this regard, the controversial 1994 book by Richard Herrnstein and Charles Murray, *The Bell Curve*, has arguably been the focus of the most heated debates about what contemporary science tells us about the biological foundations of race. One reviewer suggested it was the most extensively attacked book in the entire history of psychology (Lynn 1999). While the book actually makes little reference to race, it was viewed in the general populace (and in the popular press) as a book about "race and IQ" (Jacobs 1999). The book suggests that social status is largely the result of immutable intellectual gifts and deficits. Those at the top of the social strata, so it is argued, are naturally more intelligent; and those at the bottom, intellectually deficient. This rhetoric represented the worst fears of those within the academic community who thought the new "genetic revolution" would lead to a reification of race as a biological reality (Robinson 1994-95). The book stood as the "I told you so" example of the potential impact of genetics research on social perceptions.

However, at the same time that the concerns about the impact of genetic research on the social perceptions of race and genetic difference were being articulated, many in the scientific community were suggesting the opposite – that genetic research had, in fact, provided the best evidence that race is a biological fiction (Owens and King 1999). Genetic research (and the Human Genome Project in particular) was not reifying the notion of race, it was suggested, but providing the scientific ammunition to destroy any claims to biological legitimacy.

In this regard, many in the academic community have forcefully proposed that the broad racial categories most often used in common parlance and in the popular media – Black, Caucasian, Asian – have no biological foundation. For example, the scholars Sandra Lee, Joanna Mountain, and Barbara Koenig declare that the "widely accepted consensus among evolutionary biologists and genetic anthropologists is that biologically identifiable human races do not exist" (2001). Genetic research has, indeed, highlighted the youth and tremendous genetic homogeneity of the human species. We are a very young and similar lot. "From a genetic perspective," explains Svante Pääbo (2001), all humans are Africans, "either residing in Africa or in recent exile." Building on this portrayal of homogeneity, a number of commentators take an optimistic view of the social significance of genetic research and treat it as a truism that race is not biological and, as such, suggest that the stage is set for a fresh approach to the exploration of human variation. "The discordance between 'race' and human genome variation sets the stage for an analysis of the state of the science on human genome variation and 'race' and the relationship between genome variation and population difference in health and disease" (Royal and Dunston 2004).

Of course, not all in the academic community believe the notion that race has no biological underpinnings (Risch 2006). Most recently, and notoriously, James Watson, co-discoverer of the double-helix and Nobel laureate, suggested that individuals of African descent are genetically predisposed to have inferior intelligence. The statements led to an immediate international reaction, including the cancellation of the book tour that gave him the forum to discuss race and his suspension (and eventual resignation) as chancellor of the Cold Spring Harbor Laboratory in New York (M. Kahn 2007). Shortly after his provocative comments, Watson offered a half-hearted retraction – both apologizing for the statement and stating that his comments were really meant to underscore the need to further understand population difference. "The overwhelming desire of society today is to assume that equal powers of reason are a universal heritage of humanity. It may well be. But simply wanting this to be the case is not enough. This is not science. To question this is not to give in to racism. This is not a discussion about superiority or inferiority, it is about seeking to understand differences, about why some of us are great musicians and others great engineers" (BBC News 2007).

Naturally, Watson's "retraction" does little to soften the central premise of his original claim that there are measurable genetic differences between races. He has simply restated it as an observation about population difference instead of a claim of genetic inferiority – hardly a definitive renunciation of the biology of race.

But despite a handful of outspoken scientists such as Watson, the majority in the research community, at least those who have taken public positions, are against the idea of biologically definitive, genetically based, racial categories (Collins 2004; Cooper and Kaufman 2003). At a minimum, they have distanced themselves from idea that there are biologically discrete populations that map the social construct of race (Owens and King 1999; Pearce et al. 2004). Even Watson, when pressed in a follow-up interview after his provocative statements, said that there "there is no scientific basis for such a belief" (M. Kahn 2007).

RESEARCHING POPULATION DIFFERENCE

Set against the voices in the academic world suggesting that genetic research is destroying (or has destroyed) the biological foundations of the construct of race is the reality that much of the current genetic research is, paradoxically, based on a search for an understanding of genetic variation between discrete populations. In other words, after years of emphasizing homogeneity in the debates about race, much of the current research focus is seeking to explore the ways populations differ. For example, emerging large population genetic initiatives, including biobank projects and large longitudinal studies like UK Biobank (Biobank UK), are designed to provide the population data necessary to tease out the complex relationship between genes and the environment in the development of human disease. The international research initiative known as the HapMap is an "effort to identify and catalog genetic similarities and differences in human beings" (International HapMap Project). To this end, genetic data are being gathered from populations with "African, Asian, and European ancestry." (M. Kahn 2007)

More to the point, many of these projects' specific research objectives, as exemplified by the emerging areas of nutrigenomics and pharmacogenomics, are aimed at an exploration of how genetic predispositions may impact things like food metabolism and drug reaction. While none of the projects are overtly exploring the biology of race, the emphasis on difference, inherent in the goals and methodologies of the initiatives, has renewed "the historical emphasis on biology in concepts of race and ethnicity" (Rahemtulla and Bhopal 2005; Foster and Sharp 2004). For example, in the field of pharmacogenomics, researchers are focusing on race and ethnicity as a way to explore "whether different responses to drug treatment may be attributable to genetic differences" (Rahemtulla and Bhopal 2005). The approach is similar in the field nutrigenomics. Indeed, it has been said that "the assumption of real genetic markers that distinguish one ethnic group from another is at the philosophical heart of nutrigenomics" (Grierson 2003).

No one is denying that there is discrete genetic variation between geographically defined sub-populations that have both biological and health implications. But given the existing socially entrenched description of how the human species is sub-divided, it is easy to slip from a discussion of specific geographically defined genotypic difference (let's call it "genographic variation") to one about race (Foster and Sharp 2004).

So, after over a decade of genomic research and consistent academic assertions that the work has or will kill biological notions of race, the most recent work is, again, viewed as a potential engine of misinformation about the biology of race (Lee 2005). The irony of this reality has been recognized by a number of commentators. Allan Goodman, for instance, has suggested that the "acceptance of the notion of race as biology" faded within the academic community throughout the 1970s and '80s, but "during the past decade racialized notions of biology have made a comeback. This is especially true in human genetics, a field that paradoxically once drove the last nail into the coffin of race-as-biology" (2000).

A statement about the fact that current research methods may result in an inappropriate reification of biological difference can be found in an intriguing location, the consent template for the participants of the HapMap project. This document, or a close version of it, is presented to all individuals considering the provision of a biological sample for this international research initiative. On page four of the consent template, one of the risks of participating is described:

Some people may use the information from the HapMap or from future studies using the HapMap to exaggerate differences between groups for prejudiced or other bad reasons. Others may use the information to downplay differences between groups, to say that all people's genes are about the same, so we don't need to respect the special concerns of different groups. Biology does not provide a reason for prejudice, but discrimination does exist (International HapMap Consortium).

RESPONSE BY THE SCIENTIFIC COMMUNITY

In the face of concern that current population genetics studies will reify race, many in the scientific community have held their ground – insisting that the production of more population-based genomic knowledge will enlighten and not entrench prejudicial views (Rotimi 2004). Pääbo, for example, states:

> Genome-wide studies of genetic variation among human populations may not be so easy to abuse – in terms of using data as "scientific support" for racism or other forms of bigotry – as is currently feared. If anything, such studies will have the opposite effect because prejudice, oppression, and racism feed on ignorance. Knowledge of the genome should foster compassion, not only because our gene pool is extremely mixed, but also because a more comprehensive understanding of how our genotype relates to our phenotype will demonstrate that everyone carries at least some deleterious alleles. Consequently, stigmatizing any particular group of individuals on the basis of ethnicity or carrier status for certain alleles will be revealed as absurd. (2001)

Genetic researchers, such as Francis Collins, director of the US National Human Genome Research Institute, have also suggested that race is a social construct and, as a result, a poor proxy for identifying the true genetic variation sought in current research efforts. Indeed, in an article that was a direct response to the concern that emerging research initiatives would inappropriately use race, Collins argued that "[a] true understanding of disease risk requires a thorough examination of root causes. 'Race' and 'ethnicity' are poorly defined terms that serve as flawed surrogates for multiple environmental and genetic factors in disease causation, including ancestral geographic origins, socio-economic status, education, and access to health care" (2004, S13; see also Cooper and Kaufman 2003).

Thus, an interesting tension has emerged. On the one hand, emerging research is, rightly or not, re-igniting the race debate by placing the analysis of biological difference in the foreground (Harmon 2007). On the other hand, the scientific community remains publicly committed to the notion that the broad social notion of race (e.g., Black, White, Asian, etc.) has no definitive foundation in genetics. Of course, the genetics community is not a homogeneous collection that speaks with one voice. However, the general ethos over the past decade has been in opposition to (or, at least, a de-emphasis of) biological theories of race, as evidenced by the response of professional bodies to the recent Watson controversy. The Federation of American Scientists, for example, condemned Watson's comments and said they were "prejudices that are racist, vicious and unsupported by science" (2007).

SOCIAL TRENDS AND THE REIFICATION PROCESS

There are numerous social forces and research trends that seem likely to upset this delicate balance and facilitate the reification process – nudging public representations away from descriptions of genographic variation toward reliance on traditional notions of race. From the way genetic researchers use "race" in research protocols to how the media handles genetic stories, it will become increasingly difficult for society to walk the "tightrope" of both aggressively exploring the biology of difference and resisting the reification of racial categories. Below, I briefly review and critique several of these trends.

Race in Research

Despite assertions like those made by Collins above – that is, that race is a poor proxy for genetic difference – race is commonly used in biomedical research for precisely this purpose. In part, this is undoubtedly because it is a term that still has profound cultural resonance. When designing protocols, it is easy to fall back on already ascribed categories (Rebbeck and Sankar 2005). In addition to this kind of use, however, there is a good deal of health research investigating the role of the social construct of "race" (Sheldon and Parker 1992; Kaplan and Bennett 2003). In this context, the use of the concept makes conceptual sense – its social underpinnings are recognized and may, in fact, be a part of the study (e.g., research on racism in health care, LaVeist 2000) or the connection between socioeconomic status, race, and health (Lillie-Blanton and LaVeist 1996).

So, in this scientific literature we find race being used in a wide variety of ways, including as a term to describe study populations, results, and applications. Indeed, it is a term that is used in a tremendously inconsistent manner and often without explanation (Bhopal and Donaldson 1998; Rebbeck and Sankar, 2005). Recently, George Ellison and colleagues looked at the contemporary use of "race" in scientific literature and found "there is a lack of consensus about what race and ethnicity mean and how these should be operationalized. As a result, researchers and practitioners may conflate the utility of racial and ethnic categories for sampling diverse study populations with their ability to identify and address an etiological variation therein" (2007).

The suggestion that race is used inconsistently and often with little academic rigour is more than mere speculation. An interesting study by Hasan Shanawani and colleagues (2006) examined 268 published genomic studies involving "race" as a study variable. Of these published reports, 72 per cent did not explain their methods for assigning race or ethnicity as an independent variable. This is truly remarkable, especially when one considers that 67 per cent of the studies reached conclusions about genetics, health outcomes, and race (ibid., 724).

Fullwiley's (2007) ethnographic study of pharmacogenomic researchers, referred to above, found that despite the recognized inaccuracy of the notion of "race" to explain human variation, researchers reflexively fall back on the classic racial categories. Indeed, she found that when asked, researchers explicitly recognize the complex nature of genomic diversity but, in parallel, would use the usual, socially defined, racial classifications. For example, she asked the principal investigator of a large pharmacogenomic research initiative to explain race. "[M]y understanding of race is that there are three major races — that there's a Caucasian race, that that is a race — as opposed to European, OK. And there's an, an, an African race. And, um, and there is an Asian race. That is my understanding of race, that those are racial groups. Now are you going to ask me what characterizes a race? Are you going to ask me those kinds of things [laughing shyly]?" (ibid.).

Fullwiley concludes her study by noting that it takes a "significant intellectual leap" for researchers to move from the "notion of specificity to the idea that race is the right conceptual tool to account for such differences" (ibid.).

Race, then, lives on in biomedical research in a wide variety of forms. Arguably, when the term is used without clarity, it gives a veneer of scientific legitimacy to the breadth of meanings and, at least superficially, to the idea that an assortment of meanings has biological significance.

Race and Markets

It seems likely that market forces will be one of the most significant elements in any reification process. First, market forces will naturally push toward the classification system that creates the largest market. As noted by Collins (2004) above, race is, at best, a rough proxy for underlying genotypic variation. But the classification of "race" will inevitably be a broader, more encompassing, classification than a specific geographic group with a specific genotypic variation. For example, pharmacogenomics research may disclose that individuals from Western Africa metabolize a drug in a unique manner, thus making the drug more beneficial to them. Yet, the racial category of "black" is larger and more recognizable than "Western Africans." As such, the invisible hand of the market will naturally gravitate to the larger, more recognizable, market segment.

Second, the concept of race already has social traction, making it a powerful marketing tool as compared to the description of other, more specific and technically accurate, geographic classifications. Marketing to individuals with specific "genographic" backgrounds will have far less force than marketing to racial or ethnic groups. Indeed, there are numerous examples of this kind of "race" marketing. Emerging nutrigenomic companies are selling tests and supplements based on race and ethnicity. On the website of the GenSpec the company declares that they offer "the first genetically specific nutritional supplements made just for you." They go onto suggest that "different ethnic groups have distinct health needs and unique risk factors" (GenSpec). On the website, these statements overlie a photographic image of a number of individuals from the conventionally recognized "racial" groups, thus implying that visual phenotypes normally associated with "race" have genetic significance. In other words, the insinuation is that the visible phenotypes of the traditionally defined races, such as skin colour, have real biological meaning.

The development and marketing of BiDil, a pharmacogenomic drug that has been called the first "race-based" therapy, stands as another powerful example of how the products of genetic research may be presented to the public. The drug BiDil, which is meant to help prevent heart disease in "black" Americans, has an interesting and controversial history (Kahn 2004). The clinical trials that led to its development and Food and Drug Administration approval have been criticized as being incomplete and far from conclusive regarding the drugs exclusive effectiveness among "blacks" (Bloche 2004; Brody and Hunt 2006; Caulfield 2007). While the drug has been hailed as a positive step toward personalized medicine and an effective tool in the fight against health disparities (Daar and Singer 2005; Devine 2006), it has also been suggested that market opportunities may have been the dominant motivational factors in the drug's development

(Kahn 2004). In short, the data that suggested "African-Americans" responded well to the drug (data which remains contested, largely because of the lack of a comparator group) was viewed as both a marketing and regulatory opportunity. From the perspective of this paper, the BiDil story demonstrates how quickly biotechnology products can become "racialized," even in the face of concerns about the social impact of that process (Kahn 2007). Pamela Sankar and Jonathan Kahn suggest that the BiDil story stands as an example of the exploitation of race "to gain commercial and regulatory advantage in the pharmaceutical marketplace" (2005).

Indeed, this seems to be precisely what happened with the marketing of BiDil. The public representations of the drug rarely spoke about the specific "black" population that would benefit most from the drug. Surely, the research did not conclude that all individuals with "black" skin – the primary social signifier of "African-American" – would benefit from the drug. On the contrary, the research that surrounded the approval of BiDil has been criticized exactly because it did not accurately explore how "race" was associated with heart disease (perhaps it is the social construction of "race" that is more properly associated with the risk of heart disease – a possibility supported by studies that have shown that individuals of African descent living in the UK and the Caribbean have hypertension rates two to three times lower than those in the United States (Brooks and King 2008)). Despite this uncertainty, the drug was marketed at "blacks" (Kahn 2004).

It is interesting to note that BiDil was initially embraced by many in the African-American community, including the NAACP and the Association of Black Cardiologists. However, after the controversies associated with the drug intensified – including concern about the conduct of the clinical trials – there was less enthusiasm. For example, in the summer of 2007, Dr. Clyde Yancy, on behalf of the Association of Black Cardiologists, stated that "none of us are comfortable with race as a descriptor for drug efficacy" (quoted in Brooks and King 2008).

Of course, the decision to market a product to a specific racial group should not come as a surprise. Race has long been used as a marketing tool for myriad products, including tobacco and alcohol (Altman, Schooler, and Basil 1991). Indeed, there are marketing infrastructures in place to provide advice on how best to market to specific ethnic groups and racial communities (IMediaConnection;

Cultural Marketing Communications; Multicultural Healthcare Marketing Group) – thus facilitating gravitation toward existing and known categorizations. There is also some evidence that in the health care context, such as in the pharmaceutical industry, there is a view that racial and ethnic populations are "untapped" markets that warrant specific advertising attention (Lee 2005). For example, one of the talks at the First Annual Meeting of the Pharmaceutical Marketing Research Group (PMRG) was presented by Sheila Thorne, President and CEO of the Multicultural Healthcare Marketing Group. The talk was entitled "When the Ivory Tower goes to the Ebony Hood" and, according to the PMRG website, included a discussion of best practices for marketing to specific ethnic groups (Pharmaceutical Marketing Research Group). Similarly, an industry publication noted a "more concentrated move by pharmaceutical marketers to reach ethnic groups" (Schnuer 2001).

In total, market pressures, existing marketing frameworks, and the fact that the concept of race already has significantly more immediate social recognition than more specific geographic designations, will nudge representations of genetic difference toward conventional racial categories.

Race in the Media

Media coverage of biotechnology is everywhere. It is not surprising, then, that the media is one of the most important sources of scientific information (Holtzman et al. 2005; Caulfield 2005; Ten Eyck and Williment 2003). Though the relationship between media coverage and public perceptions is obviously complex, there seems little doubt that the media can influence popular opinion and the framing of science issues (Marks et al. 2007; Nisbet and Lewenstein 2002). As such, popular representations of genetic research and products will also play an important role in how the public views the link between race and genetics.

To date, there are ample examples of less-than-ideal media representations of the biology of race. For example, in 2006 my local paper, the *Edmonton Journal*, ran a feature story with the headline "Ethnic links provide clues to health." The article, which discussed "race-related conditions," was accompanied by a photo of three hands – apparently Black, White, and Asian (Zdeb 2006). A piece in the popular magazine *Men's Health* had the less-than-subtle title

"Race Relations" (Hobday 2006). The article opens with a provocative claim: "Ask any epidemiologist and he'll tell you that not all men are created equal. Your race affects your susceptibility to certain diseases" (ibid.). The article includes a colour-coded chart to allow Caucasians, African-Americans, Asians, and Latinos to map their health risks.

It is not that these kinds of articles are entirely inaccurate (for example, the social construct of race is obviously correlated with a variety of health disparities). However, the simplified version of the relationship between race, genetics, and disease may mislead the public – about both the nature and the strength of the relationship. More important from the perspective of this chapter, such representations imply that the traditional racial demarcations are the ones that are biologically significant.

Naturally, there are numerous reasons why media coverage may be less than accurate. Reporters work in a competitive business. Stories must be sold to editors and be interesting enough to sell publications. This reality facilitates a polarization in the story telling, such that every health and science story is framed as either a breakthrough or a social controversy (Highfield 2000). The fact that scientists are increasingly under pressure to justify work in practical and near-future terms also leads to a hyping and simplification of research results (Caulfield and Bubela 2004). The seemingly inevitable "race spin" has been noted by a variety of commentators. For example, Charles Rotimi states: "Race-based hypotheses in biomedical research sell. Reporting the nuances underlying group difference does not and, more importantly, will probably not receive the same attention in the popular press" (Rotimi, 2004).

An examination of the media coverage of BiDil stands as a good illustration of popular representations of a race and health topic. As noted above, BiDil is one of the first pharmaceuticals to be marketed and framed as a product specific to a single race. How the media covered BiDil may hint at how they will handle other race and genetic issues.

So, what did newspapers have to say about BiDil? A sampling of North American newspaper articles on BiDil reveals an interesting pattern (Harry and Caulfield 2007). A portion of the articles uncritically accept the notion of race, especially in the headlines. The *New York Times* declared: "The first race-based medicine" (2005). The *Washington Post*: "The race to market: Heart supplement targets Blacks, echoing race-based drug" (Payne 2005). And the *Wall Street Journal*: "BiDil heart drug aimed at blacks gets FDA approval" (Dooren 2005).

Many other stories, however, were explicitly framed around the race debate. Indeed, many of the articles focused on the issues associated with using the social construct of race as a proxy for underlying genetic characteristics. Some of these articles focused on justifying the use of race in this context, others were more explicitly critical. To cite just one example, in a piece published in the *New York Times*, entitled "I Am a Racially Profiling Doctor," the author argues that the use of race, while not a perfect proxy for genetic difference, is better than nothing – suggesting that it is the "poor man's clue" to actual genotypic variation (Satel 2002). "[I]n the sometimes cloudy world of medicine, a poor man's clue is all you've got" (ibid.).

In total, the reporting surrounding BiDil reflects the common practice of framing biomedical research as either a breakthrough or a controversy. If the former is the focus, the reporting is implicitly accepting of a biological role of race (e.g., some articles presented the story as a "major advance in the treatment of a slowly failing heart" (Pope 2004)). If the latter, we see an emphasis on the social issues associated with the race debate.

In some ways, one could view the coverage of the BiDil story as encouraging. The complexities of the race issue were represented in a number of articles and were much less deterministic than some might have predicted (Stein 2005) – a finding that fits well with other studies that have explored genetic determinism in the media (Condit, Ofulue, and Sheedy 1998). In addition, the idea of marketing a drug to a particular racial group was seen as controversial, because it might reinforce socially inappropriate views of race and lead to poor health outcomes.

On the other hand, a portion of the stories did transmit a simple message about a "race-based drug" – thus imparting biological significance to traditional notions of race. And even when the race issue was part of the story, the biology of race was not always analyzed – the article simply said that marketing to racial groups might create social issues. In other words, these articles did not critique the biology of race. A 2005 article in the *Boston Globe* stands as a good example (Rowland 2005). This piece starts as a story about the FDA approval of the drug and suggests that the approval is a rudimentary step toward individualized health care, the "future of medicine" (ibid.). It then notes the race issue, but does not say anything about the biology of race – the focus is on health disparity and social perception. All valid talking points, but the story leaves open an implication about the biology of race.

In the future, as more pharmacogenomic and nutrigenomic products emerge, one wonders whether the social controversy will fade and the simple reporting of the new products and genetic discoveries will dominate. Given the influence of industry on news reporting in other situations, such as in the context of pharmaceuticals (Zuckerman 2003; Caulfield 2004), this seems a reasonable prediction.

THE IMPACT OF PUBLIC REPRESENTATIONS

Why do we care about how race is presented in marketing campaigns, research reports, and the popular press? Do simplistic representations of the biology of race have a negative social consequence? Do they increase racism? Naturally, one could argue that the perpetuation of inaccurate information about race and biology is a bad thing regardless of the existence of empirical evidence that tells us whether this is so. Misinformation does not help social discourse, public engagement, or the education process. That said, there is at least some research that demonstrates that biological views of race may increase prejudicial attitudes. For example, a focus group study by Eleanor Singer and colleagues found that "the more White respondents believed 'differences between Whites and Black people' in various characteristics — drive to succeed, ability in math, tendency to act violently, and intelligence — were attributable to genes, the more prejudiced they were toward Blacks" (2007). In another study, Celeste Condit and colleagues found that "some messages linking race, genes, and health produce increases in racist attitudes in some audiences" (2004).

While such data isn't overwhelming – indeed, more research is clearly warranted – it does hint at a possible social impact of the reification process: the facilitation of racism through a legitimization of biological difference. Of course, the relationship between public representations of science and public attitudes is complex (Condit, Parrott, and Harris 2002). For example, Benjamin Bates and colleagues studied focus group reactions to direct-to-consumer advertising of pharmacogenomic products and found that responses were "based on a variety of reason-based resources, not simple acceptance" (2004). These conclusions fit well with the work of other scholars, like Matthew Nisbet and Chris Mooney, who argue that the public use "their value predispositions (such as political or religious beliefs) as perceptual screens, selecting news outlets and Web sites whose outlooks match their own. Such screening reduces the choices of what to pay attention to and accept as valid" (2007).

Such views on the role of public representations do not preclude the possible intensification of racist attitudes through inaccurate messaging. On the contrary, for those in society who already harbour prejudicial tendencies – and they are far from few – their "perceptual screen" would lead to a selection of media reports that accord with potentially racist views.

There are, of course, a number of other reasons why the use of race in genetic research may create policy challenges, including the promotion of an overly simplistic view of gene-environment interactions that could lead to poor health outcomes (Lee 2005, 2133) and the loss of research opportunities by distracting us from "information that might actually be more relevant to research, diagnosis, or therapy, such as environmental factors of finer-grained differences in ancestral origins than the crude grouping of 'race'" (Cho 2006).

WHAT DO TO?

Addressing the concerns associated with the public presentation of genetic research will be a terrific challenge. First, as noted above, many of the forces that could contribute to the reification process are systemic and well-entrenched. Indeed, in many ways, this natural gravitation toward a biological view of race is hardly surprising. The idea of race has been a consistent theme of Western culture for centuries. The social categories roughly correspond to simplistic phenotypic visual cues, such as skin colour. It is, in many ways, an easy approach to categorization. As recently noted by Brooks and King: "This misconception about race has taken hold due to the tendency to racially categorize people based upon physical appearance, in most instances skin color and hair-type (the "I know it when I see it," or phenotypical, reasoning)" (2008). And despite efforts to minimize the biological view, it has always been in the background. As genetic research moves forward, the natural inclination is to overlay the simple phenotypic classifications over the vastly more complex reality. The market will push toward the large and well-recognized proxy of race. And the media's tendency to simplify and polarize seems unlikely to become a constructive force.

Despite the existence of these significant hurdles, steps can (and should) be taken to minimize the reification process. To quote Mark Twain, "Get your facts first, then you can distort them as you please." So, for starters, the research community must be encouraged to use race (and related terms) more precisely. We need to get the facts straight, thus diminishing the chance of inappropriate extrapolation. In addition, given the profoundly destructive role the concept of race has played in Western society, it could be argued that researchers have a moral responsibility to use the term in the most careful manner possible. Thus, researchers need to be rigorous in their use of the term, the design of methodologies, and the presentation of data. As Sankar and Cho have suggested, "researchers need to be clear about the choice and definition of terms, as well as to be careful about making appropriate generalizations" (2002). Rebbeck and Sankar provide concrete recommendations for researchers in the design of genetic studies (2005). They suggest that researchers should assess the need for a particular category (e.g., does the research really demand "race" as a kind of grouping, or is the term being used out of classification habit?); decide exactly how the term will be used in the study and describe and justify its use (e.g., what term fits better – race, ancestry, or ethnicity?); and be consistent in the use of the term (e.g., don't slide between a specific categorization like "genographic history" and race).

Scientific journals and peer reviewers need to be diligent in the evaluation of the use of the term. And, finally, we need to find ways to write about race that does not facilitate stigmatization (Kaplan and Bennett 2003; Brown and the PLoS Medicine Editors 2007).

Of course, no matter how rigorously the term is used within the scientific community, some degree of simplification and distortion seems inevitable, as argued above. As such, because the exploration of genetic difference – through projects like the HapMap – is likely to be with us for decades, we should also consider mechanisms and policies that may moderate the reification process more broadly. A detailed examination of such approaches is beyond the scope and intent of this chapter, but could include policies governing the marketing of genetic products, regulatory policies for the approval of drugs and devices, and the use of public research funding guidelines.

Finally, we need more research on all aspects of this issue. Over the past fifteen years, social science research has added depth and data to the early speculations by the likes of Hubbard, Nelkin, and Duster – in some cases confirming fears, in others dispelling or redirecting them (Condit, Ofulue, and Sheedy 1998; Condit et al. 2001). But as research on genetic variation pushes forward, so too should the analysis of the ethical, legal, and social issues. This work is needed to elucidate both the nature of public representations and its actual impact on perceptions.

Thanks to Simrat Harry, Jacob Shelley, Victor Alfonso and Nola Ries for their valuable insight and research assistance and the AHFMR, AFMNet and Genome Alberta for funding support.

BIBLIOGRAPHY

Altman, D.G., Schooler, C., Basil, M.D. 1991. Alcohol and cigarette advertising on billboards. *Health Educ. Res.* 6:487-90.

BBC News. 2007. Lab suspends DNA pioneer Watson. *BBC News* 19 October: http://news.bbc.co.uk/2/hi/science/nature/7052416.stm.

Bates, B.R., Poirot, K., Harris, T.M., Condit, C.M., Achter, P.J. 2004. Evaluating direct-to-consumer marketing of race-based pharmacogenomics: A focus group study of public understandings of applied genomic medications. *J. Health Commun.* 9:541-59.

Bhopal, R., Donaldson, L. 1998. White, European, Western, Caucasian, or what? Inappropriate labeling in research on race, ethnicity, and health. *Am. J. Public Health* 88:1303-7.

Biobank UK. http://www.ukbiobank.ac.uk/.

Bloche, M.G. 2004. Raced-based therapeutics. *New Eng. J. Med.* 351:2035-7.

Brody, H., Hunt, L. 2006. BiDil: Assessing a race based pharmaceutical. *Ann. Fam. Med.* 4:556-60.

Brooks, J., King, M. 2008. *Genetisizing Disease: Implications for Racial Health Disparities* (Center for American Progress, January 2008).

Brown, M. and the PLoS Medicine Editors. 2007. Defining human differences in biomedicine. *PLoS Med.* 4:1421-2.

Caulfield, T. 2004. The commercialization of medical and scientific reporting. *PLoS Med.* 1:178-9.

– 2005. Popular media, biotechnology and the "cycle of hype". *J. Health L. and Policy* 5:213.

– 2007. Nutrigenomics, popular representations and the reification of "race"? *Health L. Rev.* (in press).

Caulfield, T., Bubela, T. 2004. Do the print media 'hype' genetic research? A comparison of newspaper stories and peer-reviewed research papers. *Can. Med. Assoc. J.* 170:1399-1407.

Cho, M. 2006. Racial and ethnic categories in biomedical research: There is no baby in the bathwater. *J. L. Med. and Ethics* 34:497-9.

Collins, F. 2004. What we do and don't know about race, ethnicity, genetics and health at the dawn of the genome era. *Nat. Genet.* 36:S13-5.

Condit, C.M., Ofulue, N., Sheedy, K.M. 1998. Determinism and mass-media portrayals of genetics. *Am. J. Hum. Genet.* 62:979-84.

Condit, C.M., Ferguson, A., Kassel, R., Thadhani, C., Gooding, H.C.,Parrott, R. 2001. An exploratory study of the impact of news headlines on genetic determinism. *Sci. Commun.* 22:379-95.

Condit, C.M., Parrott, R., Harris, T.M. 2002. Lay understandings of the relationship between race and genetics: Development of a collectivized knowledge through shared discourse. *Public Understand. Sci.* 11:373-87

Condit, C.M., Parrott, R., Bates, B.R., Bevan, J., Achter, P.J. 2004. Exploration of the impact of messages about genes and race on lay attitudes. *Clin. Genet.* 66:402-8.

Cook-Deegan, R. 1994. *The Gene Wars: Science, Politics and the Human Genome*. New York: Norton and Company.

Cooper, R.S., Kaufman, J.S. 2003. Race and genomics. *New Engl. J. Med.* 348:1166-70.

Crompton, S. 2007. Medicine that's only skin deep. *The Times* 20 October: http://women.timesonline.co.uk/tol/life_and_style/women/body_and_soul/article2693996.ece.

Cultural Marketing Communications. http://www.culturalmarketingcommunications.com/ethnicmulticultural.htm.

Daar, A.S., Singer, P.A. 2005. Race: A risk genetics must run. *The Globe and Mail* 25 June: F7.

Devine, D. 2006. NAACP goes to the grassroots for BiDil. *Boston Banner* 42: http://bostonbanner.com/archives/stories/2006/10/100506-07.htm.

Dooren, J.C. 2005. BiDil heart drug aimed at blacks gets FDA approval. *Wall Street Journal* 24 June:B3.

Duster, T. 1990. *Backdoor to eugenics*. New York: Routledge.

Ellison, G.T.H., A. Smart, R. Tutton, S.M. Outram, and R. Ashcroft. 2007. Racial categories in medicine: A failure of evidence-based practice? *PLoS Med.* 4:1434-6.

Federation of American Scientists. 2007. FAS condemns comments made by Dr. James Watson. *Federation of American Scientists* 18 October: http://fas.org/main/content.jsp?formAction=297&contentId=572.

Foster, M., Sharp, R. 2004. Beyond race: Towards a whole-genome perspective on human populations and genetic variation. *Nat. Rev. Genet.* 5:790-6.

Fullwiley, D. 2007. Race and genetics: Attempts to define the relationship. *BioSocieties* 2:221-37.

GenSpec. http://www.4genspec.com/.

Goodman, A.H. 2000. Why genes don't count (for racial differences in health). *Am. J. Public Health* 99:1699-1702.

Grierson, B. 2003. What your genes want you to eat. *New York Times* 4 May: http://query.nytimes.com/gst/fullpage.html?res=9A02E5D9133DF937A35756C0A9659C8B63.

Hacking, I. 1995. The looping effects of human kinds. In *Causal cognition: An interdisciplinary approach*, ed. D. Sperber, D. Premack, and A. Premack, 351-83. Oxford: Oxford University Press.

Harmon, A. 2007. In DNA era, new worries about prejudice. *New York Times* 11 November: http://www.nytimes.com/2007/11/11/us/11dna.html?_r=1&oref=slogin.

Harry, S., Caulfield, T. 2007. Race-marketing: BiDil and the race debate in print media. Poster presented at American Society of Human Genetics Annual Meeting, October 23-27, in San Diego, California.

Herrnstein, R., Murray, C. 1994. *The Bell Curve: Intelligence and Class Structure in American Life*. New York: Free Press.

Highfield, R. 2000. Selling science to the public. *Sci.* 289: 59.

Hobday, E. 2006. Race relations. *Men's Health* 21(6):44.

Holtzman, N.A., Bernhardt, B.A., Mountcastle-Shah, E., Rodgers, J.E., Tambor, E., Geller, G. 2005. The quality of media reports on discoveries related to human genetic diseases. *Comm. Genet.* 8:133-44.

Hubbard, R., Wald, E. 1993. *Exploding the Gene Myth: How Genetic Information Is Produced and Manipulated by Scientists, Physicians, Employers, Insurance Companies, Educators, and Law Enforcers*. Boston: Beacon Press.

IMediaConnection. http://www.imediaconnection.com/content/7202.asp.

International HapMap Project. About the HapMap. http://www.hapmap.org/thehapmap.html.en.

International HapMap Consortium. Consent Template, The HapMap Project and Other Research on Genetic Variations. The International

HapMap Project. http://www.hapmap.org/downloads/elsi/consent/Consent_Form_Template.pdf.

Jacobs, L.A. 1999. Equal opportunity, natural inequalities, and racial disadvantage: *The bell curve* and its critics. *Phil. Soc. Sci.* 29:121-45.

Kahn, J. 2004. How a drug becomes 'ethnic': Law, commerce and the production of racial categories in medicine. *Yale J. Health Policy, L. and Ethics* 4:1-46.

– 2007. Race-ing patents/patenting race: An emerging political geography of intellectual property in biotechnology. *Iowa L. Rev.* 92:353-416.

Kahn, M. 2007. Scientist Watson returns to US over race row. *Reuters* 19 October: http://www.reuters.com/article/newsOne/idUSN1844930820071019?sp=true.

Kaplan, J.B., Bennett, T. 2003. Use of race and ethnicity in biomedical publication. *J. Am. Med. Assoc.* 289:2709-16.

LaVeist, T.A. 2000. On the study of race, racism, and health: A shift from description to explanation. *Int'l J. Health Serv.* 30:217-9.

Lee, S.S-J. 2005. Racializing drug design: Implications of pharmacogenomics for health disparities. *Am. J. of Public Health* 95:2133-8.

Lee, S.S-J., Mountain, J., Koenig, B.A. 2001. The meanings of 'race' in the new genomics: Implications for health disparities research. *Yale J. Health Policy, L. and Ethics* 1:33-75.

Lillie-Blanton, M., LaVeist, T.A.. 1996. Race/ethnicity, the social environment, and health. *Soc. Sci. Med.* 43:83-91.

Lynn, R. 1999. The attack on *The Bell Curve. Personality and Individ. Diff.* 26:761-5.

Marks, L., Kalaitzandonakes, N., Wilkins, L. Zakharova, L. 2007. Mass media framing of biotechnology news. *Public Understand. Sci.* 16:183-203.

Multicultural Healthcare Marketing Group. http://www.mhmg-online.com/.

Nelkin, D. 2001. Molecular metaphors: The gene in popular discourse. *Nat. Rev. Genet.* 2:555-9.

Nelkin, D., Lindee, S. 2004. *The DNA Mystique: The Gene as a Cultural Icon.* Ann Arbor, MI: University of Michigan Press.

New York Times. 2005. The first race-based medicine. *New York Times* 19 June: 11.

Nisbet, M.C., Lewenstein, B. 2002. Biotechnology and the American media: The policy process and the elite press, 1970 to 1999. *Sci. Commun.* 23:359-91.

Nisbet, M.C., Mooney, C. 2007. Framing science. *Sci.* 316: 56.

Olson, S. 2001. The genetic archaeology of race. *Atlantic Monthly* 287:69-80.

Owens, K., King, M.C. 1999. Genomic views of human history. *Sci.* 286:451-3.

Pääbo, S. 2001. The human genome and our view of ourselves. *Sci.* 291:1219-20.

Payne, J.W. 2005. The race to market: Heart supplement targets Blacks, echoing race-based drug. *Washington Post* 13 January: F1.

Pearce, N., Foliaki, S., Sporie, A., Cunningham, C. 2004. Genetics, race, ethnicity, and health. *Brit. Med. J.* 328:1070-2.

Pharmaceutical Marketing Research Group. http://www.pmrg.org/index.php?src=gendocs&ref=2007%20Institute%20Abs%20thorne%20tbd&category=2007%20Institute&submenu=PMRG_Institute&PHPSESSID=f0f9cd00d71796a1b713fb3d5.

Pigliucci, M., Kaplan, J. 2003. On the concept of biological race and its applicability to humans. *Phil. Sci.* 70:1161-72.

Pope, J. 2004. Heart drugs benefit black patients. *Times-Picayune*, 9 November 2004:1.

Rahemtulla, T., Bhopal, R. 2005. Pharmacogenetics and ethnically targeted. *Brit. Med. J.* 330:1036-7.

Rebbeck T., Sankar, P. 2005. Ethnicity, Ancestry, and Race in Molecular Epidemiologic Research. *Cancer Epidemiol Biomarkers Prev* 14(11):2467-71.

Risch, N. 2006. Dissecting racial and ethnic differences. *New Eng. J. Med*, 354:408-11.

Robinson, D. 1994-95. Hereditary monarchy in the republic of virtue: *The bell curve: Intelligence and class structure in American life. J. Blacks Higher Educ.* 6:117-22.

Rotimi, C. 2004. Are medical and nonmedical uses of large scale genomic markers conflating genetics and 'race'? *Nat. Genet.* 36:S43-7.

Rowland, C. 2005. "Panel backs drug for blacks: BiDil heart treatment is 1st aimed at specific race; FDA expected to give OK" *Boston Globe* June 17, 2005.

Royal, C., Dunston, G. 2004. Changing the paradigm from 'race' to human genome variation. *Nat. Genet.* 36:S5-7.

Sankar, P., Kahn, J. 2005. BiDil: Race medicine or race marketing? *Health Aff.* 455-63.

Sankar, P., Cho, M. 2002. Toward a New Vocabulary of Human Genetic Variation. *Science* 298:1337-8.

Satel, S. 2002. I am a racially profiling doctor. *The New York Times*. 5 May:56.

Schnuer, J. 2001. DTC marketers eye ethnic media: Agencies, niche titles get more calls for pitches. *Advertising Age* 72(12):39.

Shanawani, H., Dame, L., Scwartz, S., Cook-Deegan, R. 2006. Non-reporting and inconsistent reporting of race and ethnicity in articles that claim association among genotype, outcome and race or ethnicity. *J. Med. Ethics* 32:724-8.

Sheldon, T.A., Parker, H. 1992. Race and ethnicity in health research. *J. of Public Health* 19:104-10.

Singer, E., Antonucci, T.C., Burmeister, M., Couper, M.P., Raghunathan, T.E., Van Hoewyk, J. 2007. Beliefs about genes and environment as determinants of behavioral characteristics. *Int'l. J. of Public Opinion Res.* 19:331-53.

Stein, R. 2005. FDA Approves Controversial Heart Medication for Blacks. Washington Post, Friday, June 24:A15

Ten Eyck, T., Willimen, M. 2003. The national media and things genetic. *Sci. Commun.* 25:129-52.

Venter, J.C., Adams, M.D., Myers, E.W., Li, P.W., Mural, R.J., Sutton, G.G., Smith, H.O., et al. 2001. The sequence of the human genome. *Sci.* 291:1304-51.

Zdeb, C. 2006. Ethnic links provide clues to health. *The Edmonton Journal* 13 November.

Zuckerman, D. 2003. Hype in health reporting: 'Checkbook science' buys distortion of medical news. *Int'l J. Health Serv.* 33:383-9.

An Interaction of Genes in Our Social Environment: Genetic Discrimination among Persons at Risk for Huntington Disease

YVONNE BOMBARD AND MICHAEL R. HAYDEN

INTRODUCTION

The interplay between genes and the environment may take on many forms. Genes may interact with environmental factors to change the direction or magnitude of the effect of a genetic variant. Alternatively, environmental factors may facilitate the phenotypic expression of disease-susceptibility genes. Taking a broader socio-behavioural perspective, it is also possible to regard genes and genetic information as interacting with the *social* "environment" to influence reaction and treatment among persons in society.

The rapid advances in genomic medicine offer many diagnostic, treatment, and reproductive options as well as the possibility of peering into our genetic futures. However, these powerful new technologies have also produced significant fear in society about the potential misuse of genetic information to discriminate against healthy individuals on the basis of genetic predisposition for a disease.

The interaction, or reaction, of the social "environment" to genetic information is not a new phenomenon; genetic discrimination has historical precedent. As history reveals, subtle influences of economic pressures along with health policies intended to improve the health of society can spiral quickly into eugenic practices across many diseases and populations. Today, with the increasing transparency of the human genome and the reliance on employers and private insurance companies to access health care, threats of genetic abuse are ever more real. It stands to reason that third parties have a direct interest in genetic information and there is potential for misuse of that information to discriminate against healthy individuals.

BACKGROUND

Indeed, the fear of genetic discrimination is widespread (Apse et al. 2004; Hall et al. 2005). Fear of genetic discrimination has prevented individuals from undergoing genetic testing (Apse et al. 2004; Peterson et al. 2002) and participating in genetic research (Hadley et al. 2003). These effects have significant public health implications, as genetic discrimination directly hinders individuals' potentially beneficial engagement with genetic medicine and the achievement of important scientific and medical advances. For example, many women at increased risk for breast cancer as well as persons at risk for Huntington Disease (HD) do not undergo genetic testing out of fear of its social implications for themselves and their families (Armstrong et al. 2003; Hall and Rich 2000; Quaid and Morris 1993).

Huntington Disease was the first adult-onset genetic disease for which a predictive test was developed. The test allows at-risk individuals to know whether they have inherited the causative CAG trinucleotide expansion in the *HD* gene (Langbehn et al. 2004; MacDonald et al. 1993). Huntington Disease is a debilitating inherited neuropsychiatric disease that usually presents in adult life with chorea, mood, and personality changes as well as cognitive impairment. HD symptoms usually become apparent between the ages of thirty-five and forty-five and then gradually progress until death approximately fifteen to twenty years after initial diagnosis (Harper 1991; Hayden 1981). Given the current lack of a treatment to prevent or interrupt the progression of the disease, significant concerns were raised about whether it was ethical to offer such testing. Initially there were warnings that predictive testing would lead to increased discriminatory practices within insurance and employment agencies against those identified with the mutation (Craufurd and Harris 1986; Perry 1981). It has been over twenty years since the inception of genetic testing for HD, yet little is known about whether predictive testing for HD actually results in discrimination.

SIGNIFICANCE OF GENETIC DISCRIMINATION

The consequences of genetic discrimination (GD), both for individuals and for the larger social "environment," have the potential to create significant social, health, and economic burdens by limiting opportunities for individuals at genetic risk in a range of contexts (Otlowski, Taylor, and Barlow-Stewart 2003). Given the likelihood that similar tests will become increasingly available for predicting risks for other diseases, exploring the nature of genetic discrimination in the context of HD is generally instructive for other disorders. Studies to date have been hampered by a lack of understanding of genetic discrimination from the perspectives of those at-risk or who have experienced genetic discrimination – the targets of discrimination. A description of the concerns and experiences of those facing these issues has surprisingly been overlooked. Moreover, the insurance and employment settings have received a disproportionate amount of attention with regards to genetic discrimination. Understandably these settings are the focus of existing discourse on genetic discrimination since they may be more tangible to determine. Yet the relationships with family members and friends following testing or knowledge of genetic risk are of equal, if not of more importance, especially in the field of genetics, and have been neglected thus far.

It would be helpful to have a better understanding of individuals' initial reactions to genetic discrimination (or the risk of it) and how they make sense of these experiences. Little is also known about how individuals found to have the HD expansion manage the risk or experience of genetic discrimination. Insight into the coping strategies used to deal with genetic discrimination can offer approaches for other persons at risk for late-onset disorders for mitigating genetic discrimination and navigating the social "environment" with respect to genetic information, in general.

CONCEPTUAL FRAMEWORK

The conceptual frame underpinning this discourse is Goffman's Stigma Theory (1963). Scholars define stigma as a distinguishing attribute that discredits or devalues a stigmatized person's identity within a particular context (Crocker, Major, and Steele 1998; Goffman 1963; Jones et al. 1987). Stigma results in labelling, negative stereotyping, exclusion, discrimination, and low status in the context of a power situation (Link and Phelan 2001). Stigma is a broad concept under which prejudice and discrimination are inextricably linked: stigma permeates many stereotypes, which are collectively held beliefs about members of a social group. Prejudice is the endorsement of negative stereotypes, and discrimination is the behavioural response based on prejudice (Arboleda-Florez 2003).

Goffman distinguishes three types of stigma: tribal identities, abominations of the body, and blemishes of individual character (1963). Tribal identities refer to the social situation into which one is born. This may include religious, ethnic, racial, or national groups. Abominations of the body represent physical ailments, such as deformities, illnesses, and paralysis. Goffman uses blemishes of individual character, such as drug addictions, to describe "moral transgressions" or "weakness of will." Furthermore, Goffman characterizes various dimensions in his definition of stigma. Such dimensions include concealability, stability, disruptiveness, and the extent to which a stigma is physically unappealing to others (1963).

Stigmatizing "marks" or diseases are further distinguished by their visibility and obtrusiveness. Goffman describes people with disorders that are stigmatizing and that cannot be hidden or disguised as discredited, and describes those with the conditions that allow people to "pass as normal" as discreditable. Whereas the discredited may deal with problems of "impression management," the discreditable may face difficulties of "information management" (Goffman 1963).

HYPOTHESES

In applying this conceptual framework in reference to genetic discrimination, persons at risk for HD can be considered to possess a form of tribal identity, as the nature of their genetic status is a matter of inheritance. They do not display overt symptoms of HD and, therefore, face issues of information management and likely use various cognitive, emotional, and behavioural strategies to manage genetic discrimination.

A longstanding question since the inception of HD predictive testing is: Does participating in predictive testing lead to increased levels of discrimination against persons who are at risk for HD? Moreover, on a fundamental level, does GD exist in persons at risk for HD and, if so, in which social "environments," and how do they cope or manage these experiences?

Given the anecdotal evidence of the existence of GD in other populations and countries (Apse et al. 2004; Lapham, Kozma, and Weiss 1996; Low, King, and Wilkie 1998; Peters et al. 2005), it is hypothesized that persons at risk for HD face genetic discrimination in multiple facets of their everyday lives. It is also likely that individuals respond to such issues by adopting cognitive, emotional, and behavioural strategies, similar to other contexts of stigmatization (Miller and Major 2000).

An understanding of individuals' perceptions, experiences, and management strategies regarding genetic discrimination is helpful in obtaining an appreciation of how genetic information may interact with the *social* "environment." It is thus the intent of this paper to review the nuances inherent to studying genetic discrimination, including the conceptual and methodological challenges, and to provide an overview of recent results exploring perceptions of genetic discrimination among individuals at risk for HD.

CONCEPTUAL AND METHODOLOGICAL CHALLENGES IN INVESTIGATING GENETIC DISCRIMINATION

Current evidence of genetic discrimination has been considerably hampered by various methodological constraints ranging from definitional issues, sampling issues, to response issues (Treloar et al. 2004).

Although the definition of genetic discrimination has been recognized and subjected to considerable debate by scholars, the concept of genetic discrimination has not been developed so as to delineate its conceptual features. Only when a concept's characteristics, boundaries, preconditions, and outcomes have been defined can the concept be measured (Morse et al. 1996). Existing literature lacks a mature conceptualization of genetic discrimination as well as an understanding of genetic discrimination, from the perspective of persons at risk for a genetic disorder.

The definitions of genetic discrimination have varied from narrow to broad, referring, for example, to the misuse of genetic information by insurers or, more broadly, to the use of genetic information for the psychosocial disadvantage of individuals as a result of prejudice or stigma (Treloar et al. 2004). Given its potential legal implications, genetic discrimination can be conceptualized as unjust distinctions that may be prohibited to varying degrees depending on the legislation available in a particular jurisdiction. From a human rights perspective, genetic discrimination may also refer to socially unacceptable distinctions, whereas an actuarial view would classify genetic discrimination as irrational distinctions (Rothstein and Anderlik 2001).

Ultimately, the generally recognized concept of genetic discrimination refers to differential treatment of asymptomatic individuals or their family members based on real or perceived genetic characteristics (Billings et al. 1992), which involve elements of social unacceptability as well as irrationality. Given the subjective nature of this social phenomenon, it is best to allow those at risk or those who have experienced genetic discrimination to define and identify the conceptual dimensions and characteristics of genetic discrimination themselves.

It is important to acknowledge that the process of making distinctions or providing differential treatment may not necessarily only involve disadvantage. Individuals may be treated differentially but in a positive way. This may be especially true in the case of HD since genetic information is inextricably linked to family, and outcomes such as increased understanding and support may also occur after disclosure of genetic information.

Targeting the appropriate subpopulations in which to investigate genetic discrimination also presents unique challenges. Although genetic discrimination includes individuals and family members, family members who may be at risk but who have not been genetically tested may not necessarily see the relevance of genetic discrimination to them. Stigma or prejudicial attitudes may occur towards an HD family, for example, but since genetic discrimination is commonly regarded as the denial of opportunities such as insurance or employment, the issue of genetic discrimination may not be considered as relevant for members who either have not had a particular experience of genetic discrimination or who have not been genetically tested or for those who have tested "negative" (Treloar et al. 2004). Thus, identifying the study population is particularly challenging, since individuals who would represent the target population of genetic discrimination may not necessarily view themselves as targets of genetic discrimination.

Furthermore, the distinction between an asymptomatic individual and a presymptomatic – or once-symptomatic but now asymptomatic – one is equally difficult to define and will likely continue to evolve as the clinical validity of genetic testing and understanding of the natural histories of diseases develop. In the context of HD, for example, the classification of asymptomatic persons continues to evolve as new insights reveal very early cognitive and psychiatric changes occurring in HD mutation carriers which even precede the unequivocal clinical diagnosis of HD (Duff et al. 2007; Hinton et al. 2007; Johnson et al. 2007; Snowden et al. 2002; Solomon et al. 2007). Likewise, the previous category of "asymptomatic" has evolved to include states such as "prediagnosed," "preclinical," and "premanifest," recognizing the continuum of sub-clinical changes that occur in persons carrying the HD mutation up to thirty-nine years from estimated onset of HD (Hinton et al. 2007).

The need to sample populations at risk for genetic conditions also presents problems since sampling frames such as support groups, clinical patients, or disease registries may be skewed towards individuals who may be more resourceful and willing to identify themselves. Thus, perhaps, those most vulnerable to genetic discrimination or those who fear genetic discrimination most may not be captured by such sampling frames and the extent of the concern or experience of genetic discrimination may not be fully ascertained. Moreover, targeting socially identifiable subpopulations at risk for genetic discrimination entails the risk of stigmatizing them (Foster, Bernsten, and Carter 1998).

In addition, genetic discrimination experiences are self-reported and may not always be validated. Although discriminatory experiences are inherently subjective experiences, self-reports of health as well as discrimination are commonly used and are increasingly being recognized as a valid (Krieger 1999; Sullivan 2003). Similar to self reports provided for other subjective somatic and mental health measures, self reports of social issues such as discrimination are considered valid precisely because they are subjective (Sullivan 2003). Previous studies have shown consistent associations between self-reports of discrimination and health consequences ranging from mental health problems, substance abuse, to physiological outcomes (Amaro, Russo, and Johnson 1987; Landrine et al. 1995; Meyer 1995; Williams 1997). Further, triangulation – the use of qualitative and quantitative methods, for example – incorporating the participants' perspectives on what constitutes genetic discrimination ultimately enhances the validity of discrimination experiences beyond any activity intended to "verify" accounts of genetic discrimination.

STUDYING GENETIC DISCRIMINATION

We undertook qualitative studies to explore the concept of genetic discrimination, the concerns and experiences of genetic discrimination, as well as the strategies individuals at risk for HD use to manage genetic discrimination.

Qualitative research approaches facilitate the conceptual exploration of otherwise unexplored phenomena and can generate insights for further development or testing on representative samples (Morse and Field 1995, 2nd ed.). Qualitative research approaches are also appropriate when the intent of the study is to gain insights into the meaning of experiences from individuals (Rubin and Rubin 1995).

Grounded theory was used as the qualitative method for this study. The choice of grounded theory is appropriate as it is typically used to explore basic social processes (Strauss and Corbin 1998, 2nd ed.) based on the theoretical assumptions of symbolic interactionism (Blumer 1969). It is also consistent with the assumption that genetic discrimination is situated in the social interactions and consequences that occur following disclosure of one's risk or genetic status.

Study Sample

Thirty-seven individuals who had the HD mutation (HD+) were sampled according to purposive sampling procedures where variation across participant demographic variables was sought (e.g., age, gender, education, and time since genetic testing) and formed the primary sample for this study. Ten people at 50 per cent risk for HD but who chose not to be tested (NT; "not tested"), as well as eight people who did not have the HD mutation (HD-), were recruited for the purpose of making theoretical comparisons. Theoretical comparisons are a vital part of discovering the properties and dimensions in the data and enable identification of variations in the developed theory (Strauss and Corbin 1998b). These comparison cases provided the opportunity to assess how family history and "negative" test results influenced concerns about and experiences of genetic discrimination. Participant recruitment continued until no new data emerged from subsequent interviews (Strauss and Corbin 1998).

Data Collection and Analysis

Data were collected through individual, semi-structured, open-ended interviews that lasted sixty-five minutes on average (range: fifty to ninety minutes). The interviews were digitally recorded, transcribed *verbatim,* and checked for accuracy. Field notes were maintained to document important contextual and behavioural information.

During the interviews, participants were encouraged to reflect on the following issues: their interpretations of genetic discrimination, their experiences of and concerns about genetic discrimination, their thoughts on genetic privacy, as well as how they responded to the risk or experience of genetic discrimination.

Constant comparison analysis was used to explore the concerns and experiences of genetic discrimination keeping with the tradition of grounded theory analysis (Strauss and Corbin 1998).

CONCERNS AND EXPERIENCES OF GENETIC DISCRIMINATION

An interview study was conducted to describe the nature of experiences, concerns, and strategies for genetic discrimination from the perspective of the HD community. Fifty individual semi-structured interviews with gene-positive, gene-negative, and untested healthy persons demonstrated that genetic discrimination is not an issue persons at risk for HD think about on a regular basis but one that they considered "occasionally" when an event sensitized them to the issue (Bombard et al. 2008). Awareness of the potential for genetic discrimination was precipitated by events that brought the potential or risk of genetic discrimination to the fore and suggested that having a genetic difference may hold consequences.

Awareness events included: observations of affected relatives' experiences of stigma and discrimination, information provided by genetic counsellors, and their own experiences of genetic discrimination. Persons' observations of affected relatives' experiences of stigma and discrimination related to their relatives being treated as though they were drunk homeless persons, and being put at a distance by their home communities (Bombard et al. 2008). Knowledge gathered through genetic counselling sessions, insurance applications, and the media formed other types of awareness events.

Participants also described their own encounters with genetic discrimination that occurred in insurance, family, social, health care, and employment settings. They shared experiences of being treated differently in insurance underwriting and being denied insurance policies and upgrades.

Individuals described subtle experiences of altered patterns of interaction, symptom-monitoring, and events where they felt their test results were used against them, such as in custody and access cases.

In the health care domain, individuals also described altered medical advice following disclosure of their HD genetic status. In the workplace individuals spoke of their beliefs that the information about their genetic status was directly related to unsuccessful bids to get a promotion, imposition of an unwanted early retirement, and increased surveillance by their employers.

ENGAGEMENT WITH GENETIC DISCRIMINATION

Awareness events like these prompted individuals to begin a cognitive and emotional process of engagement with genetic discrimination as a preliminary step toward making sense of these experiences and determining their risk for and the consequences of genetic discrimination.

Engagement with GD involved two phases. Initially, individuals formed meaningful interpretations of GD by making sense of GD, defining its various forms and validating the threat of GD. In the second phase, individuals personalized GD to determine its risk or consequences for themselves or their families. They did this by conducting a mental survey – taking into account their social, financial, employment, or familial circumstances as a way of assessing their potential for GD or for understanding the consequences of a particular GD experience. Emotional reactions often ensued in the course of engagement, which included feelings of concern, irritation, anger, frustration, or indifference.

Individuals' levels of engagement with genetic discrimination was reflected in the way they dealt with the potential for or experience of genetic discrimination. Individuals engaged with genetic discrimination from high to low levels depending on various factors which served to facilitate or impede the process. Engaged individuals acknowledged the relevance of genetic discrimination and directly attended to its potential or experience in an active fashion and frequently displayed emotional reactions. In contrast, participants who engaged with genetic discrimination to a lesser extent did not actively reflect upon the experience or its potential, and neither did they make strong connections between their experiences and genetic discrimination.

Two factors had a major influence on the degree of engagement with genetic discrimination: stage of life and the nature of the awareness events. Participants in the earlier stages of building their lives engaged actively with genetic discrimination. These included persons with young families, entering new careers, and still building relationships. However, those for whom most life- building events occurred before learning of their genetic status or risk for HD did not engage with their risk or experience of genetic discrimination, as they perceived it as less relevant.

The nature of awareness event also informed the degree to which individuals at risk for HD engaged with their risk or experience of genetic discrimination. Those who became aware of the issue of genetic discrimination in a direct manner, such as during a counselling session or by means of a personal encounter with genetic discrimination, engaged with genetic discrimination to a greater extent compared to those who learned about genetic discrimination in a removed fashion such as through a newsletter.

STRATEGIES TO MANAGE GENETIC DISCRIMINATION

To cope with issues of stigma and discrimination, persons at risk of HD used various behavioural strategies to manage the risk and experience of genetic discrimination. These strategies varied depending on the form of the genetic discrimination experience (i.e., an actual experience or merely apprehension of a potential experience) and the degree to which individuals engaged with genetic discrimination. Depending on participants' level of engagement with genetic discrimination and the nature of their experience, four discernable strategies to manage genetic discrimination were found (figure 1) (Bombard et al. 2007).

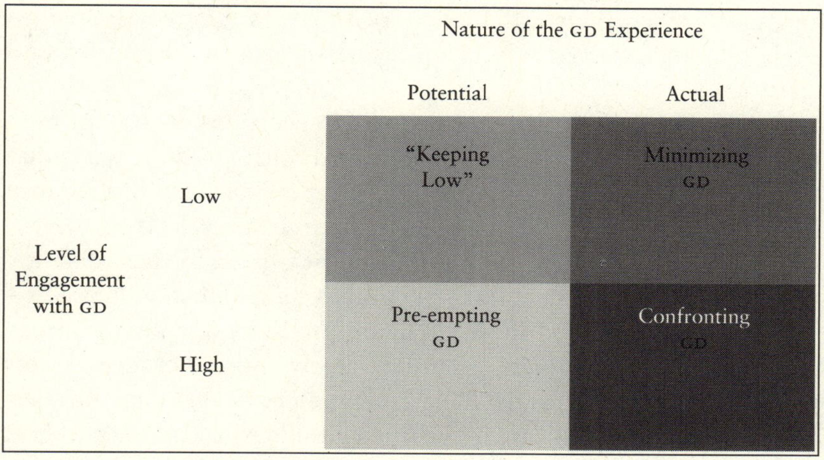

Figure 1. Strategies to manage genetic discrimination (GD)
Source: Bombard et al. 2007. (Reprinted with permission)

Keeping low described the type of strategy used to manage genetic discrimination by individuals who displayed a low level of engagement with genetic discrimination and were concerned about its potential. Individuals described keeping private about their family history or genetic test results or only sharing this information with what some referred to as the "inner circle." These people were fearful of judgment or misperceptions of their genetic risk, by employers for example. Others spoke of the potential stigma attached to their genetic risk and spoke of being "in the closet" about their genetic status. Others' strategies of "keeping low" involved staying in their present places of employment to avoid the potential loss of insurance benefits. Still others did not apply for insurance at all together because they were convinced that they would not qualify and thus avoided the probable rejection.

A second category of strategies involved *minimizing* genetic discrimination. Individuals using this behavioural strategy experienced genetic discrimination and displayed low levels of engagement with genetic discrimination. Typically, participants using this strategy were ambivalent about whether particular experiences constituted discrimination. In discussing their reactions to their experiences, individuals described screening out the incident(s), backing off, avoiding, and disregarding the encounter altogether. For example, individuals discussed avoiding confrontation to maintain relationships, such as those within the family. Others accepted and disregarded their differential treatment or offered reasons to explain others' behaviours in an effort to reduce tension around these issues.

Pre-empting genetic discrimination involved another strategy used by participants who were highly engaged with genetic discrimination and concerned about its potential. Purchasing life insurance prior to predictive testing, educating the public about HD, and ensuring one's predictive test results were not listed in their doctors' medical files characterized the approaches these individuals used.

Individuals described the strategy of qualifying for life insurance based on their family histories prior to learning of their genetic test results. They also instructed their geneticists not to send medical letters to their doctors to ensure that their results could not be accessed by insurers in the future. Participants also spoke of discussing HD and predictive testing with members of the public in an effort to increase awareness of HD and genetic information. In this respect, individuals used their genetic information to interact with their social environment by participating in a general educational campaign about HD and the implications of predictive testing.

Confronting was the category of strategies chosen by those who were highly engaged with genetic discrimination and who had had an encounter with it. Individuals who discussed confronting genetic discrimination described reactions whereby they resisted or challenged the perpetrator, sought advice, and refuted the basis for discrimination. In the context of institutional settings, for example, persons sought the advice of legal experts, unions, or clinicians to deal with discriminatory experiences. In interpersonal situations, in contrast, they described situations where they challenged others' judgmental comments or altered communication patterns or treatment.

CONCLUSIONS

These qualitative studies provide important understandings of the perspectives of persons at-risk for or who have experienced genetic discrimination. Engagement with genetic discrimination is a process that describes how individuals interpret the meaning of genetic discrimination and personalize its consequences into the context of their lives. Both these processes – interpretation and personalization – provide insight into the conceptualization of genetic discrimination and its inherent subjectivity. These studies also identify the ways in which individuals cope or manage with the risk and experiences of genetic discrimination.

Summary of Findings

ENGAGEMENT WITH GENETIC DISCRIMINATION

"Engagement with GD" describes a cognitive and emotional process individuals use to interpret the meaning of GD and personalize its risk and consequences in their lives. The process of engagement is precipitated by awareness events and results in personal formulations of the risk and effects of GD. Various factors were identified which inform the extent to which individuals engaged with genetic discrimination.

These findings demonstrate that a majority of genetically tested and untested individuals at risk for HD are concerned about and experience GD across a wide variety of contexts, and provide insight into at-risk persons' perceptions of what constitutes GD.

Genetic discrimination was conceptualized by those at-risk for or who have experienced genetic discrimination as being unfairly prevented from doing something or being treated differently. Inherent in participants' conceptualizations of genetic discrimination were elements of legal and social ideals. Human rights and privacy underpinned the perception of unjust genetic discrimination for participants since it was similar to other forms of discrimination. Genetic discrimination, according to these persons, manifests from stigma and prejudice – elements highly intertwined and fundamental to genetic discrimination. These conceptualizations resonate with broader definitions of genetic discrimination that pay due attention to the crucial elements of stigma, prejudice, and human rights.

Interpretation is, ultimately, a subjective endeavour. The nature of interpretation is dependent on the perceptions belonging to the target. What is considered "unfair," "unacceptable," "irrational," or "different" is ultimately a matter of debate, and depends on cultural context, as well as what society deems appropriate or acceptable. Moreover, genetic discrimination, being grounded in social interactions, requires individuals to make sense of others' reactions and their own responses to them. The interpretations may not necessarily include or be consistent with the intentions of the perpetrator. This process is thus inherently subjective in nature.

The theory of engagement with genetic discrimination provides a framework for understanding individuals' perceptions and experiences of genetic discrimination as well as their reactions to and strategies for genetic discrimination.

STRATEGIES TO MANAGE GENETIC DISCRIMINATION

Four main strategies – "keeping low," minimizing, pre-empting, and confronting – were identified as mechanisms to manage GD. The use of a particular strategy depended on individuals' level of engagement with GD and the nature of the experience (actual experience of GD or concern about its potential). This typology is presumed to be specific for asymptomatic individuals coping with a potentially discreditable identity as a consequence of being at increased risk for a late onset genetic disease. Given the recent attention surrounding genetic discrimination (Apse et al. 2004; Lapham, Kozma, and Weiss 1996; Peters et al. 2005), learning how individuals deal with real or potential genetic discrimination is of importance to genetics professionals in assisting individuals effectively manage these issues. Thus, these strategies may provide a framework for understanding how other individuals manage genetic discrimination for other genetic diseases for which predictive testing is available.

Ultimately, however, these qualitative studies are limited in their ability to provide generalizable and causative insight into the phenomenon of genetic discrimination. Numerous questions thus remain.

Unanswered questions

While these qualitative studies have provided a rich description of the concerns, experiences, and strategies persons at risk use to cope with genetic discrimination, there remain numerous avenues for future investigation. These include quantitative research on the extent of genetic discrimination experiences and concern, as well as the psychosocial impact of genetic discrimination.

THE EXTENT OF GENETIC DISCRIMINATION

Genetic discrimination is a topical issue that has received much debate in academic journals (Greely 2005; Harper et al. 2004; Hayden and Bombard 2005; Hudson 2007) as well as many other non-expert professional and popular press venues (Harmon 2008; Burgermeister 2003). Strikingly, all discussions point to the paucity of evidence for experiences of discrimination. Indeed, it is not yet known what the prevalence of genetic discrimination is among an asymptomatic (tested and untested) genetic population. Furthermore, from a clinical perspective, understanding the predictors and health outcomes of genetic discrimination has also been ignored. These qualitative studies demonstrate that genetic discrimination is an issue that spans beyond the traditionally examined settings of insurance and employment. Thus, an exploration of the breadth of genetic discrimination across a wide variety of settings is also required.

Further, an understanding of how often particular types of genetic discrimination occur, for how long, and at which point in time has also not been achieved. While insurance discrimination may be reported, this form of discrimination may only occur relatively infrequently, given the fact that individuals typically apply for insurance only a few times, and at particular stages in their lives. On the contrary, family and social genetic discrimination may actually occur more frequently and for longer durations. Likewise, in terms of day-to-day functioning or job-related tasks, the frequency at which this employment discrimination occurs or pervades peoples' fears and decisions is unknown. Survey instruments designed to address frequency, duration, and timing of particular forms of genetic discrimination are warranted in order to appreciate the full extent of the issue as well as its definite impact on health outcomes.

THE PSYCHOSOCIAL IMPACT OF GENETIC DISCRIMINATION

From a century of epidemiological research, it is now established that discrimination harms health (Krieger 1999). Inequality of various kinds has been shown to be associated with health consequences ranging from mental health effects, to substance abuse, to physiological outcomes. Examples include sexual discrimination resulting in elevated rates of smoking, suicide, and substance abuse (Council of Scientific Affairs 1996); disability discrimination associated with denial of health insurance thus resulting in inadequate medical care (Gill 1996); age discrimination associated with poorer survival of the elderly due to less aggressive treatment (Minkler and Estes 1991); social class discrimination associated with excess morbidity and mortality (Williams and Collins 1995); racial discrimination associated with higher mortality rates (National Center for Health Statistics 1997); and gender discrimination associated with sexual abuse and fewer years of disability-free life (adjusted for life expectancy) (Bachman and Saltzman 1995; Cosentino and Collins 1996; National Center for Health Statistics 1997). It stands to reason that genetic discrimination would also result in adverse health consequences.

It is still unknown whether psychological and possible physiological responses occur as a consequence of genetic discrimination. Moreover, it is unclear whether or how psychological, and possible physiological responses, are mediated by genetic discrimination. Examination of the heath and psychosocial outcome of genetic discrimination is an important issue. If such associations are found, this would raise the effects of GD to a level that suggests it ought to be recognized as a significant mental health concern in addition to an economic or policy issue.

CONCERN FOR GENETIC DISCRIMINATION

While findings from the present studies provide a rich description of individuals' concerns about genetic discrimination, it is unknown how these concerns influence behaviour and management strategies among persons at-risk for HD. For example, do these concerns influence at-risks persons' participation in genetic testing or genetic research? Such trends exist among other populations, and until they are examined they cannot be addressed to ensure that the concern about genetic discrimination does not hinder potentially beneficial engagement with genetic testing and research.

Furthermore, given the integral role that concern plays in responses to genetic discrimination, investigating the extent and influence of concern about genetic discrimination in the HD population will provide a more holistic appreciation of genetic discrimination. For example, do particular types of genetic discrimination lead to greater amounts of concern? Is concern about genetic discrimination associated with any psychological or physiological responses, and if so how?

OTHER TARGETS OF GENETIC DISCRIMINATION: WHAT ABOUT THE FAMILY MEMBERS?

HD and genetic discrimination affect families (Kessler and Bloch 1989; Sobel and Cowan 2000). Given that a large motivator for undergoing predictive testing among individuals at-risk for HD is to inform (and thus benefit) their children, it is likely that individuals have concerns about how their genetic test results, as well as potential subsequent genetic discrimination, may impact their children. Findings from the present study suggest that individuals have significant concerns about genetic discrimination for their children. Thus the extent of genetic discrimination may be under-represented if experiences of and concern about genetic discrimination for family members is not taken into account. Clearly, understanding how and if genetic discrimination impacts other family members is necessary to achieve a complete appreciation of how genetic discrimination, like HD, affects people's and families' lives.

Genes and environment can interact in a variety of ways. Molecular, protein, and social interactions are the multitude of levels that ought to be considered in such studies.

BIBLIOGRAPHY

Amaro, H., Russo, N.F., Johnson, J. 1987. Family and work predictors of psychological well-being among Hispanic women professionals. *Psychol Women Q* 11:505-21.

Apse, K.A., Biesecker, B.B., Giardiello, F.M., Fuller, B.P., Bernhardt, B.A. 2004. Perceptions of genetic discrimination among at-risk relatives of colorectal cancer patients. *Genet.Med.* 6, no. 6:510-16.

Arboleda-Florez, J. 2003. Considerations on the stigma of mental illness. *Can.J Psychiatry* 48, no. 10:645-50.

Armstrong, K., Weber, B., FitzGerald, G., Hershey, J.C., Pauly, M.V., Lemaire, J., Subramanian, K., Asch, D.A. 2003. Life insurance and breast cancer risk assessment: Adverse selection, genetic testing decisions, and discrimination. *Am.J.Med.Genet.* 120A, no. 3:359-64.

Bachman, R., Saltzman, H. Violence against women. NCJ-154348. 1995. Washington, DC, US Department of Justice.

Billings, P.R., Kohn, M.A., de Cuevas, M., Beckwith, J., Alper, J.S., Natowicz, M.R. 1992. Discrimination as a consequence of genetic testing. *Am.J.Hum.Genet.* 50, no. 3:476-82.

Blumer, H. 1969. *Symbolic Interactionism. Perspective and Method.* New Jersey: Prentice-Hall.

Bombard, Y., Penziner, E., Suchowersky, O., Guttman, M., Paulsen, J.S., Bottorff, J.L., Hayden, M.R. 2008. Engagement with Genetic

Discrimination: Concerns and experiences in the context of Huntington disease. *Eur.J.Hum.Genet.* 16, no. 3:279-89.

Bombard, Y., Penziner, E., Decolongon J., Klimek, M., Creighton, S., Suchowersky, O., Guttman, M., Paulsen, J., Bottorff, J., Hayden, M. 2007. Managing genetic discrimination: Strategies used by individuals found to have the Huntington disease mutation. *Clin.Genet.* 71, no. 3:220-31.

Burgermeister, J. 2003. Teacher was refused job because relatives have Huntington's disease. *BMJ* 327, no. 7419:827.

Cosentino, C.E., Collins, M. 1996. Sexual abuse of children: Prevalence, effects, and treatment. *Ann.N.Y.Acad.Sci.* 789:45-65.

Council of Scientific Affairs, American Medical Association. 1996. Health care needs of gay men and lesbians in the United States. Council on Scientific Affairs, American Medical Association. *JAMA* 275, no. 17:1354-9.

Craufurd, D.I., Harris, R. 1986. Ethics of predictive testing for Huntington's chorea: The need for more information. *Br.Med J (Clin Res.Ed)* 293, no. 6541:249-51.

Crocker, J., Major, B., Steele, C. 1998. Social Stigma and Self Esteem. In *Handbook of Social Psychology*, edited by Gilbert, D., S.T. Fiske, and G. Lindzey. Boston: McGraw Hill.

Duff, K., Paulsen, J.S., Beglinger, L.J., Langbehn, D.R., Stout, J.C. 2007. Psychiatric symptoms in Huntington's Disease before diagnosis: The Predict-HD Study. *Biol.Psychiatry.*

Foster, M.W., Bernsten, D., Carter, T.H. 1998. A model agreement for genetic research in socially identifiable populations. *Am J Hum.Genet* 63, no. 3:696-702.

Gill, C.J. 1996. Cultivating common ground: Women with disabilities. In *Man-Made Medicine: Women's Health, Public Policy, and Reform*, edited by Moss, K.L. Durham, NC: Duke University Press.

Goffman, E. 1963. *Stigma: The Management of Spoiled Identity*. Harmondsworth: Penguin.

Greely, H.T. 2005. Banning genetic discrimination. *N Engl J Med* 353, no. 9:865-7.

Hadley, D.W., Jenkins, J., Dimond, E., Nakahara, K., Grogan, L., Liewehr, D.J., Steinberg, S.M., Kirsch, I. 2003. Genetic Counseling and testing in families with hereditary nonpolyposis colorectal cancer. *Arch Intern Med* 163, no. 5:573-82.

Hall, M.A., Mcewen, J.E., Barton, J.C., Walker, A.P., Howe, E.G., Reiss, J.A., Power, T.E., Ellis, S.D., Tucker, D.C., Harrison, B.W., McLaren,

G.D., Ruggiero, A., Thomson E.J. 2005. Concerns in a primary care population about genetic discrimination by insurers. *Genet Med* 7, no. 5:311-16.

Hall, M.A., Rich, S.S. 2000. Genetic privacy laws and patients' fear of discrimination by health insurers: The view from genetic counselors. *J.Law Med.Ethics* 28, no. 3:245-57.

Harmon, A. 2008. THE DNA AGE; Fear of Insurance Trouble Leads Many to Shun or Hide DNA Tests. *The New York Times*.

Harper, P.S. 1991. *Huntington's Disease*. London: WB Saunders.

Harper, P.S., Gevers, S., de Wert, G., Creighton, S., Bombard, Y., Hayden, M.R. 2004. Genetic testing and Huntington's disease: Issues of employment. *Lancet Neurol.* 3, no. 4:249-52.

Hayden, M.R. 1981. *Huntington's Chorea*. New York: Springer-Verlag.

Hayden, M.R., Bombard, Y. 2005. Psychosocial effects of predictive testing for Huntington's disease. *Adv.Neurol.* 96:226-39.

Hinton, S.C., Paulsen, J.S., Hoffmann, R.G., Reynolds, N.C., Zimbelman, J.L., Rao, S.M. 2007. Motor timing variability increases in preclinical Huntington's disease patients as estimated onset of motor symptoms approaches. *JInt.Neuropsychol.Soc.* 13, no. 3:539-43.

Hudson, K.L. 2007. Prohibiting genetic discrimination. *N Engl J Med* 356, no. 20:2021-3.

Johnson, S.A., Stout, J.C., Solomon, A.C., Langbehn, D.R., Aylward, E.H., Cruce, C.B., Ross C.A., Nance, M., Kayson, E., Julian-Baros, E., Hayden, M.R., Kieburtz, K., Guttman, M., Oakes, D., Shoulson, I., Beglinger, L., Duff, K., Penziner, E., Paulsen, J.S. 2007. Beyond disgust: Impaired recognition of negative emotions prior to diagnosis in Huntington's disease. *Brain* 130, no. Pt 7:1732-44.

Jones, E., Farina, A., Hastorf, A., Markus, H., Miller, D., Scott, R. 1987. *Social Stigma: The Psychology of Marked Relationships*. New York: Freeman.

Kessler, S., Bloch, M.. 1989. Social system responses to Huntington Disease. *Family Process* 28, no. 1:59-68.

Krieger, N. 1999. Embodying inequality: A review of concepts, measures, and methods for studying health consequences of discrimination. *Int.J Health Serv.* 29, no. 2:295-352.

Landrine, H., Klonoff, E.A., Gibbs, J., Manning, V., Lund, M. 1995. Physical and psychiatric correlates of gender discrimination – An application of the schedule of sexist events. *Psychol Women Q* 19, no. 4:473-92.

Langbehn, D.R., Brinkman, R.R., Falush, D., Paulsen, J.S., Hayden, M.R. 2004. A new model for prediction of the age of onset and penetrance for Huntington's disease based on CAG length. *Clin.Genet.* 65, no. 4:267-77.

Lapham, E.V., Kozma, C., Weiss, J.O. 1996. Genetic discrimination: Perspectives of consumers. *Science* 274, no. 5287:621-4.

Link, B.G., Phelan, J.C. 2001. Conceptualizing stigma. *Annual Review of Sociology* 27:363-85.

Low, L., King, S., Wilkie, T. 1998. Genetic discrimination in life insurance: Empirical evidence from a cross sectional survey of genetic support groups in the United Kingdom. *BMJ* 317, no. 7173:1632-5.

MacDonald, M.E., Ambrose, C.M., Duyao, M.P., Myers, R.H., Lin, C., Srinidhi, L., Barnes, G., Taylor, S.A., James, M., Groot, N., Macfarlane, H., Jenkins, B., Anderson, M.A., Wexler, N.S. Gusella, J.F., Bates, G.P., Baxendale, S., Hummerich, H., Kirby, S., North, M., Youngman, S., Mott, R., Zehetner, G., Sedlacek, Z., Poustka, A., Frischauf, A.M., Lehrach, H., Buckler, A.J., Church, D., Doucettestamm, L., Odonovan, M.C., Ribaramirez, L., Shah, M., Stanton, V.P., Strobel, S.A., Draths, K.M., Wales, J.L., Dervan, P., Housman, D.E., Altherr, M., Shiang, R., Thompson, L., Fielder, T., Wasmuth, J.J., Tagle, D., Valdes, J., Elmer, L., Allard, M., Castilla, L., Swaroop, M., Blanchard, K., Collins, F.S., Snell, R., Holloway, T., Gillespie, K., Datson, N., Shaw, D., Harper, P.S. 1993. A novel gene containing a trinucleotide repeat that is expanded and unstable on Huntingtons-Disease chromosomes. *Cell* 72, no. 6:971-83.

Meyer, I.H. 1995. Minority stress and mental-health in gay men. *J Health Soc Behav* 36, no. 1:38-56.

Miller, C., Major, B. 2000. Coping with stigma and prejudice. In *The Social Psychology of Stigma*, edited by Heatherton, T., R. Kleck, M. Hebl, and J. Hull. New York: The Guilford Press.

Minkler, M., Estes, C.L. 1991. *Critical Perspectives on Aging: The Political and Moral Economy of Growing Old*. Amityville, NY: Baywood.

Morse, J.M., Field, P.A. 1995. *Qualitative Research Methods for Health Professional*. 2nd ed. Thousand Oaks, CA: Sage Publications.

Morse, J.M., Mitcham, C., Hupcey, J.E., Tason, M.C. 1996. Criteria for concept evaluation. *Journal of Advanced Nursing* 24, no. 2:385-90.

National Center for Health Statistics. Health, United States, 1996-1997, and injury chart book. 1997. Hyattsville, MD, National Center for Health Statistics.

Otlowski, M.F., Taylor, S.D., Barlow-Stewart, K.K. 2003. Genetic discrimination: Too few data. *Eur.J.Hum.Genet.* 11, no. 1:1-2.

Perry, T.L. 1981. Some Ethical Problems in Huntingtons-Chorea. *Can Med Assoc J* 125, no. 10:1098-1100.

Peters, K., Apse, K., Blackford, A., McHugh, B., Michalic, D., Biesecker, B. 2005. Living with Marfan syndrome: Coping with stigma. *Clin Genet* 68, no. 1:6-14.

Peterson, E.A., Milliron, K.J., Lewis, K.E., Goold, S.D., Merajver, S.D. 2002. Health insurance and discrimination concerns and BRCA1/2 testing in a clinic population. *Cancer Epidemiol Biomarkers Prev* 11, no. 1:79-87.

Quaid, K.A., Morris, M. 1993. Reluctance to undergo predictive testing: The case of Huntington disease. *Am.J.Med.Genet.* 45, no. 1:41-5.

Rothstein, M.A., Anderlik, M.R. 2001. What is genetic discrimination, and when and how can it be prevented? *Genetics in Medicine* 3, no. 5:354-8.

Rubin, H.J., Rubin, I.S. 1995. *Qualitative Interviewing: The Art of Hearing Data*. Thousand Oaks, CA: Sage Publications.

Snowden, J.S., Craufurd, D., Thompson, J., Neary, D. 2002. Psychomotor, executive, and memory function in preclinical Huntington's disease. *J Clin Exp.Neuropsychol.* 24, no. 2:133-45.

Sobel, S.K., Cowan, D.B. 2000. Impact of genetic testing for Huntington disease on the family system. *Am.J.Med.Genet.* 90, no. 1:49-59.

Solomon, A.C., Stout, J.C., Johnson, S.A., Langbehn, D.R., Aylward, E.H., Brandt, J., Ross, C.A., Beglinger, L., Hayden, M.R., Kieburtz, K., Kayson, E., Julian-Baros, E., Duff, K., Guttman, M., Nance, M., Oakes, D., Shoulson, I., Penziner, E., Paulsen, J.S. 2007. Verbal episodic memory declines prior to diagnosis in Huntington's disease. *Neuropsychologia* 45, no. 8:1767-76.

Strauss, A., Corbin, J. 1998. *Basics of Qualitative Research: Techniques and Procedures for Developing Grounded Theory*. 2nd ed. Thousand Oaks, CA: Sage Publications.

Treloar, S., Taylor, S., Otlowski, M., Barlow-Stewart, K., Stranger, M., Chenoweth, K. 2004. Methodological considerations in the study of genetic discrimination – A review. *Community Genetics* 7, no. 4:161-8.

Williams, D.R. 1997. Race and health: basic questions, emerging directions. *Ann Epidemiol* 7, no. 5:322-33.

Williams, D.R., Collins, C. 1995. US socio-economic and racial differences in health: Patterns and explanations. *Annu Rev Sociol* 21:349-86.

SECTION THREE

Interactive Models of Genes and Environment Interplays: Some Examples and Observations

This third section addresses issues for which more comprehensive and fine-grained interactive models offer promising research avenues and a robust basis for exploring the changing frontier between genes and environment as determinants of human health and behaviour.

In a first contribution, Richard Tremblay looks at the potential for more solid experimental prevention analyses of anti-social and physical aggressive behaviour. Robust data already gathered about the impacts of adverse rearing contexts on child development, including interesting developments in epigenetic studies, may suggest better research strategies for experiments aimed at the prevention of anti-social and aggressive behaviour.

Martha McClintock et al. argue for a paradigmatic shift in the conceptualization of genetically sensitive diseases and health disparities. Transdisciplinary research seems the best strategy to explain gene x environment breast cancer disparities impacting on African-American women. It does so by focusing on a comprehensive and epigenetic combination of biological channels at the organism level and of relevant environmental pathways; these range from spatial and socio-cultural elements through to a person's mental and psychological attributes.

Finally, Margaret Lock discusses general issues related to late-onset Alzheimer's disease genetic testing using ethnographic research findings on at-risk individuals who have undergone genetic testing. Epigenetic basic science results coupled to epidemiological study outcomes directly contribute to exposing the uncertainty and inconclusiveness of the knowledge derived from such genetic testing. In this conjuncture, genetically tested individuals, surprisingly unable to recall detailed information they have received about the genetics of Alzheimer's disease, tend to maintain rather than displace beliefs framed earlier in life about embodied identities and the role of genetics in shaping health outcomes.

From Social Learning Research to Experimental Epigenetic Research on Antisocial Behaviour Development: The Case of Physical Aggression

RICHARD E. TREMBLAY

Human violence is studied by many different disciplines (e.g., criminology, genetics, neuroscience, psychiatry, psychology, and sociology); however, few studies integrate these disciplines. This chapter describes how a longitudinal-experimental study based on the "social learning of aggression" hypothesis led to the integration of numerous disciplines and an epigenetic perspective.

It is well known by criminologists that the likelihood of committing a physically violent crime is highest from middle adolescence to early adulthood. This was first shown in the early nineteenth century by Adolphe Quetelet, a Belgian astronomer-mathematician-statistician who also extensively studied human physical, cognitive, and moral development. On the front cover of his 1833 book, *Research on the Propensity for Crime at Different Ages*, he wrote, "There is a budget which is paid with frightening regularity, it is that of prisons, hulks, and gallows; it is that one especially which it would be necessary to strive to reduce" (Quetelet 1984). Because adult violence is generally linked to a history of youth violence (McCord et al. 2001), and because all adults are former youths, one would expect that reducing youth violence would also reduce adult violence. Thus, the reduction of youth violence should in the long run have a very large impact on total violence in a given society.

Recently, the World Health Organization published a report on Violence and Health which concluded: "The majority of young people who become violent are adolescent-limited offenders who, in fact, show little or no evidence of high levels of aggression or other problem behaviours during their childhood" (Krug et al. 2002). This conclusion followed in the footsteps of a Surgeon General (US) 2001 report on physical violence that focused almost exclusively on adolescence and young adulthood. Indeed, most criminological studies of youth violence have focused on twelve- to eighteen-year-olds. During this period they become stronger physically, their cognitive competence increases (e.g., they become better at hiding their intentions), they become sexually mature, they ask and obtain greater freedom to use their time without adult supervision, and they have access to more resources such as money and transportation, which increases their capacity to satisfy their needs. This rapid bio-psycho-social development might be sufficient to explain why adolescence is a period of life when there are more opportunities and motives for antisocial behaviour. But in addition, adolescents lack experience and feel pressured to choose a career or to perform in school, within their peer groups, or with possible sexual partners. These factors, and many others, may explain why, compared to adults, proportionally more adolescents and young adults resort to violent behaviour.

Although a majority of adolescents will commit some delinquent acts, most of these are minor legal infractions. Population-based surveys have systematically shown that a small proportion of adolescents (approximately 6 per cent) account for the majority of violent acts and arrests (McCord et al. 2001). The challenge is to explain why some adolescents and some adults frequently resort to physically aggressive behaviour while others do not. Although adolescent criminals are relatively small in number, they frighten a large part of the population, and they represent a heavy burden of suffering for their victims, their families, and themselves. Adolescents with behavioural problems are also much more likely to be unemployed, suffer poor physical health, or have mental health problems.

DEVELOPMENTAL TRAJECTORIES OF PHYSICAL AGGRESSION

In the early 1980s, with a few colleagues, I initiated a longitudinal-experimental study to understand how kindergarten boys from low-socio-economic environments in Montreal became violent adolescents. More than 1,000 boys from fifty-three schools in poor neighbourhoods were assessed fourteen times between ages six and twenty-four. With Daniel Nagin, a criminologist from Carnegie-Mellon University in Pittsburgh (Nagin and Tremblay 1999), we described the developmental trajectories of teacher-rated physical aggression of these boys (figure 1): 17 per cent of the boys appeared never to have been physically aggressive; 4 per cent showed a high frequency of physical aggression from six to fifteen years of age; 28 per cent started with a high level of physical aggression at age six and became less and less physically aggressive with time; while the majority (52 per cent) had a low level of physical aggression at age six and also became less and less aggressive with time.

In contrast to hypotheses concerning late onset of antisocial behaviour, we did not find any group of boys in which there appeared to be an "onset" and maintenance of high levels of physical aggression for a significant number of years after age six. Self-report data during adolescence show that some individuals increase their frequency of physical aggression during adolescence. This can be seen especially with those who were already on a high trajectory of physical aggression during childhood. These boys are creating the famous peak in the age-crime curve, (Quetelet 1984; Farrington 1987; Sampson and Laub 2003) mainly because they are more likely to get arrested for physical aggressions as they grow taller and stronger. The same physical assault committed by the same boy at ages eleven and seventeen will be followed by a very different police reaction. There is a small group of boys who appear to start using physical aggression during adolescence, but the frequency of use remains below the frequency of the worst cases before they reached adolescence.

There are two other important observations from these studies. First, the boys on the high physical aggression trajectory during childhood are the most likely to be arrested and convicted for physical violence during adolescence and early adulthood. (Nagin and Tremblay 1999; Broidy et al. 2003) Second, the boys on the chronic physical aggression trajectory had the highest frequency of physical aggression during their kindergarten year (Nagin and Tremblay 2001). The researchers also observed that for every group of boys, the peak level for frequency of physical aggression was during the first year of the study, when they were in kindergarten.

These results clearly challenge the idea that the frequency of acts of physical aggression increases with age through social learning or because testosterone increases substantially in males during adolescence (van Bokhoven et al. 2006). They also challenge the notion

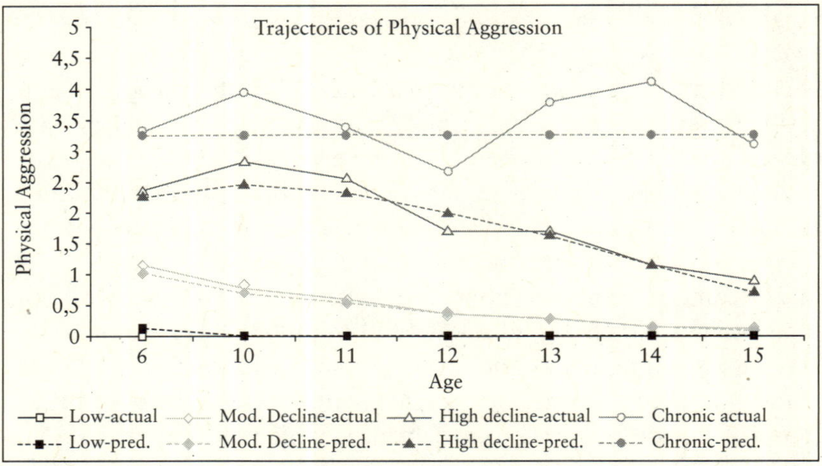

Figure 1. Developmental trajectories of physical aggression for boys from 6 to 15 years of age.

that there is a significant group of children who show chronic physical aggression during late childhood or adolescence after having successfully inhibited physical aggression throughout childhood. However, they beg the question, when do children learn to aggress physically? There are surprisingly few longitudinal studies that have tried to chart the development of physical aggression during the preschool years. This lack of attention to physical aggression during the early years appears to be the result of a long-held belief that physical aggression appears during late childhood and early adolescence as a result of bad peer influences, television violence, and increased levels of male hormones. This view of antisocial development was clearly described more than 250 years ago by Jean-Jacques Rousseau. The first sentence of his book on child development and education, *Émile*, makes his point: "Everything is good as it leaves the hands of the Author of things; everything degenerates in the hands of man" (Rousseau 1762/1979). A few pages later he is more explicit and appears to be writing the agenda for twentieth-century research on the development of antisocial behaviour: "There is no original sin in the human heart, the how and why of the entrance of every vice can be traced." Rousseau's strong stance was in clear opposition to that of Hobbes, who, a century earlier, described infants as selfish machines striving for pleasure and power, and declared: "It is evident therefore that all men (since all men are born as infants) are born unfit for society; and very many (perhaps the majority) remain so throughout their lives, because of mental illness or lack of discipline ... Therefore man is made fit for Society not by nature, but by training" (Hobbes 1647/1998).

This debate has far-reaching consequences, not only for child development investigators and educators, but also for political scientists, philosophers, and policy makers. Because the underlying debate is clearly grounded in our views of human nature, it is not surprising that investigators are likely to prefer the "origin of aggressive behaviour" that best fits their view of human nature, and their political leanings. However, since most political philosophers appear to agree that society must be built on the natural tendencies of humanity, it is surprising that research on early childhood development has not been a priority for the social sciences.

Recent longitudinal studies starting around birth are showing that there is more to the weakling's aggression than the disciples of Rousseau could imagine. In the 1990s, with colleagues from many different disciplines, I initiated longitudinal studies of large samples of newborns in order to understand the early bio-psycho-social development that leads to social maladjustment during the school years. In one of these studies we asked mothers to rate the frequency of physical aggressions at ages seventeen and thirty months and, at both times, to indicate at what age the child had started to show such behaviour. At age seventeen months, close to 90 per cent of the mothers reported that their child, at least sometimes, was physically aggressive toward others. One of the interesting results of that study was that mothers who reported that their seventeen-month-old child had started to hit others in the previous months appeared to have forgotten this early onset, since they later reported that at age 30 months their child had started to hit others *after* seventeen months of age. This memory failure as children grow older, taller, and bigger, could in part explain why parents of physically aggressive adolescents report that the aggression problems started only a year or two before (Loeber and Stouthamer-Loeber 1998).

The long-term follow-up of this cohort, as well as follow-ups of two other cohorts from Canada and the United States, shows that most children substantially increase the frequency of physical aggressions from nine to forty-eight months (Tremblay et al. 2004), and then decrease the frequency of use until adolescence (Côté et al. 2006; NICHD 2004). Figure 2 shows the different developmental

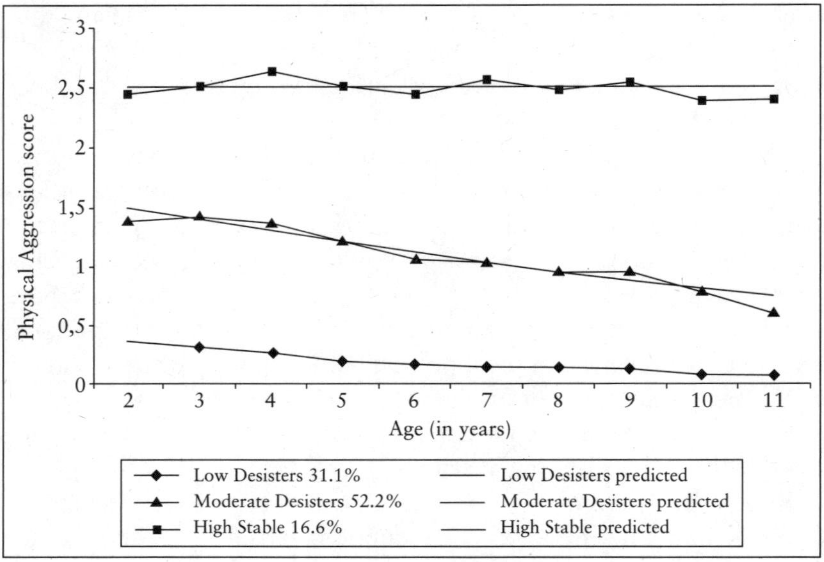

Figure 2. Physical aggression from 2 to 11 years of age

trajectories of physical aggression from two to eleven years of age for a random sample of Canadian children (N = 10,658) first assessed in 1994. We clearly see that the frequency of physical aggressions among children decreases substantially from the preschool years to pre-adolescence, except for a small group who use physical aggression most often throughout that period.

The studies of antisocial behaviour during adolescence and pre-adolescence show that family characteristics and parental behaviour are good predictors of antisocial behaviour (McCord and Widom 2001). Is this also true for preschool children on trajectories of chronic physical aggression? The predictive analyses show that the best predictor of aggression is having an older sibling, probably because one needs a target to physically aggress against. Parent separation before birth and low income, two of the classic family risks, also predict high physical aggression during early childhood. And mother characteristics before birth are among the best predictors: frequent antisocial behaviour during adolescence, giving birth before twenty-one years of age, not having finished high school, and smoking during pregnancy. Smoking apparently affects the development of the brain because of nicotine reaching the fetus' brain (Wakschlag, et al. 2002). Of course, males were more at risk than females of being on the high physical aggression trajectory, even when the assessment started at seventeen months of age. After controlling for prenatal assessments, those done at five months after birth revealed two significant predictors: family dysfunction and coercive-hostile parenting by the mothers. Thus, the traditional predictors of adolescent antisocial behaviour are predicting chronic physical aggression during the preschool years. Interestingly, the analyses of the data from our twin study also shows that at seventeen months of age more than half of the variation in frequency of physical aggression is explained by genetic factors (Dionne et al. 2003).

EPIGENETICS AND PHYSICAL AGGRESSION DEVELOPMENT

The longitudinal data on physical aggression from infancy onwards, summarized in the previous section, indicates that physical aggression is not a behaviour that children learn like reading or writing, nor an illness that children "catch" like poliomyelitis or smallpox. It is, rather, a behaviour like crying, eating, grasping, throwing, and running, that young humans engage in when the corresponding physiological structure is in place. The young human learns to regulate these "natural" behaviours with age, experience, and brain maturation. The learning-to-control process implies regulating one's needs to adjust to those of others, and this process is generally labelled "socialization."

It is not hard to imagine why the evolutionary process would have given humans a genetic program coding for all the basic mechanisms required in order to react to hunger and to threat. Young children's muscles are activated to run, push, kick, grab, hit, throw, and yell with extreme force when hungry, when angry, or when they are strongly attracted by something. However, stating that humans are genetically programmed to be able to physically aggress when needed is different from stating that the frequency of the physical aggressions they use is genetically programmed. Since all eighteen-month-olds who have developed normally can, and possibly do, physically aggress, but not all do so at the same frequency and with the same vigour, to what extent are these individual differences due to the genetic program they have inherited and to what extent are they due to the environment in which the infants have been growing?

The trajectories shown in figures 1 and 2 clearly indicate that these individual differences exist at any given point, starting in early childhood; but the most interesting phenotype is the development over time. There is obviously intra-individual change over time. Most children learn to reduce the frequency of use of a behaviour which they apparently did not need to learn. However, relatively stable differences among individuals remain. What are the gene-environment mechanisms that explain the change and stability? They are possibly very similar to the mechanisms which explain the developmental trajectories of growth in height. Genes code for growth mechanisms, but there are individual differences in these codings, as well as environmental differences (e.g., access to food) that lead to stable individual differences. Thus, the individual differences in the frequency of physical aggression at one point in time, and over time, can be due to a large number of "causes," for example, to individual differences in the genetic coding for serotonin (Pihl and Benkelfat 2005) or testosterone (van Goozen 2005), or language development (Dionne 2005), or cognitive development (Séguin and Zelazo 2005); or to environmental differences such as the mother's tobacco use during pregnancy (Wakschlag et al. 2002), birth complications, parental care (Gatti and Tremblay 2005; Zoccolillo, Paquette, et al. 2005), and peer characteristics (Boivin et al. 2005). However, the individual differences that we observe are very likely due to interactions between many of these mechanisms, that is to *epigenetic* mechanisms (Francis et al. 2002; Weaver et al. 2004).

We initiated the study that started at the earliest point during development to assess gene-environment effects on physical aggression, and used a large sample of eighteen-to-nineteen-month-old twins (Dionne et al. 2003). Results showed, with a large sample of female and male twins, that variance in mother reports of physical aggression was explained somewhat more by genetic factors (58%) than by environmental factors (42%), suggesting that there are strong genetic effects on physical aggression during early childhood. Based on the longitudinal studies described above, which show that physical aggression decreases with age, we would expect to observe increased environmental effects as children grow older, if it were the case that the pressures on learning alternatives to physical aggression come from the environment. Unfortunately, studies with older samples of twins have used global scales of antisocial behaviour (Arseneault et al. 2003; Eley et al. 1999). If their results are a true representation of genetic effects on physical aggression, we would have to conclude that learning to regulate physical aggression is largely determined by genetic factors (Arseneault et al. 2003). To settle this question, we need genetically and environmentally informative longitudinal studies, such as twin studies, that will focus on the development of physical aggression from early childhood to adulthood, to understand the role of genetic and environmental factors throughout development. The Dionne et al. study (Dionne et al. 2003) shows that both the genetic and the environmental causes of a very specific socially disruptive behaviour, physical aggressions, are in place by nineteen months of age – long before violent video games, delinquent peers, and the effects of watching war coverage on TV could be exerting any influence.

Many molecular genetic studies have attempted to identify polymorphisms related to aggressive behaviour, mainly with animal and human adult samples (Pihl and Benkelfat 2005). Caspi et al. (2002) used a longitudinal study to specifically address gene-environment interactions. They observed that the maltreated males at higher risk of being convicted of a violent crime before twenty-seven years of age were those who had the short version of the functional polymorphism in the gene coding for monoamine oxidase A (MAOA) activity. The MAOA enzyme metabolizes neurotransmitters linked in previous studies to behaviour problems (e.g., dopamine, norepinephrine, and serotonin), and the short version of the allele leads to low activity. Effects were similar for conduct disorders assessed between ten and eighteen years of age, antisocial personality symptoms, and disposition to violence measured at twenty-six years of age. Individuals with a history of chronic physical aggression may be the driving force in these associations, since they are the most likely to be found in each of the assessed categories. This study is a good illustration of gene-environment interactions related to prevention, which need to be addressed. First, although the study was a longitudinal study from birth to twenty-six years of age, the analyses did not provide information on the developmental impact of the gene-environment interaction. Was the effect of the gene-environment interaction on physical aggression present in early childhood? Did it appear later, during elementary school, adolescence, and even adulthood? These are important questions for preventive interventions.

From the developmental data presented in the preceding section, one would expect that the effects were present early, and may have grown with time. A second question concerns the intervention strategies. Let's assume that the gene-environment interaction effects appear in early childhood and will increase with time if there are no early interventions. Which type of intervention should we use? For example, we could screen pregnant women soon after conception to identify those at risk of maltreating their child and offer a support program to help prevent the family from abusing the child (Olds et al. 1998). An alternative strategy would be to give the child a chemical treatment that would correct or compensate for the low MAOA activity (Weaver et al. 2004; Caspi et al. 2002). Both strategies could also be used with some cases. Thus, much research is needed to understand the gene-environment impact on the development of physical aggression, but research is also needed on how to use that knowledge to prevent the *development* of chronic physical aggression.

Recent prevention experiments have shown that interventions with elementary school children can have relatively long-term positive impacts (e.g., Hawkins et al. 2005; Vitaro et al. 1999). However, from our present understanding of the development of physical aggression described above, we would expect that intensive preschool interventions would have more positive (or negative) long-term impacts than do intensive elementary school interventions. For example, the Perry Preschool experiment with three- and four-year-olds showed impressive long-term reduction of criminal behaviour among males; unfortunately, there is apparently no information on the development of physical aggression in this study. Olds et al. (Olds et al. 1998) experimented with an earlier intervention. They randomly allocated a nurse home-visitation program to young underprivileged pregnant women at high risk of child abuse and neglect. These children were obviously also at high risk of chronic physical aggression. The long-term follow-up of the children from the intervention group showed that they were less frequently abused and neglected, and were also less likely to exhibit delinquent behaviours during adolescence. One would expect that the intervention group learned more rapidly to regulate physical aggression and was less frequently involved in physical aggression during childhood and adolescence. Unfortunately, based on the published material, the development of physical aggression, or any other antisocial behaviour, appears not to have been included in the follow-up assessments. Regular assessments of physical aggression during childhood and adolescence in the two experiments would have helped us understand whether an intervention starting three years after birth and targeting cognitive development has as much of an impact on developmental trajectories of physical aggression as an intervention that started during pregnancy and that could therefore affect early brain development. These are important questions for assessing the costs and benefits of interventions during the developmental cycle, but they are also important questions for understanding the mechanisms that lead to or prevent chronic physical aggression. To what extent are the control mechanisms plastic, and over what period of time? The preventive study we did with disruptive children at school entry (Lacourse et al. 2002; Tremblay 2003) indicated that there can still be some plasticity at that age, but that it is somewhat limited and costly to achieve.

Weaver et al. (Weaver et al. 2004) recently showed how an environmental event during early childhood (rat pups being licked by their mothers) activated gene expression which influenced the development of the hypothalamic-pituitary-adrenal (HPA) axis and increased life expectancy. Following this work with rats, we postulated that the adverse early environmental characteristics that predict a chronic physical aggression (CPA) trajectory for human males should have an impact on gene expression. We used a sample of males from low socio-economic backgrounds who were found to be on a high physical aggression trajectory between six and twelve years of age and compared them to boys from the same background who followed a normal physical aggression trajectory (Broidy et al. 2003). Preliminary analyses indicate that males on the CPA trajectory have substantially more methylated alleles when we look at T cells and more specifically at the IL-1B cytokine. The developmental pattern of these immune system differences will be important to study. Are the differences in gene expression at the origin of the behavioural differences or are they the product of the behavioural differences? Our hypothesis from the rat licking model is that early adverse environments negatively affects gene expression, which in turn disturbs brain development and eventually prevents adequate control over aggressive responses. Experimental work with pregnant monkeys has indeed shown that stress and substance use during pregnancy has a negative impact on offspring's cognitive and behavioural development as well as on the immune system (Coe et al. 2007; Schneider et al. 2002).

Twin studies and molecular genetic studies can address the gene-environment interaction issue. However, they fail to address the causal mechanisms leading to CPA because they are limited to a statistical analysis of correlations. To test causal mechanisms we need the type of true experiments that are being regularly done with rats and monkeys (Foley et al. 2005; Weaver et al. 2006). Such studies are ethically impossible if the manipulation involves stressing healthy pregnant women, however attempts to prevent stress in high-risk pregnant women are ethical and necessary if we are to find effective preventive interventions. Thus, experimental preventive interventions can kill two birds with one stone: identify basic mechanisms leading to CPA and identify effective preventive interventions. From both perspectives they are more likely to rapidly provide useful knowledge than traditional longitudinal studies. Randomized preventive control trials that manipulate mother's behaviour pre- and post-natally are not new (Olds et al. 1986), however they are extremely rare and have failed to monitor effects on the development of gene expression, physiological structures, neurocognitive functioning, and behaviour.

CONCLUSION

More than 1600 years ago, St Augustine may have written the most sensible page of all on the development of aggression. In the seventh chapter of his *Confessions* he describes the physical aggression of infants and concludes: "Thus it is not the infant's will that is harmless, but the weakness of infant limbs ... These things are easily put up with; not because they are of little or no account, but because they will disappear with increase in age. This you can prove from the fact that the same things cannot be borne with patience when detected in an older person" (St Augustine AD 397/1960). More than a thousand years later Hobbes, in *De Cive* (Hobbes 1647/1998), makes a similar statement when he refers to a wicked man as a robust child.

In his attempt to blame the arts, sciences, and civilization in general, for inequalities among men, Rousseau invented a human child, born innocent, who had to be kept far away from society until early adolescence. Living alone with nature was the best way for a child to follow nature and avoid becoming corrupted by society (Cranston 1991). He believed children had to be kept away from peers and from books. Rousseau's romantic perception of child development appears to be an extremely common view. Many late twentieth and early twenty-first-century adults, including psychologists and psychiatrists, appear to be convinced that social behaviour is natural ("God-given" or "genetic") and antisocial behaviour is learned. For example, social learning has been one of the most influential theories in the area of aggression development in the last thirty years. In his 1973 book, *Aggression*, Albert Bandura, one of the leading social learning theorists, starts his chapter "Origins of aggression" with the following phrase: "People are not born with preformed repertoires of aggressive behaviour; they must learn them in one way or another" (Bandura 1973).

For those who believe that Rousseau is the cause of these beliefs about child development, consider the fact that 200 years before the publication of *Émile*, Erasmus in his "Declamation on the subject of early liberal education for children" criticized those "who maintained out of a false spirit of tenderness and compassion that children should be left alone until early adolescence" and argued that "one cannot emphasize too strongly the importance of those first years for the course that a child will follow throughout his entire life" (Erasmus of Rotterdam 1529/1985).

Twentieth-century longitudinal studies of thousands of subjects from childhood to adulthood have confirmed the old philosopher's experience. Children who fail to learn alternatives to physical aggression during the preschool years are at very high risk of a huge number of problems. They tend to be hyperactive, inattentive, anxious; they fail to help when others are in need; they are rejected by the majority of their classmates, they get poor grades, and their behaviour disrupts school activities (Tremblay et al. 2003). They are usually swiftly taken out of their "natural" peer group and placed in special classes, special schools and institutions with other "deviants," the ideal setting in which to reinforce marginal behaviour (Dishion et al. 1999). They are among the most delinquent from pre-adolescence onward; the first to initiate substance use, the first to become engaged in sexual intercourse; and are the most at risk of dropping out of school, having a serious accident, being violent offenders, and being diagnosed as having a psychiatric disorder (Lacourse et al., 2003; Tremblay et al. 2003).

From this perspective, failure to learn alternatives to physical aggression in the early years appears to have the long-term negative consequences on the social adjustment of an individual that Hobbes described in his 1647 *De cive*. The modern studies that have followed aggressive children into their adult years have indeed shown that there are extremely negative consequences not only for the aggressive individuals, but also for their mates, their children, and the communities in which they live (Tremblay 2000). The stage is set for early parenthood, unemployment, family violence, and a second generation of poor children brought up in a disorganized environment. We are learning from genetic and epigenetic studies with animals and humans that this intergenerational process may well be transmitted through genetic endowment, but also through maternal behaviour during pregnancy and early parenting behaviour. Indeed, the prenatal and postnatal environment has a programming impact on gene expression necessary for the development of a person who will be able to learn to adapt to the social environment, and in turn become an adequate parent.

This chapter is based on a paper presented at the Royal Society of Canada symposium "Social Sciences Facing Modern Genetics Challenges: Changing Boundaries between Genes, Behaviour and the Social Fabrics" (University of Alberta, Edmonton, 17 November 2007) and on an article published in *Canadian Journal of Policy Research* (ISUMA), 2000, vol.1, no.2, 19-24.

BIBLIOGRAPHY

Arseneault, L., Moffit, T.E., Caspi, A., et al. 2003. Strong genetic effects on cross-situational antisocial behaviour among 5-year-old children according to mothers, teachers, examiner-observers, and twins' self-reports. *Junior Child Psychiatry* 44, no. 6:832-48.

Arseneault, L., Tremblay, R.E., Boulerice, B., Saucier, J-F., 2002. Obstetrical complications and violent delinquency: Testing two developmental pathways. *Child Dev.* 73 no. 2:496-508.

Bandura, A. 1973. *Aggression: A social learning analysis*. New York: Holt.

Boivin, M., Vitaro, F., Poulin, F. 2005. Peer relationships and the development of aggressive behavior in early childhood. In: Tremblay R.E.,

Hartup W.W., Archer J., eds. *Developmental Origins of Aggression.* New York: Guilford: 376-97.

Broidy, L.M., Nagin, D.S., Tremblay, R.E., et al. 2003. Developmental trajectories of childhood disruptive behaviors and adolescent delinquency: A six site, cross national study. *Dev Psycho.* 39 no. 2:222-45.

Caspi, A., McClay, J., Moffitt, T., et al. 2002. Role of genotype in the cycle of violence in maltreated children. *Science* 297:851-4.

Coe, C.L., Lubach, G.R., Shirtcliff, E.A. 2007. Maternal stress during pregnancy predisposes for iron deficiency in infant monkeys impacting innate immunity. *Pediatr Res.* 61 no.5 Part 1:520-4.

Côté, S., Vaillancourt, T., LeBlanc, J.C., Nagi, D.S., Tremblay, R.E. 2006. The development of physical aggression from toddlerhood to pre-adolescence: A nation wide longitudinal study of Canadian children. *J Abnorm Child Psychol.* 34 no.11:71-85.

Cranston, M.W. 1991. *The Noble Savage: Jean-Jacques Rousseau, 1754-1762.* Chicago: University of Chicago Press.

Dionne, G. 2005. Language development and aggressive behavior. In Tremblay R.E., Hartup W.W., Archer J., eds. *Developmental Origins of Aggression.* New York: Guilford.

Dionne, G., Tremblay, R.E., Boivin, M., Laplante, D., Pérusse, D. 2003. Physical aggression and expressive vocabulary in 19 month-old twins. *Dev Psychol.* 39 no.2:261-73.

Dishion, T.J., McCord, J., Poulin, F. 1999. Iatrogenic effects in early adolescent interventions that aggregate peers. *Am Psychol.* 54 no. 9:755-64.

Edelbrock, C., Rende, R., Plomin, R., Thompson, L.A. 1995. A twin study of competence and problem behavior in childhood and early adolescence. *J Child Psychol Psychiatry.* 36 no.5:775-85.

Eley, T.C., Lichenstein, P., Stevenson, J. 1999. Sex differences in the etiology of aggressive and nonaggressive antisocial behavior: Results from two twin studies. *Child Dev.* 70 no. 1:155-68.

Erasmus of Rotterdam. 1529/1985. A declamation on the subject of early liberal education for children. In Sowards G.K.; ed. *Collected works of Erasmus, Literary and Educational Writings.* Vol 4. Toronto: University of Toronto Press: 297-346.

Farrington, D.P. 1987. Epidemiology. In Quay H.C., ed. *Handbook of Juvenile Delinquency.* New York: John Wiley and Sons: 33-61.

Foley, A.G., Murphy, K.J., Regan, C.M. 2005. Complex-environment rearing prevents prenatal hypoxia-induced deficits in hippocampal cellular mechanisms necessary for memory consolidation in the adult wistar rat. *J Neurosci Res.* 82:245-54.

Francis, D.D., Diorio, J., Plotsky, P.M., Meaney, M.J. 2002. Environmental enrichment reverses the effects of maternal separation on stress reactivity. *J Neurosci.* 22:7840-3.

Francis, D.D., Szegda, K., Campbell, G., Martin, W.D., Insel, T. 2003. Epigenetic sources of behavioral differences in mice. *Nat Neurosci.* 6:445-6.

Gatti, U., Tremblay, R.E. 2005. Social capital and physical violence. In Tremblay, R.E., Hartup, W.W., Archer, J., eds. *Developmental Origins of Aggression*. New York: Guilford.

Hawkins, J.D., Kosterman, R., Catalano, R.F., Hill, K.G., Abbott, R.D. 2005. Promoting positive adult finctioning through social development intervention in childhood: Long-term effects from the Seattle Social Development Project. *Arch Pediatr Adolesc Med.* 159 no.1:25-31.

Hobbes, T. 1647/1998. *De Cive; On the Citizen*. New York: Cambridge University Press.

Kellam, S.G., Rebok, G.W., Ialongo, N., Mayer, L.S. 1994. The course and malleability of aggressive behavior from early first grade into middle school: Results of a developmental epidemiologically-based preventive trial. *J Child Psychol Psychiatry.* 35 no. 2: 259-81.

Krug, E.G., Dahlberg, L.L., Mercy, J.A., Zwi, A.B., Lozano, R.E. 2002. World report on violence and health. www.who.int/violence_injury_prevention/violence/world_report/wrvh1/en.

Lacourse, E., Côté, S., Nagin, D.S., Vitaro, F., Brendgen, M., Tremblay, R.E. 2002. A longitudinal-experimental approach to testing theories of antisocial behavior development. *Dev Psychopathol.* 14:909-24.

Lacourse, E., Nagin, D.S., Tremblay, R.E., Vitaro, F., Claes, M. 2003. Developmental trajectories of boys' delinquent group membership and facilitation of violent behaviors during adolescence. *Dev Psychopathol.* 15:183-97.

Laub, J.H., Sampson, R.J. 2003. *Shared Beginnings, Divergent Lives: Delinquent Boys to Age 70*. Cambridge, MA: Harvard University Press.

Loeber, R., Stouthamer-Loeber, M. 1998. Development of juvenile aggression and violence. Some common misconceptions and controversies. *Am Psychol.* 53 no.2:242-59.

McCord, J., Widom, C.S., Crowell, N.E. 2001. *Juvenile Crime, Juvenile Justice*. Washington: National Academy Press.

Nagin, D., Tremblay, R.E. 2001. Parental and early childhood predictors of persistent physical aggression in boys from kindergarten to high school. *Arch Gen Psychiatry.* 58:389-94.

Nagin, D., Tremblay, R.E. 1999. Trajectories of boys' physical aggression, opposition, and hyperactivity on the path to physically violent and non violent juvenile delinquency. *Child Dev.* 70 no. 5:1181-96.

NICHD Early Child Care Research Network. 2004. Trajectories of physical aggression from toddlerhood to middle school: Predictors, correlates, and outcomes. *Monogr Soc Res Child Dev.* 69 no. 4 278:1-146.

Olds, D.L., Henderson, C.R., Chamberlin, R., Talelbaum, R. 1986. Preventing child abuse and neglect: A randomized trial of nurse home visitation. *Pediatrics.* 78:65-78.

Olds, D., Henderson, C.R., Cole, R., et al. 1998. Long-term effects of nurse home visitation on children's criminal and antisocial behavior: Fifteen-year follow-up of a randomized controlled trial. *JAMA.* 280 no. 14:1238-44.

Pihl, R.O., Benkelfat, C. 2005. Neuromodulators in the development and expression of inhibition and aggression. In: Tremblay R.E., Hartup W.W., Archer J., eds. *Developmental Origins of Aggression.* New York: Guilford: 261-80.

Quetelet, A. 1984. *Research on the Propensity for Crime at Different Ages.* Cincinnnati, OH: Anderson (Original work published in 1833).

Raine, A., Brennan, P., Mednick, S.A. 1997. Interaction between birth complications and early maternal rejection in predisposing individuals to adult violence: Specificity to serious, early-onset violence. *Am J Psychiatry.* 154:1265-71.

Rousseau, J-J. 1762/1979. *Emile or On Education.* New York: Basic Books.

Sampson, R.J., Laub, J.H. 2003. Life-course desisters? Trajectories of crime among delinquent boys followed to age 70. *Criminology* 41:301-39.

Schneider, M.L., Mooreb, C.F., Kraemera, G.W., Robertsd, A.D., DeJesuse, O.T. 2002. The impact of prenatal stress, fetal alcohol exposure, or both on development: Perspectives from a primate model. *Psychoneuroendocrinology* 27 no. 1-2:285-98.

Séguin, J.R., Zelazo, P. 2005. Executive function in early physical aggression. In Tremblay, R.E., Hartup, W.H., Archer, J., eds. *Developmental Origins of Aggression.* New York: Guilford, 307-29.

St Augustine. 397/1960. *Confessions.* New York: Doubleday AD.

Suomi, S.J. 2005. Genetic and environmental factors influencing the expression of impulsive aggression and serotonergic functioning in rhesus monkeys. In Tremblay, R.E., Hartup, W.W., Archer, J., eds. *Developmental Origins of Aggression.* New York: Guilford, 63-82.

Tremblay, R.E. 2003. Why socialization fails?: The case of chronic physical aggression. In Lahey B.B., Moffitt T.E., Caspi A., eds. *Causes of Conduct Disorder and Juvenile Delinquency*. New York: Guilford, 182-224.

Tremblay, R.E. 2000. The origins of youth violence (ISUMA). *Can J Policy Res.* 1 no.2:19-24.

Tremblay, R.E., Nagin, D.S., Séguin, J.R., et al. 2004. Physical aggression during early childhood: Trajectories and predictors. *Pediatrics.* 114 no.1:e43-e50.

Tremblay, R.E., Vitaro, F., Nagin, D.S., Pagani, L., Séguin, J.R. 2003. The Montreal longitudinal and experimental study: Rediscovering the power of descriptions. In Thornberry, T., ed. *Taking Stock of Delinquency: An Overview of Findings from Contemporary Longitudinal Studies*. New York: Kluwer Academic/Plenum: 205-54.

van Bokhoven, I., van Goozen, S.H.M, van Engeland, H., et al. 2006. Salivary testosterone and aggression, delinquency, and social dominance in a population-based longitudinal study of adolescent males. *Horm Behav.* 50 no. 1:118-25.

van Goozen, S.H.M. 2005. Hormones and the developmental origin of aggression. In Tremblay, R.E., Hartup, W.W., Archer, J., eds. *Developmental Origins of Aggression*. New York: Guilford, 281-306.

Vitaro, F., Brendgen, M., Tremblay, R.E. 1999. Prevention of school dropout through the reduction of disruptive behaviors and school failure in elementary school. *J School Psychol.* 37 no. 2:205-26.

Wakschlag, L., Pickett, K.E., Cook, E., Benowitz, N.L., Leventhal, B. 2002. Maternal smoking during pregnancy and severe antisocial behavior in offspring: A review. *Am J Public Health.* 92 no. 6:966-74.

Weaver, I.C.G., Cervoni, N., Champagne, F.A., et al. 2004. Epigenetic programming by maternal behavior. *Nat Neurosci.* 7 no. 8:847-54.

Weaver, I.C., Meaney, M.J., Szyf, M. 2006. Maternal care effects on the hippocampal transcriptome and anxiety-mediated behaviors in the offsrping that are reversible in adulthood. *Proc Natl Acad Sci USA.* 103:3480-5.

Zoccolillo, M., Paquette, D., Tremblay, R.E. 2005. Maternal conduct disorder and the risk for the next generation. In Pepler, D., Masden, K., Webster, C., Levene, K., eds. *Development and Treatment of Girlhood Aggression*. Mahwah, NJ: Lawrence Erlbaum Associates: 225-52.

Overcoming Health Disparities: The Power of a Transdisciplinary Approach to Environmental Regulation of Gene Expression

MARTHA K. McCLINTOCK, SARAH GEHLERT,
SUZANNE D. CONZEN,
OLUFUNMILAYO I. OLOPADE,
AND THOMAS KRAUSZ

THE CPHHD INITIATIVE

Following a report by the Institute of Medicine of the National Academies of Science, the National Institute of Health undertook in September 2003 an initiative costing $60.5 million to determine how disparities in health outcomes and disease risk have arisen among different ethnic groups within the United States. Establishing eight Centers for Population Health and Health Disparities (CPHHD), the NIH garnered support from four of its components, The National Cancer Institute (NCI), the National Institute of Environmental Health Sciences (NIEHS), the National Institute on Aging (NIA), and the Office of Behavioral and Social Sciences Research (OBSSR). The goal was to identify not only the mechanisms creating disparities in specific diseases among different ethnic and socio-economic groups of different ages within the United States, but also the potential intervention points at which these health inequities could be alleviated.

Health disparities are a major health policy concern for countries such as the United States and Canada, which enjoy ethnic diversity among their citizens. Unfortunately, with that diversity has come an unequal burden of disease that is not simply the result of unequal access to health care, but is also a consequence of the different social, economic, and political environments in which these populations live. Historically, health disparities have not been a widespread issue for such countries as France, Norway, Oman, and Japan, which have relatively homogeneous populations. Nonetheless, ethnic and socio-economic diversity is increasing in many countries following the dramatic increases in mobility, immigration, and a fluid workforce driven by economic globalization. Thus, determining effective research approaches to understanding and ameliorating health disparities in the US and Canada can also serve as a worldwide model.

Perhaps more importantly, the widest impact of understanding health disparities will be a paradigm shift in the conceptualization of mechanisms of disease. Western medicine has a profound reductionist bias, focusing its research efforts primarily on the genetic, molecular, cellular, and physiological basis of diseases and their treatments. To be sure, each of these levels of biological organization is essential. Each of these biological mechanisms, however, is regulated not only by its immediate biological environment, the cell nucleus or blood-borne hormones and immune cytokines, but also by the macro-environments within which they function: the physical world; social world; and a person's cultural practices and beliefs, cognitive and emotional appraisal of the world, mental health and psychological state.

All organisms evolved within these macro scale environments to survive physical injury and disease. Thus, genetic, cellular, and physiological mechanisms within each individual likely were selected to be responsive to and regulated by the organism's psychosocial and physical environments. Genes, for example, cannot be selected independently of their expression and regulation throughout development, which produce the specific phenotypes upon which natural and sexual selection act.

The inextricable links between environments and expression of inherited genotypes form the theoretical foundation for investigating the psychosocial causes of disease. The social and physical worlds change individual behaviour and mental states, modulating a person's brain, hormonal, and immune systems throughout their lives, thereby ultimately having epigenetic effects that increase or reduce vulnerability to disease (Gehlert et al. 2008; McClintock et al. 2005). The importance of understanding how the social environment, behaviour, and psychological states regulate gene expression was underscored and elaborated in 2006, by a panel convened by the Institute for Medicine and published as *Genes, Behavior, and the Social Environment: Moving Beyond the Nature/Nurture Debate* (The Committee on Assessing Interactions Among Social, Behavioral, and Genetic Factors in Health, 2006).

The NIH recognized that multi-level problems on such a large scale require an intensely collaborative multi-level approach in order to identify solutions. In the Request for Applications (RFA ES02-009, http://grants2.nih.gov/grants/guide/rfa-files/RFA-ES-02-009.html) and in the multiple descriptions of the eight CPHHD Centres (http://cancercontrol.cancer.gov/populationhealthcenters/cphhd/index.html), the "intensely collaborative multi-level" research strategy has been termed multidisciplinary, interdisciplinary, and transdisciplinary. Here we distinguish among these complementary pluridisciplinary approaches, and focus on the power of a transdisciplinary research paradigm for understanding psychosocial regulation of gene expression, utilizing as an exemplar our research on the particularly aggressive form of pre-menopausal breast cancer that has a disproportionately high incidence and mortality rate among African-American women.

RACE DISPARITIES IN BREAST CANCER

Epidemiology

In the past fifty years, the mortality associated with many common diseases has decreased. This has not been as true of cancer, despite major advances (see figure 1). While reasons for the limited success in reducing cancer mortality are complex, some likely are attributable to the increasing disparity seen between groups defined by race and age. Mortality rates have fallen sharply for White and Hispanic women, but not for African-American women, even though African-American women have a lower cancer incidence overall (see figure 2).

The disparity in breast cancer mortality is even more striking. In Chicago, the breast cancer mortality rates for African-American women have held steadily above 40 per 100,000 between 1982 and 2003, whereas mortality for Whites dropped to 25 per 100,000 during the same period (Hirschman et al. 2007). Similar results are reported nationwide and abroad, with death rates for African-American

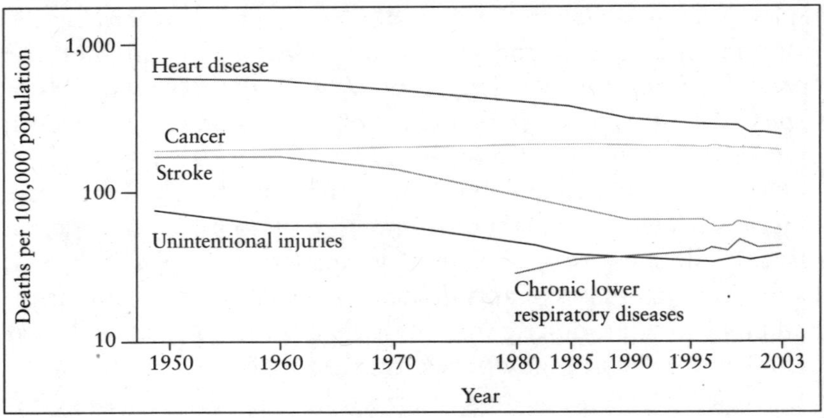

Figure 1. Leading causes of death in the US, 1950–2003 (National Center for Health Statistics, 2006). Combined, by race 2000–2004. SEER Incidence and Death Rates (Ries et al. 2007).

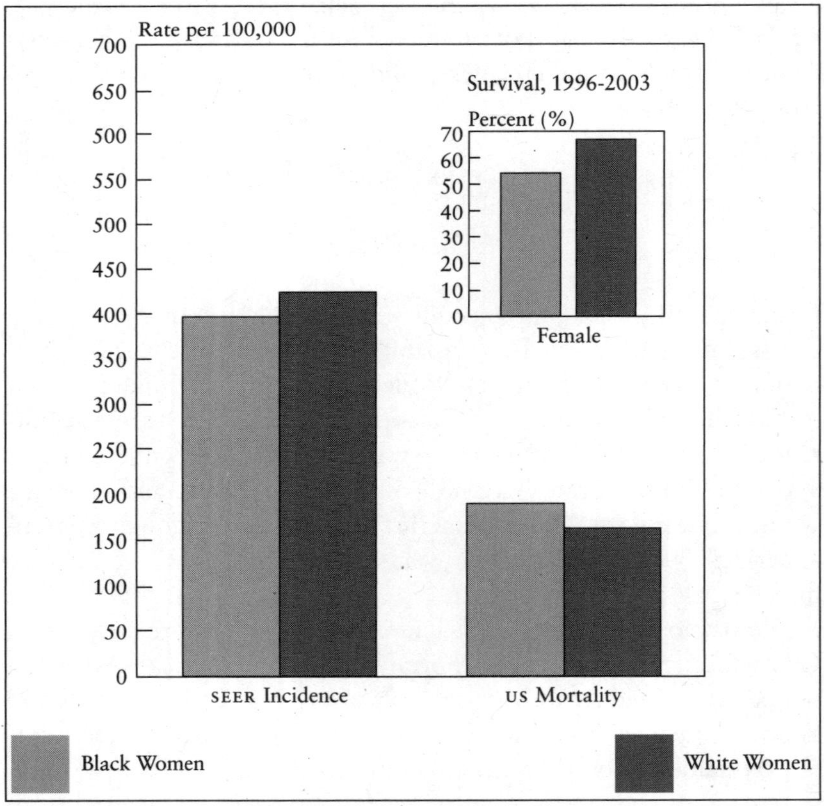

Figure 2. Five-year cancer survival rates all sites.

women at 35 per 100,000 and 25 per 100,000 for White women (Adams et al. 2006; Bowen et al. 2008; Jatoi et al. 2005; Smigal et al. 2006).

A portion of the White and African-American disparity in breast cancer mortality is attributable to access to good-quality mammograms and health care in general (Hirschman et al. 2007; Smith-Bindman et al. 2006; Whitman et al. 2007). Yet it was recently determined that breast cancer is made up of different subtypes, some of which are experienced more frequently by African-American women, a biological reality that cannot be explained by access to mammograms and healthcare alone.

Strides in Identifying Tumour Biology and Genetic Mutations

The apparent paradox between lower incidence and higher mortality is partially explainable by tumour biology and types of genetic mutations. Distinguishing breast cancer subtypes, with detailed analyses of pathology and genotype, has revealed that the prevalence of basal-like breast cancer subtype in premenopausal African-American Women (39%) is more than twice that of non-African-American women (16%)(Carey et al. 2006). In addition, evidence indicates that women with basal-like tumours have a short survival time after diagnosis (Carey et al. 2006). This is likely because basal-like tumours have a higher mitotic index (odds ratio [OR], 11.0; 95% confidence interval [CI], 5.6-21.7), more marked nuclear pleomorphism (OR, 9.7; 95% CI, 5.3-18.0), and higher combined grade (OR, 8.3; 95% CI, 4.4-15.6) than other tumour types. Interestingly, after menopause, typically around fifty years of age, the prevalence within the two populations is similar (14% and 16%).

A study in an urban health centre found "triple-negative" tumours (TNTS) to be more prevalent among African-American women in an urban cancer centre – 29.3% among AA women and 13.0% among similarly aged non-AA women (Lund et al. 2008; also reported by Bauer et al. 2007; Bowen et al. 2008; Morris et al. 2007). Triple-negative tumours lack the Estrogen Receptor alpha (ER-), Progesterone Receptor (PR-), and Human Epidermal growth factor Receptor-2 (HER2-) with which currently effective treatments interact. There are also marked differences in the genotypes of breast cancers. Basal-like tumours are more likely to have mutations of the *P53* gene (protein 53, a tumour suppressor gene normally regulating the cell cycle and reducing the risk of gene mutations; 44% vs. 15%;

Carey et al., 2006). The triple-negative phenotype and basal-like origin cancer types with distinctive gene expression signatures (Cleator et al. 2007; Kang et al. 2008) are currently thought to have independent risk factors for increased mortality and distant metastasis at diagnosis (Ihemelandu et al. 2008).

The causes of these highly proliferative tumours occur at multiple levels and their inter-relationships are poorly understood. They must explain the differences in gene expression profiles, which cannot be explained by mammogram frequency alone. An obvious question then is: How much of this type of breast cancer, suffered disproportionately by African-American women, is hereditary?

Overall, only 20 to 30 per cent of breast cancers are associated with either an inherited mutation of genes known to increase risk for breast cancer or a family cluster of the disease. Examples of inherited gene mutations are *BRCA1* and *BRCA2* (breast cancer 1, early onset, which normally suppresses tumours by maintaining genomic integrity) and *PTEN* (phosphates and tensin homolog, which normally regulate the cell cycle, preventing rapid growth and cell division). A woman can also be considered to have a high genetic risk if the women in her family pedigree have a high incidence of breast cancer, although a specific inherited somatic mutation has not yet been identified. Specifically, although 400 mutations of *BRCA1* and 200 of *BRCA2* are known to exist, African-American women with strong family histories do not possess these mutations. Because they do not have these mutations, nor do they have many relatives with the disease, they have what is termed "sporadic breast cancer." Fully 70 to 80 per cent of breast cancer cases are sporadic, lacking evidence of an inherited genetic component.

The Concept of Race in Explaining Disease Risk

The high prevalence of sporadic breast cancers suggests to us that African-American women are not at high risk for early aggressive breast cancer because of their race when it is defined by inherited alleles and mutations resulting from shared gene flow from the African continent. Rather, an epigenetic approach is needed, focusing on race as a socially and self-defined category. According to this approach, it is the social and personal experiences of being an African-American woman that have epigenetic effects in her body. That is, we hypothesize that there are particular aspects of the social environment and psychological experience of African-American women that change their physiological and cellular systems in a way that regulates expression of gene systems that accelerate the onset and growth of mammary tumours, decrease tumour differentiation, and increase malignancy. To test this hypothesis, which involves at least six levels of social and biological organization, a transdisciplinary research paradigm is essential (Gehlert et al. 2008; McClintock et al. 2005).

TYPES OF PLURIDISCIPLINARY RESEARCH

Acquiring knowledge about complex phenomena benefits from pluridisciplinary approaches, since each discipline is limited in its own way. With a multidisciplinary approach, knowledge is acquired from a variety of disciplines independently; in an interdisciplinary approach, the focus remains on a single discipline, with techniques from another discipline incorporated to supplement the central view. It is only through transdisciplinary approaches that experts from multiple disciplines come together to mutually inform one another, while at the same time changing and challenging their primary disciplinary views to create knowledge about properties that emerge from interactions between levels of organization in a complex system.

An analysis of the *Madonna Lisa* by Leonardo da Vinci (figure 3, left image) illustrates a multidisciplinary approach. Art theorists conduct analyses utilizing terms of aesthetics to explicate the basis for the painting's artistic appeal and beauty. Art historians understand the painting by studying its cultural and historical context, determining who influenced and taught da Vinci, who commissioned the painting, what its audience was, and what impact it had on culture and events at the end of the fifteenth century.

Theologians might utilize the painting to illustrate the newly developed concept of the humanity of Mary and Jesus, rather than the previous view of Mary only as an austere inaccessible empress and Jesus a divine being. A mathematician could analyze the geometry that generates the perspective and depth of the image. An economist might consider the painting's value in today's art market, and argue that Russia should make the rational choice to sell it from her Hermitage collection in order to offset national debt. Each discipline contributes a unique domain of knowledge, yet those domains are relatively independent.

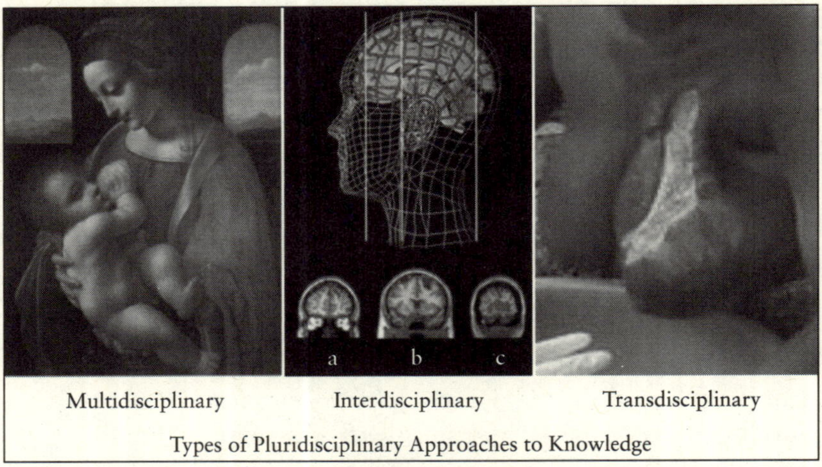

Figure 3. Three images of women, exemplifying different pluridisciplinary approaches to knowledge. Left. *Madonna Lisa*. Leonardo da Vinci 1490–1491, The Hermitage, St Petersburg, Russia. Centre. Positron emission tomography image of differential glucose utilization in specific brain regions driven by exposure to subliminal androstadienone (Jacob et al. 2001). Right. A premenopausal Nigerian woman with rapidly growing aggressive breast cancer (photo courtesy of Olufunmilayo I. Olopade).

In an interdisciplinary approach, the boundaries between disciplines are sufficiently porous to allow the primary discipline to borrow and incorporate techniques from another discipline. The interaction, however, is unidirectional. Biopsychologists can borrow the technique of positron emission tomography developed by radiologists and medical physicists (figure 3, centre) in order to understand how androstadienone, a putative human pheromone, tunes the brain to emotional information and regulates a woman's mood. The technique used to produce this image measures glucose utilization throughout a woman's brain during twenty-minute test sessions conducted on two different days. The only thing that varies between the two days is the application of nanomolar amounts of androstadienone; and by subtracting the two images the unique effect of androstadienone on brain function can be revealed. Neuroimaging is a great boon to understanding androstadienone's mechanisms of action. This knowledge, however, is not reciprocated; it does not advance knowledge in radiology or medical physics, the disciplines that created the technique.

A transdisciplinary approach is necessary to fully understand events in the world that emerge from interactions among levels of organization. Often addressing social, economic, and political problems, the solutions involve multiple disciplines yet focus on phenomena that reside between disciplines (Hirsch Hadorn, et al. 2008; Nicolescu 2002). The process of transdisciplinary research involves scientists from different disciplines mutually informing one another during the course of a shared research endeavour, changing the course of each others' experiments in order to incorporate concepts from other disciplines and ultimately achieving an integrated understanding of a complex interaction (Croyle 2008; Hall et al. 2008a; Leischow et al. 2008; Pohl 2005; Stokols et al. 2008; Syme 2008).

Reducing breast cancer mortality among African-American women requires a transdisciplinary approach. Breast cancer is a genetic disease, yet some of its subtypes are more prevalent among people living in particular social and physical environments (figure 3, right). The Nigerian woman shown in figure 3, with a rapidly growing aggressive breast cancer, similar in type to that suffered by young African-American women, graphically illustrates how this disease would progress without early detection and treatment.

Cancer is by definition a disease of dysregulated genetic mechanisms, some inherited and some epigenetic. Clearly, altered gene expression in a dislocated Nigerian woman or an African-American woman would not create her ethnic identity or her social circumstances. Rather, this aggressive pattern of cancer emerges from interactions among multiple levels of organization, ranging from the social to the genetic. In order to fully characterize and understand the bidirectional interaction between the social contexts, the built environment, psychological states, the balance of physiological systems, and gene expression within mammary tissue, a transdisciplinary approach is necessary. And pinpointing specific social and biological mechanisms and their order in a bidirectional causal pathway requires mutually informative human and animal research: studies of the lived experience of women in their own communities, and parallel animal models in a laboratory designed to study their social interactions and behaviour.

CIHDR: RESULTS OF A TRANSDISCIPLINARY RESEARCH PROCESS

Transdisciplinary research involves scientists coming together from many more levels of organization than is typically the case in interdisciplinary research. Most importantly, these disciplines are not viewed in a scientific status hierarchy nor are the relationships among them hierarchical, with one being primary and directing the contributions of the others. There are frequent and intense interactions at all phases of the research endeavour, which keeps the research endeavour focused on a common goal and speeds scientific progress.

Six Levels of Organization

The Center for Interdisciplinary Health Disparities Research (CIHDR) includes scientists and physicians covering a minimum of six levels of organization (see figure 4): 1. Neighbourhood, 2. Social groups, 3. The individual woman, 4. Physiological systems, 5. Cell anatomy and metabolism and 6. Gene function. They specialize in urban communities, neighbourhoods, and social services, psychology, endocrinology and immunology, surgical pathology and histochemistry, cancer biology, oncology, and molecular genetics. They came together specifically to understand and rectify the health disparity in breast cancer between White and African-American women, utilizing community-based participatory research, geocoding, psychosocial interviews, endocrine measures, histopathology, immunochemistry, and gene expression studies, combined with clinical care in human participants. In addition, CIHDR utilizes three rodent models, one studying the diversity of spontaneous mammary gland tumours in rats, a transgenic mouse model of ductal carcinoma of the mammary gland, and a xenograph model in which human cancer cells are transplanted into mice.

Accelerating Research and Keeping on Target

The results presented below are the direct result of a transdisciplinary research process, in which the co-authors, who represent a wide array of disciplines, have scrutinized the details of each other's experiments, modified traditional methods, created new methods to parallel those from other disciplines, and changed their experimental designs to accommodate strong differences in what constitutes scientific proof. They shared and created new analytic methods for multiple measures from different levels of organization that are nested around and within an individual, then jointly interpreted the results and designed future research.

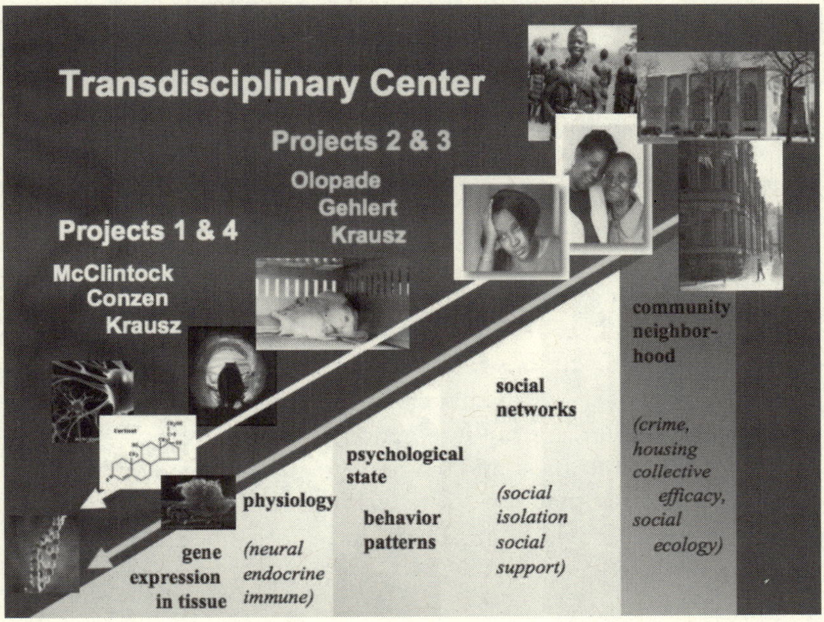

Figure 4. Organization of the Center for Interdisciplinary Health Disparities Research.

This research process of assimilation and accommodation is ongoing. Research progresses faster because changes and insights do not await publications from a distant laboratory in another discipline. Narrow assumptions from one study can be corrected by the strong preliminary data from parallel studies at a different level of organization; new measures can be added across all studies as soon as they have provided essential insights for one.

The group dynamic also keeps experiments targeted on the primary shared research question. In isolation, the research focus of a particular laboratory can drift, following the lead of unexpected and robust results – certainly an important path to scientific discovery. Nonetheless, given that time and resources are limited, these excursions can divert attention from the shared research question, particularly if its answer is not immediately obvious. The need for midcourse corrections is rapidly communicated through frequent formal and informal discussions within a transdisciplinary group, whose members range from technicians and students to the primary investigators. Propinquity is key, facilitated by building design and administrative structures that support transdisciplinary research, operating in concert with the traditional paradigms focused on training and research within departmental and disciplinary boundaries (Stokols et al., 2008).

This process of jointly pounding out research details mandated not only taking time to teach each other knowledge and critical thinking from our own disciplines but also becoming comfortable incorporating new factors that are traditionally ignored or dismissed by our own discipline. This does take time, and is an intellectual style to which some are not suited (Hall et al. 2008b; Holmes et al. 2008; Masse et al. 2008). Initially progress is slowed by the steep learning curves for all in a transdisciplinary team. The result, however, is a group of scientists that can target and make rapid progress on problems that arise from interaction between levels of organization, such as breast cancer and the social regulation of gene function, research problems that have ramifications for science, social and health policies (Croyle 2008; Hiatt and Breen 2008; Masse et al. 2008; Syme 2008).

Downward Causation

In both the rat and transgenic mouse models, we discovered that randomly assigning genetically similar rats to social isolation accelerated formation of mammary tumours (see figure 5; McClintock et al. 2005, in addition to increasing tumour size and malignancy (Hermes et al. 2009; Williams et al. 2009). In the controlled laboratory environment, we unequivocally established that social isolation preceded the development of mammary tumours and the rapid progression of ductal carcinoma *in situ*.

With this knowledge, interviews of African-American women were designed to include measures of social isolation and felt loneliness. Laboratory work also established that isolating female rats made them more vigilant, cautious, attentive and wary. Their psychological state can be inferred from their display of species-typic anxiety behaviours and is manifest by limited exploration when introduced to a novel and potentially threatening environment (see left side of figure 6; Hermes et al. 2009). This prompted the addition of environmental surveys of the built environment in a four block area around participants' homes in order to quantifying the level of threat, indexed by unprotected vacant lots, abandoned buildings,

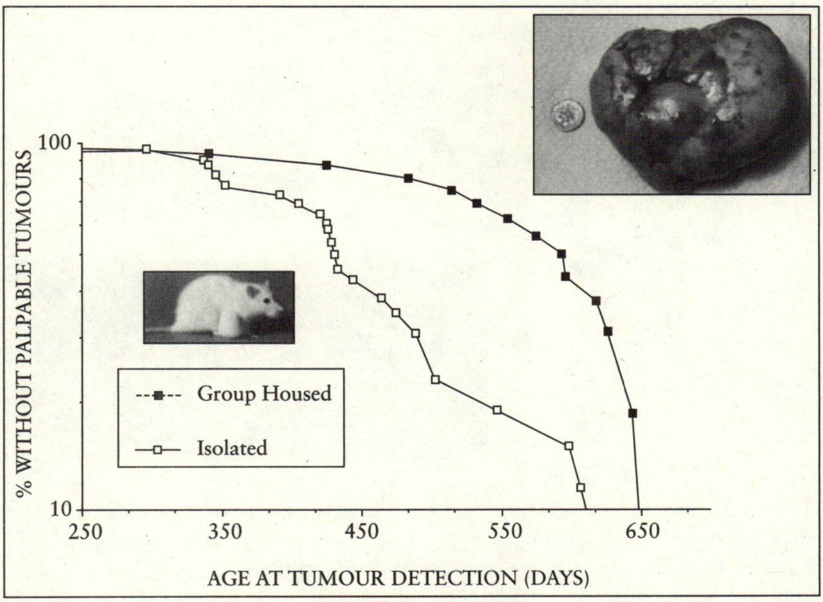

Figure 5. Isolated female rats developed palpable mammary tumours at a younger age than did their sisters randomly assigned to live in groups (McClintock et al. 2005).

heavy traffic patterns, drug trafficking, needles, loitering and broken windows (see right side of figure 6). Thereby, the full range of the built environment was quantified, namely anything that would impede or facilitate the woman's social interactions within her neighbourhood. This was coupled with uniquely human, subjectively determined measures of threats and safety.

Interviews with African-Americans residing in neighbourhoods of Chicago's South Side revealed that poverty and poor housing stock often force people to relocate, disrupting their social networks. The role of reciprocated social supports during a stressor was hypothesized to be a potential psychosocial cause of disease risk, and was modelled in rats by moving their home cages to rest next to strangers' and then observing the social dynamics among the group during this mild relocation stressor. Indeed, lack of reciprocal care with cage mates was a risk factor for accelerated disease and operated in addition to having a vigilant temperament (Yee et al. 2008).

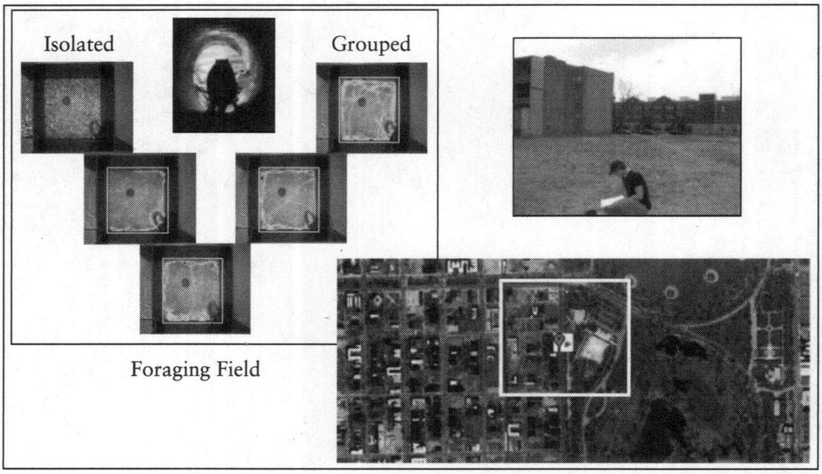

Figure 6. Vigilance: Methods for quantifying behaviour in a threatening environment. On the left, the track indicates the ground traversed by a rat after being placed in a home location in the lower right corner of the foraging field (method developed by Yee and McClintock). On the right, the white square indicates the 3-block diameter around a participant's home, which was scored for the level of threats and supports (Gehlert, unpublished data).

Dysregulated Stress Response

Isolated rats had a dysregulated stress response, responding with higher levels of glucocorticoids from the adrenal cortex, even after the stressor had ended, and then recovering more slowly to baseline (Hermes et al. 2009; Hermes et al. 2006). When transgenic mice were socially isolated following a parallel protocol, they also developed a dysregulated glucocorticoid response to stressors (see figure 7; Williams et al. 2009).

Isolated female rats with greater adrenocortical dysregulation subsequently developed larger mammary tumours (Hermes et al. 2009), as did female rats living in groups who developed greater adrenocortical dysregulation with age (Yee et al. 2009). Among isolated rats, it was not just a higher response to a stressor, but also a lower baseline level of stress hormone, potentially indicative of hypocortisolemia, which increased the number of glucocorticoid receptors.

We translated this observation into an experimental protocol for assessing glucocorticoid function in women. By donating four saliva

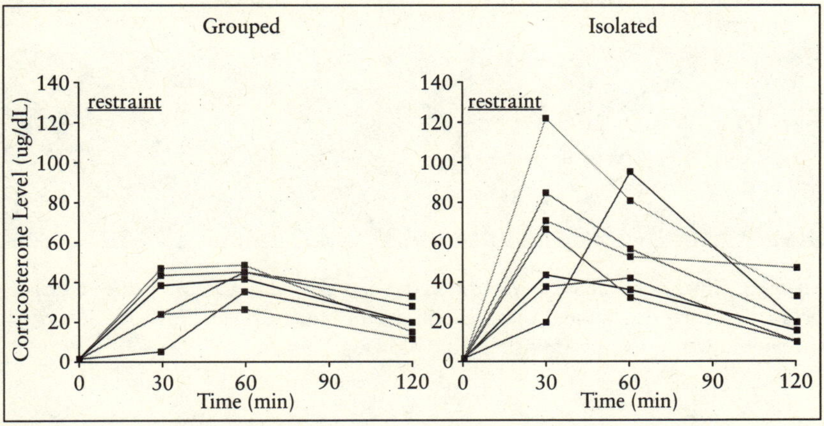

Figure 7. Dysregulated endocrine response of isolated SV40t-antigen mice. During a restraint stressor mimicking a collapsed burrow tunnel, corticosterone levels in isolates rose more quickly and higher than it did in their sisters who were assigned to live in groups (Williams et al. 2009).

samples throughout the day for three consecutive days, African-American participants enabled characterization of the circadian rhythm of their glucocorticoids. Some women did indeed have a low shallow rhythm, indicating a state of hypocortisolemia typically associated with unrelenting chronic stress (Gehlert, Unpublished Results).

Glucocorticoid Receptors: Petri Dish to Spontaneous Tumours

CIHDR focused on the dynamics of glucocorticoids, because it had been established that pretreating human cancer cells growing in a Petri dish with a synthetic glucocorticoid prevented cell death in response to a chemotherapeutic agent (Moran et al. 2000). Blocking the tumour cells' glucocorticoid receptors with the drug RU486 negated the effects of pre-treatment, leaving the cells vulnerable to chemotherapy. Moving to a xenograph model, the synthetic glucocorticoid dexamethasone also decreased apoptosis in human cancer cells grafted into a mouse (Pang et al. 2006). Without glucocorticoid receptors, dysregulated stress hormones could not directly attenuate cell death or increase proliferation, resulting in the early development of rapidly growing tumours.

The above *in vitro* and *in vivo* results prompted immunohistochemistry analysis for glucocorticoid receptors in the spontaneous

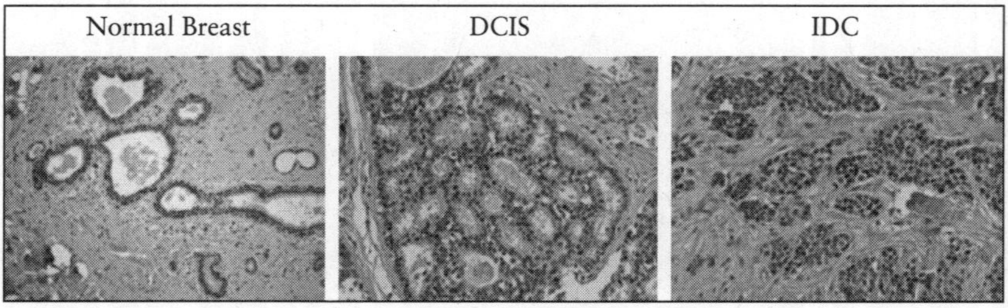

Figure 8. Glucocorticoid receptor (GR) activation in epithelial cells of three types of breast tissue: Normal tissue, ductal carcinoma in situ (DCIS) and invasive ductal carcinoma (IDC). The GR stains medium brown.

mammary tumours developed in isolated rats and the SV40tantigen-induced mammary tumours of transgenic mice. Positive results in these animal models raised the priority for glucocorticoid receptor immunohistochemistry on women's breast tumours. Glucocorticoid receptors were present in all three, particularly in the basal layer of the mammary ducts (see figure 8; (Belova et al. 2009; Yee et al. 2009; Hermes et al. 2009). Moreover, indicating bioactivity stimulated by glucocorticoids, the receptors of isolated rats were more likely to have preponderance in the nucleus, where gene regulation occurs.

Gene Expression in a Transgenic Mouse Model

The transgenic mouse model utilizes a transfected simian virus to stimulate in all animals ductal carcinoma in situ (DCIS) and then invasive ductal carcinoma (IDC), the most common form of breast cancer in women. Randomly assigning these genetically identical animals to social isolation rather than life in a stable social group accelerated development of DCIS and IDC. It also afforded the opportunity to identify mammary tissue genes that are differentially expressed before cancer develops, identifying one of the final common paths along which the social environment regulates gene expression and accelerates tumour formation and growth.

Global microarray analyses of RNA expression in the mammary glands of socially isolated and group-housed mice were compared, revealing two clusters of consistently down-regulated genes in the isolated animals: One cluster regulates pathways of fatty acid synthesis and the other the innate inflammatory response. RNA expression of a tumour suppressor gene, *PTEN*, was also down-regulated

(Williams et al. 2009). We are therefore examining whether methylation associated with the physiological changes of social isolation plays a role in silencing these genes and are preparing to measure parallel changes in human mammary tissue.

CROSS CENTRE COLLABORATION: THE SEARCH FOR A COMMON DENOMINATOR IN HEALTH DISPARITIES

The eight Centers for Population Health and Health Disparities (CPHHD) initiative also form a transdisciplinary research network. Each centre focuses on a different type of health disparity among people living in a variety of geographic and social circumstances (Warnecke et al. 2008). On the surface, the disparities seem disparate. A goal of this network of CPHHD centres is to increase research interactions within and among the centres, developing a shared model that may reveal common downward causation pathways by which social circumstances increase risk for a wide variety of diseases.

Where people live is an essential predictor of self-rated health, operating independently of individual factors. Incorporating information about place within a comprehensive multidimensional model significantly attenuates disparities in self-rated health among African-Americans by 15 to 76 per cent, particularly for young adults (Dob et al. 2008). In other words, a major source of poor health in the individual is the neighbourhood in which they live.

There is an interaction between characteristics of the neighbourhood environment, which by definition transcends the individuals within its borders, and a person's genotype, which carries a risk for disease. In Chicago, gentrification of African-American neighbourhoods on the West and North Sides is associated with increased risk of metastases when African-American women are first diagnosed with breast cancer. African-American women in nearby neighbourhoods not disrupted by gentrification are less likely to have metastases (Barrett et al. 2008).

In Philadelphia, African-American men with a germ-line mutation or sequence variant of the *MSR1* gene (Macrophage Scavenger Receptor 1, which affects the innate inflammatory system) are at greater risk for prostate cancer if they live in a neighbourhood in which least 90 per cent of its residents are below the poverty line. Those who also have the *MSR1* gene mutation and variants and live in neighbourhoods that are more affluent are at lower risk (Rebbeck, personal communication).

A key role for the innate inflammatory system is also suggested by the high incidence of cervical cancer among Appalachian women. Cervical cancer incidence and mortality among Appalachian women who smoke is associated with impairment of immune function, indexed by failure to sequester Epstein-Barr virus acquired during mononucleosis in childhood or young adulthood. Cytokines, signalling molecules in the innate inflammatory response, are produced by abdominal fat, and are thought to be involved in a wide variety of diseases, including diabetes and hypertension. Thus, having less abdominal fat may be the mechanism through which obesity, quantified by a body mass index (weight/height^2) in the 25 – 30 range, is associated with the longest disability-free life expectancy (Al Snih et al. 2007) as well as fewer body disabilities among older diabetic Hispanics living in Texas (Al Snih et al. 2007).

Given the common thread of neighbourhood quality, stressors, and impaired inflammatory function in these diverse populations, the CPHHD centres have undertaken a cross-centre study in which they all deploy the same measures of neighbourhood and place, psychosocial stressors, glucocorticoid levels, and innate inflammatory cytokines. The CPHHD initiative has dramatically increased disciplinary interactions within and between centres. This transdisciplinary process holds the promise of a much-needed parsimonious and integrated account of bi-directional interactions between place, ethnicity, stressors, and gene regulation that produce disparities in disease risk.

COMMUNITY-BASED PARTICIPATORY RESEARCH: ESSENTIAL FOR HEALTH POLICY AND ERADICATION OF HEALTH DISPARITIES

Given the progress in basic sciences that has been enabled by a change in science policy that supports a mutually informative transdisciplinary approach, how can these insights be translated into better health care, particularly for underserved populations? Essential to this goal are partnerships between academic researchers and affected communities that extend from the beginning of the basic research process to the dissemination and implementation of results. All centres have partnered with community groups, such as community-based organizations (Masi and Gehlert 2008; Warnecke et al. 2008). The goal of this community-based participatory research is multifaceted. First, such partnerships help ensure that the research questions, designs, and methods of data collection are informed by community realities. Second, they enable scientists and physicians to share their scientific findings with communities as soon as they become available in a manner that facilitates change. Finally, community collaborations are essential for framing information in the most effective way for underserved communities to partner with academic researchers in a way that allows them to harness and incorporate the insights obtained into the design and testing of effective multi-level interventions.

It is also important to consider the community's collective beliefs and their shared ideas of what distinguishes their community from others. Understanding beliefs and shared ideas is as essential for effectively framing information and designing robust interventions and effective care as it is for understanding the cause of disparities. These beliefs should be detected and framed at the level of the community itself, its collected beliefs, rather than merely instantiated within a single individual.

To this end, CIHDR investigators conducted forty-nine focus group interviews in diverse African-American neighbourhoods in Chicago's South Side, including over 500 participants (Salant and Gehlert 2008). One study based on these focus group data found three cultural beliefs to be salient: candidacy (what makes a woman at risk for breast cancer), collective memory, and victimization. There were novel risks perceived by the community — for example, the risk of "knowing" whether one was at genetic risk, with the increased risk engendered by the knowledge itself. Significant collective memories impaired trust in the available health care system and the process of biomedical research. The "Tuskegee Study of Untreated Syphilis in the Black Man," conducted by the US Public Health Service between 1932 and 1972 is often referenced as a cause of impaired trust. In order to study the progression of untreated syphilis, poor, undereducated African-American sharecroppers in Alabama, some of whom had syphilis, were studied without treatment, without being told their diagnosis and without informed consent. Finally, analysis of focus group data yielded a collective sense of victimization, substantiated by loss of job opportunities, high rates of poverty, failure to protect against crime, and provide municipal and social services, inadequate health care, woeful public education, and poor government representation in general. Understanding which of these collective cultural traits is key to addressing the disparity in the etiology, treatment, and prevention of aggressive breast cancers in African-American women is the mandate of the transdisciplinary research supported by the NIH through the Centers for Population Health and Health Disparities.

BIBLIOGRAPHY

Adams, S.A., Hebert, J.R., Bolick-Aldrich, S., Daguise, V.G., Mosley, C.M., Modayil, M.V., et al. 2006. Breast cancer disparities in South Carolina: Early detection, special programs, and descriptive epidemiology. *J S C Med Assoc, 102*(7):231-9.

Al Snih, S., Ottenbacher, K.J., Markides, K.S., Kuo, Y.F., Eschbach, K., and Goodwin, J.S. 2007. The effect of obesity on disability vs mortality in older Americans. *Arch Intern Med, 167*(8):774-80.

Al Snih, S., Raji, M.A., Markides, K.S., Ottenbacher, K.J., and Goodwin, J.S. 2005. Weight change and lower body disability in older Mexican Americans. *J Am Geriatr Soc, 53*(10):1730-7.

Barrett, R.E., Cho, Y.I., Weaver, K.E., Ryu, K., Campbell, R.T., Dolecek, T.A., et al. 2008. Neighborhood change and distant metastasis at diagnosis of breast cancer. *Ann Epidemiol, 18*(1):43-7.

Bauer, K.R., Brown, M., Cress, R.D., Parise, C.A., Caggiano, V. 2007. Descriptive analysis of estrogen receptor (er)-negative, progesterone receptor (pr)-negative, and her2-negative invasive breast cancer, the so-called triple-negative phenotype: A population-based study from the California cancer registry. *Cancer, 109*(9):1721-8.

Belova, L., Delgado, B., Kocherginsky, M., Melhem, A., Olopade, O.I., and Conzen, S.D. 2009. Glucocorticoid receptor expression in breast cancer associates with older patient age. *Breast Cancer Res Treat*, 116(2):441-7.

Bowen, R.L., Duffy, S.W., Ryan, D.A., Hart, I.R., and Jones, J.L. (2008). Early onset of breast cancer in a group of British black women. *Br J Cancer, 98*(2):277-81.

Carey, L.A., Perou, C.M., Livasy, C.A., Dressler, L.G., Cowan, D., Conway, K., et al. 2006. Race, breast cancer subtypes, and survival in the Carolina breast cancer study. *Jama, 295*(21):2492-502.

Cleator, S., Heller, W., Coombes, R.C. 2007. Triple-negative breast cancer: Therapeutic options. *Lancet Oncol, 8*(3):235-44.

Croyle, R.T. 2008. The national cancer institute's transdisciplinary centers initiatives and the need for building a science of team science. *Am J Prev Med, 35*(2 Suppl):S90-93.

Dob, D.P., Fincha, B.K., Basurto-Davilad, R., Bird, C., Escarce, J., Lurie, N. 2008. Does place explain racial health disparities? Quantifying the contribution of residential context to the black/white health gap in the United States. *Social Science and Medicine, 67*(8):1258-68.

Gehlert, S., Sohmer, D., Sacks, T., Mininger, C., McClintock, M.K., Olopade, O.I. 2008. Targeting health disparities: A model linking upstream determinants to downstream interventions. *Health Aff (Millwood),* 27(2):339-49.

Hall, K.L., Feng, A.X., Moser, R.P., Stokols, D., and Taylor, B.K. 2008a. Moving the science of team science forward: Collaboration and creativity. *Am J Prev Med, 35*(2 Suppl):S243-9.

Hall, K.L., Stokols, D., Moser, R.P., Taylor, B.K., Thornquist, M.D., Nebeling, L.C., et al. 2008b. The collaboration readiness of transdisciplinary research teams and centers findings from the national cancer institute's trec year-one evaluation study. *Am J Prev Med, 35*(2 Suppl):S161-72.

Hermes, G.L., Delgado, B., Tsakalis, M., Tretiakova, M., Krausz, T., Conzen, S.D., et al. 2009. Social isolation dysregulates endocrine and behavioral stress responses as it increases the burden and malignancy of spontaneous mammary tumors. *Submitted.*

Hermes, G.L., Rosenthal, L., Montag, A., McClintock, M.K. 2006. Social isolation and the inflammatory response: Sex differences in the enduring effects of a prior stressor. *Am J Physiol Regul Integr Comp Physiol,* 290:R273-R282.

Hiatt, R.A., Breen, N. 2008. The social determinants of cancer: A challenge for transdisciplinary science. *Am J Prev Med, 35*(2 Suppl):S141-50.

Hirsch Hadorn, G., Hoffmann-Riem, H., Biber-Klemm, S., Grossenbacher-Mansuy, W., Joye, D., Pohl, C., et al., eds. 2008. *Handbook of Transdisciplinary Research*. New York, New York: Springer.

Hirschman, J., Whitman, S., Ansell, D. 2007. The Black/White disparity in breast cancer mortality: The example of Chicago. *Cancer Causes Control, 18*(3):323-33.

Holmes, J.H., Lehman, A., Hade, E., Ferketich, A.K., Gehlert, S., Rauscher, G.H., et al. 2008. Challenges for multi-level health disparities research in a transdisciplinary environment. *Am J Prev Med, 35*(2 Suppl):S182-92.

Ihemelandu, C.U., Naab, T.J., Mezghebe, H.M., Makambi, K.H., Siram, S.M., Leffall, L.D., Jr., et al. 2008. Basal cell-like (triple-negative) breast cancer, a predictor of distant metastasis in African American women. *Am J Surg, 195*(2):153-8.

Jacob, S., Kinnunen, L.H., Metz, J., Cooper, M., McClintock, M.K. 2001. Sustained human chemosignal unconsciously alters brain function. *NeuroReport, 12*(11):2391-4.

Jatoi, I., Anderson, W.F., Rao, S.R., Devesa, S.S. 2005. Breast cancer trends among black and white women in the United States. *J Clin Oncol, 23*(31):7836-41.

Kang, S.P., Martel, M., and Harris, L.N. 2008. Triple negative breast cancer: Current understanding of biology and treatment options. *Curr Opin Obstet Gynecol, 20*(1):40-6.

Leischow, S.J., Best, A., Trochim, W.M., Clark, P.I., Gallagher, R.S., Marcus, S.E., et al. 2008. Systems thinking to improve the public's health. *Am J Prev Med, 35*(2 Suppl):S196-203.

Lund, M.J.B., Butler, EN, Bumpers, H.L., Okoli, J., Rizzo, M., Hatchett, N., Green, V.L., Brawley, O.W., Opreatlies, G.M. and Gabram, S.G.A. 2008. High prevalence of triple-negative tumors in an urban cancer center. *Cancer*, 113:608-15.

Masi, C.M., Gehlert, S. 2008. Perceptions of breast cancer treatment among African American women and men: Implications for interventions. *J Gen Intern Med.*

Masse, L.C., Moser, R.P., Stokols, D., Taylor, B.K., Marcus, S.E., Morgan, G.D., et al. 2008. Measuring collaboration and transdisciplinary integration in team science. *Am J Prev Med, 35*(2 Suppl):S151-60.

McClintock, M.K., Conzen, S.D., Gehlert, S., Masi, C., Olopade, O.I. 2005. Mammary cancer and social interactions: Identifying multiple environments that regulate gene expression throughout the life span. *J Gerontol B Psychol Sci Soc Sci, 60 Spec No 1*:32-41.

Moran, T.J., Gray, S., Mikosz, C., and Conzen, S.D. 2000. The glucocorticoid receptor mediates a survival signal in human mammary epithelial cells. *Cancer Research, 60*:867-72.

Morris, G.J., Naidu, S., Topham, A.K., Guiles, F., Xu, Y., McCue, P., et al. 2007. Differences in breast carcinoma characteristics in newly diagnosed african-american and caucasian patients: A single-institution compilation compared with the national cancer institute's surveillance, epidemiology, and end results database. *Cancer, 110*(4):876-84.

Nicolescu, B. 2002. *Manifesto of transdisciplinarity* (K.-C. Voss, Trans.). New York: State University of New York (SUNY) Press.

Pang, D., Kocherginsky, M., Krausz, T., Kim, S.Y., Conzen, S.D. 2006. Dexamethasone decreases xenograft response to paclitaxel through inhibition of tumor cell apoptosis. *Cancer Biol Ther, 5*(8):933-40.

Pohl, C. 2005. Transdisciplinary collaboration in environmental research. *Futures, 37*(10):1159-78.

Ries, L.A.G., Melbert, D., Krapcho, M., Stinchcomb, D.G., Howlader, N., Horner, M. J., et al., eds. 2007. *Seer cancer statistics review, 1975-2005*. Bethesda, Md.: National Cancer Institute.

Salant, T., Gehlert, S. 2008. Collective memory, candidacy, and victimisation: Community epidemiologies of breast cancer risk. *Sociol Health Illn, 30*(4):599-615.

Smigal, C., Jemal, A., Ward, E., Cokkinides, V., Smith, R., Howe, H.L., et al. (2006). Trends in breast cancer by race and ethnicity: Update 2006. *CA Cancer J Clin, 56*(3):168-83.

Smith-Bindman, R., Miglioretti, D. L., Lurie, N., Abraham, L., Barbash, R. B., Strzelczyk, J., et al. 2006. Does utilization of screening mammography explain racial and ethnic differences in breast cancer? *Ann Intern Med, 144*(8):541-53.

Statistics., N.C.f.H. 2006. Health, United States, 2006, with chartbook on trends in health of Americans. In C.f.D.C.a. Prevention, ed. (Figure 27): U.S. Government Printing Office, Libary of Congress Catalog Number 76–641496.

Stokols, D., Misra, S., Moser, R.P., Hall, K.L., Taylor, B.K. 2008. The ecology of team science: Understanding contextual influences on transdisciplinary collaboration. *Am J Prev Med, 35*(2 Suppl):S96-115.

Syme, S.L. 2008. The science of team science: Assessing the value of transdisciplinary research. *Am J Prev Med, 35*(2 Suppl):S94-5.

The Committee on Assessing Interactions among Social, Behavioral, and Genetic Factors in Health. 2006. *Genes, Behavior, and the Social Environment: Moving Beyond the Nature/Nurture Debate*. Washington, D.C.: The National Academies Press.

Warnecke, R.B., Oh, A., Breen, N., Gehlert, S., Paskett, E., Tucker, K.L., et al. 2008. Approaching health disparities from a population perspective: The national institutes of health centers for population health and health disparities. *Am J Public Health, 98*(9), 1608-15.

Whitman, S., Shah, A.M., Silva, A., Ansell, D. 2007. Mammography screening in six diverse communities in Chicago – a population study. *Cancer Detect Prev, 31*(2):166-72.

Williams, B., Pang, D., Delgado, B., Kocherginsky, M., He, J., Tretiakova, M., Krausz, T., Pan, D., McClintock, M.K., Couzen, S.D. 2009. A model of gene – environment interaction reveals mammary gland gene expression and increased tumor growth following social isolation. *Cancer Prevention Research*, 2(10):850–61.

Yee, J.R., Cavigelli, S.A., Delgado, B., Krausz, T., Conzen, S.D., and McClintock, M.K. 2009. Individual variation in stress-induced corticosterone dynamics and spontaneous mammary tumor risk. *Psychoneuroendocrinology (In Press).*

Yee, J.R., Cavigelli, S.A., Delgado, B., and McClintock, M.K. 2008. Reciprocal affiliation among adolescent rats during a mild group stressor predicts mammary tumors and lifespan. *Psychosom Med,* 70(9):1050-9.

Learning to Live Again with Uncertainty: Social Repercussions of Molecular Genomics

MARGARET LOCK

Social scientists whose interest is in the impact on society of the development and application of new biomedical technologies highlight the way in which many such technologies have the potential to transform our experiences of embodiment, body boundaries, identity, social relationships, and the allocation of responsibility for health and illness (Franklin and Lock 2003; Strathern 1992). Clearly, specific technologies have a range of social impacts, one of the most dramatic being organ transplantation, that challenge assumptions about the boundaries of self and other (Lock 2002). Technologies of assisted reproduction create arrangements in which biological and social parenting no longer coincide, thus generating new forms of kinship (Kahn 2000, Thompson 2005) and sonography, which permits assessment of the fetal sex in utero, has made it possible in certain parts of the world where abortion is readily available to bring about a serious imbalance in the sex ratio at birth (Sen 2003).

Genetic testing, the subject matter of this chapter, is less physically invasive than are many other biomedical technologies but it can, nevertheless, bring about profound changes in the lives of tested individuals and their families, in part because predictions about future illness are involved, inevitably bringing about repercussions for biologically related kin. Furthermore, it is has been argued that the very experience of self may be transformed on the basis of genotypic information in at least two ways: first due to learning about "embodied risk" in the form of a gene and, second, as a result of medicalization.

More than two decades ago Edward Yoxen (1982) suggested that the ability of geneticists to detect "pre-symptomatically ill" individuals by means of genetic testing and screening would mean that virtually everyone living in countries where such technologies are available would shortly be subject to increased medical surveillance. Since that time publications about real and imagined social ramifications of genetic testing have increased exponentially.

Until recently, testing has been largely limited to families affected by single-gene disorders that follow a Mendelian pattern of segregation or, alternatively, to individuals deemed to be at high risk for specific conditions, notably certain cancers, because of their genetic profiles, with the result that social science research has similarly been confined to such families. The findings of this research, insightful and important though they are, are derived from a rather small percentage of the population at large – those relatively few families affected by such disorders. The "penetrance" – in the language of genetics – of several of the genes involved in such disorders is very high, so that virtually all individuals who carry such mutations will manifest the disease in question, making predictions about risk highly reliable although, on occasion, errors are made (Waalen and Beutler 2009). However, very many others of the estimated 4,000 rare single gene disorders, exhibit medium or low penetrance, and it is often not possible to predict with any reliability if the disease will indeed become manifest phenotypically. Alternatively, when the disease does become manifest, it is often the case that the age at onset of the condition cannot be predicted and, furthermore, its severity may differ considerably among affected individuals. Research has also shown that many of the so-called single gene disorders have numerous allelic variations and are, therefore, much more complex and unpredictable than was at first realized, with the result that risk predictions are by no means as easy to make as was formerly assumed (Scriver and Waters 1999).

It is likely that in the not too distant future things will change, so that genetic testing will be routinized as part of basic clinical care for very many common conditions (Brice 2004) – already hundreds of DNA tests for identifying genes associated with disorders of numerous kinds are now available (Yoon et al. 2001). However, by far the majority of human genes are "susceptibility" genes; such genes are neither necessary nor sufficient to cause any given condition, and it is assumed in the case of complex, common diseases, that several genes are usually implicated in causation, in association with developmental and environmental variables of many kinds, although the involved mechanisms remain for the most part poorly understood. Estimating future risk for illness on the basis of the presence of a single susceptibility gene is, therefore, highly questionable, raising social repercussions of a rather different kind from those associated with single gene disorders.

This chapter is divided into three parts: the first part constitutes an overview of the social science findings to date in connection with responses of individuals and families to genetic testing for single gene disorders and for breast cancer. This is followed by a brief discussion of what is characterized by many scientists today as a paradigm shift currently taking place in molecular genetics, central to which is an argument about the "de-throning" of the gene. The final section of the paper presents findings from ethnographic research with healthy individuals who come from families where late-onset Alzheimer's disease has been diagnosed and who have undergone genetic testing to assess their individualized risk. Their insights about embodied risk after receiving their test results are discussed and contrasted with the findings in connection with single gene disorders.

THE GENETIC BODY

In the early 1990s the epidemiologist Abby Lippman coined the term "geneticization" to gloss what she perceived to be a new form of medical surveillance. Lippman characterized geneticization as a process "in which differences between individuals are reduced to their DNA codes" (Lippman 1992). Above all, she was concerned about the possibilities of an indirect reinforcement of racism, social inequalities, and discrimination against those with disabilities, the result of a rekindled conflation between social realities and an essentialized biology grounded in small differences in DNA sequences. Recent research strongly suggests that with respect to obesity and diabetes among First Nations populations in Canada, for example, Lippman's concern has proven justified (Poudrier 2007).

The sociologist Nikolas Rose, drawing on Foucaultian biopolitics, and concerned about society as a whole, suggests that in advanced liberal democracies where life is "construed as a project," values such as autonomy, self-actualization, prudence, responsibility, and choice are integral to "work on the self." He argues that genetic forms of thought have become "intertwined" into this project, and the merged language of genetics and risk "increasingly supplies a grid of perception that informs decisions on how to conduct one's life, have children, get married, or pursue a career" (Rose 2007). Life potentially becomes one of "optimization." But Rose is quick to add that there is little evidence to date that someone labelled as genetically at risk is reduced to a "passive body-machine that is merely to be the object of a dominating medical expertise" (Rose 2007), and empirical findings strongly support this position.

It is estimated that only between 15 and 20 per cent of adults designated at risk for a named genetic disease or for carrying a fetus that may be at risk for a genetic disease have been willing thus far to undergo genetic testing, a finding that has held for over ten years (these numbers vary from country to country and region to region, and differ according to the disease in question (Beeson and Doksum 2001; Quaid and Morris 1993; Wexler 1992). It has also been shown that a good number of people when tested ignore or challenge the results (Hill 1994; Rapp 1999). No doubt this situation exists because uncertainty, disbelief, doubt, and concerns about repercussions among kin as a result of the knowledge, colour people's responses to test results in connection with the majority of genetic disorders. But worry about social discrimination, including stigma, loss of insurance coverage, and possible employment difficulties, also contribute to the reluctance of many people to consider testing (Apse et al. 2004; Peterson et al. 2002). Responses also depend upon whether or not reproductive decision-making is implicated, the age of onset of the disease in question, and whether the severity of the condition or even its actual occurrence can be reliably predicted. For virtually all of the single gene disorders, there are few, if any, preventive measures that can be recommended for those who test positive, and curative treatments are largely non-existent.

Space does not permit a discussion of genetic screening, when genetic testing is made available to populations known to be at high risk for specific deadly childhood conditions such as Tay Sachs disease and ß thalassemia. However, because decisions about reproduction are at stake, the uptake of testing by such groups of people is usually very high, with the notable exception historically of sickle cell screening programs in which populations of African origin were targeted (Mitchell et al. 1996; Wailoo and Pemberton 2006).

Of Moral Pioneers

Rayna Rapp's classic ethnography about the social impact of amniocentesis exposes many of the problems associated with genetic testing that continue to be of fundamental concern today. Amniocentesis is a technology used primarily to detect Down syndrome, a chromosomal abnormality, and certain inherited disorders. Rapp shows graphically how, despite a firm policy of non-directive counselling and a resolute belief that they are "information brokers" of "rational" knowledge, American genetic counsellors convey information to women in a variety of ways that frequently depend upon the assumed ethnicity of the individual receiving the results (Rapp 1999). Counsellors often encourage, apparently inadvertently, "stratified reproduction," in which "some categories of people are empowered to nurture and reproduce, while others are disempowered" (Ginsburg and Rapp 1995). Rapp's ethnography also makes it clear that many pregnant women when forced to make a decision about genetic testing are non-cooperative and frequently re-interpret or resist risk information they are given. Counselled women and their partners must inevitably confront "the gap" created among statistical estimations of risk based on population databases, their personal concerns about undergoing the actual test, and their doubts about the meaning of the results for their individual well-being.

Several women interviewed by Rapp, including some who were well educated, misunderstood what they had been taught; however, even when the import of counselling was correctly internalized, making a "rational" decision about termination of a wanted pregnancy should the test prove positive raised an array of difficulties. Some people expressed disbelief about the accuracy of the testing; others were concerned because amniocentesis can induce pregnancy loss; some made it clear that they did not believe Down syndrome is a reason to abort a fetus and, among these people, several were particularly concerned because the test would tell them nothing about the severity of the phenotype. Others, believing that they themselves have a healthy lifestyle, did not accept that their fetus is at risk for disease. Religious beliefs also play a part in decision-making, as do family economics, the reproductive experiences of extended family members, and attitudes to disability in general. In some families, the pregnant woman is made to feel responsible for the "problem" having arisen in the first place. Rapp describes the women who undergo testing as "moral pioneers" because they are expected to make rational decisions about abortion of wanted pregnancies, when in reality they are confronted with complex, heart-rending decisions.

Carole Browner's work among Mexicans living in America has shown how the presence of male partners during genetic counselling sessions can have a profound effect on decision-making. With few exceptions, the husband's role was understood by both partners as supportive and facilitating of the decision that the woman herself had chosen. However, Browner found that when women appeared to be vacillating about having a test, clinicians tended to forge alliances with the male partner, perhaps assuming they would be more able to see reason (Browner 2007).

Many researchers, among them Rapp and Browner, have shown that when genetic information is incorporated into accounts about illness causation, such knowledge supplements rather than replaces previously held notions about kinship, heredity, and health. For example, writing about Huntington disease, a single gene disorder with adult onset (sometimes very late in life) for which there is no known treatment, Cox and McKellin (1999) make it clear that lay understandings of heredity conflict with Mendelian genetics, because the scientific account does not assuage the anxieties of families dealing with the lived experience of genetic risk. Similarly to Rapp, these authors argue on the basis of empirical findings: "theories of Mendelian inheritance frame risk in static, objective terms. They abstract risk from the messiness of human contingency and biography." These authors conclude that test candidates and their families jointly engage in a "complex social calculus or risk" that is fluid, contingent, and inter-subjective (1999).

People who come from families with Huntington disease often vacillate about testing, sometimes for many years, in part as a result of the uncertainties involved about age of onset of the condition, and because no treatment exists (Cox and McKellin 1999). Moreover, increased knowledge about molecular genetics complicate estimations of future risk, sometimes making "educated choices" about testing problematic. For example, it is now known that the autosomal dominant gene associated with Huntington disease is not 100 per cent penetrant, as was formerly believed to be the case, so that not quite everyone with the gene will manifest the disease (McNeil et al. 1997).

The anthropologist Monica Konrad also uses Huntington disease as an illustrative example of what she characterizes as "the making of the 'pre-symptomatic person'" (Konrad 2005). Inspired in part by anthropological research into divination, Konrad explores the "prophetic realities" unfolding in contemporary society as a result of genetic technologies. Konrad, like Rapp, is concerned with "moral decision-making" and her emphasis is on how, when bodies are made into oracles, "moral systems of foreknowledge" thus produced are enacted both within and across generations. Konrad is at pains to emphasize what happens in families where some people choose to be tested and others refuse. Her work, like virtually all the other social science research on genetic testing, makes it abundantly clear that the common approach in bioethics of a "right to know" and an assumption of individual autonomy with respect to decision making in connection with genetics, is extremely problematic. Konrad discusses at length the "pragmatics of uncertainty" that infuse the everyday lives of people living with genetic foreknowledge and, further, the new forms of "relational identity" that testing brings about: how and when to inform children of one's own test results; whether to be entirely "truthful" or not; whether to say nothing at all; making a decision as to whether the children be tested, and if so, when? Value is associated with the very idea of kinship, the ties of which are medicalized as a result of genetic testing, thus accounting for why "affectively charged kinship talk" (2005; see also Finkler 2000, 2001) consistently dominates gene talk.

When the sociologist Nina Hallowell interviewed women in the United Kingdom who come from families where cancer is very common and who were undergoing testing at a specialty clinic for the BRCA genes associated with increased risk for breast cancer, without exception she found that these women believed that it was their duty to themselves and to their children to undergo testing. Moreover, many women who had already borne children believed themselves to be responsible for having unknowingly put their children at risk (Hallowell 1999). On the basis of these findings, Hallowell argued that women, more so than men, are likely to develop feelings of "genetic responsibility"; that is, to experience an obligation to undergo testing and reveal the results to kin. As one woman put it:

> A large proportion of my concern is a responsibility to my daughter. And I think also it's sort of a helplessness ... I've passed

> on the gene to my daughter. I must make sure now that I alert her to what might be in store for her, because I have that responsibility.

Most women interviewed by Hallowell were frightened of undergoing the test, scared that it might affect their employment or health insurance, but nevertheless went through with it. Sometimes women were pushed to do so by their spouses or sisters:

> I said to my husband that I didn't want to know. I said, if I'm going to get cancer then I'm just going to get it. I don't want to go for this test. And my husband, he kept saying … you know, you should, because it's not just for you, but for the kids.

Kaya Finkler also interviewed women who come from families designated as being "at risk" for breast cancer, some of whom had undergone genetic testing. She describes how these women become "perpetual patients" while healthy, and how at family gatherings they discuss the genes they believe they share with extended kin. Finkler concludes that families, often dispersed and no longer in regular contact, are reunited by medicalization: "DNA joins the compartmentalized, fragmented postmodern individual to his or her ancestors" by means of medical testing, the construction of medical genealogies, and the storage of DNA samples (2001). Her findings clearly document a zone of chronic anxiety that families are liable to inhabit when some individuals carry the gene(s) that increase risk for breast cancer (Finkler et al. 2003). However, as Finkler points out, such anxiety is often exacerbated by media hype that has a tendency to misrepresent and overstate scientific findings.

Genetic Citizenship and Future Promise

Rayna Rapp and her associates have documented how networks of families increasingly coalesce as a result of shared knowledge about the rare single gene disorders that afflict their children. Such groups provide mutual social support and lobby the United States Congress for improved research funding (similar activities happen in many other countries). These activists are painfully aware that only rarely will drug companies invest in research into these kinds of diseases because there is little profit to be had in developing medications for the so-called "orphan diseases," over 1,500 of which are distributed across a mere 2 per cent of the world's population. Lobbying for public funding is deemed essential, much of it directed initially at locating the relevant mutations on the human genome. These practices often have direct links to biocapital; the state is involved only in so far as political lobbying for recognition of the disease and funding for it are indispensable (Rapp et al. 2001; Rapp 2003). Such alliances constitute what has come to be known as "genetic citizenship" in action, and involve not only mobilization of affected people, but new ways of envisioning the future, when gene therapy may possibly become a realistic option (Callon and Rabeharisoa 2004; Heath et al 2004; Rapp 2003; Taussig et al 2003).

One of the citizen support groups investigated by Taussig and her colleagues is LPA (Little People of America), founded in 1957. Members of LPA do not all make similar decisions with respect to the choices now available to them in connection with treatment, such as limb lengthening, and also about genetic testing. Many LPA members fear genetic testing may be used inappropriately, and that pressure will be brought to bear on couples to undergo abortions when testing proves positive for dwarfing. Furthermore, when LPA couples choose to have genetic testing, "choice" is inevitably compounded by uncertainty, because several dwarfing conditions exist in which different genes are implicated, but there is virtually no knowledge, other than that of the isolated experiences of some families, about how these genes are likely to interact during reproduction (Taussig et al 2003). Research of this kind shows how, even among politically active groups, concerns about persisting uncertainties and the outcomes of technological interventions are dominant and, further, that within activist groups people are by no means of one mind.

Biosociality and the Affiliation of Genes

In putting forward the concept of biosociality, the anthropologist Paul Rabinow cited the geneticist Neil Holtzman who argued that early detection of genetic susceptibility and predispositions would shortly become routine. Rabinow chose to give particular emphasis to only one of the many issues raised by Holtzman: "the likely formation of new group and individual identities and practices arising out of these new truths (Rabinow 1996)." Rabinow is careful to note that groups formed on the basis of individual experiences with disease were already in existence some time before genotyping became available and will clearly continue to function with respect to "pastoral" and political activities. But, he suggests, new congeries of people will emerge as a result of knowledge founded in molecular genetics: "it is not hard to imagine groups formed around chromosome 17, locus 16,256, site 654,376 allele variant, with a guanine substitution." Such groups will have "medical specialists, laboratories, narrative traditions, and a heavy panoply of pastoral keepers to help them experience, share, intervene, and 'understand' their fate" (1996).

At the time when Rabinow first introduced the concept of biosociality, the idea of groups literally coming together on the basis of a specified chromosomal abnormality as Rabinow suggested (with a touch of irony one assumes) seemed far-fetched to many. In retrospect his insight appears to have been prescient. An article in the *New York Times* in December 2007 discusses the experiences of certain families with *extremely* rare genetic mutations who, as a result of a new diagnostic technology, learn about the DNA mutation that has affected one or more of their children and, with access to email and the Internet, have made contact with similarly affected families. These families readily agreed that contact with other affected families, even though indirect, was an extremely supportive experience (Harmon 2007).

Raspberry and Skinner, who carried out research with ethnically diverse families in the southeastern United States where a child had been diagnosed with a genetic disorder (2007), similar to the findings reported in the *New York Times*, found that a genetic diagnosis frequently gives legitimacy to a disorder as "truly" biological. Families are then able to escape from catch-all "soft" diagnostic categories such as autism and ADHD (attention deficit and hyperactivity disorder), and sustain hope for a "cure" in the not too distant future, perhaps by means of genetic engineering. Nevertheless, these researchers argue that such families maintain a "hybrid notion of causality," even when it is undeniable that chromosomal deletions have brought about very real bodily changes. Inevitably, questions about the range of phenotypic expression, severity, and individual compensatory capabilities are uppermost in people's minds.

A decade on, Rabinow admits to limitations associated with the concept of biosociality, although it is a concept that has been made extensive use of by many researchers – a measured critique of which appears in the book edited by Sahra Gibbon and Carlos Novas (2007).

In reassessing the situation, Rabinow (2007) notes that there has been a shift in the time horizon that he formerly assumed was unfolding, brought about in large part by the "demise of the gene" and the emergence of a postgenomic era – a topic to be expanded upon below.

Global Testing

Although genetic testing is not an inordinately expensive technology, only relatively recently has it begun to be carried out in economically deprived countries. Duana Fullwiley has carried out ethnographic research in connection with attitudes towards genetic testing in Senegal, West Africa, where this technology was introduced several years ago. She notes that the physicians she interviewed, the majority of whom were trained in France, were frustrated with the effects of what Fullwiley describes as "discriminate biopower" (2004). Although Senegal has one of the lowest rates of HIV in Africa, at a little over 1 per cent of the population, and sickle cell disease, a genetic disease common in malarial regions, affects 10 per cent or more of the population, the funding provided by NGOS, following UN and WHO directives was, until recently, almost exclusively for HIV/AIDS and not for sickle cell disease.

Fullwiley points out that Senegalese physicians with whom she talked assume that young married women do not want to be tested for the sickle cell gene because abortion is not acceptable to this Muslim population and, further, Wolof "tradition" is that women should have many children. Although the majority of women interviewed by Fullwiley cited religion as a major influence on their thinking, she found that, even among those opposed to abortion, some thought that testing would be helpful in order to know what the future had in store for them. Others thought testing of male partners might give women just cause to divorce unsympathetic or disagreeable husbands. Alternatively, reluctant young women might be able to avoid entering a marriage arranged by the family in which it was proven with genetic testing that children could well be born homozygous for sickle cell disease. Among those women who agreed that selective abortion would be acceptable, Muslim teaching was cited in which it is argued that, prior to "ensoulment," embryos are simply "life." After a period of gestation (there is disagreement among the women as to how long), once embryos become "human life" and not simply life, only then is abortion regarded as murder.

Fullwiley found that the principal matters that concern families when discussing genetic testing include "recent family history and present family character, spiritual conviction and religious interpretation, marital problems and familial pressure to resolve them, and the social obligation to raise healthy children" (2004). These convictions, although clearly local in kind, are strikingly similar in some ways to narratives elicited by anthropologists working in the West in that, notably, it is the well being of the family as a whole, and not simply of individuals, that may well be uppermost in mind when seeking out genetic testing. This is particularly apparent, not surprisingly, when decisions about reproduction are at issue.

BEYOND THE DOGMA OF GENETIC DETERMINISM

As is now well known, when mapping the human genome, involved scientists labelled 98 per cent of the DNA they had isolated as "junk" because it did not conform with their idea of how the blueprint for life was assumed to work. In recent years the situation has changed dramatically, and junk DNA, thrust summarily to one side in order to focus on the task of mapping only those genes that code directly for proteins, is no longer ignored. The function of non-coding DNA is still by no means fully understood, but some of it is now known to be converted into non-coding RNA that is in turn deeply implicated in gene expression and regulation (Eddy 2001; Mattick 2003, 2004). The activities of ncRNA are thought to comprise the most comprehensive regulatory system in complex organisms; they function to create the "architecture" of organisms, without which chaos would reign (Mattick 2003). ncRNA frequently brings about regulation by acting as a signalling system that profoundly affects the timing of processes that take place during development, including stem cell maintenance, cell proliferation, apoptosis (programmed cell death), and the onset of cancer and other complex ailments (Petronis 2001). Consequently, the research interests of the majority of molecular and population biologists are no longer confined to mapping the structure of genomes, but are now focused on the elucidation of the mechanisms of sub-cellular, cellular, and organ functioning throughout the life span of individuals, and also through evolutionary time.

In their important book *Genomes and What to Make of Them*, the sociologist/philosopher team of Barnes and Dupré argue "DNA is not simply involved with heredity; one now has to ask what does DNA do 'all the time,' throughout the life cycle? How, when, and under what circumstances does DNA become expressed or, alternatively, when is it switched off (2008)?" In a related vein, Richard Strohman, a Berkeley molecular biologist asks: "if the program for life is not in our genes, then where is it?" He notes that many of his colleagues have been arguing quietly for a long time that "there is no program in the sense of an inherited, pre-existing script waiting to be read." Rather, he argues, "there are regulatory networks of proteins that sense or measure changes in the cellular environment and interpret those signals so that the cell makes an appropriate response." This regulatory system, a "dynamic-epigenetic network," has a life of its own, so to speak, with rules that are not specified by DNA (2001).

The biologist Scott Gilbert suggests that in light of this major conceptual shift our "self" is best understood as permeable. We are each, in effect, "a complex community, indeed, a collection of ecosystems," as he puts it (2002). Contingency is the name of this game and, further, it is apparent, perhaps to the majority of researchers in molecular biology, that genes do not have clearly demarcated beginnings or ends; nor are they stable, and only very rarely indeed do they determine either individual phenotypes or the biological make up of future generations (Stotz et al. 2006; Jablonka and Lamb 2005; Neumann-Held and Rehmann-Sutter 2006). Furthermore, a segment of DNA demarcated as a gene can code for multiple proteins used in multiple pathways (Buchanan et al. 2009). Quite simply, then, genes are not *us* in any straightforward manner, and the gene, although it continues to be a useful concept, can no longer pass as the fundamental animating force of all human life. Systematic research into molecular epigenetics is just beginning to take off and, although genetics and genomics play an indispensable role in this research, ultimately the objective is to explain what it is about inheritance, health, and illness that genes alone do not explain.

One well-documented, frequently cited case that illustrates the above position involves findings that have accumulated over the years in connection with what is known as the Dutch famine of 1944 (Lumey 1992). Thirty thousand people died from starvation as a result of a World War II German food embargo that brought about the complete breakdown of local food supplies, adding to the misery of an already harsh winter. Birth records collected in Holland since that time have shown that children born of women who were pregnant during the famine not only had low birth weights, but also exhibited a range of developmental and adult disorders later in life including diabetes, coronary heart disease, and cancers. Furthermore, it has been shown that this second generation, even though prosperous and well nourished, themselves produced low birth weight children who inherited similar health problems (Harding 2001).

Researchers argue that these findings strongly suggest that expression of crucial DNA sequences had been repressed due to radically reduced nutritional intake during pregnancy. It is now recognized that such changes are the result of a molecular process known as methylation, crucial to both the expression and silencing of genes, and it has been shown convincingly that environmental variables can alter this complex process and, further, that the changes that result may be inherited independently of DNA. These findings are currently attracting a great deal of attention among researchers (Champagne and Meaney 2001; Szyf et al. 2008) and have opened the door to what is being described positively by some as neo-Lamarckianism. Increased knowledge about methylation and other key processes at the level of the cell are beginning to make clear some of the crucial mechanisms involved in dynamic epigenetics and, furthermore, are exposing both the indivisibility of culture and the material world, and the means by which extensive variation is produced over time (Jablonka and Lamb 1995; Oyama et al. 2001). However, as Strohman makes clear, scientists are currently suspended between paradigms: genetic determinism is a failed paradigm, he argues (although the majority of involved scientists quite possibly take issue with him), and research into dynamic epigenetics is only just taking shape – in short, we are betwixt and between, and the current generation of scientists, especially when they work in alliance with the corporate world have, for the most part, been trained for and remain firmly embedded in a deterministic framework. And yet, even Craig Venter is on record as commenting that genes cannot possibly explain that which makes us who we are, and similarly, Strohman insists that while the Human Genome Project did indeed tell us a great deal about our genome, it tells us nothing about who we are and how we got this way (2001).

Commentary of this kind brings us firmly into the realms of anthropology and philosophy. The fundamental question for many becomes one of whether or not DNA has "agency" – a position that Neumann-Held and Rehmann-Sutter argue as in any case thoroughly anthropomorphic (2006).

One can argue that Mendelian genetics, particularly the hard-nosed, reductionist, deterministic version – the creation of James Watson and Francis Crick – "fit" very neatly into the sweep of modernity. Genes make us what we are in this vision. The hope of some, especially with the mapping of the Human Genome, was that we would be able to engage in fundamental genetic engineering and manufacture genomes designed to eradicate disease, poverty, ignorance, and criminality (as the past editor of *Science*, Daniel Koshland, so infamously wrote (1988)), while at the same time enhancing our desire for aesthetically pleasing, perfect offspring. But the molecularized universe has turned out to be so very much more complicated, and exciting, than most people had imagined. It is a universe entirely in tune with postmodernity – an environment of the unexpected in which boundaries formerly thought to be stable are dissolved. Increasingly it has become clear that multiple factors, including events both internal and external to the body, contribute, almost without exception, to the enhancement or inhibition of gene expression, with the result that it is now agreed by many molecular biologists that research into what it is that brings about phenotypic expression must make use of a "wide-angled lens." These emerging insights strongly suggest that our efforts to divine individual futures by means of genetic testing for any condition other than the rare Mendelian disorders are precarious indeed, and the majority of clinicians and basic scientists, with some notable exceptions, are well aware of this.

In her book *The Century of the Gene* Evelyn Fox Keller summed up, already a decade ago, where she believes we now stand: "Genes have had a glorious run in the twentieth century, and they have inspired incomparable and astonishing advances in our understanding of living systems. Indeed, they have carried us to the edge of a new era in biology, one that holds out the promise of even more astonishing advances. But these very advances will necessitate the introduction of other concepts, other terms, and other ways of thinking about biological organization, thereby loosening the grip that genes have had on the imagination of the life sciences these many decades" (Keller 2000).

Keller, while she is clear that the concept of the gene is "good enough" for many experimental purposes, concludes that it is time to think about adopting new concepts to bring about more appropriate insights into the workings of living systems. Gelbart insists that the term "gene" may have become a hindrance to the understanding of many biologists (1998) and Keller adds that this problem is no doubt even more marked among "lay readers" (2000). However, the research findings set out below suggest, at least in connection with certain diseases, that people from affected families are by no means wedded to the idea of the gene as a powerful deterministic force.

The genetics of Alzheimer's disease is introduced in the following section to illustrate a little of the complexity that we are now confronted with in connection with susceptibility genes.

THE GENETICS OF ALZHEIMER'S DISEASE

Before presenting empirical findings about the impact on individuals of being given a risk assessment for Alzheimer's disease based on genotyping, it is necessary to briefly set out details about the genetics of this disease, as it is currently understood. It will become readily apparent that knowledge about ones genotype alone is by no means a powerful predictor for the disease, and it should be born in mind that age is without doubt the greatest overall risk factor for dementia, and that many other variables are routinely implicated including head trauma, education levels, diet, toxic environments, and family history, among others.

Alois Alzheimer originally observed a case of what is now known as "early onset" Alzheimer's disease. This form of dementia occurs in only approximately 170 extended families worldwide, has long been thought of as a "genetic disease," and is associated with three specific, genetic mutations each of which has been mapped (St George-Hyslop 2000). It is not strictly true to claim that the gene determines even this autosomal dominant form of the disease, because the age of onset for identical twins can vary by as much as a decade (Tilley et al. 1998). Early onset AD usually (but not inevitably) manifests itself somewhere between the ages of 35 and 60, progresses relatively quickly to death, and accounts for up to 5% of all diagnosed cases of the disease.

In 1993 the first publication appeared that explicitly made an association between a variation of the gene known as APOE and increased risk for the common, late onset form of AD (Corder et al.

1993). This finding forced some revisions of the received wisdom of the time – namely that Alzheimer's disease in older people is "sporadic," and does not "run in families." The APOE gene, present in all mammals, is located in humans on chromosome 19, and is essential for lipid metabolism. This gene comes in three universally distributed forms APOEε2, APOEε3, and APOEε4, and evidence from over 100 laboratories indicates that it is the APOEε4 allele that puts individuals at increased risk for AD. Between 14 and 16 per cent of so-called Caucasian populations (the most extensively studied population) carry at least one ε4 allele, however, it is unanimously agreed that the presence of the allele is neither necessary nor sufficient to cause the disease, for reasons that remain poorly understood. In other words, the ε4 allele is an example of a "susceptibility gene," one that contributes to disease causation only under certain, as yet unknown, circumstances.

It is estimated that at least 50 per cent of ε4 carriers never get Alzheimer's disease. Research in connection with the allele shows that when it is implicated in AD, exactly the same final biological pathway is involved as that set in motion by the autosomal dominant genes associated with the early onset form of the disease; but the biological changes in which APOEε4 in its homozygous form is implicated become manifest later in life, usually between the ages of 65 and 75 (Selkoe 2002). For individuals who are heterozygous and have only one ε4 allele, the age of onset is usually later. Given that somewhere between 30 and 60 per cent of patients diagnosed with late onset AD do not have the ε4 allele (Myers et al. 1996), there must be at least one other, and probably several more pathways to Alzheimer's disease. Involved scientists assume today that such pathways are constituted by mutually interactive genes and non-coding DNA, in conjunction with environmental factors, internal and/or external to the body. These alternative pathways become evident late in life, usually after age 70 or later, but they too result in the same final common pathway as that for early onset, and ε4 linked AD.

In 2004 the situation with respect to the genetics of Alzheimer's disease was summarized by two neurogeneticists as follows: "First, and most importantly, the heritability of AD is high…this had been demonstrated in various studies…over the past decades. But, these experts go on to note, "most of the research currently being done has faulty methodology, lacks replication, and is inattentive to haplotype structure" (Bertram and Tanzi, 2004). Using the citation index

PubMed, Bertram and Tanzi showed that in 2003 alone a total of 1037 studies were carried out on the genetics of AD, out of which 55 analyzed genes were reported to have a positive association with increased risk for the disease, while 68 tested negative. On repeat testing most of the positive associations could not be shown again (Bertram and Tanzi 2004).

Currently the approach known as genome-wide association studies (GWAS) is being applied to Alzheimer genetics. To date findings from eight such studies, several of which have sample sizes of well over 1000 cases, have been published, all of which confirm that the APOE gene alone clearly puts certain individuals at risk, especially in its homozygous form. One of the studies was carried out by Bertram and Tanzi who have also published a review article summarizing what they believe is the present situation with respect to GWAS:

> As additional GWAS are carried out on larger datasets and higher-resolution arrays, we can expect the list of novel AD gene candidates to keep growing over the coming years. For all of these putative associations, replication attempts and meta-analyses across multiple independent samples will be essential to determine the identity of *bona fide* AD susceptibility genes. Despite the rapid progress being made in these still early days of the GWAS era, it should be emphasized that for none of the novel AD candidate genes that have thus far emerged from genome-wide screening, do we have conclusive functional genetic evidence that would allow us to unequivocally establish any of these loci as genuine AD risk genes. (Bertram and Tanzi 2009)

One thing becomes dramatically clear from GWAS research – the hundreds of biological pathways that are potentially implicated on the road to dementia including, possibly, one or more of those involved in activation of the immune system and also with inflammatory processes.

Despite the undeniable complexity, the genetic epidemiologist, Richard Mayeux, commenting on the genetics of AD in a New Yorker article, made it clear that he does not believe researchers will be held back too much longer from genuinely insightful knowledge: "a decade from now your doctor will look up your gene profile and decide whether you have a high risk for Alzheimer's, and then give you a prophylactic treatment of some sort." But, he adds, "Right now, you don't know what the hell to do!" (Halpern 2005).

However, population research in connection with the genetics of both early and late onset AD suggests that no straightforward solution is in sight. This epidemiologically-based approach has amply demonstrated that genes are shape-shifters without peer, the products of evolutionary and recent human history, dietary and climatic patterns, possibly of toxic environments and, at times, of serendipitous mutations. Most epidemiological research into the genetics of AD has been carried out since the early 1990s, when the significance of the e4 allele was first identified, but these studies have been confined largely to what are known among population geneticists as Caucasian populations (Growden 1998; Korovaitseva et al. 2001; Roses 1998; Saunders 2000; Silverman et al. 2003). The research methodology has been criticized, but even so, it appears that the relationship between APOEe4 and AD incidence is probably significantly weaker than is commonly assumed. For example, one community-based study found that 85 per cent of elderly homozygous e4 individuals whose average age was 81 showed no sign of dementia when given standard tests for cognitive functioning (Hyman et al. 1996).

Adding to the uncertainties, APOEε4 has been shown to work in unexpected ways in specific populations. Among Pygmies and other groups of people whose subsistence economy was until relatively recently predominantly that of hunting and gathering, possession of an e4 genotype *apparently* protects against AD. This finding holds when controlled for age (Corbo and Scacchi 1999). Low rates of AD have been reported for parts of Nigeria, and the presence of an ε4 allele does not appear to place individuals at increased risk (Farrer et al. 1997). On the other hand, APOEε4 is significantly associated with dementia among African-Americans, although less so than in Caucasian populations (Farrer 2000). Once again, the methodology of this research has been criticized, but the data appear sufficiently robust to conclude that risk reducing factors (in Africa) and risk enhancing factors (in North America) must be implicated, among them other genes, their protein products, diet, environment, and quite possibly yet other variables.

The Indianapolis-Ibadan project headed up by Hugh Hendrie for over 17 years, has shown that the incidence rates of AD and dementia in Yoruba are less than half the incidence rates for AD and dementia in African-Americans when controlled for age, although the ε4 allele frequency is not significantly different in the two cohorts (Hendrie 2009). Furthermore, the Yoruba have a lower incidence of both vascular disease and vascular risk factors, including hypertension, than do African-Americans and, significantly, cholesterol and lipid levels are much lower in the Yoruba. Hendrie's group concludes, reasonably, that *both* genetic and environmental factors may be responsible for these differences. They note that there may well be considerable variation among the genomes of studied Yorubans, as has been well established for African populations in general. As yet, they do not know how well the African-American admixed population corresponds to the Yorubans under study. This calls for further investigation, as does the relationship between diet and vascular disease in the two populations.

It is evident that basic science and epidemiological findings about the genetics of late-onset Alzheimer's disease (AD) are subject to continual revision and are far from conclusive. Moreover, adding greatly to the uncertainty, although usually not openly acknowledged, the accuracy of a diagnosis of AD is disputed by certain researchers, particularly because, even though it is the most commonly diagnosed of the dementias, it is nevertheless a "waste basket" category applied after other diagnoses have been ruled out (Savva et al. 2009; Whitehouse 2008). It is no surprise then that current guidelines about genetic testing for APOE status do not support its routinization in clinical care, particularly because there is no known treatment for the disease. However, it is possible that this situation may change in the not too distant future; several private companies already offer testing for APOE, and an "Early Alert Alzheimer's Home Screening Test" kit is marketed directly to consumers (Kier and Molinari 2003).

What does this current state of knowledge about late-onset AD genetics imply for biosociality, embodied identity, and worry about becoming demented in the future? Clearly, learning that one carries an e4 allele should not bring about as dramatic an effect as learning that you have one of the deadly genes associated with early-onset Alzheimer's disease or the mutation associated with Huntington Disease. Learning about one's APOE status cannot provide accurate information about the probable future, but rather only introduces a possible scenario involving the kind of uncertainty that anyone living in a family where AD is present inevitably confronts as part of daily life. The final part of this chapter presents a summary of responses by individuals who have been informed as part of a randomized controlled trial about the status of their APOE gene.

EMBODYING KNOWLEDGE ABOUT THE APOE GENE

A National Institutes of Health (NIH) approved randomized controlled trial that goes under the name REVEAL (Risk Evaluation and Education for Alzheimer's disease) was recently carried out in the United States. Healthy individuals from families in which one or more members have been affected by AD are enrolled as subjects for this research. The REVEAL trial was originally a three-sited project at Boston University Medical School; Case Western Reserve Medical School, Cleveland; and Cornell University Medical School, New York, but has been extended to include Howard University in Washington DC, for a total of 442 participants. Subjects for this trial were recruited either through systematic ascertainment from American AD research registries kept at the respective medical schools, or through self-referral at each site (Cupples et al. 2004). Upon recruitment into Phase I of the project, research subjects were randomized into intervention and control groups. In the original three-sited sample everyone self-identified as "white," and the majority are women. Participants are highly educated, with a mean of seventeen years of education. The Howard sample identify themselves as African-Americans, and also have a high mean education level of fifteen years.

All participants reported that they are eager to assist with medical research about Alzheimer's disease. Upon recruitment to the trial, they attended an educational session about Alzheimer's disease in the form of a PowerPoint presentation that emphasized theories about AD causation and about risk for AD based on gender, family history, and genotype, after which they were asked to return to the research site at a later date for a blood draw. People in the intervention group were informed a few weeks later about their APOE status. Those assigned to be controls were not given this information until after the study was completed.

Reactions of the subjects to APOE testing were systematically monitored by means of three follow-up structured interviews conducted by genetic counsellors over the course of twelve months, and then compared with the reactions of individuals in the control group. In phase II of the project, when the four sites were involved, everyone was informed of their APOE status from the outset, and both clinicians and counsellors were involved in disclosing to research subjects their APOE status. In order to carry out the "risk disclosure" portion of the study all subjects are shown one of several specially designed "risk curves." The population database from which these curves were created was derived from a meta-analysis of studies involving very large samples of Caucasian subjects (Green et al. 1997) (a modified curve is used with the Howard sample). The curves were sub-divided on the basis of age, gender, and the six possible combinations of APOE genotype, giving a total of twelve curves (Farrer et al. 1997). Results from the follow up questionnaires suggest that people do not experience increased anxiety levels that extend much beyond the time of receiving their result (Larusse et al. 2005).

After the REVEAL trial had already been in progress for approaching one year, I was asked by one of the principal investigators to contribute a qualitative component to the study. After considerable thought I agreed, having obtained an understanding from REVEAL researchers that the qualitative findings might well not support the original objectives of the project, or the quantitative findings.[1] The qualitative project consisted of open-ended interviews carried out with a sub-sample of seventy-nine of the REVEAL subjects twelve

1 One justification for this research, it is argued, is that testing for susceptibility genes is likely to become increasingly common, especially in the private sector, and therefore knowledge about how people deal with risk information when it is not possible to make predictions with a high degree of confidence is urgently needed. A second justification is that to withhold information about their bodies from people is patronizing. A third justification is that in many families where someone has died of AD some members of the next generation believe that they have a virtually 100 per cent chance of contracting the disease. If individuals can be taught that, even if they are homozygous for APOEε4, their lifetime risk for getting AD is never more than approximately 52 per cent for men and 58 per cent for women, then their anxiety levels may well be lowered. The fourth explicit justification for the research is to create a pool of APOE ε4 individuals whose bloods can be used at any time to enrich clinical trials.

months or more after participants had initially received their genotype results (Lock et al. 2007). When interviewed, it was clear that the majority of participants had transformed the results they had been given into accounts that "fit" with their experience of being related to someone with Alzheimer's disease; personal assessments of their own family history; and accumulated knowledge about the disease that they had gathered from a variety of sources, including AD societies, their physicians, and the media. In other words, risk estimates provided in the REVEAL study rarely displace "lay knowledge" about who in their family is particularly at risk – knowledge that participants bring with them to the project. Rather, the "scientific" information is either nested into pre-existing knowledge, simply forgotten, or even actively rejected, as has also been shown for single-gene disorders.

Furthermore, it is difficult to imagine how genetic information given out as part of REVEAL might radically transform the way individuals perceive their own risk when only 27 per cent of the interviewed sample were able to recall their genetic results correctly, and an almost equal number (23 per cent) either remembered incorrectly or did not remember anything at all. The remaining participants retained the "gist" of the information they were given. This is despite the fact that many volunteered to participate in REVEAL specifically because they wanted the genetic test done, although the main reason for participation was to assist in scientific research. When asked about their genetic results, responses like that of Vicki are not uncommon:

> I was just thinking on my way in here today, oh I bet they're going to ask me about which genes I have. And I can't remember! ... I should have reviewed.

Paul also emphasizes the difficulty he had recalling his results:

> Even though she [the genetic counsellor] has explained this to me several times, I still couldn't tell you which one of the markers, of the four, they were watching – you know, she just handed me some information and said, "Here are your markers." ... we had gotten all this information at the opening meeting. And we all dutifully took home our notes of this. And come back three months later or whatever, and they'd throw out these things

> again and I said, "Oh, cripe." And I still don't know whether I have a 10 per cent or a 20 per cent or a 50 per cent chance.

While few accurately remember their APOE status or risk assessment, 50 per cent retain the gist of the information – often expressing their results in general terms such as "having a lower risk than I imagined," "having the bad gene." For example, Tessa says:

> I keep forgetting. I have problems with it, I know I'm either an e2 or e4, but keep forgetting which. The thing that I do remember is whichever one I am, that it's not a factor.

This inability to remember their APOE status is equally the case for people who were given higher risk estimates because they have at least one e4 allele. Jacqueline said:

> You know, I can't even remember. I would come in from one meeting to the next, and I couldn't remember what my risk was. And to this day, I'm not 100 percent sure, but I know that it's elevated.

Similarly, Helen's comment reveals considerable confusion:

> In fact, when I first came back to have the follow-up study after we found out the results they asked me that percent and whether it was 3/4, 2/2 or whatever. I don't even remember. The number didn't stick ... to me it was simply like a 50/50 probability ... okay, it's 3/4 – so I put that down. It's more like a parrot thing than a, "yes, I know what this means."

Elizabeth has seven relatives with AD and, not surprisingly, despite learning from the REVEAL education session that e4 does not *cause* AD, she finds it difficult to come to terms with this information, particularly as she was informed that she is heterozygous for e4. But Elizabeth made it clear that she had already known for a "fact" that she will get AD *before* being genotyped, and that genotyping in effect changed nothing.

Other participants did not trust the results they were given. Rebecca, who was told that she is a 3/3 and at a relatively low risk said, somewhat angrily:

> According to that test, I don't have a whole lot of risk, okay? So, technically I should feel better. But I don't believe it. If I had all the confidence in the world in that test, I would say, "Oh maybe it's not going to happen." But I don't believe it.

Rebecca has four affected relatives, and is right to be concerned. Possibly she has forgotten that she was taught in the educational session that approximately 50 per cent of people diagnosed with AD do not have the e4 allele.

In contrast, some subjects clearly learnt a valuable piece of information, as the following quote suggests, even though they did not always understand exactly what was explained to them:

> I guess I thought before testing I might have a 90 per cent chance of having AD...Now I know its fifty-fifty, just like flipping a coin.

Given that there is little that can be done to either prevent or treat AD, responses of the following kind are not uncommon:

> I think [REVEAL] provides useful information ... Just don't ask me how I would use it ... I honestly don't know.

And another said, "Well, I know where I stand, and my children know where they stand – maybe get it, maybe not."

EXPLANATIONS FOR ALZHEIMER'S CAUSATION

Although some REVEAL subjects entered the study precisely because they believe that AD is intimately related to genetic constitution, upon completion of the project, with one exception only, everyone considered genetics to be just one of several possible causes for late-onset AD, and it appears that they held this opinion before they underwent the REVEAL education session that emphasized multi-causality. Theories about causation aside from genetics included diet (35%), environment (29%), level of physical activity (19%), aluminum (19%), age (16%), depression (17%), and mental activity (17%). Stress, head injuries, smoking, and alcohol consumption were also frequently mentioned.

Muriel juggles with several different ideas based on her experience with her affected mother:

> I mean there's always the diet thing and I do somewhat watch that because I'm certainly aware of the diet connections … there is this other thing about keeping your mental activity up as you get older, you know, stimulate the brain; do crossword puzzles, learn new things, and keep your brain working. My mother did that though. She watched her diet and she was very careful and doggone it, it didn't keep it from happening. And the genetic side, of course, is also not understood. There's not just one cause.

Rosie speculates about the role environmental pollutants play in causing AD. She takes vitamins, exercises, and avoids using aluminum cookware in the hope of preventing the disease, but she links her mother's illness primarily to the stress of having many children late in life, to smoking, and "slowing down" as she got older. For Rosie, the role of genetics is complicated and ambiguous:

> I think (genetics) are a minute aspect of it. It's genetics and environment. People want to say a lot about genetics, and I have to say, we don't know enough. I think that genetics is the big buzz word … Now, with my mom, I think that it could have been a predisposition, but with the stress of having three little ones in her fifties and I guess going through the change of life or whatever, I don't know, all of that could have played a role. Maybe she got depressed and the depression could have led – I don't know. I can't say that I a hundred percent think that it's genetics, even though I did the APOE test. And I forgot what I had! But I refuse to buy into that paradigm. I think there are other things that they don't know about … and I think that stress and environment helps make a weakness into a disease.

Ideas of "susceptibility" and "predisposition" are very common among REVEAL participants and Julia's understanding of genetic risk perhaps represents some acquaintance on her part with the new scientific knowledge discussed above about the significance of genetic signalling and gene expression:

> I think at some point that genes act up. And I don't know what the trigger is, but it's going to send some message that's going to

> cause something else to happen. I think we can recognize the gene, but I don't know that they know what causes the gene to do the bad stuff ... so I think there's something larger happening that allows these abhorrent genes or whatever, to run havoc in your body ... I don't think they really know how to take a mixture of factors of genetics and gender and whatever, to say, okay, this is what really sparks this clogging of your brain.

Similarly, Lila speaks of "genetic potential," but believes she may have some control over the actual manifestation of the disease. She draws an analogy with her experience of diabetes:

> I'd like to think that I have something to do with how [AD] manifests itself. It's sort of like diabetes, which I have a very strong family history for. And knowing that there's certain things in terms of diet or exercise that research has shown may avoid triggering that genetic potential helps. You have the genetic potential, no question. Whether or not it shows up or not has a lot to do with what you do; and your environment. I'd like to think the same way about Alzheimer's.

Clearly, genetic determinism does not loom large in the minds of these respondents who believe strongly in multi-causality. Poor recall of their genotype and risk estimates suggests, I believe, not that they are stupid (as genetic counsellors who have heard these findings presented often say), but that this information is of little relevance to most of them in their daily lives. The mean age of these individuals is in the mid-fifties, and hence a descent into dementia is, no doubt, many years away, if indeed it happens at all. Furthermore, many people are preoccupied with care giving for their affected relatives, while holding down a job, raising children, and sometimes living in strained economic circumstances. The uncertainty associated with the genotype results is simply filed away (literally in the case of many respondents, in the back of a drawer) where it may *possibly* gain significance as these individuals grow older.

Blended Inheritance

The qualitative interviews not only made it clear that many individuals are not able to accurately recall what they had been taught about their supposed personalized risk for AD, but also showed that many continue to hold beliefs that they held prior to entering the study about who in their family is at particular risk for AD, based on physical appearance or purported personality types. For example, Katherine said:

> I showed you the picture of me and my dad. We look like clones, practically, physically. And nobody's really said – I don't know whether or not that makes a difference, a person's physical appearance. But I have a suspicion that it does.

Robert commented:

> Do I think I have a higher than normal chance? Yes. Heredity. And also I'm so much like my mother, who had Alzheimer's. There's a very high likelihood that one or more of her children will have a predisposition toward it. And I would say I'm front-runner because of so many other characteristics I have that are very much like my mother's.

Findings such as these have been noted in other research into the impact of genetic testing, and illustrate resort to "blended inheritance," a concept created some years ago by Martin Richards. He documented a common understanding held among the British public about a mixing or blending of influences inherited from both parents, rather than one entailing a Mendelian transmission of genes (Richards 1996). Such ideas stem from a long tradition of such reasoning, in evidence as early as classical times (Turney 1995). Like earlier work on single gene disorders, including that of Richards and of Cox and McKellin cited above, there is a tendency among many REVEAL respondents to identify a family member who in some way resembles the afflicted person as the individual most likely to be at risk for developing the disorder, whether individual genotypes are known or not.

Given the scientific uncertainty about how exactly and under what circumstances the APOE gene contributes to AD causation, and the emphasis given in the REVEAL study to the undoubted contribution of other involved variables, it is perhaps not surprising that narratives about risk for AD quite often draw on ideas about blended inheritance, despite the high education level of the REVEAL participants. Furthermore, contributing greatly to the uncertainty is not only the lack of clarity associated with the scientific knowledge available, but also the late onset of the disease. Many informants assume they may well die of some other disease before they become very old. Even more important, it seems, is the fact that the increased risk estimates given to these research subjects exceed a "normal" population by only 10 per cent by age 70, and 30 per cent by age 85, for all but the five individuals who are homozygous for the e4 allele. Everyone in the trial is well aware of this situation.

Unless knowledge about AD causation advances considerably, it seems that in families where AD has been diagnosed, even after genotyping, few of the next generation will think of themselves in any straightforward way as "genetically at risk." Their position is similar to that of several researchers who argue that family history continues to be a much more important signifier of AD risk than does genotyping (Clarke 2009). It is the expression of the phenotype, and not the genotype, that brings people up short in connection with this particular disease, for only then are vague and distant uncertainties about the future brought to an abrupt end. In a related vein, the biosociality that takes place among AD families is almost exclusively to do with care giving, and is most often managed by AD societies that, without exception, because of the complexity and uncertainties involved, downplay the contribution of genetics to dementia (Lock et al. 2007). In contrast to families dealing with rare single gene disorders, there is no need for AD families to rally together to lobby for research funding. Genetic citizenship is not required of them because governments are running scared about the mounting cases of dementia and, though many researchers regard it as insufficient, funding is not regularly in short supply. It is also worth noting for late-onset Alzheimer's disease that decisions about reproduction are not involved. People may wonder if they have passed on an e4 allele to their children, but most hope, and indeed often assume, that by the time their children and grandchildren are seventy-five this disease will have been conquered.

CONCLUSIONS

The hubris associated with the Human Genome Project was always misplaced. Most involved scientists knew from the outset that mapping the genome was a relatively straightforward step towards a second challenge of a much bigger order, namely, understanding how genes function *in vivo*. As the extent of the complexity of functional genomics was increasingly appreciated, it became abundantly evident that there were going to be few, if any, easy answers to the problems confronting society in connection with complex disease. DNA is one actor among very many others internal and external to all organisms that influence disease causation, and the boundaries of organisms are permeable (Keller 2006). Aside from a handful of rare mutations, DNA alone cannot be understood as a reliable signifier for individual futures (Lock 2005).

The REVEAL researchers argue as part of their justification for carrying out the trial that it is patronizing *not* to hand out information that can readily be made available to people. But what kind of knowledge is this genetic information, embedded as it is in abundant uncertainty? And, given the contingency associated with the action of APOE, and that the risk estimates REVEAL participants were given were created on the basis of age, gender, family history, and APOE genotype alone, can these estimates be considered to have much value? Should such genotyping, even though it is clearly of use for basic science research, count as disinformation as far as individuals are concerned? Should the situation that holds at present persist, wherein patients agree, with informed consent, to donate their blood anonymously for research purposes, but forgo receiving information about what DNA testing reveals with respect to the APOE gene?

Given that the interview results make it clear that little or no change appears to take place in embodied identity or sense of self on the basis of knowledge about what form of the APOE gene one carries and, further, that family histories, family likeness, past experiences, and care giving duties trump genotypic information (Lock et al. 2007), it appears that the guidelines as they exist are appropriate. But, as genetic profiling becomes cheaper, it is highly likely that APOE genotyping will become a routine part of medical care and, moreover, that many members of the public may demand to know which of the APOE alleles they are carrying. Should it prove in the future that medication is somewhat effective with only one of the APOE variants, as is not all that unlikely, then genetic testing will rapidly be incorporated into standard care and everyone tested will learn of their genotype. The extended counselling and education sessions that the REVEAL participants received as part of the clinical trial will not be available for the public at large, making it an urgent matter that knowledge about susceptibility genes and the uncertainties associated with them be widely disseminated in every way possible. It is encouraging to find that among those individuals who participated in the REVEAL study, many apparently already had an intuitive, if somewhat inchoate, grasp of what is at stake, before they entered the trial.

The epigenetic model strongly suggests that, for complex disease, DNA will never, on its own, be a powerful divinatory tool, even when gene functioning is better understood. As research in molecular biology surges forward, the interpenetration of nature with history and culture, and the permeable boundaries of self and other become increasingly apparent. The image of the "genetic code" is one of the most powerful metaphors of our time (Neumann-Held and Rehmann Sutter 2006). But we can hope, perhaps with the assistance of new and different captivating metaphors, and an increasingly successful dissemination of recent scientific insights, that the fascination that genes have exerted for so long (on scientists and the public alike) in which they are anthropomorphized as extraordinarily powerful agents, will begin to abate. However, this change will be uneven, because in the case of the rare single gene disorders, the genetic contribution clearly outweighs other variables. And the fear associated with certain genes, such as the symbolically powerful BRCA genes linked to breast cancer, will not easily dissipate; understandably, perhaps, in families that are directly implicated.

However, to persist in taking a reductionistic approach to complex disease causation and its management would be perverse and short-sighted in the extreme in light of emerging knowledge about human biology. As Richard Lewontin noted several years ago, the entanglement among genes, organisms, and environments means that these variables will always be, inevitably and inseparably, in cause and effect relationships (2000). The APOE gene, which is pleiotropic, and contributes not only to the incidence of Alzheimer's disease under certain circumstances, but also to several other conditions, beautifully illustrates this claim. It may be necessary to reduce the involved complexity to its component parts for research purposes but the larger, dynamic picture should never be lost sight of.

Funding for this research was provided by the Social Science and Humanities Research Council of Canada (SSHRC), grant # 205806. The REVEAL project was supported by National Institutes of Health grants HG/AG02213 (The REVEAL Study), AG09029 (The MIRAGE

Study), AG13846 (Boston University Alzheimer's Disease Center), and M01 RR00533 (Boston University General Clinical Research Center).

BIBLIOGRAPHY

Apse, K., Biesecker, B.B., Giardiello, F.M., Fuller, B.P., Bernhardt, B.A. 2004. Perceptions of genetic discrimination among at-risk relatives of colorectal cancer patients. *Genetics in Medicine* 6:510–16.

Barnes, B., Dupré, J. 2008. *Genomes and What to Make of Them.* Chicago: University of Chicago Press.

Beeson, D., Doksum, T. 2001. Family values and resistance to genetic testing. In *Bioethics in Social Context.* Barry Hoffmaster, ed, 153–79. Philadelphia: Temple University Press.

Bertram, L., Tanzi, R.E. 2004. Alzheimer's disease: One disorder, too many genes? *Human Molecular Genetics* 13:R135-R141.

Brice, P. 2004. Barcode babies: Prospects for genetic profiling. *Biolines,* http://www.cambridgenetwork.co.uk/pooled/profiles/BF_COMP/view.asp?Q=BF_COMP_9786.

Browner, C. 2007. Can gender "equity" in prenatal genetic services unintentionally reinforce male authority? In *Reproductive Disruptions: Gender, Technology, and Biopolitics in the New Millennium.* M. Inhorn, ed., 147–64. New York: Berghahn Books.

Buchanan, A., Sholtis, S., Richtsmeier, J., Weiss, K. 2009. What are genes "for" or where are traits "from"? What is the question? *BioEssays* 31:198-208.

Callon, M., Rabeharisoa, V. 2004. Gino's lesson on humanity: Genetics, mutual entanglements and the sociologists's role. *Economy and Society* 33(1):1–27.

Champagne, F., Meany, M. 2001. Like mother, like daughter: Evidence for non-genomic transmission of parental behavior and stress responsivity. *Progress in Brain Research* 133:287-302.

Corbo, R.M., Scacchi, R. 1999. Apolipoprotein E (APOE) allele distribution in the world: Is APOEe4 a "thrifty" allele? *Annals of Human Genetics* 63:301-10.

Corder, E.H., Saunders, A.M., Strittmatter, W.J., Schmechel, D.E., Gaskell, P.C., Small, G.W., Roses, A.D., Haines, J.L., Pericak-Vance, M.A. 1993. Gene dose of apolipoprotein E type 4 allele and the risk of Alzheimer's disease in late onset families. *Science* 261 (5123):921-3.

Cox, S., McKellin, W. 1999. "There's this thing in our family": Predictive testing and the construction of risk for Huntington Disease. In *Sociological Perspectives on the New Genetics*. P. Conrad and J. Gabe, eds. London: Blackwell Publishers.

Cupples, A.L., Farrer, L.A., Sadovnick, D.A., Relkin, N., Whitehouse, P., Green, R.C. 2004. Estimating risk curves for first-degree relatives of patients with Alzheimer's disease: The REVEAL Study. *Genetics in Medicine* 6(4):192–6.

Eddy, S.R. 2001. Non-coding RNA genes and the modern RNA world. *Nature Reviews/Genetics* 2:919-29.

Farrer, L.A. 2000. Familial risk for Alzheimer's disease in ethnic minorities: Nondiscriminating genes. *Archives of Neurology* (57).

Farrer, L.A., Cupples, L.A., Haines, J.L., Hyman, B., Kukull, W.A., Mayeux, R., et al. 1997. Effects of age, sex, and ethnicity on the association between apolipoprotein E genotype and Alzheimer's disease: A meta-analysis. *Journal of the American Medical Association* 278:1349-56.

Finkler, K. 2000. *Experiencing the New Genetics: Kinship and Family on the Medical Frontier*. Philadelphia: University of Pennsylvania Press.

– The kin in the gene: The medicalization of family and kinship in American society. *Current Anthropology* 42(2):235–63.

Finkler, K., Skrzynia, C., Evans, J.P. 2003. The new genetics and its consequences for family, kinship, medicine, and medical genetics. *Social Science and Medicine* 57(3):403–12.

Franklin, S., Lock, M. 2003. *Remaking Life and Death: Toward and Anthropology of the Biosciences* Santa Fe: School of American Research.

Fullwiley, D. 2004. Discriminate biopower and everyday politics: Views on sickle cell testing in Dakar. *Medical Anthropology* 23:157–94.

Gelbart, W. 1998. Data bases in genomic research. *Science* (282):660.

Gibbon, S., Novas, C., eds. 2007. *Biosocialities, Genetics and the Social Sciences: Making Biologies and Identities*. London: Routledge.

Gilbert, S.F. 2002. The genome in its ecological context: Philosophical perspectives on interspecies epigenisis. *Annals of the New York Academy of Sciences* 981:202-18.

Ginsburg, F.D. Rapp, R., eds. 1995. *Conceiving the New World Order: The Global Politics of Reproduction*. Berkeley: University of California Press.

Green, J., Richards, M., Murton, F., Statham, H., Hallowell, N. 1997. Family communication and genetic counseling: The case of hereditary breast and ovarian cancer. *Journal of Genetic Counseling* 6(1):45-60.

Growdon, J.H. 1998. Apolipoprotein E and Alzheimer's Disease. *Archives of Neurology* 55:1053-4.

Hallowell, N. 1999. Doing the right thing: Genetic risk and responsibility. *Sociology of Health and Illness* 21(5):597–621.
Halpern, S. 2005. The gene hunters: Closing in on the origins of Alzheimer's disease. *The New Yorker*, 12 December, 84-93.
Harding, J. E. 2001. The nutritional basis of the fetal origins of adult disease. *International Journal of Epidemiology* 30:15–23.
Harmon, A. 2007. After DNA diagnosis: 'Hello, 16p11.2. Are you just like me?' *The New York Times*, 28 December.
Heath, D., Rapp, R., Taussig, K-S. 2004. Genetic citizenship. In *A Companion to the Anthropology of Politics*. David Nugent and Joan Vincent, eds., 152–67. London: Blackwell.
Hendrie, H. 2009. Diagnosis of dementia and Alzheimer's disease in Indianapolis and Ibadan: Challenges in cross-cultural studies of aging and dementia. *Alzheimer's and Dementia* 5(4):P122.
Hill, S.A. 1994. *Managing Sickle Cell Disease in Low-Income Families*. Philadelphia: Temple University Press.
Hyman, B.T., Gomez-Isla, T., Briggs, M., Chung, H., Nichols, S., Kohout, F., Wallace, R. 1996. Apolipoprotein E and cognitive change in an elderly population. *Annals of Neurology* 40 (1):55-66.
Jablonka, E., Lamb, M.J. 2005. *Evolution in Four Dimensions: Genetic, Epigenetic, Behavioral, and Symbolic Variation in the History of Life and Mind*. Cambridge, MA: MIT Press.
Kahn, Susan. 2000. *Reproducing Jews: A Cultural Account of Assisted Conception in Israel*. Durham, NC: Duke University Press.
Keller, E.F. 2000. *The Century of the Gene*. Cambridge: Harvard University Press.
– 2006. Beyond the gene but beneath the skin. In *Genes in Development: Rereading the Molecular Paradigm*, E. M. Neumann-Held and C. Rehmann-Sutter, eds., 290-312. Durham and London: Duke University Press.
Kier, F.J., Molinari, V. 2003. "Do-it-yourself" dementia testing: issues regarding an Alzheimer's home screening test. *Gerontologist* 43 (3):295-301.
Konrad, M. 2005. *Narrating the New Predictive Genetics: Ethics, Ethnography, and Science*. Cambridge: Cambridge University Press.
Korovaitseva, G.I., Sherbatich, T.V., Selezneva, N.V., Gavrilova, S.I., Golimbet V.E., Voskresenskaya, N.I., Rogaev, E.I. 2001. Genetic association between the Apolipoprotein E (APOE) gene and different forms of Alzheimer's disease. *Russian Journal of Genetics* 37(4):422-7.
Koshland, D. 1989. Sequences and consequences of the human genome. *Science* 246:189.

LaRusse, S., Roberts, J.S., Marteau, T.M., Katzen, H., Linnenbringer, E.L., Barber, M., Whitehouse, P., Quaid, K., Brown, T., Green, R.C., Relkin, N.R. 2005. Genetic susceptibility testing versus family history-based risk assessment: Impact on perceived risk of Alzheimer disease. *Genetics in Medicine* 7(1):48-53.

Lewontin, Rç. 2000. *The Triple Helix: Gene, Organism and Envionment.* Cambridge MA: Harvard University Press.

Lippman, A. 1992. Led (astray) by genetic maps: The cartography of the human genome and human care. *Social Science and Medicine* 35:1469–96.

Lock, M. 2002. *Twice Dead: Organ Transplants and the Reinvention of Death*. Berkeley: University of California Press.

– 2005. Eclipse of the gene and the return of divination. *Current Anthropology* 46 (5):S47-S70.

– 2007. Biosociality and susceptibility genes: A cautionary tale. In *Biosocialities, Genetics and the Social Sciences*, S. Gibbon and C. Novas, eds. London: Routledge.

– 2008. Globalization and the state: Is an era of neo-eugenics in the offing? In *Embodiment and the State. Health, Politics and the Intimate life of State Powers*, G. Pizza and H. Johannessen, eds. Oxford and New York: Berghahn Books.

Lock, M., Freeman, J., Chilibeck, G., Beveridge, B., Padolsky, M. 2007. Susceptibility genes and the question of embodied identity. *Medical Anthropology Quarterly* 21 (3):256-76.

Lumey, L.H. 1992. Decreased birth weights in infants after maternal in utero exposure to the Dutch famine of 1944–45. *Paediatric Perinatal Epidemiology* 6(2):240–53.

Mattick, J. 2004. The hidden genetic program of complex organisms. *Scientific American* 291:60-7.

– 2003. Challenging the dogma: The hidden layer of non-protein-coding RNAs in complex organisms. *Bioessays* 25:930-9.

McNeil, S.M., Novelletto, A., Srinidhi, J., Barnes, G., Kornbluth, I., Altherr, M.R., Wasmuth, J.J., Gusella, J.F., MacDonald M.E., Myers, R.H. 1997. Reduced penetrance of the Huntington's Disease mutation. *Human Molecular Genetics 6*:775-9.

Mitchell, J.J., Capua, A., Clow, C., Scriver, C.R. 1996. Twenty-year outcome analysis of genetic screening programs for Tay-Sachs and ß-Thalassemia disease carriers in high schools. *American Journal of Human Genetics 59*:793–8.

Myers, R.H., Schaefer, E.J., Wilson, P.W., D'Agostino, R., Ordovas, J.M., Espino, A., Au, R., White, R.F., Knoefel, J.E., Cobb, J.L., McNulty, K.A.,

Beiser, A., Wolf, P.A. 1996. Apolipoprotein E epsilon4 association with dementia in a population-based study: The Framingham study. *Neurology* 46 (3):673-7.

Neumann-Held, E.M., Rehmann-Sutter, C. 2006. *Genes in Development: Rereading the Molecular Paradigm*. Durham and London: Duke University Press.

Oyama, S. 2001. Terms in tension: What do you do when all the good words are taken? In *Cycles of Contingency: Developmental Systems and Evolution*. Susan Oyama, Paul E. Griffiths, and Russell D. Gray, eds. Cambridge, MA: MIT Press. 177–94.

Peterson, E.A., Milliron, K.J., Lewis, K.E., Goold, S.D., Merajver, S.D. 2002. Health insurance and discrimination concerns and BRCA1/2 testing in a clinic population. *Cancer Epidemiology, Biomarkers, and Prevention* 11: 79–87.

Petronis, A. 2001. Human morbid genetics revisited: Revelence of epigenetics. *Trends in Genetics* 17:142-6.

Poudrier, J. 2007. The geneticization of Aboriginal diabetes and obesity: Adding another scene to the story of the thrifty gene. *Canadian Review of Sociology and Anthropology* 44:237-61.

Quaid, K.A., Morris, M. 1993. Reluctance to undergo predictive testing: The case of Huntington's Disease. *American Journal of Medical Genetics* 45:41-5.

Rabinow, P. 1996. Artificiality and enlightenment: From sociobiology to biosociality. In *Essays on the Anthropology of Reason*. New Jersey: Princeton University Press.

– 2007. Afterword: Concept Work. In *Biosocialities, Genetics and the Social Sciences: Making Biologies and Identities*. Sahra Gibbon and Carlos Novas, eds. London: Routledge. 188-92.

Rapp, R. 1999. *Testing Women, Testing the Fetus: The Social Impact of Amniocentesis*. New York: Routledge Press.

– 2003. Cell life and death, child life and death: Genomic horizons, genetic diseases, family stories. In *Remaking Life and Death: Toward an Anthropology of the Biosciences*. Sarah Franklin and Margaret Lock, eds., 23–60. Santa Fe: School of American Research Press.

Rapp, R., Heath, D., Taussig, K-S. 2001. Genealogical disease: Where hereditary abnormality, biomedical explanation, and family responsibility meet. I, *Relative Matters: New Directions in the Study of Kinship*. Sarah Franklin and Susan MacKinnon, eds., 384–412. Durham, NC: Duke University Press.

Raspberry, K., Skinner, D. 2007. Experiencing the genetic Body: Parents' encounters with pediatric clinical genetics *Medical Anthropology* (26):355-91.

Richards, M. 1996. Lay and Professional Knowledge of Genetics and Inheritannce. *Public Understanding of Science* 5:217-30.

Rose, N. 2007. *The Politics of Life Itself: Biomedicine, Power, and Subjectivity in the Twenty-First Century*. Princeton: Princeton University Press.

Roses, A.D. 1998. Apolipoprotein E and Alzheimer's disease: The tip of the susceptibility iceberg. *Annals of the New York Academy of Sciences* 8:738-43.

Saunders, A.M. 2000. Apolipoprotein E and Alzheimer disease: an update on genetic and functional analyses. *Journal of Neuropathology and Experimental Neurology* 59 (9):751-8.

Savva G.M., Wharton, S.B., Ince, P.G., et al. 2009. Age, neuropathology, and dementia. *New England Journal of Medicine* 360: 2302-9.

Scriver, C.R. Waters, P.J. 1999. Monogenetic traits are not simple: Lessons from phenylketonuria. *Trends in Genetics* 15: 267-72.

Selkoe, D.J. 2002. The pathophysiology of Alzheimer's disease. In *Early Diagnosis of Alzheimer's Disease*, edited by L.F.M. Scinto and K.R. Daffner. Totawa, New Jersey: Humana Press.

Sen, A. 2003. Missing women – revisited: Reduction in female mortality has been counterbalanced by sex selective abortions. *British Medical Journal* 327:1297–8.

Silverman, J.M., Smith, C.J., Marin, D.B., Mohs, R.C., Propper, C.B. 2003. Familial patterns of risk in very late-onset Alzheimer's disease. *Archives of General Pyschiatry* 60:190-7.

St. George-Hyslop, P. 2000. Molecular genetics of Alzheimer's disease. *Biological Psychiatry* 47:183-99.

Stotz, K., Adam B., Griffiths, P. 2006. Tracking the shift to postgenomics. *Community Genetics* (9):190-6.

Strathern, M. 1992. *After Nature: English Kinship in the Late Twentieth Century*. Cambridge: Cambridge University Press.

Strohman, R. 2001. A new paradigm for life: beyond genetic determinism. *California Monthly* 111:4-27.

Szyf, M., McGowan, P., Meaney, M.J. 2008. The social environment and the epigenome. *Environmental and Molecular Mutagenesis* 49:46-60.

Taussig, K-S., Rapp, R., Heath, D. 2003. Flexible eugenics: Technologies of the self in the age of genetics. In *Genetic Nature/Culture: Anthropology and Science beyond the Two Culture Divide*. Alan H. Goodman, Deborah Heath, and M. Susan Lindee, eds., 58–76. Berkeley: University of California Press.

Thompson, C. 2005. *The Ontological Choreography of Reproductive Technologies*. Cambridge, MA: MIT Press.

Tilley, L., Morgan, K., Kalsheker, N. 1998. Genetic risk factors in Alzheimer's disease. *Journal of Clinical Pathology: Molecular Pathology* 51:293-304.

Turney, J. 1995. The public understanding of science – where next? *European Journal of Genetics in Society* 1 (2):5-22.

Waalen, J., Beutler, E. 2009. Genetic screening for low-penetrance variants of protein-coding genes. *Annual Review of Genomics and Human Genetics* 10:431-50.

Wailoo, K., Pemberton, S.G. 2006. *The Troubled Dream of Genetic Medicine: Ethnicity and Innovation in Tay-Sachs, Cystic Fibrosis, and Sickle Cell Disease*. Baltimore: Johns Hopkins University Press.

Wexler, N. 1992. Clairvoyance and caution: Repercussions from the Human Genome Project. In *The Code of Codes: Scientific and Social Issues in the Human Genome Project*. D.J. Kevles and L. Hood, eds., 211–43. Cambridge, MA: Harvard University Press.

Whitehouse, P.J. In Press. *The Myth of Alzheimer's*. New York: St. Martin's Press.

Yoon, P., Bin Chen, W., Faucett, A., Clyne, M., Gwinn, M., Lubin, I., Burke, W., Khoury, M.J. 2001. Public health impact of genetic tests at the end of the 20th century. *Genetics in Medicine* (3):405-10.

Yoxen, .J. 1982. Constructing genetic diseases. In *The Problem of Medical Knowledge: Examining the Social Construction of Medicine*. P. Wright and A. Treacher, eds., 144–61. Edinburgh: University of Edinburgh.

Conclusion

RODERICK A. MACDONALD AND LOUIS MAHEU

This collection of essays is the result of collaboration between leading scholars drawn from fields as diverse as biology, epidemiology, anthropology, sociology, law, and ethics. Scholars from many other disciplines, notably in the health sciences, history, policy studies, economics, and philosophy, have also attended to the themes raised here, as have playwrights, painters, sculptors, musicians, poets, and film-makers to name only some. As editors, we believe that each field of knowledge and artistic expression has a role to play in addressing the relationships among gene expressions, behaviour, and the social fabric.

But this collection is much more than simply a contribution to our substantive understanding of a particular field of human experience. Our authors have challenged each other, and each of us, to reflect on how knowledge is produced, disseminated, and deployed for tactical, strategic, and public policy purposes. Their rich dialogue has revealed both the rewards of integrated crossdisciplinary inquiry and the indispensible character of rigorous disciplinary scholarship. Knowledge and frameworks of knowledge production are deeply contextual; yet no context determines the content *per se* of knowledge. Without proper attention to the protocols and conceptual armature of disciplines, research driven by testable hypotheses, replication studies, and critique is implausible. Without the discipline of disciplines the line between fact and fancy is difficult to draw, and ideological claims proffered by the "faith-based constituency" are dangerously advanced as plausible substitutes for knowledge and theory generated by what has been concomitantly derided as the "evidence-based constituency."

A central characteristic of those who work in the precincts of the "evidence-based constituency" is their recognition of plurality. While there may be but a single "faith-based constituency" with a single comprehensive explanation of all that is and all that may be, no such monotheism afflicts disciplinary scholars. Evidence is always contextual; explanations and theories are always contingent; predictive extrapolations are always hypothetical; and policy recommendations are always offered with the explicit caveat: "to the best of our knowledge and understanding today." Many Canadian governments (although not all) have recently recognized the foundational character of research and have reinvested in scholarly endeavours. In so doing, they are not acting naïvely. They now know that fundamental research does not typically translate into immediate policy outcomes; that fundamental research tends, more often than not, to be disciplinary; and that fundamental research means supporting several disciplines focusing on different dimensions of a problem.

Leading scholars today acknowledge the limits of their understanding. In recognizing the necessity of rigorous disciplinary scholarship, they also acknowledge the necessary partiality of disciplinary perspectives. The essays in this collection are all rooted in particular disciplines, yet in the spirit of interdisciplinary inquiry that shaped the design of the Symposium that spawned them, most also traverse disciplinary boundaries. To a further reflection on this second, meta-contribution of our authors, we now turn.

LEARNING THE DISCIPLINE OF DISCIPLINARY KNOWLEDGE

The fundamental epistemological challenge of our various intellectual and expressive attempts to understand human beings and their environment has long vexed scholars and artists: How is it possible to investigate any aspect of human behaviour without understanding the entire material and socio-psychological context of human action and interaction?

It seems that we cannot know everything under a single analytical framework with sufficient subtlety and fidelity to be able to offer plausible and testable diagnostic hypotheses that can then be deployed either to produce robust advances in knowledge or to inform State policy formation. As we observed in the Introduction, what we purchase in terms of coverage when we propound a meta-theory, we lose in terms of detailed knowledge that can be replicated or operationalized. Specific disciplinary knowledge seems to be an indispensible step for building more comprehensive understandings of complex phenomena. Yet the pursuit of disciplinary insight is not cost-free either. Paradoxically, it seems that we can only gain a clearer picture of our world by consciously adopting strategies of exclusion: disciplinary and sub-disciplinary field-theories, conceptual apparati, methodologies, research protocols, and the promotion of communities of shared understanding all serve to perfect partial knowledge so that it may be instrumentalized. These markers of orthodoxy enable us identify the relevant core of our disciplines, to recognize and attend to the research that is most likely to inform our own, and to remain ignorant of, to discount, or to dismiss what we consider the peripheral.

Contemporary debate about disciplines is the scholarly reflection of the age-old conundrum presented by the story of the Tower of Babel. Is the message that, absent a multiplicity of disciplines (and of the knowledge embedded in multiple scholarly discourses) we could build to the Heavens? Should we abandon disciplines and seek only integrated, non-disciplinary knowledge (and shared scholarly discourse)? Or does the story of Babel simply teach us a prudential lesson about the limits of disciplines as mechanisms for sharing knowledge and the necessary humility that should accompany the human quest to "know"? Put differently, is the story a cautionary tale about the partiality of understanding and the difficulties of human communication resulting from our multiple disciplinary discourses? Indeed, might Babel be a reassurance that pursuing our different disciplines, and then having to negotiate multiple disciplinary discourses, will have a liberating effect on our intellect?

According to the story of Babel, in the beginning all human beings had one language. In a similar way, according to the story of the Garden of Eden, in the beginning all human beings had a primal and shared, though limited, knowledge. With one exception, all that could be known was known, and all that was known could be known by all people. Just as the story of Babel can be used to reconcile us to linguistic diversity, to explain away the possibility that the human species may not have had a single origin, to explain away how it is that language, culture, and knowledge are revealed in geographic diversity, or even to explain why humans can never be divine, the biblical presentation of Eden can be interpreted as a parallel story meant to explain the diversity of human knowledge. Having succumbed to the temptation to eat from the fruit of the tree of knowledge of good and evil, Adam and Eve were expelled from Eden. As in Babel, expulsion fractured the primal, the undifferentiated, and the uniform.

Biblical allegory can serve to illuminate – perhaps even suggest a moral foundation for – the differentiation of knowledge systems, but it tells us nothing about how human beings have come to deploy the differentiated knowledge they have created. Nor does it tell us much about our motivations in seeking (or, more often, refusing to seek) more general knowledge frameworks. What arrogance accounts for the fact that we do not use the existence of competing professional knowledge systems to enrich our own understanding? What arrogance leads us to claim the primacy of our chosen knowledge system, and the preponderance (if not the exclusivity) of the explanatory hypotheses it provides? And again, why our insistent urge to confound knowledge with partial perspectives and willingly to become disciples rather than skeptics?

There is no simple, or universal, or singular answer to these questions. We do appear to have an inborn capacity to learn, to know, and to recall. This human capability is nurtured by our families, by our peers, and by mass media. Much of what we initially learn is both unself-conscious and undifferentiated. Concepts like time, space, causation, and computation affect our lives and are actually deployed by us in daily activities long before we either identify them as such, or understand their basic protocols. Prior to identification and understanding, these concepts are not disaggregated; they are part of the "big, blooming, buzzing confusion" of everyday experience. Yet they are no less present in, and no less directive of, that everyday experience. How often we forget that the expression "muddling through" implies success, not failure, in a purposive endeavour.

Later in life, learning becomes more self-conscious and differentiated – indeed, more disciplined. This disciplined learning typically arises in schools and is reinforced by the categories of entertainment and recreation we come to indulge. We learn arithmetic, learn to read, learn about history and basic science in a structured tuition that is most often disconnected from the other tuition we receive. These various subjects are islands of specialized knowledge, forming in an ocean of general experience and cultural indoctrination.

Our initial acquisition of general knowledge is culturally grounded, but unconsciously; of course, the more specialized bits of disciplinary learning whose assumptions are not part of our consciousness until a later stage in our lives are also culturally grounded. Moreover, even as we acquire this specialized knowledge we continue to learn unconsciously. One may go further. It is this continual acquisition of specialized knowledge that provides the primary spur to unselfconscious learning. The paradox of life-long unselfconscious learning is that what is learned actually cannot speak its name (its cultural content). The expression "common sense" captures the two elements of the paradox. Our sense is *common* in that it pretends to be shared with others; it is also *common* in the sense that it is undifferentiated.

Throughout our lives we confront the relationship between these two modes of knowledge acquisition. On the one hand, there is a vast body of knowledge that we have learned unconsciously and that, in the manner of the slave boy in Plato's dialogue *The Meno*, we do not know that we know until we have need to, or are invited to, recall what we know. On the other hand, there is a vast body of knowledge that we have learned consciously in a disciplined manner and that, in the manner of Locke's *Essay on Human Understanding*, we know that we know, and we can deploy to solve puzzles that confront us as mere hypotheses.

In attending to this relationship of tacit and explicit knowledge, admittedly, we have already placed ourselves on the terrain of "uncommon" sense (Polanyi 1958, 1966). What is most revealing about our inquiries into the origins of the knowledge we can wield is the manner in which we develop instincts of unity and diversity, of connectedness and distinctiveness, of similarity and individuation, of orthodoxy and heresy, in our different knowledge fields. In committing ourselves to this inquiry into origins we privilege consciously learned knowledge and become disciples of the discipline we adopt as our default epistemological register. This commitment to specified modes of inquiry is as true of particularistic knowledge fields as it is of philosophy itself.

ASSUMPTIONS, HYPOTHESES, EXPERIMENTS, AND DATA

One of the distinctive characteristics of the contemporary knowledge establishment (universities, scholarly think tanks, learned societies, research laboratories) is its preoccupation, especially in the biomedical, natural, and social sciences, with experimentation and verification. Even those who take an anti-positivist approach to knowledge formation are committed to testing hypotheses within a given "conceptual scheme." By contrast with the cottage-industry of intellectual inquiry preceding the industrial revolution, we now devote enormous intellectual effort to frameworks of inquiry, to methodology, and to refining protocols for data collection and analysis. The objective is not, however, simply methodological perfection. All this scholarly activity presupposes that the development and deployment of rigorous research methods furthers some end, if only the end of obtaining increased understanding. Hence, the need for hypotheses to propound and test.

Since Hume and Kant, however, we know that all empirical hypotheses rest on prior assumptions about the character of the world and the character of human beings. Whatever the origin of these assumptions – in theology, in philosophy, in superstition, in irrational prejudice, in apparently rational projection from that which we take to be definitively established – they remain just that: assumptions. Because the human mind seeks to make sense of human experience, and because human experience is as various as the number of human beings, we typically aggregate our different particular experiences into more general categories of experience grounded in shared assumptions. These shared assumptions (and not the specific knowledge derived from the application of research methodologies they justify, let alone the research methodologies themselves) are the foundation of disciplines (Kuhn 1974). Yet we often pass over such foundations, easily impressed as we are by what we gain from disciplinary theory building and settled research methodologies.

Consider the following "thought experiment" relating to the idea of measurement (Macdonald 2000). The fact of humans measuring (distances, weights, volumes, temperature, and time) is hardly of recent vintage. Sizing up the world around us is a central survival skill, and developing the means to make comparative evaluations of the physical environment through measurement appears to have been a relatively early human achievement. Non-conjunctural measurement protocols and tools are not only a valuable shortcut for assessing opportunity, danger, and risk to ourselves; they are helpful for communicating this information to others.

On the basis of anthropological studies, we can hypothesize that early measurement systems were essentially pragmatic: based on days, moons, and years, for example. Just as it took several millennia (and much theological bludgeoning) for the seven-day week to emerge, so too it took a long time for a true base-ten system of computation to overtake more empirical systems (Ifrah 1998). Recall that our inherited Roman symbols of calculation, based on fingers (I), hands (V), and pairs of hands (X) was typical even in cultures that depended on rapid computation. The capacity to abstract from experience and to systematize experience is an amazing human accomplishment.

And yet, this type of rationality has its experiential limitations. Certainly a system for counting days, months, and years does not need external reference points – biblical or astronomical – to validate its aggregating structures. Given the way we count, it would have been more rational had ten-day weeks, and ten-hour days of 100 minutes each, with 100 seconds to each minute been adopted as a complement to our base-ten system of decades and centuries. Indeed, exactly such a system was proposed by French revolutionaries on October 24, 1793, as a way instantiating revolutionary political rationality in everyday life.

The experiential constraints on measuring systems were not (and even today are not) just physiological, theological, and political. Often occupational need was the key driver of measurement systems and protocols. And these needs were often discrete – focused on length, or area, or volume, or weight, or time, or temperature, and so on. It took a long time before people began to think of measuring as an "integrated" activity. In early Mediterranean life, it really did not matter that short and long linear distances were calculated on a different logic: a ready conversion of a thumb, a hand, a foot, or a cubit into a league was hardly a preoccupation. So also, the transposition of distance to volume to weight.

What, then, drove the quest to integrate measurement systems? It appears that the commercial requirements of the Industrial Revolution played a major role: It became useful to know, for example, how much a cubic foot of water weighs, how many cubic inches comprised a gallon, and how many acres made a square mile. Of course, in the integrative endeavour, many domain-specific units of measurement – pecks, gills, fathoms, chains, stones – began to disappear. Economic need combined with enlightenment rationality to produce what we now know of as the metric system (SI). Today, the world trading system exerts enormous pressure for a universal conversion to SI – an essentially analytic *a priori* base-ten scale that integrates distance, volume, and weight, and to which are added a temperature scale in which the difference between the freezing and boiling points of water is divided into 100 units, as well as the measurement of thermal energy (calories).

In the adoption of the SI system, it would appear that the rational "theory" of integrated scientific measurement has apparently trumped the everyday "need" for pragmatic measurement. But even the metric system had an empirical root: the metre was initially (mis) calculated as 1/10,000,000th of the distance between equator and pole on the meridian passing through Paris. Moreover, while the definition of the litre is still tied directly to the definition of a metre, the original definition of a kilogram by reference to the absolute weight of a litre of water has been overtaken by a definition relating to the mass of a physical prototype preserved by the *International Bureau of Weights and Measures*. As such, it is now the only SI unit that is defined in relation to an object of experience, rather than to a fundamental physical property.

This reflection on systems of measurement carries two key messages for those who would ruthlessly pursue a uniform scientific methodology. First, even in a field of inquiry that purports to organize knowledge of the world according to *a priori* rational hypotheses that may be applied across human activity, the standard protocols can be trumped by politics, past practice, technology, and convenience. Yet our assumptions about measurement, our methods and protocols for measuring, and the evaluative units by which we measure retain their integrity even when they lose their utility. In other words, knowledge is normally contextualized but its content is relatively autonomous from the pragmatic needs it serves. Second, to recognize that all disciplinary protocols and assumptions, like all measurement systems, are susceptible to being trumped or modulated by experience is also to recognize their contingency. As already implied, physiology, theology, economics, and politics have each had their say in the configuration of even the most "rational" of measurement systems.

ON BECOMING A DISCIPLE IN THE AGE OF TECHNOLOGY

Our choices of disciplinary rationalities are grounded not just in socio-psychological factors like religion, culture, tradition, and economics and material circumstances like physiology, climate, and the natural environment (Montesquieu, 1977). Sometimes technical capacity (or its lack) is the driving logic.

Where imagination and invention outstrip measurement technology, our response is to seek relational simplicity. Where we can imagine processes, ideas, and things that require the integration of several logical frames or measurement systems (in the present context, several disciplinary perspectives), but where the integration of these frames and systems is beyond our existing computational ability, we react by seeking abstraction. Sometimes we reorder these logics under a meta-logic that operates more as a slogan than as the fount of hypotheses (for example, religion, self-interest, survival of the fittest). Sometimes we convert these frames and systems into an explicitly correlated meta-system (for example, the metric system, the market, Esperanto). And sometimes we seek a meta-protocol to provide a lexicon for translating multiple discourses (for example, the concepts of interdisciplinarity and transdisciplinarity).

Let us turn again to measurement. Suppose that we had developed the computer in 1700. What would have been the impact on the way we measure at that date of our capacity to convert instantaneously all measurements? If instantaneous unit conversion – say from liquid ounces to *avoirdupoids* ounces to stones to tons to flagons – were possible and easily done, the impetus for measurement rationalization would no longer have had an economic rationale. It would no longer have been necessary to adopt measurement systems anchored in our base-ten system of arithmetic in order to achieve the required integration of length, weight, and volume in easily transposable units. More significantly, once technology frees us from any given computational structure, there is no predicting the factors that might generate a new measurement logic. It is even possible that accessible computation at an earlier time might have simply rendered redundant the quest for integrated measurement systems.

From the perspective of the semi-numerate public, history shows that pragmatic, experience-based systems will always be preferred to integrated measurement systems as a way of understanding the world. From the perspective of the professional engineer deploying the slide rule, a rational system has most appeal. From the perspective of the infinite calculation capacities of the computer, it is irrelevant whether the empirical *a posteriori* or the rational *a priori* should prevail as the organizing logic. With a computer there is no need either to seek relational simplicity in order to assist the expert, or to impose this expert rationality on the everyday measurement activities of a lay audience.

Today, however, metric measurement systems, decimal currency systems, and base-ten arithmetical systems have acquired global predominance. Most people have come to accept metric measurement because of various other factors that have little to do with measurement *per se*. The creation and imposition of metric measurement can be understood as an example of the ambiguous relationship between disciplinary culture and popular culture. From one perspective it might be thought that the discipline of scientific measurement has overruled the pragmatic measurement of action. But what we have cast as the pragmatic measurement of human action – the concepts of pints, ounces, and tonnes – is not exclusively a vernacular of popular culture. Many, perhaps most, pragmatic measures originated in response to expert, or disciplinary, need. Whether it was the needs of the brewers of beer or the needs of bakers and ship-owners, the rationale for each system was found in local knowledge serving local needs.

One might conclude that what is at stake is not predominantly a conflict between disciplinary knowledge and popular knowledge, but rather a conflict between competing disciplinary rationalities. In contrast with the universal meta-rational discipline of the metric system, the discrete, pragmatically rational discipline emerging from specialized knowledge fields was connected to the key assessment needs of those who deployed it. The story of measurement reminds us that we constantly confront competing *a priori* disciplinary rationalities (however experience-driven their origins or reasons for success) and that these rationalities generate competing pragmatic effects.

The development of measurement and computation as an endeavour of its own, and its dissociation from the particular contexts where specific measuring protocols were needed and used, was accompanied by a corresponding loss of the richness of the language of measurement. This loss of language that reflected the culture of the measurer has also led to the loss of the culture that was carried by this language. "A country mile" has not yet found its metric equivalent. Perhaps in time we shall learn to say a "gram of proactivity is equivalent to a kilogram of reactivity." If we do, make no mistake, the expression will not be coined in scientific publications. It will, like the expression "an ounce of prevention is worth a pound of cure" arise in literary usage as taken on board by popular culture.

To become a disciple in the age of technology is to commit oneself to the internal logic of one's own system of consciously learned disciplined knowledge. It is to imagine that the rationality of disciplinary method is not, and need not be, grounded in the "common knowledge" of pragmatic experience. For some, it is also to assume that the value of the particular partial knowledge revealed by one's disciplined scholarly inquiry sufficiently justifies a lack of interest in, if not disdain for, the partial knowledge of others, whether they be scholars or members of the lay public. Happily, the contributors to this collection have no such *hubris*. Each is sensitive to the partiality of disciplinary knowledge and to the importance of pursuing complementarity in research endeavours.

INDISCIPLINE AND INTERDISCIPLINARITY

In any field of human action there will be those who question received knowledge. Christian theology characterizes such indiscipline either as heresy or apostasy. Both challenges to orthodoxy call forth immediate sanction: excommunication. The sinner is cast out of the community of believers. Scholarly disciplines are no less brutal with apostates, although more tolerant of heretics – as long as the heretical belief only challenges methods, research protocols, and analytical frameworks. These heretical beliefs, after all, can be put to the Popperian test. If rigorous experimentation fails to falsify them, they may be contingently or provisionally accepted. Ultimately, they may even become a new orthodoxy.

No such solicitude is granted to apostates. Too much is at stake. And so, employment, scholarly rewards, recognition, and research funding flow only to those who accept the fundamental assumptions of their chosen field of inquiry. Furthermore, the contemporary research establishment is typically structured so that its atomic knowledge-units are the already recognized and established disciplines. In such an environment, the worst form of apostasy is to question the logic of one's discipline and the function of disciplines as the ground of all acquired knowledge. In an extreme form, this questioning, this apostasy is, of course, the sin of *interdisciplinarity*.

The conception that there could be a unified knowledge and that, in consequence, there could be a unified methodology for apprehending and transmitting this knowledge derives from the commitment of the enlightenment encyclopedists to the idea of objective knowledge – of knowledge not dependent on status, gender, locality, or any other human differentiator. While the notion in Western culture that a person might know many things is as old as the Greeks, the encyclopedists contested sharply the view that Aristotle "knew it all" or that da Vinci "knew it all." In neither case was the knowledge they possessed comprehensive. Nor was it, in the spirit of Bacon, rigorously tested by replicable experimentation. Aristotle and da Vinci may have "understood" all that they knew; they did not, however, "know it all."

The eighteenth century encyclopedists accepted that there could be no denial of disciplines and no reinvention of a unified, nondisciplinary knowledge. By contrast, the great integrative projects of the nineteenth century, whether in the humanities, the social sciences, or the physical sciences did aim at expounding a single "theory of everything." At that time, the search for integration originated with *a priori* meta-theory. Today the quest for comprehensive understanding continues, yet is grounded in a different set of assumptions from that held by Marx and Darwin. We now seek to build integrated knowledge from its components. In this endeavour we concede that integrated knowledge flows from interdisciplinarity, and that before there can be interdisciplinarity there must be disciplinarity.

Most social scientific disciplines assert their capacity to provide explanations across the entire range of human action. An economist may claim, for example, that the tools of economic analysis can be applied to any social setting – from the family to the international trading system. Similarly, a sociologist may claim that the tools of sociological analysis can be deployed in any setting of human interaction – from the neighbourhood to the corporation. That most economists and sociologists tend to focus on one or another of these settings (family, global trade, neighbourhood, corporation), and tend to develop sub-specialities identified by these foci does not mean that they have renounced the ambition of being able to explain any human phenomenon through their disciplinary lens. Disciplinary disciples accept that their discipline does not provide a comprehensive explanation of human action; they claim only that the potential scope of its partial explanation is comprehensive.

Today, in other words, most social science disciplines do not require disciples to make a profession of faith in a comprehensive world view. We have been taught to believe that it is possible to engage in disciplinary analysis without ultimately having to commit ourselves to contemplating our place in the universe. Disciplinarity enables us to deploy knowledge systems grounded in a relatively limited number of concepts that are held to have general explanatory power when applied to the world of experience. It does not require us to undertake the boundary-breaking exercise ourselves.

The distinctive character of interdisciplinarity, by contrast, is that it involves a different epistemology and a different intellectual practice. It imposes a new discipline upon our thinking. Interdisciplinarity demands from its disciples a commitment to contemplating the place of their initial discipline in the universe imagined by some other discipline. The precondition to interdisciplinary discipleship is disciplinary indiscipline.

INTERDISCIPLINARY KNOWLEDGE AND TRUST

In any complex society there are multiple levels of interdependence between people, both as individuals and with respect to the social or professional roles they may occupy. We in Canada, like people in most societies, assume as a rule, and in the absence of evidence suggesting the contrary, that others are not psychopaths. Normally, we also presume that those who claim expertise are both competent and well-motivated. We are prepared to take on faith that the building we are in was well-designed, well-built, and well-maintained; that the food we eat has been properly grown, properly prepared, and properly presented. None of us are able to know everything and to do everything ourselves. Interdependence is a necessary feature of modern life (Govier 1997, 1998).

But this interdependence is almost always just below the surface of our consciousness and perceptions. Because buildings do not collapse and because we do not routinely suffer from salmonella poisoning, we are not aware of how much we trust others all the time. Scholarly disciplines serve, more than anything else, to discipline our trust; this occurs in the vocabulary we deploy, the ideas we advance, the standards of proof we accept, and the credentials we demand of those who claim expertise.

When someone who is a biologist, for example, speaks to other biologists in the language of sociology, the basic disciplinary conditions for trust (for credibility) are usually absent and the discussion is greeted skeptically. Note the point that the lack of trust is not in the expertise of a sociologist; nor is it really in sociology; it is in the capacity, or for that matter, the incapacity, we have to evaluate the degree of trust that our erstwhile biology professor colleague should be afforded *extra muros* as a sociologist.

By contrast, when the sociology professor speaks in the language of sociology to the biologist (assuming the credentializing of the speaker has been assured), the reaction is rarely one of mistrust. Rather it is often one of disengagement; sometimes apathy, sometimes condescension. The mistrust is not personal but epistemic. We are prepared to accept the messenger, and perhaps even listen to the message, but not to afford it the commitment of our own lives. We decline to learn enough sociology either to appreciate the meaning of the message for our own discipline or to frame the meaning of our own discipline for the sociologist.

In the end, the lessons of interdisciplinarity are no different from the lessons of Babel. There can never be a workable *Esperanto* – a language created *a priori* that is good for all times, all places, and all occasions: Likewise there can never be a successful new discipline of interdisciplinarity that is *a priori*; the more this new discipline of interdisciplinarity has *a priori* contours, the more it resembles traditional disciplines. Even a *lingua franca* as an *a posteriori* construct cannot be a closed normative system: Latin soon developed its nativist variants and its foreign dialects; today we are reliably informed that there are thirty-seven distinct forms of English, not counting innumerable "pidgin" versions (Crystal 2003). Where the new discipline of interdisciplinarity is dominated by a *lingua franca*, it risks becoming a theology; disciplinary pidgins cluster on the margins of the "true." Any new discipline of interdisciplinarity will reflect manifold *lingua franca,* each of which will be always open for revision.

To say that there can never be a single interdisciplinarity does not mean, however, that there can never be protocols, understandings, concepts, and attitudes by which diverse disciplinary protocols, understandings, concepts, and attitudes may be enabled to focus jointly and productively on complex problems. But here, the endeavour is neither to create a comprehensive body of integrated knowledge or even a general theory of interdisciplinarity of the type suggested by Somerville and Rapport (Somerville 2000). The foundational trust necessary for interdisciplinary indiscipline depends on the building and diffusion of elemental socio-cultural components.

Under such an epistemology, what is to be accepted as valid and relevant knowledge for addressing the case in hand is not given as scientific fact, but has to be negotiated and judged (McDonell 1997).

INTERDISCIPLINARY REFLECTIONS ABOUT GENES AND SOCIAL ENVIRONMENT

The various essays in this collection focus on scholarly debates and research outcomes that point the way to the development of more sophisticated explanatory models of gene and environment interplays. They acknowledge and attend to the complex neurobiological and behavioural conduits through which bi-directional genetic and environmental influences have an impact on human behaviour. Every paper, in its own way, exemplifies the powerful contribution that disciplinary knowledge can make to the development of these models. But every paper, also in its own way, locates itself on the terrain of interdisciplinarity.

The first section contains three essays discussing human personality traits or disorder behaviours underlined by genetic and environmental factors interplays. The possibility of discovering links between personality traits, genes, and environment factors has been an important part of the history of human as well as of animal-model genetics.

Two geneticists brought wide-ranging contributions to this section. David Goldman examined multiple intermediary phenotypes underlying gene and stress interactions. This meant a psychiatric disorder, the incapacity to cope with stress, would reveal a genetically related character through physiological, endocrinal, neuropsychological, pharmacological, and at-the-cell-level intermediary markers. The call from those who are investigating neurogenetic psychiatric disorders for research that transgresses disciplinary boundaries will extend promising experimental strategies to a vast area of biomedical science. In turn, this more comprehensive approach stands to better explain the complex intermediary phenotypes intervening in outcomes like high levels of stress, and of alcohol and drug abuse.

Jonathan Flint's paper reviewed a range of research endeavours within developmental and neuro- psychology and psychiatry focusing on specific personality traits. He specifically critiqued questionable research studies and denounced the flawed results they generated as to the relationship between personality traits and genetic factors.

However, to complete the picture of these flawed results, he went on to highlight both the potential strengths but also the limitations of molecular genetic research that appears to show an indisputable link between personality traits, and genetic and environmental factors. He marshalled a broad range of disciplines to paint a robust critical picture of weak scientific outcomes and to hypothesize more promising research strategies. These new strategies would demand a broader epigenetic twist, which might then deliver more rigorous explanations for gene, environment, and personality trait interplay.

This is a conclusion reinforced in this first section of the collection by a cognitive and developmental psychology essay focusing on human intelligence inheritance. The genetic deterministic explanation models too often found in this literature can only be successfully challenged by attending to molecular genetic techniques and models as applied to human intelligence. That is, the paper by Douglas Wahlsten, a cognitive development psychology scholar, would not have been convincing in establishing the significant shortcomings of studies tying human intelligence inheritance to genetic factors had he not ventured onto the terrain of neurosciences and mastered social statistics' techniques. All three of these papers on personality traits and genetic factors rest on the premise that meaningful explanatory models depend on research that integrates multiple disciplinary perspectives drawn from the humanities and social sciences and genetics.

The second section of this collection contains three chapters that emphasize social and ethical issues pertaining to research relating to genetic and environmental determinants of human behaviour. An expert in health law issues, Timothy Caulfield integrated the perspectives of public health with those of communication and public opinion studies and that of public understanding of science. His paper directly questions genetically influenced reification explanations as applied to notions of race in public representations of disease. Although many of the proponents of genetic research cited by Caulfield have expressed clear reservations about positing a directly affirmative impact of genetic factors on human behaviour, as Caulfield notes, race geneticization is still a significant feature of popular and commercial discourse.

The paper by Françoise Baylis, a philosopher and bio-ethicist, draws on many human and social sciences approaches to health and disease issues, as well as on medical studies and ethics to challenge research results supposedly establishing that genetic factors directly influence human behaviour. And here again, despite the opposition of some genetics scholars she referred to, there remains a resilient geneticization of many processes and behaviours. As Baylis also argues, transdisciplinarity research – embedded in a new research culture of trust and esteem for the work of scholars from other disciplines – should open new and more promising ways of addressing gene and environment interplays as well as many other research questions regarding human behaviours.

These essays from the second section of the collection nicely marry humanities and social science viewpoints to genetic perspectives in order to reveal the continuing power of genetic determinism as an explanatory model. Yvonne Bombard and Michael Hayden combined social science understandings of stigma; labelling; marked social relationships, especially as revealed by scholars of symbolic interactionism, with in-depth molecular and cellular genetic knowledge about clinical, neurological, and biological features of Huntington Disease. The fruitful collaboration between a molecular biologist and a scholar trained in interdisciplinary studies of health behaviour has led to a rich contribution to our understanding of a relatively understudied dimension of genetic discrimination, using individuals undergoing genetic tests related to Huntington Disease as a case study.

A final series of three chapters addresses issues for which still more comprehensive and fine-grained interactive models offer promising avenues for future research. These chapters explore new possibilities for hypothesizing and testing the combined impacts of genetic and environmental factors on human behaviour. Richard Tremblay, a psychologist with a mastery of advances in social sciences about aggressive, delinquent, and criminal youth behaviours, explored many developmental psychology and psychiatry studies documenting personality traits and behaviours of specific youth populations displaying aggression, or at risk of delinquent behaviour. The experimental prevention analyses he called for can find analogous relevant inputs from other research fields. Indeed, some recent epigenetic studies of environmental and genetic interplays conditioning aggressive and disorderly behaviour highlight factors and behaviour settings that should be included in more robust experimental prevention research designs.

As for Martha McClintock et al. they proposed a systematic transdisciplinary approach for understanding the genetically sensitive disease, cancer. The Center for Population Health and Health Disparities they belong to favoured the combination of many research teams and strategies deriving from various disciplines. The active cooperation of hematology, oncology, tumour pathology, genetics, psychology, and other social sciences scholars engaged a comprehensive and epigenetic understanding of breast cancer disparities. Could such interweaving of multiple disciplinary channels and pathways pave the way in the future, as argued by these contributors, to more robust models for understanding the interplays of gene and environment in the shaping of human behaviour?

A final essay is by Margaret Lock, a cultural anthropologist with a particular interest in studies of the body in health and illness, and especially versed in the social sciences of health and medicine. Lock offered a rich and comprehensive study of molecular genomic effects as related to late-onset Alzheimer's disease. Her chapter conveyed in-depth knowledge of epidemiological study results, of intermediary pharmacological and neuropathological phenotype findings, and, more globally, of recent molecular epigenetic advances to establish how the complicated nature of gene and environment interplays intensively confront modern embodied identities with ambivalence and uncertainty. The large and dynamic breadth of disciplines she expertly referred to provides a bedrock foundation for her discussion of a much more disputable link than normally assumed between a susceptibility gene and the onset of disease and behaviour.

What emerges from all these papers is the recognition by leading scholars in the humanities and social sciences and in genetic research that the study of gene and environment interplays is a dynamic field of inquiry. The intellectual and research challenges posed by the new molecular genetics are substantial. The papers prepared by scholars working in the field of epidemiology have posed significant questions that derive from taking molecular findings out of the laboratory and trying to observe them as experienced by populations in situated social contexts. Those prepared by ethicists and lawyers attempt to engage with the key research outcomes of this field and the misleading interpretations often placed on these results by popular media. Moreover, scholars working within basic humanities and social science disciplines have made substantial contributions to our understanding of gene and environment interplays in the context of everyday social interactions.

As a collection, these essays compel the following two conclusions about interdisciplinary reflections on gene and environment interplays. First, the new molecular genetics poses challenges as much within the traditional biomedical scientific domains as within the humanities and social sciences. Interdisciplinarity is not just an affair of what has been summarily described as the two cultures (Snow, 1965). Second, within the social sciences and humanities to date, the challenges have been engaged by philosophers, ethicists, lawyers, and scholars working in basic social science disciplines. In many cases, however, one perceives a greater interdisciplinarity between the "two cultures" than between disciplines within the humanities and social sciences. It is as if it is easier to establish what Galison calls a "trading zone" between biomedical and natural sciences, on the one hand, and the social sciences and humanities on the other, than it is between sub-disciplines of one or other of these scholarly fields (Galison 1997).

As noted by contributors to this collection of essays, the fundamental challenge of building interdisciplinary research is the challenge of trust. The failure to trust the commitments of those with whom we work attests to our failure to trust ourselves. A failure to make ourselves vulnerable in the presence of the "disciplinary other," induces us to distrust the sincerity even of the "disciplinary other" who renders herself or himself vulnerable to us. In a disciplinary trading zone theorists and experimenters meet, strategically coordinating parts of their partial knowledge systems with each other. In an interdisciplinary trading zone, there are no disciplinary assumptions, concepts, and practices that can claim authority to exclude other disciplinary assumptions, concepts, and practices. As the contributions of the authors of this collection attest, the very fact of working together in investigating complex problems occasions, evidences, and reinforces the trust without which intellectual trading will not flourish. Moments, modes, and sites for sharing research and debating assumptions, findings, and explanations constitute the zone in which we can build significant knowledge advances.

ACKNOWLEDGING AND MEETING THE CHALLENGES

The creation of a fruitful dialogue between genetics and the humanities and social sciences confronts researchers, knowledge entrepreneurs, scholarly institutions and associations, and universities with numerous challenges. These are at once intellectual and material.

In this conclusion, our primary attention has been given over to the intellectual challenges. How can we create the conditions for promoting new scholarly communities that draw together expertise and insight from multiple disciplines to engage deeply with complex problems? We have argued that interdisciplinarity cannot flourish where scholars either uncritically adhere to the pre-determined *ex ante* of their discipline, or where they uncritically embrace a pre-bounded *ex post* of their emerging interdiscipline. Interdisciplinarity is how we symbolize the human desire to communicate across the vast intellectual spaces over which we have been scattered by our disciplinary arrogance. And a first step to achieving interdisciplinarity is to recognize the cultural groundedness and partiality of all that one does as a scholar – including editing collections of essays about gene expressions, behaviour, and the social fabric.

Self-recognition is just the first step. We must also put into place structural and material resources. In the days of shrinking research budgets, of increasing corporate-sponsored research in universities, and of the redeployment of resources of peer-managed granting councils to programs mandated by governments, the prospects are not favourable. Each of these tendencies needs to be challenged, resisted, and reversed. But success in reorienting spending priorities will not follow the mere identification of need by scholars. Money follows outcomes. Universities and scholars must take the lead. It is not enough simply to shift resources from disciplinary to interdisciplinary research.

Public debates – carried out in community forums, in newspapers, on television programs, and especially whenever some new "scientific discovery" is reported of "a gene for X" – are essential for mobilizing public support for cross-disciplinary research funding. Informing citizens about the dangers of too quickly moving from laboratory to policy, about the bidirectional aspects of gene and environment interplays, and about the need to invest even more in research projects exploring these ideas are equally important.

Already, through symposia such as that which gave rise to these papers, scholarly organizations like the *Royal Society of Canada* can lay the groundwork for the trust and understanding needed to tackle these complex ideas and problems. But this is just the start. There are significant bodies of literature in the health sciences field, in the science and technology field, in biological anthropology, and in the sociology of medicine that have interrogated these issues. Expanding the horizons of interdisciplinary and transdisciplinary inquiry even beyond those disciplines represented in this collection is an imperative. We hope, nonetheless, that the Symposium and the papers published here will make an important contribution to advancing knowledge about gene and environment interplays. Finally, and more generally, we hope that this collection will make a contribution to advancing understanding about the conditions and prospects of interdisciplinary dialogue in the sciences, the humanities, and the arts.

BIBLIOGRAPHY

Crystal, D. 2003. *English as a Global Language*. Cambridge: Cambridge University Press.

Galison, P. 1997. *Image and Logic: A Material Culture of Microphysics*. Chicago: University of Chicago Press.

Govier, T. 1997. *Social Trust and Human Communities*. Montreal: McGill-Queen's University Press.

– 1998. *Dilemmas of Trust*. Montreal: McGill-Queen's University Press.

Ifrah, G. 1998. *The Universal History of Numbers: From Prehistory to the Invention of the Computer*. London: Harvill.

Kuhn, T. 1974. Second thoughts on paradigms. In F. Suppe, ed., *The Structure of Scientific Theories*, 459. Urbana: University of Illinois Press.

Locke, J. 1989. *An Essay Concerning Human Understanding*. Oxford. Clarendon Press.

Macdonald, R. 2000. Transdisciplinarity and trust. In M. Somerville and D. Rapport, eds, *Transdisciplinarity: Recreating Integrated Knowledge*, 61. Oxford, EOLSS Publishers.

McDonell, G. 1997. Scientific and everyday knowledge: Trust and the politics of environmental initiatives. *Social Studies of Science* 27 (December): 819.

Montesquieu, Baron C. de S. 1977. *The Spirit of the Laws*. Berkeley, University of California Press.

Plato. 2006. *Meno*. Cambridge. Cambridge University Press.

Polanyi, M. 1958. *Personal Knowledge*. Chicago: University of Chicago Press.

– 1966. *The Tacit Dimension*. Garden City, N.Y. Doubleday.

Snow, C.P. 1965. *Two Cultures: and a Second Look: An Expanded Version of the Two Cultures and the Scientific Revolution*. London: Cambridge University Press.

Somerville, M. and Rapport, D., eds. 2000. *Transdisciplinarity: Recreating Integrated Knowledge*. Oxford, EOLSS Publishers.

Index

f = figure
t = table